Ethics and Politics
Cases and Comments

The Nelson-Hall Series in Political Science

Consulting editor: **Samuel C. Patterson**
The Ohio State University

Ethics and Politics
Cases and Comments

Second Edition

Edited by

Amy Gutmann

PRINCETON UNIVERSITY

and

Dennis Thompson

HARVARD UNIVERSITY

Nelson-Hall Publishers nh Chicago

Project Editor: Dorothy Anderson
Typesetter: Fine Print
Manufacturer: BookCrafters, Inc.

LIBRARY OF CONGRESS CATALOGING-IN-PUBLICATION DATA

Ethics and politics : cases and comments / edited by Amy Gutmann and
Dennis Thompson. – 2nd ed.
p. cm.
Bibliography: p.
Includes index.
ISBN 0-8304-1224-7
1. Political ethics–Case studies. I. Gutmann, Amy.
II. Thompson, Dennis F. (Dennis Frank), 1940-
JA79.E823 1989
172–dc20

Reprinted 1991

Manufactured in the United States of America

10 9 8 7 6 5 4 3 2

Hardcover: ISBN 0-8304-1224-7
Paperback: ISBN 0-8304-1230-1

Contents

Acknowledgments

This book grew out of courses we have taught at Princeton and Harvard. We are grateful to our students who helped us recognize the importance of cases in understanding political ethics and who helped us choose (and in some instances write) the cases we present here. For able and creative research assistance, we are indebted to Mike Comiskey, Ted Aaberg, and Michael McNally. Donald E. Stokes, Dean of the Woodrow Wilson School at Princeton, encouraged this project from the beginning, and we are grateful to him and to the School for their support. We also appreciate the contributions of Marc Roberts, Dorothy Robyn, and the staff of the Case Program at the Kennedy School of Government at Harvard.

Introduction

Dean Acheson, Secretary of State under President Truman, once described the place of morality in making foreign policy in this way: "Our discussions centered on the appraisal of dangers and risks, the weighing of the need for decisive and effective action against considerations of prudence. . . . Moral talk did not bear on the issue." When one of his colleagues objected to a course of action charging that it was morally wrong, Acheson's reply probably reflected the conventional wisdom of American policymakers at the time. He told his colleague that on the Day of Judgment his view might be confirmed and that he was free to go forth and preach the necessity of salvation, but that "it was not, however, a view which I would entertain as a public servant."

The public servants whose views are revealed in the Pentagon Papers and the Watergate Transcripts apparently accepted—with a vengeance—Acheson's view that ethics has no place in politics. One has to look long and hard to find any hint of "moral talk" in these or similar documents of government at that time. To preserve national honor or to keep a president in office seemed to be the noblest aims to which these officials aspired. Its use as a technique of public relations appeared to be the most important role for ethics. Certainly, many officials continued to serve conscientiously, and many policies fulfilled the public interest. But insofar as officials heeded ethics, they did so tacitly. They were, at best, closet moralists.

Partly because of public reaction to Vietnam and Watergate, the climate is now more favorable for ethics, or at least for talk about ethics. Public officials are less hesitant to raise ethical questions and are less reluctant to accept ethical constraints on at least some of their conduct. In 1977, Congress passed the toughest code of ethics in its history. And in 1978, it imposed a strict code on the executive branch, setting up an Office of Government Ethics to enforce it. Ethics became a salient issue in the 1988 presidential campaign. Several presidents and executive agencies have appointed commissions, councils, and aides to advise them on questions of ethics. These developments have hardly brought an end to official misconduct: it remains at least as frequent and no less flagrant (as the Iran-Contra Affair illustrates). But public officials no longer find it so easy to avoid answering for their questionable conduct. Even more significantly, questions of undeniable moral content have captured a prominent place on the political agenda. Officials cannot escape talking about ethics when they address, for example, issues of nuclear deterrence, affirmative action, abortion, surrogate parenting, or AIDS-testing.

One reason for some of these changes is, no doubt, that politicians have discovered that moral talk, and sometimes even moral action, help them win or stay in office. But there are also, as there have always been, good moral reasons for public officials to be guided by ethical considerations in making policy. The reasons are now even more compelling, because the scope and stakes of American politics are greater than ever.

Public officials use means—such as violence and the threat of violence—that affect the fate of all of us and future generations as well. And the goods that our political institutions distribute—such as health care and employment opportunities—are among those that people value the most. Because officials and institutions act in ways that seriously affect the well-being of many other people and societies, we want their actions to be guided by rules that prevent them from subordinating other people's interests to their own, or the interests of some people to those of others. Because in a democracy officials and institutions are supposed to act in our name and only on our authority, we want their actions to conform to the moral principles we share with each other.

Moral or ethical principles, broadly speaking, express the rights and duties that individuals should respect when they act in ways that seriously affect the well-being of other individuals and society, and the conditions that collective practices and policies should satisfy when these similarly affect the well-being of individuals and society. Those who reject the relevance of ethics to politics do not necessarily reject all principled approaches to politics. They often recommend that public officials use principles of prudence to tell them how to achieve their own goals, or the goals of their institutions, in the most efficient way possible. What distinguishes ethical principles is the disinterested perspective they embody. Prudence asks whether an action or policy serves the interests of some particular individual or group or nation. Ethics asks whether an action or policy could be accepted by anyone who did not know his or her particular circumstances (such as social class, race, or nationality).

When prudence opposes morality in politics, we sometimes describe this as a conflict between expedience and principle. In a conflict so described, almost no one wants to argue in favor of expedience over principle. But some may argue that the free pursuit of self-interest will contribute to the public interest—at least if social and political institutions are designed correctly. But this claim does not fundamentally challenge the relevance of morality to politics; it simply proposes a (supposedly) more effective means of achieving moral ends in politics. If there is a dispute, it is over the devices of moralists, not their desires.

Should we try to change the principles that motivate public officials, or should we try to restructure political institutions to elicit ethical behavior from those who are self-interested? Presumably we have to attempt both, and perhaps we should want to change the structures of power in government and society so that citizens and officials can live together in a genuinely moral community. Whatever ways we choose to realize morality in politics, we must understand the meaning, justification, and application of moral principles in political life. This is the subject of political ethics.

Discussions of political ethics are hard to find in the literature on American politics or moral philosophy. Texts in American government tend to concentrate on the mechanics of power. If they do not banish ethics from politics, they keep it safely segregated in a realm of ideals that rarely intrude into the real world of politics. The literature of moral philosophy often takes the opposite, equally mistaken, approach. It introduces the principles of ordinary morality into politics without change. It attends to none of the special features of political life—neither the necessities of politics in general nor the imperatives of democratic politics in particular. The moral values of the political process itself, so important in a democracy, usually meet with benign neglect.

Although political ethics must be consistent with a more general theory of ethics, it cannot be the same as ordinary ethics because political life differs in morally significant ways from private life. More than most citizens, public officials assume responsibility for protecting the rights and interests of all of us. They act in our name and on our behalf. And the environment in which they act is largely impersonal and intractable. Often it is populated with powerful people and institutions that are hostile, sometimes extremely hostile, to the purposes of public-spirited officials. These and other differences between public and private life do not make ethics irrelevant to politics. If anything they make it all the more important. But they do require us to take account of the special characteristics of politics as we frame our moral judgments.

We make these moral judgments about two different aspects of politics—the ethics of the process and the ethics of policy. The first part of this book considers the moral problems of the methods used to achieve political goals, while the second part examines problems of the content of the goals themselves. The cases focus on problems of public policy and the officials who make it. Public policy is not necessarily the most important part of politics, but it plays an increasingly important role in the modern state. Knowing how to think ethically about the means and ends of public policy is essential not only for officials but for all participants in the democratic process.

The moral problem of process is that politics often requires public officials to use bad means to achieve good ends—means, such as violence, that ordinary citizens may not use except under the most extraordinary circumstances. The moral demands of ordinary politics may include a willingness to use and threaten to use violence, to deceive and manipulate, to break promises and disobey orders—in short, to harm some people for the sake of helping more people or protecting the same people from even greater harm.

If we recognize that public officials cannot avoid using bad means to achieve good ends, we must seek moral limits on the use of these means. Machiavelli's advice to the Prince is inadequate: "He should not depart from the good if he can hold to it, but he should be ready to enter on evil *if he has to.*" Political necessity is at best a vague and at worst a misleading standard. We want to prevent public officials not only from pursuing their self-interest with impunity but also from unfairly sacrificing the interests of some people or societies for the sake of advancing the interests of others. To admit that politicians must get their hands dirty, therefore, is not to agree with Machiavelli that "when the effect is good . . . it always justifies the action." Both utilitarians and their critics agree that politicians cannot so easily or frequently justify using morally bad methods to achieve good ends. Utilitarians insist on a strict calculation of the costs and benefits of such means; politicians must employ only those means that maximize benefits to all people who are affected by their use. The leading critics of utilitarianism argue that some means, such as torturing innocent persons, are not justified, even when the gain in social benefits outweighs the costs.

The cases in the first three chapters of Part One invite you to examine the morally questionable means that are most commonly used in the political process: violence and the threat of violence, deception, manipulation, and promise-breaking. We encounter more rarely the method illustrated in chapter 4 in the protests by Daniel Ellsberg, Otto Otepka, and the sixty-five lawyers who worked for the Justice Department in the late 1960s. The occasion for "civil disobedience" by public officials is generally a governmental policy that they believe to be seriously unjust. But their decision to disobey is itself an instance of the problem of dirty hands. We (and they) must decide whether they are justified in doing wrong in order to do good. Faced with what they reasonably believe to be a morally wrong policy, should they disobey while remaining in office, leave office (silently or in protest), threaten to resign (as did Secretary of State Shultz over the President's proposal to give lie detector tests to government employees), or comply with the policy for the sake of furthering better policies in the future (as did several of the engineers who opposed the decision to launch the space shuttle *Challenger*)?

The cases in Part Two illustrate the ethical problems of determining the goals of public policy. In everyday life we must choose among the many things that we ideally would like to accomplish. But our choices generally do not raise the same difficult moral questions as in politics, because in private life we are not responsible for acting in the interests of so many other people and reconciling their conflicts over such a wide range of goals. Competing preferences, scarce resources, and stakes as high as life and death combine with the duties of office to make the choices among policy goals morally hard ones.

Utilitarianism is attractive as a theory for guiding hard choices in politics because it offers a single simple principle—maximize social happiness—by which to resolve all conflicts among policies. The first case in Part Two, which assesses the risks of nuclear power, suggests that, for both empirical and moral reasons, this hope of theoretical simplicity may be illusory. Even if the experts appointed by the Atomic Energy Commission had been able to estimate the level of risk accurately, they seemed to concede that they could not decide, by using policy analysis (based on utilitarianism), whether that level was socially acceptable. The second case in chapter 5 features a public official who acknowledges this limitation of policy analysis. William Ruckelshaus, as the head of the Environmental Protection Agency, was charged with setting standards to regulate the American Smelting and Refining Company (Asarco), whose arsenic emissions were polluting the air in the Tacoma, Washington, area. "For me to sit here in Washington and tell the people of Tacoma what is an acceptable risk," he said, "would be at best arrogant and at worst inexcusable." Ruckelshaus held public workshops to inform concerned citizens and to help the EPA decide upon pollution standards. Yet the political process could not fully answer the questions that policy analysis had failed to answer, and Ruckelshaus had to combine the results of both to make his decision. The case calls into question not whether policy analysis should be used at all, but what place it should have in the broader process of policy-making.

Many critics of policy analysis question whether the utilitarian principle is a desirable standard for choosing among policy options even in theory. They take issue with two assumptions of policy analysis as it is commonly practiced: that all competing goods can be reduced to a common measure (generally money) and that justice entails maximizing social welfare rather than distributing goods in a fair way among individuals. But utilitarians, in turn, challenge their critics to supply a better principle or set of principles by which public officials can make hard choices among competing goods.

This challenge is taken up by Arizona legislators who, as portrayed in chapter 6, faced a hard choice in calculating the costs and benefits of alternative uses of scarce social resources. Should state tax monies be used to fund expensive organ transplants, basic health care for the poor, or both? The Arizona legislature decided to expand basic health care for poor, pregnant women and for children, rather than to fund organ transplants for a smaller number of citizens in need of more expensive, catastrophic health care. When an Arizona resident died after being denied a liver transplant, a public controversy erupted. Many of the critics of the legislature implicitly appealed to the egalitarian principle of distribution according to need. An egalitarian principle (prohibiting discrimination) is explicitly invoked by opponents of AIDS-testing by insurance companies, the subject of the second case in chapter 6. The insurance companies deny that setting higher rates for applicants who test positive for AIDS constitutes unfair discrimination; they argue that doing so is no different than denying coverage to applicants who have cancer, heart disease, or diabetes. To decide who is right in these two cases and why, we must not only evaluate but also give more content to the egalitarian moral principles that figure in the debates.

The egalitarian principle that is commonly applied to employment policy is equal opportunity. But in a society where past discrimination has prevented some minorities and women from developing their talents and obtaining the same jobs as equally talented white men, it is not obvious whether equal opportunity in employment requires nondiscrimination or preferential treatment. The cases in chapter 7 ask you to choose between competing views of what constitutes fair employment practices in industry and in government.

No choice is harder to justify in a liberal democracy than the choice between saving life and protecting liberty. The cases in chapters 8 and 9 illustrate significant variations of this conflict. "Legalizing Laetrile" poses a problem of legislative paternalism: Should government restrict the liberty of some citizens for the sake of prolonging or saving their lives? The Food and Drug Administration's prohibition on marketing of a "do-it-yourself kit for AIDS testing" poses the parallel problem of bureaucratic paternalism. Authorized by Congress to set standards for marketing of health care products, should the FDA restrict liberty for the sake of protecting citizens from false information or psychic trauma?

Abortion raises the even more difficult problem of choosing between life and liberty when citizens disagree over what constitutes a human life. Joseph Califano's account of his own struggle with this dilemma while secretary of health, education and welfare exemplifies a problem of hard choices, and also brings us back to the problem of dirty hands with a new twist: should citizens accept a public office that requires them to pursue policies contrary to their own moral principles? From the perspective of a different office, members of Congress faced the no less difficult problem of determining the government's policy on funding abortion. The 1988 congressional debate over Medicaid funding of abortions in cases of rape or incest brings out the complexity of the political conflict between life and liberty. If we assume that the legalization of abortion is morally justified, we must ask whether the government should give poor women the financial means to exercise their freedom to obtain an abortion. The question becomes especially difficult when we recognize that citizens reasonably disagree over the morality of legalized abortion and therefore over the value of the liberty that is at stake in the funding policy.

Recent controversies over the commercial practice of surrogate parenting present another variation on the conflict between life and liberty. Proponents defend the practice as an exercise of the fundamental freedoms of procreation and contract, while critics argue that it degrades human life by exploiting women and treating children as commodities. Two sets of proposals before the New York State legislature, one recommending and the other opposing the legal enforcement of surrogate parenting contracts, reveal some of the moral and political dimensions of the conflict.

This case, like most of the cases in the book, is full of details, ranging from scientific and legal technicalities to biographical facts about the officials who are featured. The cases are designed to represent, as far as possible, actual decisions and policies rather than hypothetical ones. The value of examining real cases is, first of all, to come to appreciate the complexity that confronts officials who make policy and citizens who assess it. One of the most difficult but least examined steps in political ethics is to identify and frame the ethical issues themselves. Issues do not usually announce themselves as moral dilemmas; they often lie buried in a mass of facts and a welter of claims and counterclaims. The cases call for some moral detective work to discover the ethical suspects among the many leads the facts may suggest.

The complexity of the cases also serves a second purpose. Moral principles in their pristine form often seem to have little critical force in politics. Either they are so general that everyone readily accepts them as truisms, or they are so extreme that almost no one takes them seriously. By trying to apply the principles to particular cases, we can begin to see exactly what difference which principles make in our political judgments. Finally, the complexity should remind us that context matters in political ethics. The cases, of course, cannot give a full account of the history of the events and institutions or the structures of social and economic power. But they provide enough information to prompt us to ask what more must be known about the context to reach ethical conclusions. After reading each case, one should always ask what further information is necessary to arrive at an adequately informed conclusion. The information provided in the case is intended to be as much an invitation to further research as an account of the facts relevant to the case.

The subjects of some of the cases are officials at the highest levels of government, making decisions of great historical significance—as in the decision to use the atomic bomb against Japan. And some are statements of policies with far-reaching implications for society now and in the future—as in the reports on nuclear energy. We have included such cases because they raise important issues in themselves and because they illustrate principles that have wider application. But equally important are the cases that describe less famous and less momentous events in which lower level officials make decisions that directly affect relatively few people, such as the Denver Income Maintenance Experiment, which included fewer than two hundred families. Such cases represent the more typical moral world of politics. It is a world that both citizens and officials can more often influence because the scale of its problems is more manageable and because the patterns of its problems are more predictable. Though less dramatic than the once-in-a-lifetime dilemmas we more often hear about, these decisions of normal politics cumulatively affect at least as many people.

The range of cases is intended to indicate that ethical problems may appear almost any place in political life. Behind the seemingly tedious and technical dispute over the accounting practices in the New York City fiscal crisis lay large questions of democratic accountability. In Califano's story of the abortion battles, the seemingly petty disputes over legislative language (for example, whether rape must be reported within thirty, sixty, or ninety days) actually affect the welfare of many citizens and reveal disagreements of fundamental principle. Ethical issues do not arrive only at great moments in history; they also dwell in the routine of everyday politics.

However valuable cases may be, they cannot stand alone. All of the selections in this book are meant to be read in conjunction with works in moral philosophy and political theory. Such works provide principles to help assess the cases, and the cases may sometimes suggest revisions in the principles to take account of the special features of politics. Recommended readings accompany each set of cases. The recommendations are neither exclusive nor exhaustive, and other works not mentioned may be equally appropriate. But without some substantial basis in theory, any analysis of the cases is likely to be superficial.

At the end of each set of cases are comments and questions designed to encourage discussions of the ethical issues that the cases raise. Since ethical analysis should be viewed as a process of deliberation, it is best conducted (at least in part) through discussion with other people. This is especially true for political ethics. In a democracy, it is only through persuading other citizens of the moral worth of our cause that we can legitimately win their support in the making of public policies.

Recommended Reading

The best brief introduction to moral philosophy is still William K. Frankena, *Ethics*, 2d ed. (Englewood Cliffs, N.J.: Prentice Hall, 1973). Also see J. L. Mackie, *Ethics* (New York: Penguin, 1977), and Bernard Williams, *Morality* (New York: Harper and Row, 1972). Two useful readers are: Tom L. Beauchamp (ed.), *Philosophical Ethics* (New York: McGraw-Hill, 1982), and Peter Singer (ed.), *Applied Ethics* (New York: Oxford University Press, 1986). For some interesting applications of moral theory to a wide range of topics, see Jonathan Glover, *Causing Death and Saving Lives* (New York: Penguin, 1978). Generally on political ethics, see Joel Fleishman et al. (eds.), *Public Duties: The Moral Obligations of Government Officials* (Cambridge, Mass.: Harvard University Press, 1981), and Dennis F. Thompson, *Political Ethics and Public Office* (Cambridge, Mass.: Harvard University Press, 1987).

A general framework for questions about the ethics of process should be informed by the literature on the problem of dirty hands. The classic sources are Machiavelli, *The Prince* (New York: Random House, 1950), and Max Weber, "Politics as a Vocation," in H. H. Gerth and C. W. Mills (eds.), *From Max Weber* (New York: Oxford University Press, 1958). If you read only one modern work on the subject, it should be Michael Walzer, "Political Action: The Problem of Dirty Hands," *Philosophy & Public Affairs* 1 (Winter 1972), pp. 160–80; reprinted in Marshall Cohen et al. (eds.) *War and Moral Responsibility* (Princeton, N.J.: Princeton University Press, 1974). Some other contemporary discussions are the articles by Stuart Hampshire, Bernard Williams, and Thomas Nagel in Hampshire et al. (eds.), *Public and Private Morality* (New York: Cambridge University Press, 1978), and Dennis F. Thompson, "Democratic Dirty Hands," in *Political Ethics and Public Office*, pp. 11-39.

The ethics of policy has generated a large literature in recent years, in part stimulated by the revival of moral and political philosophy. For a provocative view, see Robert E. Goodin, *Political Theory and Public Policy* (Chicago: University of Chicago Press, 1982). A general approach is presented by Brian Barry and Douglas W. Rae, "Political Evaluation," in F. I. Greenstein and N. W. Polsby (eds.), *Handbook of Political Science* (Reading, Mass.: Addison Wesley, 1975), vol. I, pp. 337–401. On the strengths and weaknesses of utilitarianism, the foundation of the dominant approach to policy analysis, see J. J. C. Smart and Bernard Williams, *Utilitarianism For and Against* (New York: Cambridge University Press, 1973). More recent discussions of these issues are Samuel Scheffler, *The Rejection of Consequentialism* (Oxford: Clarendon Press, 1984), and Thomas Nagel, *The View from Nowhere* (New York: Oxford University Press, 1986).

The philosophical work that has been most influential on the study of the ethics of policy is John Rawls, *A Theory of Justice* (Cambridge, Mass.: Harvard University Press, 1971). For commentaries on Rawls, see Norman Daniels (ed.), *Reading Rawls* (New York: Basic Books, 1976).

A selection of philosophical writing on particular policies appears in the readers compiled by the editors of *Philosophy & Public Affairs* and published by Princeton University Press. See Marshall Cohen et al. (eds.), *Equality and Preferential Treatment* (1978); *Medicine and Moral Philosophy* (1982); *Rights and Wrongs of Abortion* (1974); *War and Moral Responsibility* (1974); and Charles R. Beitz et al. (eds.), *International Ethics* (1985). Also see the series of books, Maryland Studies in Public Philosophy, edited by the Center for Philosophy and Public Policy, University of Maryland, and published by Rowman and Allanheld.

Students can keep up with current work in this subject by regularly reading the journals *Ethics* (University of Chicago Press) and *Philosophy & Public Affairs* (Princeton University Press).

Part One

The Ethics of Process

1 Violence

Introduction

Violence violates the fundamental moral prohibition against harming persons, yet governments must sometimes use violent means to defend that same fundamental principle. The most dramatic instance of the use of violence is war, and the most terrifying kind of war is nuclear war. The cases in this chapter raise questions about nuclear war and the means used to prevent it.

"War is cruel and you cannot refine it," General Sherman told the citizens of Atlanta who protested against the brutality of his invasion of their city. Many other military and political leaders as well as moral philosophers have agreed with Sherman. If your cause is just in a war, you should use any means necessary to win it. To place moral constraints on the fighting of a war, the argument goes, would simply prolong it and could increase the chances of war in the future by making war more morally respectable.

In most wars most nations nevertheless have accepted some moral constraints on their conduct (such as not torturing prisoners) and the philosophical writing on just war has long distinguished the justice of a war from the justice of the means used to fight it. The former does not necessarily determine the latter. Even in the war against the Nazis, we should condemn some methods—for example, the practice of the Free French forces who enlisted Moroccan mercenaries by promising that they could, with impunity, rape Italian women. And we want to distinguish moral from immoral actions of men fighting on the side of the aggressor nation: we praise General Rommel for ignoring Hitler's order to shoot all prisoners captured behind the lines.

The basic principle underlying most rules of war is that it is morally wrong to attack noncombatants. Noncombatants are defined as those who are not fighting or not supplying the means of fighting the war. Farmers and nurses are noncombatants, while munitions workers and soldiers are combatants. Different moral traditions give different reasons for this prohibition, but all regard it as important.

At the same time most philosophers of just wars recognize that noncombatants will inevitably be killed in modern warfare—sometimes justifiably so. The major problem then becomes either (1) to formulate the prohibition so as to justify some deaths of noncombatants or (2) to specify the conditions under which the prohibition may be suspended. The most prominent example of the first alternative is the doctrine of double-effect, which holds that the death of noncombatants is permissible if it is an unintended (though foreseen) side effect of a morally legitimate end. The doctrine, for example, would permit an air strike against an enemy missile site even if civilians lived nearby. The other alternative would allow civilians to be killed directly only if necessary to stop the imminent destruction of a nation. In this view, British bombing of German cities may have been justified until 1942 but not thereafter.

Nuclear weapons, some have argued, make obsolete all these fine distinctions and the rules of war that depend on them. With the possible exception of tactical weapons, nuclear forces strike directly at civilian populations. The destruction of Hiroshima and Nagasaki could hardly be described as an unintended side effect; nor was the bombing necessary to prevent the defeat of the United States. But the new technology may increase the need to take the old rules of war seriously. Even some of those who favored the bombing of Hiroshima and Nagasaki recognized that it called for moral justification and believed they could provide it. Writing only a few months before President Harry S. Truman accepted his advice to use the bomb against Japan, Secretary of State Henry Stimson insisted that the "rule of sparing the civilian population should be applied as far as possible to the use of any new weapon." Stimson's own defense of the use of that weapon, reprinted as the first selection in this chapter, shows how he came to terms with that moral rule.

Nuclear deterrence also creates problems for the rules of war—or perhaps we should say the rules create problems for deterrence. The essence of deterrence, some say, is an immoral threat: if the enemy launches a nuclear attack against us, we will retaliate by destroying the enemy's population. Deterrence, others in turn argue, is morally justified because to threaten evil consequences is the best way, or the only way, to prevent them from occurring. But critics of deterrence object that the threat itself (if it is credible as it must be) increases the likelihood of nuclear war. In any case, the critics say, the threat remains immoral, and we should not accept indefinitely any system of defense based on such a threat.

The Strategic Defense Initiative (SDI), announced by President Reagan in the spring of 1983 in a statement reprinted in this chapter, holds out the promise of a future in which the United States (and its allies) no longer rely on the threat of nuclear attack or retaliation. The prevailing system of nuclear deterrence would become obsolete if the United States developed a strategic space shield that "missiles could not penetrate, a shield that could protect us from nuclear missiles just as a roof protects a family from rain." Advocates of SDI acknowledge that the vision will not soon become a reality, but they argue that the potential moral and strategic benefits are great enough to justify large-scale investment in research and development. Critics argue that the development of SDI raises moral problems similar to those affecting familiar forms of nuclear deterrence: parts of the SDI system may be used for offensive purposes; other countries may reasonably regard the system as a threat even if the United States does not intend to use it offensively; SDI, a defense system the effectiveness of which will remain uncertain for a decade or more, requires an enormous investment of scarce social resources.

The Decision to Use the Atomic Bomb

Henry L. Stimson

In recent months there has been much comment about the decision to use atomic bombs in attacks on the Japanese cities of Hiroshima and Nagasaki. This decision was one of the gravest made by our government in recent years, and it is entirely proper that it should be widely discussed. I have therefore decided to record for all who may be interested my understanding of the events which led up to the attack on Hiroshima on August 6, 1945, on Nagasaki on August 9, and the Japanese decision to surrender on August 10. No single individual can hope to know exactly what took place in the minds of all of those who had a share in these events, but what follows is an exact description of our thoughts and actions as I find them in the records and in my clearest recollection.

It was in the fall of 1941 that the question of atomic energy was first brought directly to my attention. At that time President Roosevelt appointed a committee consisting of Vice President Wallace, General Marshall, Dr. Vannevar Bush, Dr. James B. Conant, and myself. The function of this committee was to advise the President on questions of policy relating to the study of nuclear fission which was then proceeding both in this country and in Great Britain. For nearly four years thereafter I was directly connected with all major decisions of policy on the development and use of atomic energy, and from May 1, 1943, until my resignation as Secretary of War on September 21, 1945, I was directly responsible to the President for the administration of the entire undertaking; my chief advisers in this period were General Marshall, Dr. Bush, Dr. Conant, and Major General Leslie R. Groves, the officer in charge of the project. At the same time I was the President's adviser on the military employment of atomic energy.

The policy adopted and steadily pursued by President Roosevelt and his advisers was a simple one. It was to spare no effort in securing the earliest possible successful development of an atomic weapon. The reasons for this policy were equally simple. The original experimental achievement of atomic fission had occurred in Germany in 1938, and it was known that the Germans had continued their experiments. In 1941 and 1942 they were believed to be ahead of us, and it was vital that they should not be the first to bring atomic weapons into the field of battle. Furthermore, if we should be the first to develop the weapon, we should have a great new instrument for shortening the war and minimizing destruction. At no time from 1941 to 1945 did I ever hear it suggested by the President, or by any other responsible member of the government, that atomic energy should not be used in the war. All of us of course understood the terrible responsibility involved in our attempt to unlock the doors to such a devastating weapon; President Roosevelt particularly spoke to me many times of his own awareness of the catastrophic potentialities of our work. But we were at war, and the work must be done. I therefore emphasize that it was our common objective through-

"The Decision to Use the Atomic Bomb" as it appeared in *Harper's Magazine*, later incorporated in chapter "The Atomic Bomb and the Surrender of Japan" in *On Active Service in Peace and War*, by Henry L. Stimson and McGeorge Bundy.

out the war to be the first to produce an atomic weapon and use it. The possible atomic weapon was considered to be a new and tremendously powerful explosive, as legitimate as any other of the deadly explosive weapons of modern war. The entire purpose was the production of a military weapon; on no other ground could the wartime expenditure of so much time and money have been justified. The exact circumstances in which that weapon might be used were unknown to any of us until the middle of 1945, and when that time came, as we shall presently see, the military use of atomic energy was connected with larger questions of national policy.

The extraordinary story of the successful development of the atomic bomb has been well told elsewhere. As time went on it became clear that the weapon would not be available in time for use in the European theater, and the war against Germany was successfully ended by the use of what are now called conventional means. But in the spring of 1945 it became evident that the climax of our prolonged atomic effort was at hand. By the nature of atomic chain reactions, it was impossible to state with certainty that we had succeeded until a bomb had actually exploded in a full-scale experiment; nevertheless it was considered exceedingly probable that we should by midsummer have successfully detonated the first atomic bomb. This was to be done at the Alamogordo Reservation in New Mexico. It was thus time for detailed consideration of our future plans. What had begun as a well-founded hope was now developing into a reality.

On March 15, 1945, I had my last talk with President Roosevelt. My diary record of this conversation gives a fairly clear picture of the state of our thinking at that time. I have removed the name of the distinguished public servant who was fearful lest the Manhattan (atomic) project be "a lemon"; it was an opinion common among those not fully informed.

"The President. . . had suggested that I come over to lunch today. . . First I took up with him a memorandum which he sent to me from ________, who had been alarmed at the rumors of extravagance in the Manhattan project. ________ suggested that it might become disastrous and he suggested that we get a body of 'outside' scientists to pass upon the project because rumors are going around that Vannevar Bush and Jim Conant have sold the President a lemon on the subject and ought to be checked up on. It was rather a jittery and nervous memorandum and rather silly, and I was prepared for it and I gave the President a list of the scientists who were actually engaged on it to show the very high standing of them and it comprised four Nobel Prize men, and also how practically every physicist of standing was engaged with us in the project. Then I outlined to him the future of it and when it was likely to come off and told him how important it was to get ready. I went over with him the two schools of thought that exist in respect to the future control after the war of this project, in case it is successful, one of them being the secret close-in attempted control of the project by those who control it now, and the other being the international control based upon freedom both of science and of access. I told him that those things must be settled before the first projectile is used and that he must be ready with a statement to come out to the people on it just as soon as that is done. He agreed to that. . . ."

This conversation covered the three aspects of the question which were then uppermost in our minds. First, it was always necessary to suppress a lingering doubt that any such titanic undertaking could be successful. Second, we must consider the implications of success in terms of its long-range postwar effect. Third, we must face the problem that would be presented at the time of our first use of the weapon, for with that first use there must be some public statement.

I did not see Franklin Roosevelt again. The next time I went to the White House to discuss atomic energy was April 25, 1945, and I went to explain the nature of the problem to a man whose only previous knowledge of our activities was that of a Senator who had loyally accepted our assurance that the matter must be kept a secret from him. Now he was President and Commander-in-Chief, and the final responsibility in this as in so many other matters must be his. President Truman accepted this responsibility with the same fine spirit that Senator Truman had shown before in accepting our refusal to inform him.

I discussed with him the whole history of the project. We had with us General Groves, who explained in detail the progress which had been made and the probable future course of the work. I also discussed with President Truman the broader aspects of the subject, and the memorandum which I used in this discussion is again a fair sample of the state of our thinking at the time.

Memorandum discussed with President Truman April 25, 1945:

"1. Within four months we shall in all probability have completed the most terrible weapon ever known in human history, one bomb of which could destroy a whole city.

"2. Although we have shared its development with the U.K., physically the U.S. is at present in the position of controlling the resources with which to construct and use it and no other nation could reach this position for some years.

"3. Nevertheless it is practically certain that we could not remain in this position indefinitely.

"a. Various segments of its discovery and production are widely known among many scientists in many countries, although few scientists are now acquainted with the whole process which we have developed.

"b. Although its construction under present methods requires great scientific and industrial effort and raw materials, which are temporarily mainly within the possession and knowledge of U.S. and U.K., it is extremely probable that much easier and cheaper methods of production will be discovered by scientists in the future, together with the use of materials of much wider distribution. As a result, it is extremely probable that the future will make it possible for atomic bombs to be constructed by smaller nations or even groups, or at least by a larger nation in a much shorter time.

"4. As a result, it is indicated that the future may see a time when such a weapon may be constructed in secret and used suddenly and effectively with devastating power by a willful nation or group against an unsuspecting nation or group of much greater size and material power. With its aid even a very powerful unsuspecting nation might be conquered within a very few days by a very much smaller one. [A brief reference to the estimated capabilities of other nations is here omitted; it in no way affects the course of the argument.]

"5. The world in its present state of moral advancement compared with its technical development would be eventually at the mercy of such a weapon. In other words, modern civilization might be completely destroyed.

"6. To approach any world peace organization of any pattern now likely to be considered, without an appreciation by the leaders of our country of the power of this new weapon, would seem to be unrealistic. No system of control heretofore considered would be adequate to control this menace. Both inside any particular country and between the nations of the world, the control of this weapon will undoubtedly be a matter of the greatest difficulty and would involve such thoroughgoing rights of inspection and internal controls as we have never heretofore contemplated.

"7. Furthermore, in the light of our present position with reference to this weapon, the question of sharing it with other nations and, if so shared, upon what terms, becomes a primary question of our foreign relations. Also our leadership in the war and in the development of this weapon has placed a certain moral responsibility upon us which we cannot shirk without very serious responsibility for any disaster to civilization which it would further.

"8. On the other hand, if the problem of the proper use of this weapon can be solved, we would have the opportunity to bring the world into a pattern in which the peace of the world and our civilization can be saved.

"9. As stated in General Groves' report, steps are under way looking towards the establishment of a select committee of particular qualifications for recommending action to the executive and legislative branches of our government when secrecy is no longer in full effect. The committee would also recommend the actions to be taken by the War Department prior to that time in anticipation of the postwar problems. All recommendations would of course be first submitted to the President."

The next step in our preparations was the appointment of the committee referred to in paragraph 9 above. This committee, which was known as the Interim Committee, was charged with the function of advising the President on the various questions raised by our apparently imminent success in developing the atomic weapon. I was its chairman, but the principal labor of guiding its extended deliberations fell to George L. Harrison, who acted as chairman in my absence. It will be useful to consider the work of the committee in some detail. Its members were the following, in addition to Mr. Harrison and myself:

James F. Byrnes (then a private citizen) as personal representative of the President.

Ralph A. Byrd, Under Secretary of the Navy.

William L. Clayton, Assistant Secretary of State.

Dr. Vannevar Bush, Director, Office of Scientific Research and Development, and president of the Carnegie Institution of Washington.

Dr. Karl Compton, Chief of the Office of Field Service in the Office of Scientific Research and Development, and president of the Massachusetts Institute of Technology.

Dr. James B. Conant, Chairman of the National Defense Research Committee, and president of Harvard University.

The discussions of the committee ranged over the whole field of atomic energy, in its political, military, and scientific aspects. That part of its work which particularly concerns us here relates to its recommendations for the use of atomic energy against Japan, but it should be borne in mind that these recommendations were not made in a vacuum. The committee's work included the drafting of the statements which were published immediately after the first bombs were dropped, the drafting of a bill for the domestic control of atomic energy, and recommendations looking toward the international control of atomic energy. The Interim Committee was assisted in its work by a Scientific Panel whose members were the following: Dr. A. H. Compton, Dr. Enrico Fermi, Dr. E. O. Lawrence, and Dr. J. R. Oppenheimer. All four were nuclear physicists of the first rank; all four had held positions of great importance in the atomic project from its inception. At a meeting with the Interim Committee and the Scientific Panel on May 31, 1945, I urged all those present to feel free to express themselves on any phase of the subject, scientific or political. Both General Marshall and I at this meeting expressed the view that atomic energy could not be considered simply in terms of military weapons but must also be considered in terms of a new relationship of man to the universe.

On June 1, after its discussions with the Scientific Panel, the Interim Committee unanimously adopted the following recommendations:

1. The bomb should be used against Japan as soon as possible.

2. It should be used on a dual target—that is, a military installation or war plant surrounded by or adjacent to houses and other buildings most susceptible to damage, and

3. It should be used without prior warning [of the nature of the weapon]. (One member of the committee, Mr. Bard, later changed his view and dissented from the third recommendation.)

In reaching these conclusions the Interim Committee carefully considered such alternatives as a detailed advance warning or a demonstration in some uninhabited area. Both of these suggestions were discarded as impractical. They were not regarded as likely to be effective in compelling a surrender of Japan and both of them involved serious risks. Even the New Mexico test would not give final proof that any given bomb was certain to explode when dropped from an airplane. Quite apart from the generally unfamiliar nature of atomic explosives, there was the whole problem of exploding a bomb at a predetermined height in the air by a complicated mechanism which could not be tested in the static test of New Mexico. Nothing would have been more damaging to our effort to obtain surrender than a warning or a demonstration followed by a dud—and this was a real possibility. Furthermore, we had no bombs to waste. It was vital that a sufficient effect be quickly obtained with the few we had.

The Interim Committee and the Scientific Panel also served as a channel through which suggestions from other scientists working on the atomic project were forwarded to me and to the President. Among the suggestions thus forwarded was one memorandum which questioned using the bomb at all against the enemy. On June 16, 1945, after consideration of that memorandum, the Scientific Panel made a report, from which I quote the following paragraphs:

"The opinions of our scientific colleagues on the initial use of these weapons are not unanimous: they range from the proposal of a purely technical demonstration to that of the military application best designed to induce surrender. Those who advocate a purely technical demonstration would wish to outlaw the use of atomic weapons, and have feared that if we use the weapons now our position in future negotiations will be prejudiced. Others emphasize the opportunity of saving American lives by immediate military use, and believe that such use will improve the international prospects, in that they are more concerned with the prevention of war than with the elimination of this special weapon. We find ourselves closer to these latter views: *we can propose no technical demonstration likely to bring an end to the war; we see no acceptable alternative to direct military use.* [Italics mine.]

"With regard to these general aspects of the use of atomic energy, it is clear that we, as scientific men, have no proprietary rights. It is true that we are among the few citizens who have had occasion to give thoughtful consideration to these problems during the past few years. We have, however, no claim to special competence in solving the political, social, and military problems which are presented by the advent of atomic power."

The foregoing discussion presents the reasoning of the Interim Committee and its advisers. I have discussed the work of these gentlemen at length in order to make it clear that we sought the best advice that we could find. The committee's function was, of course, entirely advisory. The ultimate responsibility for the recommendation to the President rested upon me, and I have no desire to veil it. The conclusions of the committee were similar to my own, although I reached mine independently. I felt that to extract a genuine surrender from the Emperor and his military advisers, they must be administered a tremendous shock which would carry convincing proof of our power to destroy the Empire. Such an effective shock would save many times the number of lives, both American and Japanese, that it would cost.

The facts upon which my reasoning was based and steps taken to carry it out now follow.

The principal political, social, and military objective of the United States in the summer of 1945 was the prompt and complete surrender of Japan. Only the complete destruction of her military power could open the way to lasting peace.

Japan, in July 1945, had been seriously weakened by our increasingly violent attacks. It was known to us that she had gone so far as to make tentative proposals to the Soviet government, hoping to use the Russians as mediators in a negotiated peace. These vague proposals contemplated the retention by Japan of important conquered areas and were therefore not considered seriously. There was as yet no indication of any weakening in the Japanese determination to fight rather than accept unconditional surrender. If she should persist in her fight to the end, she had still a great military force.

In the middle of July 1945, the intelligence section of the War Department General Staff estimated Japanese military strength as follows: in the home islands, slightly under two million; in Korea, Manchuria, China proper, and Formosa, slightly over two million; in French Indo-China, Thailand, and Burma, over 200,000; in the East Indies area, including the Philippines, over 500,000; in the by-passed Pacific islands, over 100,000. The total strength of the Japanese Army was estimated at about five million men. These estimates later proved to be in very close agreement with official Japanese figures.

The Japanese Army was in much better condition than the Japanese Navy and Air Force. The Navy had practically ceased to exist except as a harrying force against an invasion fleet. The Air Force had been reduced mainly to reliance upon Kamikaze, or suicide, attacks. These latter, however, had already inflicted serious damage on our seagoing forces, and their possible effectiveness in a last ditch fight was a matter of real concern to our naval leaders.

As we understood it in July, there was a very strong possibility that the Japanese government might determine upon resistance to the end, in all the areas of the Far East under its control. In such an event the Allies would be faced with the enormous task of destroying an armed force of five million men and five thousand suicide aircraft, belonging to a race which had already demonstrated its ability to fight literally to the death.

The strategic plans of our armed forces for the defeat of Japan as they stood in July had been prepared without reliance upon the atomic bomb, which had not yet been tested in New Mexico. We were planning an intensified sea and air blockade and greatly intensified strategic air bombing through the summer and early fall, to be followed on November 1 by an invasion of the southern island of Kyushu. This would be followed in turn by an invasion of the main island of Honshu in the spring of 1946. The total U.S. military and naval force involved in this grand design was of the order of five million men; if all those indirectly concerned are included, it was larger still.

We estimated that if we should be forced to carry this plan to its conclusion, the major fighting force would not end until the latter part of 1946, at the earliest. I was informed that such operations might be expected to cost over a million casualties, to American forces alone. Additional large losses might be expected among our allies, and, of course, if our campaign were successful and if we could judge by previous experience, enemy casualties would be much larger than our own.

It was already clear in July that even before the invasion, we should be able to inflict enormously severe damage on the Japanese homeland by the combined application of "conventional" sea and air power. The critical question was whether this kind of action would induce surrender. It therefore became necessary to consider very carefully the probable state of mind of the enemy, and to assess with accuracy the line of conduct which might end his will to resist.

With these considerations in mind, I wrote a memorandum for the President, on July 2, which I believe fairly represents the thinking of the American government as it finally took shape in action. This memorandum was prepared after discussion and general agreement with Joseph C. Grew, Acting Secretary of State, and Secretary of the Navy Forrestal, and when I discussed it with the President, he expressed his general approval.

Memorandum for the President, July 2, 1945, on proposed program for Japan:

"1. The plans of operation up to and including the first landing have been authorized and the preparations for the operation are now actually going on. This situation was accepted by all members of your conference on Monday, June 18.

"2. There is reason to believe that the operation for occupation of Japan following the landing may be a very long, costly, and arduous struggle on our part. The terrain, much of which I have visited several times, has left the impression on my memory of being one which would be susceptible to a last ditch defense such as has been made on Iwo Jima and Okinawa and which of course is very much larger than either of those two areas. According to my recollection it will be much more unfavorable with regard to tank maneuvering than either the Philippines or Germany.

"3. If we once land on one of the main islands and begin a forceful occupation of Japan, we shall probably have cast the die of last ditch resistance. The Japanese are highly patriotic and certainly susceptible to calls for fanatical resistance to repel an invasion. Once started in actual invasion, we shall in my opinion have to go through with an even more bitter finish fight than in Germany. We shall incur the losses incident to such a war and we shall have to leave the Japanese islands even more thoroughly destroyed than was the case with Germany. This would be due both to the difference in the Japanese and German personal character and the differences in the size and character of the terrain through which the operations will take place.

"4. A question then comes: Is there any alternative to such a forceful occupation of Japan which will secure for us the equivalent of an unconditional surrender of her forces and a permanent destruction of her power again to strike an aggressive blow at the 'peace of the Pacific'? I am inclined to think that there is enough such chance to make it well worthwhile our giving them a warning of what is to come and a definite opportunity to capitulate. As above suggested, it should be tried before the actual forceful occupation of the homeland islands is begun and furthermore the warning should be given in ample time to permit a national reaction to set in.

"We have the following enormously favorable factors on our side—factors much weightier than those we had against Germany:

"Japan has no allies.

"Her navy is nearly destroyed and she is vulnerable to a surface and underwater blockade which can deprive her of sufficient food and supplies for her population.

"She is terribly vulnerable to our concentrated air attack upon her crowded cities, industrial and food resources.

"She has against her not only the Anglo-American forces but the rising forces of China and the ominous threat of Russia.

"We have inexhaustible and untouched industrial resources to bring to bear against her diminishing potential.

"We have great moral superiority through being the victim of her first sneak attack.

"The problem is to translate these advantages into prompt and economical achievement of our objectives. I believe Japan is susceptible to reason in such a crisis to a much greater extent than is indicated by our current press and other current comment. Japan is not a nation composed wholly of mad fanatics of an entirely different mentality from ours. On the contrary, she has within the past century shown herself to possess extremely intelligent people, capable in an unprecedentedly short time of adopting not only the complicated technique of Occidental civilization but to a substantial extent their culture and their political and social ideas. Her advance in all these respects during the short period of sixty or seventy years has been one of the most astounding feats of national progress in history—a leap from the isolated feudalism of centuries into the position of one of the six or seven great powers of the world. She has not only built up powerful armies and navies. She has maintained an honest and effective national finance and respected position in many of the sciences in which we pride ourselves. Prior to the forcible seizure of power over her government by the fanatical military group in 1931, she had for ten years lived a reasonably responsible and respectable international life.

"My own opinion is in her favor on the two points involved in this question:

"a. I think the Japanese nation has the mental intelligence and versatile capacity in such a crisis to recognize the folly of a fight to the finish and to accept the proffer of what will amount to an unconditional surrender; and

"b. I think she has within her population enough liberal leaders (although now submerged by the terrorists) to be depended upon for her reconstruction as a responsible member of the family of nations. I think she is better in this respect than Germany was. Her liberals yielded only at the point of the pistol and, so far as I am aware, their liberal attitude has not been personally subverted in the way which was so general in Germany.

"On the other hand, I think that the attempt to exterminate her armies and her population by gunfire or other means will tend to produce a fusion of race solidity and antipathy which has no analogy in the case of Germany. We have a national interest in creating, if possible, a condition wherein the Japanese nation may live as a peaceful and useful member of the future Pacific community.

"5. It is therefore my conclusion that a carefully timed warning be given to Japan by the chief representatives of the United States, Great Britain, China, and, if then a belligerent, Russia by calling upon Japan to surrender and permit the occupation of her country in order to insure its complete demilitarization for the sake of the future peace.

"This warning should contain the following elements:

"The varied and overwhelming character of the force we are about to bring to bear on the islands.

"The inevitability and completeness of the destruction which the full application of this force will entail.

"The determination of the Allies to destroy permanently all authority and influence of those who have deceived and misled the country into embarking on world conquest.

"The determination of the Allies to limit Japanese sovereignty to her main islands and to render them powerless to mount and support another war.

"The disavowal of any attempt to extirpate the Japanese as a race or to destroy them as a nation.

"A statement of our readiness, once her economy is purged of its militaristic influence, to permit the Japanese to maintain such industries, particularly of a light consumer character, as offer no threat of aggression against their neighbors, but which can produce a sustaining economy, and provide a reasonable standard of living. The statement should indicate our willingness, for this purpose, to give Japan trade access to external raw materials, but no longer any control over the sources of supply outside her main islands. It should also indicate our willingness, in accordance with our now established foreign policy, in due course to enter into mutually advantageous trade relations with her.

"The withdrawal from their country as soon as the above objectives of the Allies are accomplished, and as soon as there has been established a peacefully inclined government, of a character representative of the masses of the Japanese people. I personally think that if in saying this we should add that we do not exclude a constitutional monarchy under her present dynasty, it would substantially add to the chances of acceptance.

"6. Success of course will depend on the potency of the warning which we give her. She has an extremely sensitive national pride and, as we are now seeing every day, when actually locked with the enemy will fight to the very death. For that reason the warning must be tendered before the actual invasion has occurred and while the impending destruction, though clear beyond peradventure, has not yet reduced her to fanatical despair. If Russia is part of the threat, the Russian attack, if actual, must not have progressed too far. Our own bombing should be confined to military objectives as far as possible."

It is important to emphasize the double character of the suggested warning. It was designed to promise destruction if Japan resisted, and hope, if she surrendered.

It will be noted that the atomic bomb is not mentioned in this memorandum. On grounds of secrecy the bomb was never mentioned except when absolutely necessary and furthermore, it had not yet been tested. It was of course well forward in our minds as the memorandum was written and discussed that the bomb would be the best possible sanction if our warning were rejected.

The adoption of the policy outlined in the memorandum of July 2 was a decision of high politics; once it was accepted by the President, the position of the atomic bomb in our planning became quite clear. I find that I stated in my diary, as early as June 19, that "the last chance warning. . . must be given before an actual landing of the ground forces in Japan, and fortunately the plans provide for enough time to bring in the sanctions to our warning in the shape of heavy ordinary bombing attack and an attack of S-1." S-1 was a code name for the atomic bomb.

There was much discussion in Washington about the timing of the warning to Japan. The controlling factor in the end was the date already set for the Potsdam meeting of the Big Three. It was President Truman's decision that such a warning should be solemnly issued by the U.S. and the U.K. from this meeting, with the concurrence of the head of the Chinese government, so that it would be plain that *all* of Japan's principal enemies were in entire unity. This was done in the Potsdam ultimatum of July 26, which very closely followed the above memorandum of July 2 with the exception that it made no mention of the Japanese Emperor.

On July 28 the Premier of Japan, Suzuki, rejected the Potsdam ultimatum by announcing that it was "unworthy of public notice." In the face of this rejection we could only proceed to demonstrate that the ultimatum had meant exactly what it said when it stated that if the Japanese continued the war, "the full application of our military power, backed by our resolve, will mean the inevitable and complete destruction of the Japanese armed forces and just as inevitably the utter devastation of the Japanese homeland."

For such a purpose the atomic bomb was an entirely suitable weapon. The New Mexico test occurred while we were at Potsdam, on July 16. It was immediately clear that the power of the bomb measured up to our highest estimates. We had developed a weapon of such a revolutionary character that its use against the enemy might well be expected to produce exactly the kind of shock on the Japanese ruling oligarchy which we desired, strengthening the position of those who wished peace, and weakening that of the military party.

Because of the importance of the atomic mission against Japan, the detailed plans were brought to me by the military staff for approval. With President Truman's warm support I struck off the list of suggested targets the city of Kyoto. Although it was a target of considerable military importance, it had been the ancient capital of Japan and was a shrine of Japanese art and culture. We determined that it should be spared. I approved four other targets including the cities of Hiroshima and Nagasaki.

Hiroshima was bombed on August 6, and Nagasaki on August 9. These two cities were active working parts of the Japanese war effort. One was an army center; the other was naval and industrial. Hiroshima was the headquarters of the Japanese Army defending southern Japan and was a major military storage and assembly point. Nagasaki was a major seaport and it contained several large industrial plants of great wartime importance. We believed that our attacks had struck cities which must certainly be important to the Japanese military leaders, both Army and Navy, and we waited for a result. We waited one day.

Many accounts have been written about the Japanese surrender. After a prolonged Japanese cabinet session in which the deadlock was broken by the Emperor himself, the offer to surrender was made on August 10. It was based on the Potsdam terms, with a reservation concerning the sovereignty of the Emperor. While the Allied reply made no promises other than those already given, it implicitly recognized the Emperor's position by prescribing that his power must be subject to the orders of the Allied Supreme Commander. These terms were accepted on August 14 by the Japanese, and the instrument of surrender was formally signed on September 2, in Tokyo Bay. Our great objective was thus achieved, and all the evidence I have seen indicates that the controlling factor in the final Japanese decision to accept our terms of surrender was the atomic bomb.

The two atomic bombs which we had dropped were the only ones we had ready, and our rate of production at the time was very small. Had the war continued until the projected invasion on November 1, additional fire raids of B-29s would have been more destructive of life and property than the very limited number of atomic raids which we could have executed in the same period. But the atomic bomb was more than a weapon of terrible destruction; it was a psychological weapon. In March 1945, our Air Force had launched its first great incendiary raid on the Tokyo area. In this raid more damage was done and more casualties were inflicted than was the case at Hiroshima. Hundreds of bombers took part and hundreds of tons of incendiaries were dropped. Similar successive raids burned out a great part of the urban area of Japan, but the Japanese fought on. On August 6 one B-29 dropped a single atomic weapon on Hiroshima. Three days later a second bomb was dropped on Nagasaki and the war was over. So far as the Japanese could know, our ability to execute atomic attacks, if necessary by many planes at a time, was unlimited. As Dr. Karl Compton has said, "it was not one atomic bomb, or two, which brought surrender; it was the experience of what an atomic bomb will actually do to a community, *plus the dread of many more,* that was effective."

The bomb thus served exactly the purpose we intended. The peace part was able to take the path of surrender, and the whole weight of the Emperor's prestige was exerted in favor of peace. When the Emperor ordered surrender, and the small but dangerous group of fanatics who opposed him were brought under control, the Japanese became so subdued that the great undertaking of occupation and disarmament was completed with unprecedented ease.

In the foregoing pages I have tried to give an accurate account of my own personal observations of the circumstances which led up to the use of the atomic bomb and the reasons which underlay our use of it. To me they have always seemed compelling and clear, and I cannot see how any person vested with such responsibilities as mine could have taken any other course or given any other advice to his chiefs.

The Bomb, the War, and the Russians

Martin J. Sherwin

"The Bottom Facts"

Many of the questions that have plagued later commentators on the atomic bombings of Hiroshima and Nagasaki simply do not seem to have occurred at the time to the policymakers responsible for those decisions. Nowhere in Stimson's meticulous diary, for example, is there any suggestion of doubt or questioning of the assumption that the bomb should be used against Germany or Japan if the weapon was ready before the end of the war. From the time of the first organizational meeting for the atomic energy project held at the White House on October 9, 1941, members of the Top Policy Group conceived of the development of the weapon as an essential part of the total war effort. They asked whether it would be ready in time, not whether it should be used if it was; what were the diplomatic consequences of its development, not the moral implications of its military use.

This was not simply due to an absence of reflection. Stimson, for one, began to ponder seriously the revolutionary aspects of the atomic bomb during the winter of 1944–45. By March he was convinced that its development raised issues that "went right down to the bottom facts of human nature, morals and government." And yet this awareness of its profound implications apparently did not lead him to raise the sort of questions that might naturally seem to follow from such awareness. He never suggested to Roosevelt or Truman that its military use might incur a moral liability (an issue the Secretary did raise with regard to the manner in which conventional weapons were used), or that chances of securing Soviet postwar cooperation might be diminished if Stalin did not receive a commitment to international control prior to an atomic attack on Japan. The question naturally arises, why were these alternative policy choices not considered? Perhaps what Frankfurter once referred to as Stimson's habit of setting his mind "at one thing like the needle of an old victrola caught in a single groove" may help to

---

explain how he overlooked exactly what he sought to avoid—an atomic energy policy that contributed to the destruction of the Grand Alliance. Yet it must be pointed out that Bush and Conant never seriously questioned the assumption of the bomb's use either. Like Niels Bohr, they made a clear distinction between, on the one hand, its military application, which they took to be a wartime strategic decision, and, on the other, its moral and diplomatic implications, which bore on the longer-range issues of world peace and security and relations among nations. "What role it [the bomb] may play in the present war," Bohr had written to Roosevelt in July 1944, was a question "quite apart" from the overriding concern: the need to avoid an atomic arms race.

The preoccupation with winning the war obviously helped to foster this dichotomy in the minds of these men. But a closer look at how Bohr and Stimson respectively defined the nature of the diplomatic problem created by the bomb suggests that for the Secretary of War and his advisers (and ultimately for the President they advised) the dichotomy was, after all, more apparent than real. As a scientist, Bohr apprehended the significance of the new weapon even before it was developed, and he had no doubt that scientists in the Soviet Union would also understand its profound implications for the postwar world. He also was certain that they would convey the meaning of the development to Stalin, just as scientists in the United States and Great Britain had explained it to Roosevelt and Churchill. Thus the diplomatic problem, as Bohr analyzed it, was not the need to convince Stalin that the atomic bomb was an unprecedented weapon that threatened the life of the world, but the need to assure the Soviet leader that he had nothing to fear from the circumstances of its development. It was by informing Stalin during the war that the United States intended to cooperate with him in neutralizing the bomb through international control, Bohr reasoned, that it then became possible to consider its wartime use apart from its postwar role.

Stimson approached the issue differently. Without Bohr's training and without his faith in science and in scientists, atomic energy in its *un*developed state had a different meaning for him. Memoranda and interviews could not instill in a non-scientist with policymaking responsibilities the intuitive understanding of a nuclear physicist whose work had led directly to the Manhattan Project. The very aspect of the atomic bomb upon which Bohr placed so much hope for achieving a new departure in international affairs—its uniqueness—made it unlikely that non-scientists would grasp its full implications and therefore act upon his proposals. In this sense Bohr was correct when he said that he did not speak the same language as Churchill, or as any other statesman, for that matter.

It was only after Bohr's proposal was rejected at the Hyde Park meeting in September 1944 that events forced Stimson to think deeply about the weapon under his charge. Beginning with the fixed assumption that the bomb would be used in the war, he developed a view of the relationship between it and American diplomacy that reinforced that assumption, or at least gave him no cause to question it. For he could not consider an untried weapon an effective diplomatic bargaining counter; on the contrary, its diplomatic value was related to, if not primarily dependent upon, its demonstrated worth as a military force. Only when its "actual certainty [was] fixed," Stimson believed, could it carry weight in dealings with the Soviet Union.

The need for assurance that the bomb would work raises the central question: Did Stimson's understanding that the bomb would play an important diplomatic role after the war actually prevent him from questioning the assumption that the bomb ought to be used during the war? It must be stressed, in considering this question, that Stimson harbored no crude hatred or racial antagonism for the Japanese people. Nor was he blind to moral considerations that might affect world public opinion. On May 16 he reported to Truman that he was anxious to hold the Air Force to "precision bombing" in Japan because "the reputation of the United States for fair play and humanitarianism is the world's biggest asset for peace in the coming decades." But his concern here, it is evident, was not with the use as such of weapons of mass destruction, but simply with the manner in which they were used. "The same rule of sparing the civilian population should be applied as far as possible to the use of any new weapon," he wrote in reference to the bomb. The possibility that its extraordinary and indiscriminate destructiveness represented a profound qualitative difference, and so cried out for its governance by a higher morality than guided the use of conventional weapons, simply did not occur to him. On the contrary, the problem of the bomb as he perceived it was how to effectively subsume its management under the existing canons of international behavior. His diary suggests why:

May 13, 1945: Having copied into his diary Grew's memorandum raising questions about the role of the Soviet Union in the Far East during and after the war, Stimson noted: "These are very vital questions. . . . [They] cut very deep and in my opinion are powerfully connected *with our success with S-1.*"

May 15, 1945: Recounting the meeting between the Secretaries of State, War, and the Navy, he described "a pretty red hot session first over the questions which Grew had propounded to use in relation to the Yalta Conference and our relations with Russia." He then remarked: "Over any such tangled wave of problems the S-1 secret would be dominant and yet we will not know until after that time [the beginning of July] probably, until after that meeting [the Potsdam Conference] whether this is a weapon in our hands or not. We think it will be shortly afterwards, but it seems a terrible thing to gamble with such big stakes in diplomacy without having your *master card* in your hand."

Stimson's diary reveals further that following that May 15 meeting, he discussed the war against Japan with Marshall. He noted that while the Navy did not favor an invasion, Marshall "has got the straightforward view and I think he is right and he feels that we must go ahead," adding, "Fortunately the actual invasion will not take place until after my secret is out. The Japanese campaign involves therefore two great uncertainties; first whether Russia will come in though we think that will be all right; and second, when and how S-1 will resolve itself."

May 16, 1945: Summarizing the discussion with Truman about precision bombing and new weapons noted above, he wrote: "We must find some way of persuading Russia to play ball."

Was the conveying of an implicit warning to Moscow, then, the *principal* reason — as some historians have argued — for deciding to use the atomic bomb against Japan? The weight of the evidence available suggests not. Stimson's own account of his decision seems more accurate: "My *chief purpose,*" he wrote in 1947, in defense of the bombings of Hiroshima and Nagasaki, "was to end the war in victory with the least possible cost in the lives of the men in the armies which I had helped to raise." But if the conclusion of the war was Stimson's *chief* purpose, what other purposes were there? And did they prevent him from questioning the assumption that the bomb ought to be used?

The problem raised by these latter questions — the influence of secondary considerations reinforcing the decision — defies an unequivocal answer. What can be said, however, is that, along with Truman and Byrnes and several others involved, Stimson consciously considered two diplomatic effects of a combat demonstration of the atomic bomb: first, the impact of the attack on Japan's leaders, who might be persuaded thereby to end the war; and second, the impact of that attack on the Soviet Union's leaders, who might then prove to be more cooperative. It is likely that the contemplation together of the anticipated effects upon both Japanese and Soviet leaders was what turned aside any inclination to question the use of the bomb.

In addition, however, to the diplomatic advantages policymakers anticipated, there were domestic political reactions they feared, and these, too, discouraged any policy other than the most devastating and rapid use of the bomb. Everyone involved in administering the atomic energy program lived with the thought that a congressional inquiry was the penalty he might pay for his labors. It was in preparation for just such an eventuality that the Briggs Committee, even before the Project was underway, had excluded émigré and even recently naturalized scientists from its meetings. At the time the Army assumed responsibility for the development of the bomb, and on several occasions thereafter, Under Secretary of War Robert P. Patterson informed Groves that the "greatest care should be taken in keeping thorough records, with detailed entries of decisions made, of conferences with persons concerned in the Project, of all progress made and of all financial transactions and expenditures... [for] the most exact accounting would be demanded by Congress at sometime in the future." Even Bohr's association with the Manhattan Project was a product of this concern. He was invited to join the Project, Richard Tolman wrote to Conant in October 1943, because Groves "would like to be able to say that everything possible had been done to get the best men." That these anxieties were not the result of mere bureaucratic paranoia is made clear by the wartime correspondence between the Secretary of War and the chairman of the Senate Special Committee Investigating the National Defense Program. "The responsibility therefore [sic] and for any waste or improper action which might otherwise be avoided rests squarely upon the War Department," Senator Harry Truman warned Stimson in March 1944. Then there was the warning to Roosevelt a year later from the director of the Office of War Mobilization, James Byrnes: "If the project proves a failure, it will then be subjected to relentless investigation and criticism." It is all the more necessary to remember the possible influence of these warnings by Truman and Byrnes in the ironic aftermath of events.

Beyond reasons directly related to the war, to postwar diplomacy, or to domestic policies, there was another, more subtle consideration moving some advisers to favor a combat demonstration of the bomb. "President Conant has written me," Stimson informed news commentator Raymond Swing in February 1974, "that one of the principal reasons he had for advising me that the bomb *must be used* was that that was the only way to awaken the world to the necessity of abolishing war altogether. No technological demonstration, even if it had been possible under the conditions of war—which it was not—could take the place of the actual use with its horrible results.... I think he was right and I think that was one of the main things which differentiated the eminent scientists who concurred with President Conant from the less realistic ones who didn't."

Among the most prominent of the "less realistic" scientists Stimson was referring to here was, of course, Leo Szilard, a premature realist on atomic energy matters since the thirties. On May 28, 1945, Szilard and two associates (Walter Bartky, Associate Dean of the Physical Sciences at the University of Chicago, and Harold Urey, head of the Manhattan Project's Gaseous

Diffusion Laboratory at Columbia) traveled to Spartanburg, South Carolina, to discuss atomic energy matters with Byrnes. They were directed there by Matt Connelly, the President's appointments secretary, after an unsuccessful attempt to speak personally with Truman.

Since March 1945, Szilard had been applying his analytical energies to the problem of predicting the impact of the new weapon on American security, and on devising a workable plan for the international control of atomic energy. In a remarkably perceptive memorandum written in March he had discussed a number of central problems: the transition of nuclear weapons technology from atomic to hydrogen bombs, the greater vulnerability of an urbanized nation to nuclear attack, systems of control that ought to be considered, including control of raw materials and on-site inspection, and several other issues basic to any international control program. Having concluded that there was "no point" in trying to discuss his ideas with Groves, Conant, or Bush, he contacted Einstein. He needed a letter of introduction to the President, Szilard told his colleague, for there was "trouble ahead." A request for an interview with Roosevelt was then sent to Mrs. Roosevelt, who had intervened earlier in the war to bring the criticisms of the Chicago scientists to her husband's attention. "Perhaps the greatest immediate danger which faces us is the probability that our 'demonstration' of atomic bombs will precipitate a race in the production of these devices between the United States and Russia," Szilard warned in a memorandum prepared for a conference with Roosevelt scheduled for May 8. The United States government was about to arrive at decisions, he warned, that would control the course of events after the war. Those decisions ought to be based on careful estimates of future possibilities, not simply "on the present evidence relating to atomic bombs." Always conscious of power considerations, and well aware of potential diplomatic weight of the bomb, Szilard concluded a series of questions with the query: "Should. . .our 'demonstration' of atomic bombs and their use against Japan be delayed until a certain further stage in the political and technical development has been reached so that the United States shall be in a more favorable position in negotiations aimed at setting up a system of control?"

Szilard's reasoning here was not very different from Stimson's. They both looked to the bomb's power to persuade the Soviets to accept an American blueprint for world peace. But whereas the Secretary of War expected the early demonstration of that power to suffice to produce the desired effect, Szilard reasoned that the American lead in development would have to be overwhelming and unapproachable before such a demonstration had even a chance of having the desired effect.

At the Spartanburg interview the hopelessness of having such a calculated policy adopted became clear to Szilard. Byrnes seemed grossly ignorant about the implications of atomic energy and its diplomatic value. In response to the Secretary of State-designate's view that "our possessing and demonstrating the bomb would make Russia more manageable in Europe," Szilard argued that the "interests of peace might best be served and an arms race avoided by not using the bomb against Japan, keeping it secret, and letting the Russians think that our work on it had not succeeded." Byrnes responded that the nation had spent $2-billion on its development and Congress would want to know the results. "How would you get Congress to appropriate money for atomic energy research if you do not show results for the money which has been spent already?" he asked the astonished scientists.* They returned to Chicago convinced that Byrnes was inclined toward a policy that would make a postwar atomic arms race inevitable. As a direct result of the Spartanburg interview, Szilard initiated a movement among scientists at the University of Chicago to prevent the use of the atomic bomb against Japan. In the meantime, however, decisions were being taken that would outdistance any attempt to block the military use of the bomb.

"LOOKING AT THIS LIKE STATESMEN"

On May 31, 1945, three days after Truman set the date for the Potsdam Conference, the Interim Committee submitted a formal recommendation that the atomic bomb be used without warning against Japan. The Committee had met officially on three previous occasions—May 9, 14, and 18. Its members had reviewed the history of the Manhattan Project; received background briefings from Groves, Bush, Conant, and others; discussed the Quebec Agreement and the Combined Development Trust; appointed a Scientific Panel; considered the appointment of industrial and military panels; and designated William L. Laurence, science editor of *The New York Times,* to prepare statements to be issued *after* the atomic attacks. Yet the question of whether the bomb should be used at all had never actually been discussed. The minutes of the Interim Committee suggest why. The committee members had come together as advocates, the responsible advisers of a new force in world affairs, convinced of the weapon's diplomatic and military potential, aware of its fantastic cost, and awed by their responsibilities. They were also constrained in their choices by several shared but unstated assumptions reinforced for scientists and policymakers alike by the entire history of the Manhattan Project: First, that the bomb was a legitimate weapon that would have been used against the Allies if Germany had won the race to develop it. Second, that its use would have a profound impact upon Japan's leaders as they debated whether or not to surrender. Third, that the American public would want it used under the circumstances. And fourth (an assumption from which one member of the Committee subsequently dissented), that its use ultimately would have a salutary effect on relations with the Soviet Union. These assumptions suggested, at least obliquely, that there were neither military, diplomatic, nor domestic reasons to oppose the use of the weapon. On the contrary, four years of war and the pressures to end it, four years of secrecy and the prospect of more; $2-billion and the question "For what?"; Japan's tenacious resistance and America's commitment to unconditional surrender; Soviet behavior and the need for international control—all these factors served to bolster the accepted point of view. And the structure of the Committee itself made the introduction of alternatives extremely difficult: its tight organization and crowded agenda; its wide-ranging responsibilities for atomic energy policy and its limited knowledge of the military situation; its clear mandate to recommend postwar programs and the ambiguity, at best, of its responsibility for wartime decisions.

Stimson organized, chaired, and drew up agendas for the Committee's meetings. Although he did seek to create an atmosphere in which everyone felt free to discuss any problem related to atomic energy, the minutes of the meetings indicate that discussions closely adhered to the questions Stimson presented. The task

*Byrnes was not the only person associated with the Manhattan Project to express this attitude. Irving Stewart, a special assistant to Bush, suggested: "if the military importance [of the atomic bomb] is demonstrated, it may provide the necessary Constitutional [sic] support [to create a Commission on Atomic Energy]." Stewart to Bush, Aug. 25, 1944, AEC doc. no. 299.

before the Committee was enormous, and time was short. There was little inclination to pursue unscheduled issues.

Stimson had prepared very carefully for the meeting of May 31, to which Arthur Compton, Enrico Fermi, Ernest Lawrence, and Robert Oppenheimer, the membership of the Scientific Panel, had been invited. He was anxious to impress upon them "that we are looking at this like statesmen and not like merely soldiers anxious to win the war at any cost." He had worked with Harrison, Bundy, and Groves throughout the previous day preparing the agenda, which included a statement summarizing the Committee's purpose in general—"to study and report on the whole problem of temporary controls and publicity during the war and to survey and make recommendations on post-war research, development and controls, both national and international"—and a second statement explaining a major purpose of this meeting in particular—"to give the Committee a chance to get acquainted with the [invited] scientists and vice versa." The memorandum also contained a list of questions that might arise. These included future military prospects, international competition, future research, future controls, the possibility that "they might be used to extend democratic rights and the dignity of man," and future nonmilitary uses. There is no suggestion in the memorandum, or in the questions the Secretary placed before the assembled group, that his memory was serving him well when he wrote in his autobiography: "The first and greatest problem [for the Interim Committee] was the decision on the use of the bomb—should it be used against the Japanese, and if so, in what manner?" The fact is that a discussion of this question was placed on the agenda only after it was raised casually in the course of conversation during lunch.

At 10:00 A.M. the members of the Interim Committee, the Scientific Panel, and invited guests Marshall, Groves, Bundy, and Arthur W. Page (a friend and assistant to Stimson) assembled in the Secretary of War's office. For the benefit of the Scientific Panel, Stimson opened the meeting with a general explanation of his own and Marshall's responsibility for recommendations on military matters to the President; he went on to assure them that the Committee did not regard the bomb "as a new weapon merely but as a revolutionary change in the relations of man to the universe" and that he wanted to take advantage of this; it might be "a Frankenstein which would eat us up" or it might be a project "by which the peace of the world would be helped in becoming secure." The implications of the bomb, he understood, "went far beyond the *needs* of the present war."

After these introductory remarks the members of the Scientific Panel expressed their views on questions related to postwar planning. Their orientation was toward expansion. Arthur Compton sketched the future of military weapons by outlining three stages of development. The bombs currently under production would soon be surpassed by a second generation of more powerful weapons. "While bombs produced from the products of the second stage had not yet been proven in actual operation," the minutes report, "such bombs were considered a *scientific certainty*." And a "third stage" for which nuclear fission would serve merely as a detonator, though far more difficult to achieve, might—Oppenheimer reported—reach production within a minimum of three years. There is no hint in the minutes that the eventual development of even the hydrogen bomb lay in doubt: the question was merely how soon it could be developed.

Oppenheimer's review of the explosive force for each stage must have strained the imaginations of the non-scientists present. A single bomb produced in the first stage was expected to have an explosive force of

2,000–20,000 tons of TNT. The second generation of weapons would yield the equivalent of 50,000–100,000 tons of TNT. It was possible that a bomb developed in the third stage might produce an explosive force equal to 10,000,000–100,000,000 tons of TNT.

No one, then, sitting at that table in the Pentagon on May 31 could have entertained serious doubts that atomic weapons would be available within months. Of this, the scientists were absolutely certain. Even a year earlier, Ernest Lawrence had confidently written: "The primary fact now is that the element of gamble in the overall picture no longer exists." The uncertainty that remained in May 1945 was merely as to how efficiently the initial bombs would work. Under these circumstances the sort of atomic energy programs the United States chose to pursue after the war was a pressing issue. Lawrence, as always, urged development on every front, and in the discussion that ensued, his opinion found support. Within a short time Stimson was able to conclude that there was a general agreement that after the war the industrial facilities of the atomic energy program should remain intact, that a sizable stockpile of material for military, industrial, and technical use should be acquired, and that the door to industrial development should be opened.

During the remainder of the morning, as the Committee moved from a general discussion of control and inspection to the problem of how to obtain international control, the "question of paramount concern was the attitude of Russia." Adopting the line of reasoning that Bohr had advocated during his visits to Los Alamos, Oppenheimer suggested that the United States approach the Russians about international control without giving them details of the progress achieved. He firmly believed that the Russian attitude in this matter should not be prejudged; they had always been friendly to science.

Marshall supported this general point of view by drawing on his own experience. The history of charges and countercharges that were typical of American-Soviet relations, he related, were based on allegations that had generally proved to be unfounded. The seemingly uncooperative attitude of Russia in military matters resulted from their felt necessity to maintain security. He had accepted this and had acted accordingly. As to the postwar situation, and in matters other than purely military, he was in no position to express a view. He was inclined, however, to favor the buildup of a coalition of like-minded powers that could compel Russia to fall in line. He was confident that the United States need not fear that the Russians, if they were informed about the Manhattan Project, would disclose this information to the Japanese. Finally, he raised the question whether it might be desirable to invite two prominent Russian scientists to witness the first atomic bomb test scheduled for July at Alamogordo, New Mexico.

Byrnes, who heretofore had said little, strenuously objected. If information were given to the Russians, even in general terms, he feared that Stalin would ask to be brought into the partnership. This likelihood, he felt, was increased in view of American commitments and pledges of cooperation with the British, though he did not explain how the Soviets would know about them. Although Bush noted that not even the British had any blueprints of our plants, Byrnes could not be dissuaded. He did not explain his position further, yet subsequent events suggest that he believed the bomb's diplomatic value would be diluted if Stalin were informed of the weapon prior to its use. The most desirable program for him was to maintain superiority by pushing ahead as fast as possible in production and research, while at the same time making every effort to better our political relations with Russia. In any case, the issue appears to have been settled by his forthright stand. The morning session ended shortly afterwards, at approximately 1:15 P.M., after Arthur Compton summarized as the Committee's consensus that the United States had to assure itself a dominant position while working toward political agreements. No one saw any conflict between these two objectives. "Throughout the morning's discussion," Arthur Compton has written, "it seemed to be a foregone conclusion that the bomb would be used. It was regarding only the details of strategy and tactics that differing views were expressed."

There are two extant accounts of how the luncheon conversation turned to the question of using the bomb against Japan: a letter of August 17, 1945, from Lawrence to a friend, and a description published by Compton in 1956. Lawrence claims that Byrnes asked him to elaborate on a brief proposal he had made for a nonmilitary demonstration during the morning session; Compton recalls that he asked Stimson whether it might not be possible to arrange something less than a surprise atomic attack that would so impress the Japanese that they would see the uselessness of continuing the war. Whatever the case, the issue was discussed by those at the table, including at least Byrnes, Stimson, Compton, Lawrence, Oppenheimer, and Groves. Various possibilities were brought forward, but were discarded one after the other. Inured to the brutality of war by conventional means, someone countered that the "number of people that would be killed by the bomb would not be greater in general magnitude than the number already killed in fire raids [on Tokyo]."* Another problem was that Oppenheimer could not think of a sufficiently spectacular demonstration. Groves and others at the table were convinced that a real target of built-up structures would be the most effective demonstration.

There were other considerations as well, Compton reports. If the Japanese received a warning that such a weapon would be exploded somewhere over Japan, their aircraft might create problems that could lead to the failure of the mission. If the test were conducted on neutral ground, it was hard to believe that the "determined and fanatical military men of Japan would be impressed." No one could think of any way to employ the new weapon that offered the same attractive combination of low risk and high gain as a surprise attack; and no one was willing to argue that a higher risk should be accepted.

When the Committee members returned to Stimson's office at 2:15 P.M., the Secretary altered the agenda. The first topic he now wanted considered was the effect of the atomic bomb on the Japanese and their will to fight. The initial discussion revolved around the explosive force of the weapon. One atomic bomb, it was pointed out, would not be very different from current Air Force strikes. But Oppenheimer suggested that the visual effect of an atomic bomb would be tremendous. It would be accompanied by "a brilliant luminescence which would rise to 10,000 or 20,000 feet," and the neutron effect would be lethal for a radius of nearly a mile.

There was also a discussion of attempting several simultaneous attacks. Oppenheimer considered such a plan feasible, but Groves objected on the grounds that the advantage of gaining additional knowledge by successive bombings would be lost, and that such a program would require too much of those assembling the bomb.

After considerable discussion of types of targets and the desired effect, Stimson expressed the conclusion, on which there was general agreement, that the Japanese would not be given any warning; and that

*On March 9–10 a quarter of that city had been destroyed by incendiary bombs; 83,000 persons were killed and 40,000 were injured in the most destructive conventional air raid in history. A. Russell Buchanan, *The United States and World War II,* 2 (New York), 1964, 577–78.

the bombing would not concentrate on a civilian area, but that an attempt would be made to make a profound psychological impression on as many Japanese as possible. Stimson accepted Conant's suggestion that the most desirable target would be a vital war plant employing a large number of workers and closely surrounded by workers' homes. No member of the Committee spoke to the contradiction between this conclusion and their earlier decision not to concentrate on a civilian area.

This critical discussion on the use of the bomb was over. It had not only confirmed the assumption that the new weapon was to be used, but that the *two* bombs that would be available early in August should be used. The destruction of both Hiroshima and Nagasaki was the result of a *single* decision. On the following day Byrnes suggested, and the members of the Interim Committee agreed, that the Secretary of War should be advised that, "while recognizing that the final selection of the target was essentially a military decision, the present view of the Committee was that the bomb should be used against Japan as soon as possible; that it be used on a war plant surrounded by workers' homes; and that it be used without prior warning."* On June 6 Stimson informed Truman of the Committee's decision.

*Why was Japan rather than Germany selected as the target for the atomic bomb? The minutes of the Military Policy Committee meeting of May 5, 1943 (declassified in March 1976), offer the most direct answer to this question: "The point of use of the first bomb was discussed and the general view appeared to be that its best point of use would be on a Japanese fleet concentration in the Harbor of Truk. General Styer suggested Tokio [sic], but it was pointed out that the bomb should be used where, if it failed to go off, it would land in water of sufficient depth to prevent easy salvage. The Japanese were selected as they would not be so apt to secure knowledge from it as would the Germans." MED-TS, folder 23A. Other reasons that may have contributed to the decision, settled on in the spring of 1944, are: (1) the war in Europe was expected to end first; (2) it was safer to assemble the bomb on a Pacific island than in England; (3) delivery against a target in a U.S. theater of war by a U.S. aircraft (B-29) emphasized "American" primacy in this Anglo-American development.

Bush makes an ambiguous reference to the use of the bomb on June 24, 1943: "We [he and FDR] then spoke briefly of the possible use against Japan, or the Japanese fleet, and I brought out, or I tried to, because at this point I do not think I was really successful in getting the idea across, that our point of view or our emphasis on the program would shift if we had in mind use against Japan as compared with use against Germany." "Memorandum of Conference with the President," AEC doc. no. 133. However, on April 23, 1945, Groves informed Stimson that "the target is and was always expected to be Japan." MED-TS folder 25, tab M. See also Hewlett and Anderson, *The New World,* pp. 252–53.

Comment

The damage and loss of lives that the atomic bomb caused in Hiroshima and Nagasaki were no greater than the destruction caused by some conventional attacks such as the firebombing of Tokyo or Dresden. What (if any) features of nuclear weapons make their use more morally questionable than the use of conventional weapons?

Compare Stimson's argument for the bombing with this defense given by Truman:

> We have used [the bomb] against those who attacked us without warning at Pearl Harbor, against those who have starved and beaten and executed American prisoners

of war, against those who have abandoned all pretense of obeying international laws of warfare. We have used it in order to shorten the agony of the war.

Recently revealed documents suggest that Stimson's recollection of the estimates of probable casualties from an invasion (over a million Americans and even more Japanese) was much higher than the estimates that Truman actually received from high military officials at the time. The joint war planners of the Joint Chiefs of Staff, for example, estimated that there would be 193,500 casualties (including 40,000 deaths) from an invasion of both Kyushu and Honshu. Other military officials argued that even these estimates were too high. Should these differences in estimates make any difference in our moral assessment of Truman's decision?

Assume that dropping the bombs actually saved more American and Allied lives than any other option open to Truman. Would that justify his decision? What if the decision reduced the total number of lives lost (including Japanese lives)? Although Truman did not say so publicly, one reason he may have decided to use the bomb was to end the war quickly before Russia could enter and gain control over territory in the region. Would this have been a morally acceptable motive?

Evaluate the alternative courses of action that Truman considered or could have considered: (1) bombing only one city, (2) bombing an exclusively military target, (3) detonating one or two bombs over the ocean as a "demonstration," (4) intensifying the naval and air blockade, or (5) abandoning the demand for unconditional surrender.

James Conant, then president of Harvard and an influential science adviser to President Truman, argued that the bomb "must be used." It was "the only way to awaken the world to the necessity of abolishing war altogether." How would you at that time have assessed the effect of the bombing on postwar efforts to prevent nuclear war? Should such effects have been a morally relevant factor in Truman's decision?

The Role of Nuclear Weapons in Strategy

Caspar W. Weinberger

1. A Viable Deterrence Policy: Lessening Dependence on Nuclear Weapons

In the wake of World War II, the United States and the Western democracies developed a policy intended to prevent any recurrence of the tremendous carnage and devastation which the war had caused. To that end, the United States made clear that it would use its atomic weapons not for conquest or coercion, but for discouraging—for *deterring*—aggression and attack against ourselves and our allies.

Today, deterrence remains—as it has for the past 37 years—the cornerstone of our strategic nuclear policy. To deter successfully, we must be able—and must be seen to be able—to respond to any potential aggression in such a manner that the costs we will exact will substantially exceed any gains the aggressor might hope to achieve. We, for our part, are under no illusions about the dangers of a nuclear war be-

From Secretary of Defense Caspar Weinberger's *Annual Report to Congress,* fiscal year 1984.

tween the major powers; we believe that neither side could win such a war. But this recognition on *our* part is not sufficient to prevent the outbreak of nuclear war; it is essential that the Soviet leadership understand this as well. We must make sure that the Soviet leadership, in calculating the risks of aggression, recognizes that because of our retaliatory capability, there can be no circumstance in which it would benefit by beginning a nuclear war at any level or of any duration. If the Soviets recognize that our forces can and will deny them their objectives at whatever level of nuclear conflict they contemplate and, in addition, that such a conflict could lead to the destruction of those political, military, and economic assets that they value most highly, then deterrence is effective and the risk of war diminished. It is this outcome we seek to achieve.

2. The Evolution of U.S. Nuclear Policy

During the late 1940s and early 1950s, America's virtual monopoly of intercontinental nuclear systems meant that our requirements for conventional war were relatively small. The Soviet Union understood that, under our policy of "massive retaliation," we might respond to a Soviet conventional attack on the U.S. or our allies with an atomic attack on the USSR. As the 1950s ended, however, the Soviets began developing and acquiring long-range nuclear capabilities. As their capacity for nuclear and conventional attack continued to grow, the U.S. threat to respond to a conventional, or even a limited nuclear, attack with massive nuclear retaliation became less and less credible; hence, it was not a stable deterrent. Accordingly, in the 1960s the U.S. and the NATO allies adopted the concept of "flexible response." This concept had two goals: first, U.S. nuclear planning was modified in order to provide the President with the option of using nuclear forces selectively (rather than massively), thereby restoring credibility and stability to our nuclear deterrent. Additionally, the United States and the allies hoped that by improving conventional forces, they would reduce reliance on nuclear weapons to deter or cope with non-nuclear attack. Unfortunately, neither we nor our allies ever fully met this key goal. Thus, with our present effort to increase our conventional strength, the Reagan Administration is essentially trying to secure a long-established but elusive goal of American policy.

By the early 1960s, the U.S. had over 7,000 strategic nuclear weapons, most of which were carried by B-47s and the then-new B-52s. The Soviet Union had fewer than 500 strategic warheads. Throughout the 1960s, our nuclear posture presented the Soviet Union with a compelling deterrent if it considered launching a nuclear strike against the United States: because of the relatively small number of weapons the Soviet Union possessed and their ineffectiveness against any U.S. strategic forces, such an attack was impossible to execute successfully. If the Soviet planner targeted our missile silos and alert bomber bases with the systems he then possessed, he found that he would deplete his nuclear arsenal while not significantly reducing U.S. retaliatory forces. In other words, his ability to limit the certain, massive retaliatory destruction of his own forces and assets was rather small. If, on the other hand, the Soviet planner targeted U.S. cities, he would have to expect a U.S. retaliatory strike against his own cities, a strike by a U.S. arsenal considerably larger and much more capable than his own, by any measure. Again, he was deterred.

During the course of the 1970s the Soviet arsenal grew both in quantity and in quality (although the U.S. qualitative edge remained). The Soviets expanded their land-based missile force and hardened their protective silos, and continued the improvement of their defenses against air attack. At the same time, the United States made a choice to restrict its improvements to the yield and accuracy of its own missile forces so as not to threaten the Soviet Union with a sudden, disarming first strike. The net result of this was to allow the Soviet Union a "sanctuary" for its ICBM force, since U.S. forces by now could not attack them effectively. The Soviets, however, did not follow our self-imposed restraint. They developed a new generation of ICBMs specifically designed to destroy U.S. missile silos, which were hardened far less than Soviet silos, and the B-52 bases. By the late 1970s, this combination of vulnerable U.S. missiles and a Soviet missile "sanctuary" had reduced the effectiveness of our earlier deterrent and eased the problems of the Soviet war planners. Now, the Soviets could envision a potential nuclear confrontation in which they would threaten to destroy a very large part of our force in a first strike, while retaining overwhelming nuclear force to deter any retaliation we could carry out.

We cannot overemphasize the importance of a multiplicity of survivable strategic forces. Over the last 20 years, we have maintained a Triad of land-based ICBMs, manned bombers, and submarine-launched ballistic missiles as an effective means of preserving a stable deterrent. The unique characteristics of the independent and separate strategic components that make up the Triad bolster deterrence by acting in concert to complicate severely Soviet attack planning, making it more difficult, on the one hand, for them to plan and execute a successful attack, on all these components and, on the other hand, to defend against their combined and complementary retaliatory effects. The Triad also acts as a hedge against a possible technological breakthrough that the Soviets might develop or obtain that could threaten the viability of any single strategic system. The importance of the Triad to deterrence is no more apparent than today, when each leg is in need of modernization.

3. Nuclear Weapons Issues

What has been said so far illustrates the complexity of the continuing task of maintaining an American nuclear force capable of surviving a Soviet attack that is aimed at destroying it. However, the maintenance of a persuasive capability to deter a Soviet nuclear attack directed solely at an ally is even more demanding. It should be most obvious in this connection that we need to be able to use force responsibly and discriminately, in a manner appropriate to the nature of a nuclear attack.

Yet, some believe that we must threaten explicitly, even solely, the mass destruction of civilians on the adversary side, thus inviting a corresponding destruction of civilian populations on our side, and that such a posture will achieve stability in deterrence. This is incorrect. Such a threat is neither moral nor prudent. The Reagan Administration's policy is that under no circumstances may such weapons be used deliberately for the purpose of destroying populations.

For this reason, we disagree with those who hold that deterrence should be based on nuclear weapons designed to destroy cities rather than military targets. Deliberately designing weapons aimed at populations is neither necessary nor sufficient for deterrence. If we are forced to retaliate and can only respond by destroying population centers, we invite the destruction of our own population. Such a deterrent strategy is hardly likely to carry conviction as a deterrent, particularly as a deterrent to nuclear—let alone conventional—attack on an ally.

To maintain a sound deterrent, we must make clear to our adversary that we would decisively and effectively answer his attack. To talk of actions that the U.S. Government could not, in good conscience, and in prudence, undertake tends to defeat the goal of deterrence.

Some of the same ambiguities cloud recent proposals that we abandon longstanding Alliance policy and pledge "No First Use" of nuclear weapons in response to Soviet conventional attacks in Europe. Indeed, if the Soviets thought that we would be so constrained, they might mass forces more heavily for offensive actions and gain a unilateral conventional advantage. To reduce further the prospects of nuclear war, we must strengthen NATO's conventional forces—not exchange unenforceable and unverifiable pledges. The danger of a "No First Use" pledge remains that it could increase the chances of war and thus increase the chances of nuclear conflict.

A Prudent Approach to Nuclear Weapons

If we are to maintain a responsible nuclear deterrent against nuclear attacks on our allies, as well as against nuclear attacks on the United States, we will need to continue to exploit our comparative advantage in technology. The movement for a nuclear freeze has been inspired in part by the mistaken belief that the United States has been steadily piling up more and more nuclear weapons. In fact, the United States has not been accumulating more weapons. The number in our stockpile was one-third higher in 1967 than in 1980. Nor have we been accumulating more destructive weapons. The average number of kilotons per weapon has declined since the late 1950s, and the total number of megatons in our stockpile was four times as high in 1960 than in 1980. With the retirement of the Titans, this total will decline even further. Moreover, the United States has had an intensive and consistent program to improve the safety of the nuclear weapons in its stockpile against accidental detonation and its consequences, as well as to improve the security of these weapons against seizure and use by terrorists or other unauthorized persons. The weapons in our stockpile today have an average age of about 13 years. It is essential that we continue to replace them with new, safer, more secure, and less vulnerable weapons.

The various proposals for a nuclear freeze would prevent us from carrying out these programs and thus improving the safety and security of our weapons, reducing the vulnerability of our delivery systems in the face of increasing threats, and replacing systems as they reach the end of their service life due simply to their age. Such proposals, hence, would reduce the stability of our deterrent against both "accidents" and deliberate destruction.

Nuclear Arms Control

It is the objective of the United States to maintain the lowest level of armaments compatible with the preservation of our, and our allies', security. While President Reagan is forced by the Soviet threat to pursue a force augmentation and modernization program, he has also undertaken a serious effort designed to reduce armaments through negotiation. In the nuclear area, the Reagan Administration took two important new arms control initiatives, on intermediate-range and strategic nuclear forces.

We can never, much as we would desire it, return to the kind of world that existed before the secrets of the atom were unlocked. But we can work to ensure that nuclear weapons are never used, by maintaining the forces necessary to convince any adversary that the cost of aggression would be far higher than any possible benefit. The United States has pursued this strategy of deterrence since the dawn of the nuclear age; and since that time deterrence has preserved the peace.

The primacy of deterrence has not changed, but the conditions for ensuring it have. The Reagan Administration's strategic modernization program is designed to preserve deterrence, in the face of an evolving threat, by increasing the survivability, accuracy, and credibility of our nuclear forces, and to offer the Soviet Union an incentive for genuine arms reduction, by demonstrating our commitment to maintaining a strategic balance.

Deterrence in Principle and Practice

National Conference of Catholic Bishops

The evolution of deterrence strategy has passed through several stages of declaratory policy. Using the U.S. case as an example, there is a significant difference between "massive retaliation" and "flexible response," and between "mutual assured destruction" and "countervailing strategy." It is also possible to distinguish between "counterforce" and "countervalue" targeting policies; and to contrast a posture of "minimum deterrence" with "extended deterrence." These terms are well known in the technical debate on nuclear policy; they are less well known and sometimes loosely used in the wider public debate. It is important to recognize that there has been substantial continuity in U.S. action policy in spite of real changes in declaratory policy....

The moral and political paradox posed by deterrence was concisely stated by Vatican II:

"Undoubtedly, armaments are not amassed merely for use in wartime. Since the defensive strength of any nation is thought to depend on its capacity for immediate retaliation, the stockpiling of arms which grows from year to year serves, in a way hitherto unthought of, as a deterrent to potential attackers. Many people look upon this as the most effective way known at the present time for maintaining some sort of peace among nations. Whatever one may think of this form of deterrent, people are convinced that the arms race, which quite a few countries have entered, is no infallible way of maintaining real peace and that the resulting so-called balance of power is no sure genuine path to achieving it. Rather than eliminate the causes of war, the arms race serves only to aggravate the position...."

Without making a specific moral judgment on deterrence, the council clearly designated the elements of the arms race: the tension between "peace of a sort" preserved by deterrence and "genuine peace" required for a stable international life; the contradiction between what is spent for destructive capacity and what is needed for constructive development.

In the post-conciliar assessment of war and peace and specifically of deterrence, different parties to the political-moral debate within the church and in civil society have focused on one or another aspect of the problem. For some, the fact that nuclear weapons have not been used since 1945 means that deterrence has worked, and this fact satisfies the demands of both the political and the moral order. Others contest this assessment by highlighting the risk of failure involved in continued reliance on deterrence and pointing out how politically and morally catastrophic even a single failure would be. Still others note that the absence of nuclear war is not necessarily proof that the policy of deterrence has prevented it. Indeed, some would find in the policy of deterrence the driving force in the superpower arms race. Still other observers, many of them Catholic moralists, have stressed that deterrence may not morally include the intention of deliberately attacking civilian populations or noncombatants....

Pope John Paul II makes this statement about the morality of deterrence:

"In current conditions 'deterrence' based on balance, certainly not as an end in itself but as a step on the way toward a progressive disarmament, may still be judged morally acceptable. Nonetheless in order to ensure peace, it is indispensable not to

From *The Challenge of Peace—The Pastoral Letter on War and Peace,* May 3, 1983.

be satisfied with this minimum, which is always susceptible to the real danger of explosion."

In Pope John Paul II's assessment we perceive two dimensions of the contemporary dilemma of deterrence. One dimension is the danger of nuclear war with its human and moral costs. The possession of nuclear weapons, the continuing quantitative growth of the arms race and the danger of nuclear proliferation all point to the grave danger of basing "peace of a sort" on deterrence. The other dimension is the independence and freedom of nations and entire peoples, including the need to protect smaller nations from threats to their independence and integrity. Deterrence reflects the radical distrust which marks international politics. . . .

MORAL PRINCIPLES AND POLICY CHOICES

Targeting doctrine raises significant moral questions because it is a significant determinant of what would occur if nuclear weapons were ever to be used. Although we acknowledge the need for deterrent, not all forms of deterrence are morally acceptable. There are moral limits to deterrence policy as well as to policy regarding use. Specifically, it is not morally acceptable to intend to kill the innocent as part of a strategy of deterring nuclear war. The question of whether U.S. policy involves an intention to strike civilian centers (directly targeting civilian populations) has been one of our factual concerns.

This complex question has always produced a variety of responses, official and unofficial in character. The NCCB committee has received a series of statements of clarification of policy from U.S. government officials.* Essentially these statements declare that it is not U.S. strategic policy to target the Soviet civilian population as such or to use nuclear weapons deliberately for the purpose of destroying population centers.

These statements respond, in principle at least, to one moral criterion for assessing deterrence policy: the immunity of noncombatants from direct attack either by conventional or nuclear weapons.

These statements do not address or resolve another very troublesome moral problem, namely, that an attack on military targets or militarily significant industrial targets could involve "indirect" (i.e., unintended) but massive civilian casualties. We are advised, for example, that the U.S. strategic nuclear targeting plan (SIOP—Single Integrated Operational Plan) has identified 60 "military" targets within the city of Moscow alone, and that 40,000 "military" targets for nuclear weapons have been identified in the whole of the Soviet Union. It is important to recognize that Soviet policy is subject to the same moral judgment; attacks on several "industrial targets" or politically significant targets in the United States could produce massive civilian casualties. The number of civilians who would necessarily be killed by such strikes is horrendous. This problem is unavoidable because of the way modern military facilities and production centers are so thoroughly interspersed with civilian living and working areas. It is aggravated if one side deliberately positions military targets in the midst of a civilian population.

---

*Particularly helpful was the letter of Jan. 15, 1983, of William Clark, national security adviser, to Cardinal Bernardin. Clark stated: "For moral, political and military reasons, the United States does not target the Soviet population as such. There is no deliberately opaque meaning conveyed in the last two words. We do not threaten the existence of Soviet civilization by threatening Soviet cities. Rather, we hold at risk the warmaking capability of the Soviet Union—its armed forces, and the industrial capacity to sustain war. It would be irresponsible for us to issue policy statements which might suggest to the Soviets that it would be to their advantage to establish privileged sanctuaries within heavily populated areas, thus inducing them to locate much of their war-fighting capability within those urban sanctuaries."

In our constitutions, administration officials readily admitted that while they hoped any nuclear exchange could be kept limited, they were prepared to retaliate in a massive way if necessary. They also agreed that once any substantial numbers of weapons were used, the civilian casualty levels would quickly become truly catastrophic and that even with attacks limited to "military" targets the number of deaths in a substantial exchange would be almost indistinguishable from what might occur if civilian centers had been deliberately and directly struck. These possibilities pose a different moral question and are to be judged by a different moral criterion: the principle of proportionality.

While any judgment of proportionality is always open to differing evaluations, there are actions which can be decisively judged to be disproportionate. A narrow adherence exclusively to the principle of non-combatant immunity as a criterion for policy is an inadequate moral posture for it ignores some evil and unacceptable consequences. Hence, we cannot be satisfied that the assertion of an intention not to strike civilians directly or even the most honest effort to implement that intention by itself constitutes a "moral policy" for the use of nuclear weapons.

The location of industrial or militarily significant economic targets within heavily populated areas or in those areas affected by radioactive fallout could well involve such massive civilian casualties that in our judgment such a strike would be deemed morally disproportionate, even though not intentionally indiscriminate.

The problem is not simply one of producing highly accurate weapons that might minimize civilian casualties in any single explosion, but one of increasing the likelihood of escalation at a level where many, even "discriminating," weapons would cumulatively kill very large numbers of civilians. Those civilian deaths would occur both immediately and from the long-term effects of social and economic devastation.

A second issue of concern to us is the relationship of deterrence doctrine to war-fighting strategies. We are aware of the argument that war-fighting capabilities enhance the credibility of the deterrent, particularly the strategy of extended deterrence. But the development of such capabilities raises other strategic and moral questions. The relationship of war-fighting capabilities and targeting doctrine exemplifies the difficult choices in this area of policy. Targeting civilian populations would violate the principle of discrimination—one of the central moral principles of a Christian ethic of war. But "counterforce targeting," while preferable from the perspective of protecting civilians, is often joined with a declaratory policy which conveys the notion that nuclear war is subject to precise rational and moral limits. We have already expressed our severe doubts about such a concept. Furthermore, a purely counterforce strategy may seem to threaten the viability of other nations' retaliatory forces, making deterrence unstable in a crisis and war more likely.

While we welcome any effort to protect civilian populations, we do not want to legitimize or encourage moves which extend deterrence beyond the specific objective of preventing the use of nuclear weapons or other actions which would lead directly to a nuclear exchange.

These considerations of concrete elements of nuclear deterrence policy, made in light of John Paul II's evaluation, but applying it through our own prudential judgments, lead us to a strictly conditioned moral acceptance of nuclear deterrence. We cannot consider it adequate as a long-term basis for peace.

This strictly conditioned judgment yields *criteria* for morally assessing the elements of deterrence strategy. Clearly, these criteria demonstrate that we cannot approve of every weapons system, strategic doctrine or policy initiative advanced in the name of strengthening deterrence. On the contrary, these criteria require continual public scrutiny of what our government proposes to do with the deterrent.

On the basis of these criteria we wish now to make some specific evaluations:

1. If nuclear deterrence exists only to prevent the *use* of nuclear weapons by others, then proposals to go beyond this to planning for prolonged periods of repeated nuclear strikes and counterstrikes or "prevailing" in nuclear war, are not acceptable. They encourage notions that nuclear war can be engaged in with tolerable human and moral consequences. Rather, we must continually say no to the idea of nuclear war.

2. If nuclear deterrence is our goal, "sufficiency" to deter is an adequate strategy; the quest for nuclear superiority must be rejected.

3. Nuclear deterrence should be used as a step on our way toward progressive disarmament. Each proposed addition to our strategic system or change in strategic doctrine must be assessed precisely in light of whether it will render steps toward "progressive disarmament" more or less likely.

Moreover, these criteria provide us with the means to make some judgments and recommendations about the present direction of U.S. strategic policy. Progress toward a world freed of dependence on nuclear deterrence must be carefully carried out. But it must not be delayed. There is an urgent moral and political responsibility to use the "peace of a sort" we have as a framework to move toward authentic peace through nuclear arms control, reductions and disarmament. Of primary importance in this process is the need to prevent the development and deployment of destabilizing weapons systems on either side; a second requirement is to ensure that the more sophisticated command and control systems do not become mere hair triggers for automatic launch on warning; a third is the need to prevent the proliferation of nuclear weapons in the international system.

In light of these general judgements *we oppose* some specific proposals in respect to our present deterrence posture:

1. The addition of weapons which are likely to be vulnerable to attack, yet also possess a "prompt hard-target kill" capability that threatens to make the other side's retaliatory forces vulnerable. Such weapons may seem to be useful primarily in a first strike; we resist such weapons for this reason and we oppose Soviet deployment of such weapons which generate fear of a first strike against U.S. forces.

2. The willingness to foster strategic planning which seeks a nuclear war-fighting capability that goes beyond the limited function of deterrence outlined in this letter.

3. Proposals which have the effect of lowering the nuclear threshold and blurring the difference between nuclear and conventional weapons.

In support of the concept of "sufficiency" as an adequate deterrent and in light of the present size and composition of both the U.S. and Soviet strategic arsenals, *we recommend:*

1. Support for immediate, bilateral, verifiable agreements to halt the testing, production and deployment of new nuclear weapons systems.

2. Support for negotiated bilateral deep cuts in the arsenals of both superpowers, particularly those weapons systems which have destabilizing characteristics; U.S. proposals like those for START (Strategic Arms Reduction Talks) and INF (Intermediate-Range Nuclear Forces) negotiations in Geneva are said to be designed to achieve deep cuts; our hope is that they will be pursued in a manner which will realize these goals.

3. Support for early and successful conclusion of negotiations of a comprehensive test ban treaty.

4. Removal by all parties of short-range nuclear weapons which multiply dangers disproportionate to their deterrent value.

5. Removal by all parties of nuclear weapons from areas where they are likely to be overrun in the early stages of war, thus forcing rapid and uncontrollable decisions on their use.

6. Strengthening of command and control over nuclear weapons to prevent inadvertent and unauthorized use.

These judgments are meant to exemplify how a lack of unequivocal condemnation of deterrence is meant only to be an attempt to acknowledge the role attributed to deterrence, but not to support its extension beyond the limited purpose discussed above. Some have urged us to condemn all aspects of nuclear deterrence.

This urging has been based on a variety of reasons, but has emphasized particularly the high and terrible risks that either deliberate use or accidental detonation of nuclear weapons could quickly escalate to something utterly disproportionate to any acceptable moral purpose. That determination requires highly technical judgments about hypothetical events. Although reasons exist which move some to condemn reliance on nuclear weapons for deterrence, we have not reached this conclusion for the reasons outlined in this letter.

Nevertheless, there must be no misunderstanding of our profound skepticism about the moral acceptability of any use of nuclear weapons. It is obvious that the use of any weapons which violate the principle of discrimination merits unequivocal condemnation. We are told that some weapons are designed for purely "counterforce" use against military forces and targets. The moral issue, however, is not resolved by the design of weapons or the planned intention for use; there are also consequences which must be assessed. It would be a perverted political policy or moral casuistry which tried to justify using a weapon which "indirectly" or "unintentionally" killed a million innocent people because they happened to live near a "militarily significant target."

Even the "indirect effects" of initiating nuclear war are sufficient to make it an unjustifiable moral risk in any form. It is not sufficient, for example, to contend that "our" side has plans for "limited" or "discriminate" use. Modern warfare is not readily contained by good intentions or technological designs. The psychological climate of the world is such that mention of the term "nuclear" generates uneasiness. Many contend that the use of one tactical nuclear weapon could produce panic, with completely unpredictable consequences. It is precisely this mix of political, psychological and technological uncertainty which has moved us in this letter to reinforce with moral prohibitions and prescriptions the prevailing political barrier against resort to nuclear weapons. Our support for enhanced command and control facilities, for major reductions in strategic and tactical nuclear forces, and for a "no first use" policy (as set forth in this letter) is meant to be seen as a complement to our desire to draw a moral line against nuclear war....

Arms control and disarmament must be a process of verifiable agreements especially between two superpowers. While we do not advocate a policy of unilateral disarmament, we believe the urgent need for control of the arms race requires a willingness for each side to take some first steps. The United States has already taken a number of important independent initiatives to reduce some of the gravest dangers and to encourage a constructive Soviet response; additional initiatives are encouraged. By independent initiatives we mean carefully chosen limited steps which the United States could take for a defined period of time, seeking to elicit a comparable step from the Soviet Union. If an appropriate response is not forthcoming, the United States would no longer be bound by steps taken.

The Strategic Defense Initiative

Ronald Reagan

ADDRESS TO THE NATION ON DEFENSE AND NATIONAL SECURITY (1983)

. . .The subject I want to discuss with you, peace and national security, is both timely and important. Timely, because I've reached a decision which offers a new hope for our children in the 21st century, a decision I'll tell you about in a few minutes. And important because there's a very big decision that you must make for yourselves. This subject involves the most basic duty that any President and any people share, the duty to protect and strengthen the peace. . . .

The defense policy of the United States is based on a simple premise: The United States does not start fights. We will never be an aggressor. We maintain our strength in order to deter and defend against aggression—to preserve freedom and peace.

Since the dawn of the atomic age, we've sought to reduce the risk of war by maintaining a strong deterrent and by seeking genuine arms control. "Deterrence" means simply this: making sure any adversary who thinks about attacking the United States, or our allies, or our vital interests, concludes that the risks to him outweigh any potential gains. Once he understands that, he won't attack. We maintain the peace through our strength; weakness only invites aggression.

This strategy of deterrence has not changed. It still works. But what it takes to maintain deterrence has changed. It took one kind of military force to deter an attack when we had far more nuclear weapons than any other power; it takes another kind now that the Soviets, for example, have enough accurate and powerful nuclear weapons to destroy virtually all of our missiles on the ground. Now, this is not to say that the Soviet Union is planning to make war on us. Nor do I believe a war is inevitable—quite the contrary. But what must be recognized is that our security is based on being prepared to meet all threats.

There was a time when we depended on coastal forts and artillery batteries, because, with the weaponry of that day, any attack would have had to come by sea. Well, this is a different world, and our defenses must be based on recognition and awareness of the weaponry possessed by other nations in the nuclear age.

We can't afford to believe that we will never be threatened. There have been two world wars in my lifetime. We didn't start them and, indeed, did everything we could to avoid being drawn into them. But we were ill-prepared for both. Had we been better prepared, peace might have been preserved.

For 20 years the Soviet Union has been accumulating enormous military might. They didn't stop when their forces exceeded all requirements of a legitimate defensive capability. And they haven't stopped now. During the past decade and a half, the Soviets have built up a massive arsenal of new strategic nuclear weapons—weapons that can strike directly at the United States. . . .My predecessors in the Oval Office have appeared before you on other occasions to describe the threat posed by Soviet power and have proposed steps to address that threat. But since the advent

From "Address to the Nation on Defense and National Security," March 23, 1983, in *Public Papers of the Presidents of the U.S., 1983* (Washington, D.C.: U.S. Government Printing Office, 1984), Bk I, pp. 437-43; and "Statement on the Strategic Defense Initiative," March 23, 1988, *Weekly Compilation of Presidential Documents,* Office of the Federal Register, Washington, D.C., pp. 381-82.

of nuclear weapons, those steps have been increasingly directed toward deterrence of aggression through the promise of retaliation.

This approach to stability through offensive threat has worked. We and our allies have succeeded in preventing nuclear war for more than three decades. In recent months, however, my advisers, including in particular the Joint Chiefs of Staff, have underscored the necessity to break out of a future that relies solely on offensive retaliation for security.

Over the course of these discussions, I've become more and more deeply convinced that the human spirit must be capable of rising above dealing with other nations and human beings by threatening their existence. Feeling this way, I believe we must thoroughly examine every opportunity for reducing tensions and for introducing greater stability into the strategic calculus on both sides.

One of the most important contributions we can make is, of course, to lower the level of all arms, and particularly nuclear arms. We're engaged right now in several negotiations with the Soviet Union to bring about a mutual reduction of weapons. I will report to you a week from tomorrow my thoughts on that score. But let me just say, I'm totally committed to this course.

If the Soviet Union will join with us in our effort to achieve major arms reduction, we will have succeeded in stabilizing the nuclear balance. Nevertheless, it will still be necessary to rely on the specter of retaliation, on mutual threat. And that's a sad commentary on the human condition. Wouldn't it be better to save lives than to avenge them? Are we not capable of demonstrating our peaceful intentions by applying all our abilities and our ingenuity to achieving a truly lasting stability? I think we are. Indeed, we must.

After careful consultation with my advisers, including the Joint Chiefs of Staff, I believe there is a way. Let me share with you a vision of the future which offers hope. It is that we embark on a program to counter the awesome Soviet missile threat with measures that are defensive. Let us turn to the very strengths in technology that spawned our great industrial base and that have given us the quality of life we enjoy today.

What if free people could live secure in the knowledge that their security did not rest upon the threat of instant U.S. retaliation to deter a Soviet attack, that we could intercept and destroy strategic ballistic missiles before they reached our own soil or that of our allies?

I know this is a formidable, technical task, one that may not be accomplished before the end of this century. Yet, current technology has attained a level of sophistication where it's reasonable for us to begin this effort. It will take years, probably decades of effort on many fronts. There will be failures and setbacks, just as there will be successes and breakthroughs. And as we proceed, we must remain constant in preserving the nuclear deterrent and maintaining a solid capability for flexible response. But isn't it worth every investment necessary to free the world from the threat of nuclear war? We know it is.

In the meantime, we will continue to pursue real reductions in nuclear arms, negotiating from a position of strength that can be ensured only by modernizing our strategic forces. At the same time, we must take steps to reduce the risk of a conventional military conflict escalating to nuclear war by improving our nonnuclear capabilities.

America does possess—now—the technologies to attain very significant improvements in the effectiveness of our conventional, nonnuclear forces. Proceeding boldly with these new technologies, we can significantly reduce any incentive that the Soviet Union may have to threaten attack against the United States or its allies.

As we pursue our goal of defensive technologies, we recognize that our allies rely upon our strategic offensive power to deter attacks against them. Their vital interests and ours are inextricably linked. Their safety and ours are one. And no change in technology can or will alter that reality. We must and shall continue to honor our commitments.

I clearly recognize that defensive systems have limitations and raise certain problems and ambiguities. If paired with offensive systems, they can be viewed as fostering an aggressive policy, and no one wants that. But with these considerations firmly in mind, I call upon the scientific community in our country, those who gave us nuclear weapons, to turn their great talents now to the cause of mankind and world peace, to give us the means of rendering these nuclear weapons impotent and obsolete.

Tonight, consistent with our obligations of the ABM treaty and recognizing the need for closer consultation with our allies, I'm taking an important first step. I am directing a comprehensive and intensive effort to define a long-term research and development program to begin to achieve our ultimate goal of eliminating the threat posed by strategic nuclear missiles. This could pave the way for arms control measures to eliminate the weapons themselves. We seek neither military superiority nor political advantage. Our only purpose—one all people share—is to search for ways to reduce the danger of nuclear war.

My fellow Americans, tonight we're launching an effort which holds the promise of changing the course of human history. There will be risks, and results take time. But I believe we can do it. As we cross this threshold, I ask for your prayers and your support.

STATEMENT ON THE STRATEGIC DEFENSE INITIATIVE (1988)

Today marks the 5th anniversary of a program vital to our future security. On March 23, 1983, in announcing our Strategic Defense Initiative—SDI—I put forward the vision of a safer and more secure future for our children and our grandchildren, a future free from the threat of the most dangerous weapon mankind has invented: fast-flying ballistic missiles. It was on that date that I challenged our best and brightest scientific minds to undertake a rigorous program of research, development, and testing to find a way to keep the peace through defensive systems, which threaten no one. If we can accomplish this, and I am more and more convinced that we can, we will no longer have to face a future that relies on the threat of nuclear retaliation to ensure our security.

The Soviets not only are ahead of us in ballistic missiles but also are deeply engaged in their own SDI-like program. If they are allowed to keep their near monopoly in defenses, we will be left without an effective means to protect our cherished freedoms in the future. But with our own investigation of defenses well underway, we have been able to propose to the Soviets at our arms negotiations in Geneva that both of us protect our nations through increasingly effective defenses, even as we cut back deeply our strategic offensive arms. SDI, in fact, provided a valuable incentive for the Soviets to return to the bargaining table and to negotiate seriously over strategic arms reductions. And as we move toward lower levels of offense, it will be all the more important to have an effective defense.

The SDI program is progressing technologically even faster than we expected. We have demonstrated the feasibility of intercepting an attacker's ballistic missiles. We have made rapid progress on sensors, the eyes and ears of a future defensive system. And our research has produced useful spinoffs for conventional defenses and for medicine, air traffic control, and high speed computing. The problems we face now are largely political. Every year, Congress has cut back the SDI budget. We are now 1-2 years behind schedule. Some of our critics question SDI because they believe we are going too fast and doing too much, while others say we should move now to deploy limited defenses—perhaps to protect our own missiles. While such a defense may initially strengthen today's uneasy balance, SDI's goal is to create a stronger, safer, and morally preferable basis for deterrence by making ballistic missiles obsolete. Thus, we seek to establish truly comprehensive defenses, defenses which will protect the American people and our allies.

The American people can never be satisfied with a strategic situation where, to keep the peace, we rely on a threat of vengeance. And we must recognize that we live in an imperfect, often violent world, one in which ballistic missile technology is proliferating despite our efforts to prevent this. We would be doing a grave and dangerous disservice to future generations if we assumed that national leaders everywhere, for all time, will be both peaceful and rational. The challenge before us is of course difficult, but with SDI, we are showing already that we have the technological know-how, the courage, and the patience to change the course of human history.

Comment

Identify any positions in the documents that might be regarded as political compromises, and indicate whether you think they are morally justified. Consider, for example, Weinberger's advocacy of both (1) a "force augmentation and modernization program" and (2) reduction of armaments through negotiation. Consider Reagan's claim that the American "approach to stability through offensive threat has worked" and his advocacy of "every investment necessary to free the world from the threat of nuclear war." The bishops resisted those "who urged us to condemn all aspects of nuclear deterrence"; is their more moderate position consistent with their own moral principles? With yours?

Weinberger writes that deterrence based on a threat against cities is "neither moral nor prudent." Does actual U.S. targeting doctrine differ in morally significant ways from the kind of deterrence that Weinberger rejects? Is a threat against military targets located near cities morally justifiable?

To some extent the disagreements about the acceptability of deterrence turn on differences in appraisals of the intentions of the Soviet Union. Should Soviet intentions be a decisive factor in our judgments about nuclear deterrence? To oppose nuclear deterrence, must one believe that full-scale nuclear war is worse than Soviet defeat of the United States? Worse in what sense?

Disagreements about the Strategic Defense Initiative (SDI) turn partly on differences in appraisals of the likelihood of developing an effective and survivable strategic defense shield in the foreseeable future. If we agree with Reagan that it would "be better to save lives than to avenge them," must we also support research, development, and testing of a strategic defense shield? Some of Reagan's scientific and military advisers claimed that he did not engage in adequate consultation before publicly committing himself to SDI. Upon what scientific and military facts does the justification of SDI depend? How would you assess the argument of some of the defenders of SDI who concede that the potential effectiveness and survivability of a strategic space shield is uncertain but insist that the high moral value of the goal—"rendering nuclear weapons impotent and obsolete"—justifies large-scale investment into research, development, and testing of parts of a strategic defense shield?

Even if you conclude that the current system of deterrence is immoral, you need not be committed to the view that the United States should immediately dismantle its nuclear weapons. Such a move could destabilize the nuclear balance and increase the risk of nuclear war. What policy implications do follow from the conclusion that deterrence (or some form of it) is immoral? Evaluate these proposals: (1) full-scale research and development of a strategic defense shield; (2) increase in capacity to fight limited nuclear wars; (3) bilateral arms control negotiations and agreements; (4) declaration of "no first use"; (5) nuclear freeze; (6) unilateral reduction of nuclear weapons; (7) unilateral disarmament.

Recommended Reading

The best contemporary discussion of the morality of war is Michael Walzer, *Just and Unjust Wars* (New York: Basic Books, 1977). The chapters most relevant to the question of the means of fighting war are 1 to 3, 8 to 13, 16, and 17. Three collections that present a variety of views on the topic are: Charles Beitz et al. (eds.), *International Ethics* (Princeton, N.J.: Princeton University Press, 1985), especially Parts 2 and 3; Marshall Cohen et al. (eds.), *War and Moral Responsibility* (Princeton, N.J.: Princeton University Press, 1974), especially the articles by Nagel and Brandt; and Richard Wasserstrom (ed.), *War and Morality* (Belmont, Calif.: Wadsworth, 1970), especially the articles by Ford, Narveson, and Wasserstrom. A good general survey of the problem from a utilitarian perspective is Jonathan Glover, *Causing Death and Saving Lives* (New York: Penguin, 1977), chapter 19 (see also the bibliography, pp. 318–24).

On the historical background of the decision to drop the bomb, see Martin Sherwin, *A World Destroyed* (New York: Random House, 1977). An account sympathetic to the decision makers is McGeorge Bundy, *Danger and Survival: Choices about the Bomb in the First Fifty Years* (New York: Random House, 1988), chapter 2. A philosopher's criticism of Truman is Elisabeth Anscombe, "Mr. Truman's Degree," in Anscombe, *Ethics, Religion and Politics* (Minneapolis: University of Minnesota Press, 1981), pp. 62–71.

A useful selection of articles as well as bibliography is James P. Sterba (ed.), *The Ethics of War and Nuclear Deterrence* (Belmont, Ca.: Wadsworth, 1985). Also, Germain Grisez, John Finnis, Joseph M. Boyle, Jr., *Nuclear Deterrence, Morality and Realism* (New York: Oxford University Press, 1987); Gregory Kavka, *Moral Problems of Nuclear Deterrence* (New York: Cambridge University Press, 1987); and Joseph S. Nye, Jr., *Nuclear Ethics* (New York: Free Press, 1986). A critique of the Bishop's Letter is Albert Wohlstetter, "Bishops, Statesmen, and Other Strategists on the Bombing of Innocents," *Commentary*, 75 (June 1983), pp. 15–35.

2 Deception

Introduction

The successful ruler, according to Machiavelli, must be "a great liar and hypocrite." Politicians have to appear to be moral even though they are not, because politics requires methods that citizens would find morally objectionable if they knew about them. We do not know how many politicians follow Machiavelli's advice today (those who do so most successfully may seem to be the least machiavellian). We do know that many public officials have tried to justify deception, and so have some political commentators and political theorists.

Deception involves intentionally causing (or attempting to cause) someone to believe something that you know (or should know) to be false. Political deception is not always easy to recognize, since it seldom comes in the form of an outright lie. More often, officials give us half-truths, which they hope we will not see are half-lies; or they offer us silence, which they hope will cause us to ignore inconvenient truths. Sometimes officials provide so much information that the truth is deliberately obscured, lost in a plethora of facts and figures. Thus the first task in analyzing a case of alleged deception is to decide whether deception actually occurred and precisely in what ways.

Those who want to justify political deception usually grant what ordinary morality maintains—that lying is generally wrong. But they go on to argue that no one (except perhaps Kant) believes that deception is always wrong. The general presumption against it can therefore be rebutted in certain circumstances, such as those that typically characterize politics. Politics is supposed to make deception more justifiable for several reasons: (1) political issues are complex and difficult to understand, especially when they must be presented in the mass media or in a short time; (2) the harmful effects of some political truths can be severe and irreversible; (3) the political effects result as much from what people believe as from what is actually true; and (4) organizing coalitions and other kinds of political action requires leaders to emphasize some parts of the truth to some people and different parts to others; telling the whole truth and nothing but the truth would make compromise almost impossible.

But, at least in a democracy, these reasons cannot give political leaders a general license to deceive whenever and wherever they think it necessary. Unless we can find out what officials have actually done—not just what they appear to have done—we cannot hold them accountable. At most, the special features of politics may justify exceptions to a general presumption against deception in a democracy.

If we conclude that deception may sometimes be necessary, our task should be to define carefully the conditions under which citizens should permit public officials to engage in deception. The main factors we should consider are: (1) the importance of the goal of the deception; (2) the availability of alternative means for achieving the goal; (3) the identity of the victims of the deception (other officials, other governments, all citizens); (4) the accountability of the deceivers (the possibility of approving the deception in advance or discovering it later); and (5) the containment of the deception (its effects on other actions by officials).

The cases in this section offer the chance to identify various kinds of deception and to discover what, if any, conditions would justify deception. The first selection is a group of minicases. They are simplified versions of actual episodes in American politics, and they provide an indication of the variety of the kinds of deception and circumstances in which politicians have tried to justify it.

"Disinformation for Qaddafi" and "The Iran-Contra Affair" describe two recent foreign policy ventures in which deception was a key element; the first was formally approved by the president and key administration officials, while the second was kept secret even from some responsible officials within the administration. The two episodes also differ with respect to their goals, the victims of the deception, the possibilities of holding the deceivers accountable, and the chances of containing the deception.

Moral difficulties often do not come neatly packaged with labels announcing "This is a dilemma of deception." In "The New York City Fiscal Crisis," many of the ethical issues lie buried in the intricate and sometimes tedious details of accounting routines. It is important to work through these details while keeping in mind the larger issues that they imply—such as the conflict between the obligation to keep the public informed and the obligation to protect the public welfare.

Lying in Office

Graham T. Allison and Lance M. Liebman

1. JFK, THE "DEAL," AND THE DENIAL

On Saturday, October 27, 1962, at the height of the Cuban Missile Crisis, President John F. Kennedy receives a letter from the Soviet government proposing to strike a deal. The Soviet Union, the letter offers, will dismantle and remove its missiles from Cuba if the United States agrees to a similar withdrawal of its nuclear-armed missiles stationed in Turkey. In fact, Kennedy twice ordered the removal of these obsolescent and vulnerable missiles in the months prior to the October crisis. But each time the Turkish government had objected, and so the missiles remained—an easy target for Soviet retaliation should the United States be forced to take military action against the missiles in Cuba.

Kennedy believes, along with virtually all of his advisers, that the Soviet offer is

Reprinted by permission of the authors.

unacceptable. To back down under fire, he reasons, would be to demonstrate that the United States was willing to trade off European security for its own. It would undermine the credibility of America's pledge to defend Europe against Soviet attack, and would invite the Soviets to stage another missile crisis elsewhere—only this time in a situation where the military deck was not so heavily stacked in America's favor. But he also knows that tens of millions of Russians and Americans might soon be dead if he cannot find some other way to resolve the crisis.

Kennedy decides to ignore the Soviet proposal and to respond favorably to an earlier, private letter from Premier Khrushchev to himself, in which the Soviet leader had offered to withdraw the missiles in Cuba in return only for an American pledge not to invade the island. But to sweeten the deal, guessing that Khrushchev's colleagues may have subsequently raised the price of Soviet withdrawal, Kennedy has his brother Robert inform Soviet Ambassador Anatoly Dobrynin privately that, while there can be no Cuba-for-Turkey exchange made under pressure, the President had already ordered the removal of the American missiles in Turkey and would make sure the order was carried out speedily.

At a press conference on November 20, after the crisis had passed and after the congressional elections that were on Kennedy's mind during October 1962, the following exchange occurred:

> Q. Mr. President, in the various exchanges of the past three weeks, either between yourself and Chairman Khrushchev or at the United Nations, have any issues been touched on besides that of Cuba, and could you say how the events of these past three weeks might affect such an issue as Berlin or disarmament or nuclear testing?
>
> The President: No. I instructed the negotiators to confine themselves to the matter of Cuba completely, and therefore no other matters were discussed. Disarmament, any matters affecting Western Europe, relations between the Warsaw pact countries and NATO, all the rest—none of these matters was to be in any way referred to or negotiated about until we had made progress and come to some sort of a solution on Cuba. So that has been all we have done diplomatically with the Soviet Union the last month.
>
> Now if we're successful in Cuba, as I said, we would be hopeful that some of the other areas of tension could be relaxed. Obviously when you make progress in any area, then you have hopes that you can continue it. But up till now we have confined ourselves to Cuba, and we'll continue to do so until we feel the situation has reached a satisfactory state.

2. The Election Debate

It is November 1969. John Lindsay is running for reelection as mayor of New York. His principal opponent is Mario Procaccino, a conservative Democrat. In a TV debate the Sunday before election day, Procaccino charges that Lindsay has "made a deal with the landlords." More specifically, he claims that (1) Lindsay has a secret report on housing in New York City, (2) the report states that rent control is at the heart of the city's housing problem, and recommends revisions of the rent control law which will result in massive rent increases, and (3) the report is being suppressed until after the election.

In fact, Lindsay knows that two city consultants (RAND and McKinsey) have done such a study for the Housing and Development Administration. He has not seen their report, but has seen a preliminary summary of their findings, which do find that rent control is aggravating the city's housing shortage, and do recommend substantial revision of the rent control law in such a way that many rents will be significantly increased. At the recommendation of the Housing and Development Administrator, the reports have been labeled "highly confidential" and publication is being withheld until after the election. On the basis of the report's findings and the recommendations of other analysts in the city government, Lindsay believes that the report's analyses are essentially correct, and plans to seek substantial changes in rent control—after the election.

Lindsay knows that to announce his intention prior to the election would cost many votes. He suspects that to acknowledge the existence of the report will raise serious doubts in many voters' minds about his support for rent control. He believes that Procaccino would be a disastrous mayor for New York City. He replies:

> I haven't seen this so-called report; there could well be such a report. The mayor sees thousands of reports from various persons, and it's the mayor's decision that counts in this whole matter of governing New York City, and my decisions have been constant, not only to be firm on rent control, which I am. I believe in it. I think we must have it.

Two hours after the debate, Lindsay and his staff are at campaign headquarters. A young aide says, "The Mayor's answer to the rent control question was ambiguous. We'd better put out a firmer denial. How about this?" He then proposes the following press release:

> Mayor Lindsay today branded as ridiculous the charge that he is soft on rent control. He said the city is not studying the watering down of controls, and if any recommendation for higher rents is made, he will reject it out of hand.

3. Miller and Furloughs

It is early 1970. Jerome Miller has just taken office as head of Massachusetts' Department of Youth Services, the agency responsible for managing the state's programs for juvenile offenders. After fifteen years of child-treatment experience, Miller—like many other progressives in his field—has come to believe that institutionalization is a disastrous policy, and that almost any environment outside the large state detention centers is better for the child and cheaper for the state. He believes the old, prison-like "reform schools" are brutal, oppressive institutions that teach little more than the finer points of crime; his ultimate goal is to shut them down entirely and replace them with a network of smaller scale, community-based halfway houses. But first he must prove to the legislature and the communities in which the houses will be located that the kids can be trusted.

Miller's first step toward deinstitutionalization is a program of weekend furloughs for confined teenage offenders. One hundred boys and girls go home on Friday afternoon, and ninety-one come back Monday morning. Miller is not alarmed, since this result conforms to his expectations, based on similar programs elsewhere, in which virtually all of the wanderers have returned within a week. But the press wants to know what the "count" was immediately, and Miller fears that published reports of a 9% AWOL rate will kill any chances for deinstitutionalization. He tells the press on Monday afternoon that all the furlough children were back on time. By Friday, the nine missing offenders have all returned.

4. Fiddling the Rules Committee Chairman

Elizabeth Jackson is a private citizen, head of an ad hoc lobbying group formed to support the Equal Rights Amendment in her state. It is December 1975. Her state has not yet ratified the ERA, but ratification is closer than it has ever been in the three years since Congress sent the amendment to the states.

(Background note: The ERA was passed by both houses of Congress in 1972. The Congressional resolution provided that the amendment would become effective if ratified by the required three-fourths of the states, thirty-eight, within seven years. By the end of 1973, thirty-four states had ratified the ERA. After a flurry of ratifications in the first two years, the battle for the ERA has come down to a grinding effort to win the few more states needed. Time seems to be on the side of the opponents. The women's movement no longer enjoys the media attention which helped win the initial passage of the ERA by projecting the image of a potent new political force. The ERA opponents seem to be getting stronger, and are able to use delaying tactics to their advantage as the 1979 deadline approaches.)

In Jackson's state, the ERA forces have had little success until this year. Although most legislators are unwilling to be recorded against the ERA, its opponents have bottled it up in committee in both houses, preventing any floor votes. Last election, the key opponent in the House retired, perhaps because he was unwilling to face the vigorous campaign of an opponent whom Jackson helped recruit. With him gone, and with the help of the Majority Leader, Jackson's group forced the bill out of committee, and the full House approved it. Now the end of the session is a day away, and the ERA languishes in the Senate Rules Committee.

The chairman of the Rules Committee, Senator Henderson, is a progressive force in the generally conservative Senate. Although he is personally ambivalent about the ERA, he has indicated to Jackson that it will reach the Senate floor. His cordiality and cooperative attitude have encouraged Jackson to be optimistic, but the end of the session is near, and the ERA still sits in Rules. Jackson now suspects that Henderson is holding the bill as a favor to his colleagues who would rather not vote on it.

Jackson is desperate to get the ERA approved this year. She knows that the national campaign against the ERA, led by Phyllis Schafly, is raising funds to support a more intensive lobbying effort next year. Moreover, her key supporter in the House, the Majority Leader, is leaving to run for Governor next year, and the Judiciary Committee chairman is running for Congress. Both of them helped to line up the necessary votes in the House, and without them next year, the prospects for the ERA look bleak. It looks to Jackson as if it's now or never.

She decides to change her tactics. She challenges Senator Henderson in his office. He's deliberately deceiving her, she charges, and she will make sure that he pays for it. He tells her that it is the Rules Committee members who are blocking the ERA, but she refuses to believe him. She tells him that her group is prepared to back Chris Carter, a young attorney active in local politics, who has agreed to run against Senator Henderson if he has sufficient funds and volunteers. She tells Senator Henderson that her group will contribute heavily to Carter unless ERA reaches the Senate floor.

In fact, she knows that her threat is pure fiction. While Carter has been rumored to be considering the race, she has not talked with him. The reason she has not is that she can see that her organization is running out of steam. They have no funds left, and fund-raising lately has been hardly worth the effort. Volunteers are tiring of the struggle, and will probably disappear if they are not successful this time. Furthermore, she herself would find it difficult to oppose Senator Henderson because of his critical role in the passage of a wide variety of progressive legislation.

5. Herman Fiddles Finnegan

Suppose that the Acting Director of the Bureau of Consular and Security Affairs in the Department of State, Philip Herman, is trying to substitute a permanent visa for foreign visitors to the United States in place of the existing renewable visa. Only the United States, among its major allies and trading partners, maintains such a restrictive policy, a legacy of McCarthyist fear of Communist infiltration and subversion, and Herman is attempting to eliminate this imbalance. To do so, he needs Congressional approval. But the man he must convince is Representative Michael Finnegan, a fierce anti-Communist who heads the House Appropriations Subcommittee for the State Department. Finnegan is virulently opposed to any change in visa requirements that would make it possible for a single additional Communist to enter the country, no matter what benefits the United States might derive from increased foreign visitation. In fact, he has blocked such efforts before. Without Finnegan's approval, there can be no change in the visa. Thus, Herman falsely tells Finnegan that the State Department is under heavy foreign pressure to abolish visas entirely, that unless the U.S. liberalizes its visa regulations, other countries might retaliate by making it increasingly difficult for Americans to travel abroad, and that the best way to beat this pressure would be to adopt a permanent visa system, which would at least permit an initial check on suspect foreigners. Finnegan buys the story.

6. Covert Action in Chile

It is early 1973. CIA Director Richard Helms has just been nominated by President Richard Nixon to be U.S. Ambassador to Iran, but before he can take the post, he must be approved by the Senate. During his confirmation hearings before the Foreign Relations Committee, he is asked questions about alleged CIA covert activity in Chile.

In 1970, the CIA had spent over $8 million to prevent the election of Dr. Salvador Allende Gossens, a Marxist, as Chile's President. Despite the CIA money, Allende won the election by a small plurality. But since no candidate won a majority of the vote, the Chilean Congress was required to choose between the top two vote-getters in the general election. In the past, the Congress had always selected the leading candidate, and 1970 appeared to be no exception.

Shortly after the election, President Nixon informed Director Helms that an Allende regime would not be acceptable to the United States and instructed him to organize a military coup d'etat in Chile to prevent Allende's accession to the presidency. The CIA was to take this highly sensitive action without coordination with the Departments of State or Defense and without informing the U.S. Ambassador to Chile. Instead, the Agency was to report, both for informational and approval purposes, only to the President's Assistant for National Security Affairs, Dr. Henry Kissinger, or his deputy.

Despite Helms' belief, expressed later, that the Agency was "being asked to almost do the impossible," he attempted to carry out the President's order. In a flurry of activity immediately prior to the scheduled meeting of the Chilean Congress, the CIA made twenty-one contacts with key military and police officials in Chile. Those Chileans who were inclined to stage a coup were given assurances of strong support at the highest levels of the U.S. government, both before and after a coup. Yet the coup never took place, and Dr. Allende took office. After the death in an abortive kidnap attempt of Chilean Army Commander-in-Chief General Rene Schneider, who opposed the coup, the plot was uncovered. CIA support for the conspirators was rumored, but the allegations were unconfirmed.

Now, in early 1973, with Allende still in power but facing increasing domestic opposition, Helms is asked about the CIA's alleged role in the 1970 coup attempt:

> Senator Symington: Did you try in the Central Intelligence Agency to overthrow the government in Chile?
>
> Mr. Helms: No, sir.
>
> Senator Symington: Did you have any money passed to the opponents of Allende?
>
> Mr. Helms: No, sir.
>
> Senator Symington: So the stories you were involved in that war are wrong?
>
> Mr. Helms: Yes, sir. I said to Senator Fulbright many months ago that if the Agency had really gotten in behind the other candidates and spent a lot of money and so forth the election might have come out differently.

Comment

Denial is often the first response of public officials accused of deception. Richard Helms (Case 6) claimed that he literally told the truth: the CIA did not try to overthrow the government of Chile, only to dissuade the Chilean Congress from confirming Allende's electoral victory; and the CIA did not give any money directly to the candidates, but only to groups that supported or opposed candidates. On what grounds should we decide that technically true statements count as deception? When should failure to disclose be considered deceptive?

In most of the cases, justifications for the deception typically mention the beneficial consequences of the deception. But we should distinguish: appeals to one's own reelection (Lindsay in Case 2), the success of a public cause (the ERA in Case 4), and the avoidance of nuclear war (Kennedy in Case 1). On what basis should we make such distinctions? Another kind of justification refers to features of the act of deception itself—such as the relations of the deceiver to the deceived. Perhaps enemies do not deserve the truth (but if so, does this include political enemies as in Case 5?). Politicians, like poker players, may know that the rules of the game allow some bluffing, as in Case 4, but, if so, are citizens playing the game too?

In each case, consider whether there were any reasonable alternatives to the deception. Perhaps Kennedy could not have given a more accurate answer or could not even have declined to comment without undermining the "deal" that resolved the crisis. Can the same be said about Lindsay, Miller, and Helms? No doubt these officials felt themselves in a bind: to reply "no comment" would bring about the same result as if they fully disclosed what they wished to conceal. We should also look at the context in which such dilemmas arise. Could the officials have taken steps earlier that would have prevented the dilemma from ever arising? If so, how does that affect our evaluation of their later deception?

Disinformation for Qaddafi

Christine Huang

By the spring of 1986, the Reagan administration had evidence that Libya's leader Colonel Muammar el-Qaddafi had supported and encouraged terrorist acts against U.S. citizens and U.S. installations abroad. Fearing a resurgence of terrorist activity and wishing to capitalize on the deterrent value of the April 14 U.S. air raid on Libya, the administration seized on the opportunity provided by a new intelligence report in July questioning Qaddafi's mental stability. The report triggered an interagency review of U.S.-Libyan policy. The State and Defense Departments, the Central Intelligence Agency, and the White House began to consider what steps might be taken to maintain the National Security Council, launching a new phase of the

 This account relies on reports in the *National Journal*, the *New York Times*, the *Wall Street Journal* and the *Washington Post.*

administration policy, first adopted in 1985, to undermine the Qaddafi regime.

On August 6, the State Department's Office of Intelligence and Research distributed a seven-page memorandum to senior mid-level officials in advance of an upcoming interagency meeting. The memo called for a "disinformation" and "deception" campaign to bring attention to Qaddafi's continuing terrorist activities, to exaggerate his vulnerability to internal opposition, and to play up the possibility of new American military action against him. Under the heading of Qaddafi's vulnerability to internal opposition, the State Department memorandum explicitly stated as its goal: "to continue Qaddafi's paranoia so that he remains preoccupied, off balance." If, according to the memo, Qaddafi believed that the army and other elements in Libya may be plotting against him, he might increase the pressure on the Libyan army thus prompting a "coup or assassination attempt."

The Crisis Pre-Planning Group (CPPG) of senior representatives from the State and Defense Departments, the CIA, and the White House met on August 7 at 4:30 p.m. in the White House situation room and endorsed the overall plan outlined in the State Department memo. A meeting of the National Security Planning Group (NSPG) was scheduled for August 14 to consider the next steps the administration would take against Qaddafi. (The NSPG is the key cabinet-level forum in which the president and his top aides discuss and make decisions on the most sensitive policy matters.)

On August 12, President Reagan received a memorandum from his national security affairs advisor, Admiral John Poindexter, summarizing a proposed program of disinformation against Libya. "One of the key elements" of the new strategy, the Poindexter memo said, "is that it combines real and imaginary events through a disinformation program—with the basic goal of making Qaddafi think that there is a high degree of internal opposition to him within Libya, that his long trusted aides are disloyal, that the U.S. is about to move against him militarily." The purpose of taking additional steps against Libya, according to the memo, was to deter terrorism, moderate Libyan policies, and "bring about a change of leadership in Libya."

The president, Poindexter, and nine other key officials met at the White House on August 14 at 11 A.M. The overall plan as outlined by Poindexter was approved by Reagan and codified in general terms in a formal National Security Decision Directive signed by the president. Details of the plan were left to Poindexter, the State Department, and the CIA. The Reagan directive ordered covert, diplomatic and economic steps designed to deter Libyan-sponsored terrorism and to bring about a change of leadership. The principal means outlined in the directive was a campaign of disinformation. Neither the memoranda themselves nor the meetings held to discuss them addressed the details of any strategy on the dissemination of false stories to reporters.

Although Poindexter's memo said that "the current intelligence community assessment is that Qaddafi is temporarily quiescent in his support of terrorism," soon after the meeting, one or two members of the NSC staff told reporters that the United States had new intelligence indicating that Qaddafi was stepping up his terrorist plans.

On August 25, the *Wall Street Journal* on page one reported that "the U.S. and Libya are on a collision course again" and added that "the Reagan administration is preparing to teach the mercurial Libyan leader another lesson. Right now, the Pentagon is completing plans for a new and larger bombing of Libya in case the President orders it." The report quoted a senior U.S. official as saying of Qaddafi,

"There are increasing signs that he's renewed planning and preparations for terrorist acts." The article went on to describe the administration's new "three-pronged program of military, covert, and economic actions" intended "to pre-empt more Libyan-sponsored terrorism, exacerbate growing political and economic tensions in Libya, and remind Col. Qaddafi and his inner circle that promoting terrorism may be hazardous to their health." The program included joint exercises with Egypt in the Mediterranean, possible joint action with France to drive Libyan troops out of Chad, increased support for dissident military officers, businessmen, and technocrats inside Libya and for Libyan exiles who wanted "to oust Col. Qaddafi," and with European cooperation, tightening the economic and political sanctions adopted in the spring of 1985 by the Common Market and by the Tokyo economic summit.

All three network television evening news programs repeated the substance of the *Journal's* report that night, citing unidentified administration officials. The August 26 issues of many major newspapers quoted unidentified and identified officials who seemed to confirm the *Journal's* article, though there was no explicit official confirmation.

On August 25, in Santa Barbara near the ranch where President Reagan was on a three-week vacation, White House spokesman Larry Speakes said, "Our policy toward Libyan-backed terrorism is unequivocal and unchanged. We will employ all appropriate measures to cause Libya to cease its terrorist policies. We certainly have reason to believe that the Libyan state, headed by Col. Qaddafi, has not forsaken its desire to cause—to create—terrorist activities worldwide, and the capability is still there to do so." In an off-the-record statement at a news conference the next day, Speakes described the *Journal's* article as being "highly authoritative, but not authorized."

Fearing that reports of impending American military action against Libya might produce more concern in Europe than in Libya, administration officials in Washington sought to soften the public line on August 27. White House, State Department, and Pentagon officials said they had indications of planned new Libyan terrorist activities aimed at Americans. They stressed, however, that they had nothing approximating a "smoking gun" to justify sending American bombers once again to strike Libya. The officials described new American diplomatic efforts to toughen economic and political sanctions against Libya as the main thrust of administration policy. Vernon A. Walters, the U.S. delegate to the United Nations, was expected to travel to Europe the following week to explore widening these sanctions. One key official expressed the fear that "these panic stories will undercut the Walters mission. The Europeans will ask us for the hard evidence, and we won't have any. It will look like we are crying wolf once again."

Bob Woodward in the *Washington Post* on October 2 disclosed the details of the administration's "secret and unusual plan of deception." The *Post* account said that beginning with the *Journal's* August 25 report, the American news media reported as fact much of the false information generated by the deception plan described in the August memos.

The White House denied that the administration had planted false reports with news organizations in the United States as a means of bringing pressure on Qaddafi. Mr. Speakes said that the information provided to the *Wall Street Journal* "was not a part of any plan or memo drafted by Poindexter and approved by the President and the U.S. Government." Defending the statements he made in August, the White House spokesman reiterated that "the information contained in the *Wall Street Journal* in these various intelligence reports was information from intelligence sources. That was hard, that was firm."

Responding to the *Post's* article in an interview on October 2 at the White House with select news columnists and broadcast commentators, President Reagan at first said, "I challenge the veracity of that entire story," but acknowledged that "there are memos back and forth. I can't deny that here and there they're going to have something to hang it on."

Secretary of State George Shultz told reporters on the same day in New York that he knew of "no decision to have people go out and tell lies to the media" but that "if there are ways in which we can make Qaddafi nervous, why shouldn't we?" He noted Winston Churchill's statement in World War II that "in time of war the truth is so precious it must be attended by a bodyguard of lies," adding that "insofar as Qaddafi is concerned we don't have a declaration of war but we have something darn close to it."

In a statement issued on October 2 in reference to the August 25 report, *Wall Street Journal* managing editor Norman Pearlstine said, "We remain convinced, as reported in the *Journal,* that the U.S. government in late summer believed Libya had resumed its active support for terrorism and that the U.S. was considering a range of options aimed at deterring such Libyan actions. We reported this based on not one source, but on information provided by a number of sources here and abroad." Pearlstine concluded by saying, "If, indeed, our government conducted such a domestic disinformation campaign, we were among its many victims." Leaving for a weekend retreat at Camp David, Maryland, on October 3, the President insisted for the second consecutive day that the administration had been trying merely to deceive Qaddafi rather than to mislead the press into printing inaccurate reports. "We are not telling lies or doing any of these disinformation things that we are cited with doing."

The Justice Department asked the Federal Bureau of Investigation to conduct an inquiry into the *Post's* October 2 report and the *Journal's* August 25 article. The probe was referred to a new unit in the FBI's Washington field office that was set up under a reorganization in the spring of 1985 to assign veteran agents to pursue leaks of classified information.

The Senate Select Committee on Intelligence initiated an inquiry. Bernie McMahon, the committee staff director, told the Associated Press on October 3 that the staff had concluded that the administration had not deliberately attempted to plant false stories in the U.S. news media. In an interview on the same day, the chairman of the Senate Intelligence Committee, Dave Durenberger, said that individual White House aides may have provided false information without the approval of their superiors, leading to inaccurate stories about Libya by major news organizations, but added that it would take "a quantum leap" to assume that the actions of a few White House officials constituted a formal administration policy of lying to American reporters.

The Iran-Contra Affair

David Nacht

The Iran-Contra Affair was a set of American foreign policy initiatives conducted in secret by a small number of executive branch officials, mainly members of the National Security Council Staff, during the Reagan administration between 1984 and 1986. The affair involved two principal parts: (1) the secret sale of arms to Iran in order to gain the release of American hostages held by Iranian allies in Lebanon and (2) the establishment of a covert mechanism to fund and arm the Nicaraguan insurgency, known as the Contras, at a time when the Congress had cut off funds to the Contras.

This case highlights the actions of two main officials in the affair, Admiral John Poindexter, the national security advisor to the president of the United States, and his aide, Lieutenant Colonel Oliver North. After the affair became public knowledge, two committees of Congress held joint hearings for eight months, at which the "star" witnesses were Adm. Poindexter and Lt. Col. North. Testifying under oath, they were granted immunity for their statements under the terms of the Fifth Amendment preventing self-incrimination.[1] North was fired from his post on the NSC staff, and Poindexter was forced to resign.

In order to preserve the secrecy of the Iran and Nicaragua activities, Adm. Poindexter made sure that few individuals knew about them. The secretary of state, for instance, apparently lacked detailed knowledge of almost all of the activities; the same was true for the chairman of the Joint Chiefs and the secretary of defense. In his relentless effort at compartmentalization, Admiral Poindexter even appears to have excluded the president from knowledge of major aspects of the affair. The director of the Central Intelligence Agency, William Casey, knew about—and in fact may have planned—many of the activities, although this may not have been in accord with Poindexter's wishes, but rather because of Casey's special friendship with Lt. Col. North. Selected members of the CIA, Defense Department, State Department, private individuals and members of certain foreign governments, all of whose participation was deemed by Poindexter and North to be necessary for the success of the mission, were also made aware of the initiatives. However, Congress was not told, even though there are legally required procedures for informing congressional leaders of highly secretive covert operations. Moreover, after an investigation began, Casey, North, and Poindexter fabricated cover stories, and the latter two destroyed documents in an effort to deceive the investigators.[2]

THE SETTING

Public disclosure of both the Iran and the Nicaraguan initiatives was bound to cause controversy. The United States and Iran had been on uncomfortable terms since the seizure of the American diplomats in Tehran in 1979 by the Iranian Revolutionary Guards. Moreover, the Reagan administration had been pursuing a vocal antiterrorism campaign waged largely against Iran and Libya. President Reagan had officially designated Iran as a terrorist nation, forbidding it, under the terms of the amended Arms Export Control Act, to receive arms from the United States. Moreover, the president had personally asked the West European allies not to sell arms to Iran.

The diversion of funds to the Contras, although closer in spirit to stated American foreign policy, concerned many because it flouted a congressional ban on such assistance, and Reagan administration officials had falsely testified that the administration was not arming the Contras. The administration had actively opposed the ruling Sandanista regime in Nicaragua by successively condemning the regime, boycotting Nicaraguan goods in the United States, mining Nicaraguan harbors, and organizing and funding the Contras. The administration's efforts to obtain material support for the rebel force had been hampered by congressional resistance. Congress voted down a number of administration requests to arm the Contras. In December 1981, President Reagan authorized a National Intelligence Finding establishing U.S. support for the Contras. A year later on December 21, 1982, Congress passed the first of five Boland Amendments, named after the congressman who wrote the legislation, barring the CIA or the Department of Defense from spending money directed "toward overthrowing the government of Nicaragua or provoking a military exchange between Nicaragua and Honduras." In September 1983, President Reagan signed another finding authorizing "the provision of material support and guidance to the Nicaraguan resistance groups." On December 8, 1983, Congress responded by placing a $24 million cap on funds to be used for supporting the Contras directly or indirectly by "DOD or CIA or any other agency involved in intelligence activities." In October 1984, Congress stopped all funding for the Contras "by any agency involved in intelligence activities."[2] It was at this point that Lt. Col. North essentially took over the role which the CIA had been performing as the logistics coordinator for the Contras.

AIDING THE CONTRAS

Lt. Col. North was a marine who had been "detailed" to the NSC staff. His boss, Robert "Bud" McFarlane, the national security advisor, was another marine colonel. North served on a committee on the NSC staff charged with combatting terrorism abroad. Although his position was not very senior, North was self-confident and eager to take the initiative in carrying out policies. He formed friendships with McFarlane, with McFarlane's successor, Adm. Poindexter, and with the director of the CIA, William Casey. North used his personal relationships to learn the priorities of the senior policymakers and to build their trust in him. He appears to have had at least tacit approval for most or all of his activities from the successive national security advisors.

North became the NSC liaison to the Contras. He was charged with "keeping them alive, body and soul" in spite of the cutoff in congressional funding. He interpreted the legal limitation as a prohibition on funding the Contras with money appropriated by Congress. Therefore, his strategy was to get money from other sources—foreign governments and private citizens: "I made every effort, counsel, to avoid the use of appropriated funds. And, as I said, that was why the decision was made in 1984, before this proscription ever became law, to set up outside entities, and to raise non-U.S. government monies by which the Nicaraguan freedom fighters could be supported."[3]

In December 1984, he initiated the effort to raise foreign funds by asking Secretary Shultz to solicit funds from the sultan of Brunei for Contra use. (Shultz's meeting with the sultan and the payment that followed actually did not occur until June 1986.) North, State Department officials, and private citizens solicited a total of $34 million dollars for the Contras from foreign sources between June 1984 and the beginning of 1986. An additional $2.7 million was raised from private contributors.[4]

President Reagan authorized the policy to raise funds from foreign sources and private contributors for the Contras; however, he may not have had the legal authority to conduct these activities. (No Court ruling has yet been issued). President Reagan himself took part briefly in the fundraising, meeting with large donors of both the foreign and private domestic variety, and Adm. Poindexter has testified that "I am confident that he [the president] was aware that these people were making contributions to support the Contras."[5] However, this activity was kept from the Congress. Elliot Abrams, the assistant secretary of state, actively misled a congressional committee about administration fundraising efforts. He later acknowledged his distortions, stating that unless members of Congress asked "exactly the right question, using exactly the right words, they weren't going to get the right answers."[6]

Rumors of NSC staff support for the Contras reached Congress and the press by June 1985. In August 1985, representatives Michael Barnes and Lee Hamilton wrote separate letters to National Security Advisor McFarlane asking for information about these rumors. In October, McFarlane received three additional requests. McFarlane responded to these requests with statements that Col. North later described as "false, erroneous, misleading, evasive, and wrong."[7] Col. North maintains that Col. McFarlane authorized him to submit misleading documents to Congressman Barnes. Col. McFarlane has testified in response that he was unaware of the full extent of the activities of Col. North. Col. McFarlane has admitted, however, that he lied in his letter of response to Congressman Hamilton of October 7, denying NSC participation in third-country fundraising for the Contras. There is also convincing evidence that he lied regarding his knowledge of Col. North's activities in coordinating logistics for the Contras.[8]

Col. McFarlane repeated these false denials in meetings with senators Leahy and Durenberger on September 5, 1985, and with members of the House Intelligence Committee on September 10. He also gave false testimony after he resigned to the Senate Select Committee on Intelligence in December 1986 concerning his knowledge of NSC staff activities. Although he claimed that he relied on press accounts for his information, McFarlane actually received memos from Col. North via computer notes, which turned up after McFarlane testified. McFarlane worked closely with North and Poindexter to cover up the NSC role in the arms sale.[9]

From July 1985 until the operation was discovered in November 1986, North, with the clear approval of Adm. Poindexter, Robert McFarlane's successor as national security advisor, employed a network of private firms, CIA agents, CIA proprietary firms, nonprofit anticommunist organizations, some State Department officials—notably Assistant Secretary of State Elliot Abrams and the U.S. ambassador to Costa Rica, Lewis Tambs—and a few private individuals to aid the Nicaraguan rebels with logistics and fundraising efforts. The bulk of the money was handled by two individuals who controlled a network of firms, known to the congressional committees investigating the Iran-Contra Affair as "The Enterprise." The Enterprise was a partnership between Albert Hakim, an Iranian-born businessman, and ex-U.S. General Richard Secord, in close coordination with Lt. Col. North. The Enterprise served in a covert capacity as an informal contractor to the U.S. government and to the Contras.

The president was not told about The Enterprise because, according to Adm. Poindexter, it was an "unnecessary detail." William Casey was informed, although Poindexter instructed North not to tell Casey because as director of the CIA, he could be called on to testify before Congress. Poindexter also hid the operation from Donald Regan, the president's chief of staff, because "he talked to the press too much. I was afraid he'd make a slip."[10] The Congress and public were not informed of The Enterprise until the Iran-Contra investigation.

At an undetermined point in 1985, Col. North decided, with the approval of Adm. Poindexter, that the residual profits from the Iran arms sale ought to go toward assisting the Contras. Only a small fraction of the total Iran arms profits actually reached the Contras. According to the congressional committees' investigation, about $3.8 million out of the $16.1 million profit from the Iran arms sales went to support the Contras![11]

Adm. Poindexter has testified that he did not distinguish among funds coming from private donations, the Iranian arms sales or foreign sources in terms of their ownership. He argues that he had the authority to let Col. North and The Enterprise use the funds as they saw fit. The funds were used to cover expenses for the many operations, for buying arms for the Contras, for public relations in the United States on behalf of the Contras, and as a source of profits for Secord and Hakim. Some were also spent on a security system for the home of Col. North.[12]

Secord and Hakim controlled most of the money raised for the Contras. At one time when North visited Contra forces and wrote that "the picture is, in short, very dismal, unless a source of bridge funding can be found," there were over $4.8 million in funds in accounts controlled by Secord and Hakim of which North did not know.[13] The Enterprise took in total revenues of $48 million from the arms sales to Iran and the Contras, and private donations from people who thought they were contributing to the Contras.[14]

All of these operations were kept secret from the Congress. Except for some of the fundraising from foreign sources, and the domestic public relations effort, the State Department was also not informed. The president was not told at this time about the diversion of funds from the Iran arms sale to the Contras.

Based on further press accounts, a new congressional inquiry was launched in June 1986. In the House Intelligence Committee's "Resolution of Inquiry," dated July 1, the president was directed to provide the House of Representatives with information and documents on: contacts between NSC staff and private individuals or foreign governments about Contra provisions; the extent to which NSC staff provided military advice to the Contras; and contacts between NSC staff and certain private individuals who were known consultants to the Contras.

Adm. Poindexter replied to the request by referring to McFarlane's response from the previous year and not mentioning any details. Since Poindexter knew that McFarlane's letter had not been accurate, he continued the deception that his predecessor had begun. The House Intelligence Committee also interviewed Col. North as part of their inquiry. Months later, in his testimony to the Iran-Contra committees, North admitted to lying in that interview.[15]

Both Col. North and Adm. Poindexter acknowledge that they misled Congress, and both defend their actions. In his testimony North defended the right of the executive to resist informing the Congress about sensitive matters: "[I sent]. . .answers . . .to the Congress that were clearly misleading. . . .I believed then, and I believe now that the executive was fully legitimate in giving no answer to those queries."[16] When Mr. Nields, the House chief counsel, asked Col. North how he could reconcile lying to Congress with a belief in democratic principles, North responded:

> . . .I did it because we have had incredible leaks, from discussions with closed committees of the Congress. I. . .was a part of, as some people know, the coordination for the mining of the harbors in Nicaragua. When that one leaked, there were American lives at stake, and it leaked from a member of one of the committees, who eventually admitted it. When there was a leak on the sensitive intelligence methods that we used to help capture the Achille Lauro terrorists, it almost wiped out that whole channel of communications. I mean, those kinds of things are devastating. They are devastating to the national security of the United States, and I desperately hope that one of the things that can derive from all of this ordeal is that we can find a better way by which we can communicate those things properly with the Congress.[17]

In a celebrated statement, Col. North concluded that "I think we had to weigh in the balance the difference between lies and lives."[18]

Critics, including the Senate counsel, Arthur Liman, have argued that Col. North could have revealed to Congress the general policy of aiding the Contras without revealing specific information that would have threatened lives. North maintains that a flaw in the oversight mechanism of Congress prevents the executive from feeling confident that Congress can maintain the confidentiality of sensitive matters. Moreover, he argued that a national debate on the subject would inevitably have led to the leaking of sensitive material.

Adm. Poindexter also admits to deceiving Congress, and he expected Col. North to do the same: "I did think he would withhold information and be evasive, frankly, in answering questions. My objective all along was to withhold from the Congress exactly what the NSC staff was doing in carrying out the president's policy."[19] Poindexter justifies this deception on the grounds that had Congress known the truth, it would have acted to stop the NSC activities. Since those activities, did not, in his view, violate the law, they could be conducted in secret:

> that what Colonel North was doing in terms of supporting the democratic resistance was within the letter of the law at the time, although obviously very sensitive, very controversial. We wanted to avoid more restrictive legislation, and so any activity that he would have been involved with on Central America we wanted to keep highly compartmented.[20]

The Iran Initiative[21]

In spite of strident rhetoric on the part of both countries, Iran and the United States each had interests in reestablishing ties with one another. Iran wanted weapons and diplomatic support in its war against Iraq, and the United States wanted to diminish the likelihood that Iran would turn pro-Soviet. There were discussions underway between Israeli and American officials concerning the possibility of U.S. sale of arms to Iran in 1984 and 1985. The Israelis maintained a secret communications channel with senior Iranian officials, about which the senior officials of the NSC gradually became aware. Throughout 1985, the number of American hostages taken increased dramatically, placing great pressure on the Reagan administration to do something to bring them home, in spite of public commitments not to give in to terrorist demands. The change in attitude within the administration was expressed in the context of broader U.S.-Iranian relations in a memo to McFarlane by two NSC staffers, Howard Teicher and Donald Fortier, dated June 11, 1985. They called for a radical shift in U.S. policy toward Iran in order to advance American and limit Soviet influence in Iran. One of the steps they recommended was the occasional shipment of arms to Iran. In June, the Iranians transmitted their desire to obtain U.S.-made weapons such as the TOW and HAWK missiles. A number of private businessmen including an Israeli, an Iranian, and a Saudi exerted their influence on NSC officials in an effort to broker a deal. National Security Advisor McFarlane circulated a draft memo on June 17 to Secretaries Shultz (State) and Weinberger (Defense) and the director of central intelligence, Mr. Casey, suggesting that the United States could sell arms via the Israelis to Iran as part of a broader strategy for improving U.S.-Iranian relations and to help bring the hostages home. Both Shultz and Weinberger replied in memos that they opposed the arms sales.

After a briefing by McFarlane, President Reagan approved, on a still undetermined date in August, the shipment of U.S.-manufactured arms by Israel to Iran. On August 30, 1985, the Israelis shipped 100 TOW missiles to Iran. They sent an additional 408 TOWs on September 14. On September 15, a U.S. hostage, the Reverend Benjamin Weir, was released. In November, there was another arms sale. It remains unclear whether the president was informed of this sale; he does not remember. North, McFarlane and Poindexter were all directly involved in the sale, and Shultz was briefed. Eighteen HAWK missiles were transferred to Iran, but they did not meet Iranian specifications, and the Iranians returned all but one of them to the Israelis. After this sale, a covert action finding was prepared by the CIA for the president to sign, approving the arms sales.

On December 7, the president met with senior officials, including McFarlane, who had just resigned as national security advisor, and Poindexter, concerning arms sales to Iran. As a result of the meeting, McFarlane, now a private citizen acting as an agent of the U.S. government, was sent to London to negotiate with a Mr. Ghorbanifar, an Iranian middleman who had brokered the previous sales.

According to his own accounts, the president was interested in proceeding with the Iran arms sales if the hostages could be freed. He signed another finding on January 17, 1986, authorizing the direct sale of American arms via the CIA to the Iranians. This decision marked a change from the previous policy of agreeing to resupply Israel with arms that they sold to Iran. Neither Secretary Shultz nor Secretary Weinberger was informed of this shift in policy, which was developed by the president and Adm. Poindexter. At this point the arms sales became coordinated within the NSC staff, as part of a broader policy aimed at the release of the hostages entitled Operation Recovery. Col. North assumed direct control over the operation under the authority of Adm. Poindexter. North brought in The Enterprise to help with the shipments.

Negotiations with the Iranians had been strained since the unsuccessful shipment of the HAWKS in November. North and McFarlane arranged a meeting with the Iranians to attempt to improve relations. Adm. Poindexter briefed the president in May 1986 in the two weeks preceding the trip, but he did not inform Shultz or Weinberger, and neither did the president. Although no U.S. hostages had been taken during the summer, three more were taken in September and October.

The taking of these hostages led North, McFarlane, and Poindexter, and probably Casey, to mistrust Ghorbanifar. Col. North sought to establish a "second channel" to Iran to replace Ghorbanifar. Acting under presidential authorization, North, along with a CIA agent and Secord, met with the second channel, an individual whose identity has not been revealed, in Frankfurt on October 5-7, 1986. They set up a second meeting in Frankfurt, at which, without presidential authorization, but possibly with Adm. Poindexter's approval, Col. North agreed that the United States would ship more TOWs and HAWKS, supply military intelligence, and pressure the Kuwaiti government to release some terrorist prisoners in exchange for the release of one or two American hostages. U.S. officials continued to negotiate with the Iranian officials through December 1986, after the affair had been made public. The talks broke down, however, and U.S. policy turned actively anti-Iran in the summer of 1987.

On November 3, 1986, the Lebanese paper Al-Shiraa disclosed that the United States had been selling arms to Iran in exchange for the release of hostages held in Lebanon. The White House issued a series of statements the following week denying the reports; the statements had been prepared in large measure by Poindexter.[22] On November 12 and 13 the cover-up continued, as Poindexter spread inaccurate accounts of the affair to the cabinet, members of Congress, and the press. He did not mention the Nicaragua connection, and he did not refer to two of the three findings signed by the president. He also omitted most of the arms shipments to Iran. On November 18, Poindexter withheld information from State Department counsel, Abraham Sofaer. That same day, Poindexter spoke with Casey about preparing false testimony for a congressional appearance.[23]

On November 19, the president held a news conference reiterating the false claims he had made during his televised address.[24] Secretary Shultz confronted the president about his factual errors on the following day. Meanwhile, McFarlane, Poindexter and North were constructing inaccurate chronologies of the affair. Because they communicated with each other via computer messages which the congressional committees later retrieved, we have a record of their attempt. The record strongly suggests that their intention was to cover up what they could. For example, in some of their accounts, they claimed the HAWK shipments were really oil equipment, when they had been the officials who had devised the oil equipment deception to preserve secrecy in the first place.[25] On November 21, Director Casey made the same false claim in his testimony to the Intelligence Committee.

Under considerable public pressure, the attorney general, Edwin Meese, decided to launch an investigation into the affair because of conflicting stories about what had actually taken place. When he informed Poindexter of this, Poindexter and North began a massive effort to destroy the evidence of their actions. They both shredded documents; North also altered the documents, deleting references to the NSC staff's ties to the Contras.[26]

When testifying, North admitted that he shredded documents for reasons other than to preserve national security:

> LIMAN: Do you deny, Colonel, that one of the reasons that you were shredding documents that Saturday, was to avoid the political embarrassment of having those documents be seen by the attorney general's staff?
>
> NORTH: I do not deny that.[27]

Moreover, North lied to Meese during his interview with the attorney general. Meese confronted North with a document, which Bradford Reynolds, the assistant attorney general, had uncovered, mentioning the diversion of funds from Iran to Nicaragua. North claimed that "no one at CIA knew about it," when Casey, in fact, had known. North also lied about the nature of the Contra supply operations.[28]

BUREAUCRATIC IRREGULARITIES

In the Iran-Contra Affair, many normal bureaucratic procedures were ignored in an effort to maintain secrecy. Both initiatives, which could be considered to be major acts of foreign policy, were handled as covert operations and kept secret from as many senior officials in the government as possible. For instance, U.S. officials negotiated with high-level Israeli and Iranian politicians without the knowledge of the secretary of state. To maintain this secrecy, Adm. Poindexter and Director Casey evidently believed that they had to deceive Secretary Shultz, with whom they dealt on a regular basis, about the activities of Lt. Col. North.

The National Security Council staff was not formed with the purpose of undertaking covert operations or foreign policy initiatives, but for easing the presidential decision-making process, yet the NSC staff took over the job of resupplying the Contras when the CIA was expressly barred from doing so by Congress. The answer to the legal question of whether the NSC staff was included in the cut-off remains uncertain: the Boland Amendment cut-off included "DOD, CIA and other agencies engaged in intelligence activities." In general, the NSC is not considered an intelligence agency, but Executive Order 12333 stated that the NSC was "the highest Executive Branch entity that provides review of, guidance for, and direction to the conduct of all national foreign intelligence, counter-intelligence, and special activities, and attendant policies and programs."[29] Moreover, the covert operations conducted by Col. North included CIA and ex-CIA personnel and were of the type which might normally be conducted by the CIA. Poindexter and North, however, received legal advice from the president's Foreign Intelligence Advisory Board to the effect that the NSC was not covered by the Boland Amendment.

JUSTIFIABLE DECEPTION?

In the congressional hearings, Adm. Poindexter and Lt. Col. North acknowledged their attempts to deceive executive branch officials, the Congress, and the public, but they maintained that their acts of deception were justifiable. The House counsel, John Nields, asked Col. North about the covert operations:

> MR. NIELDS: And these operations—they were covert operations?
> LT. COL. NORTH: Yes they were.
> NIELDS: And covert operations are designed to be secret from our enemies?
> NORTH: That is correct.
> NIELDS: But these operations were designed to be secrets from the American people?
> NORTH: Mr. Nields, I'm at a loss as to how we could announce it to the American people and not have the Soviets know about it...
> NIELDS: Well, in fact, Col. North, you believed that the Soviets were aware of our sale of arms to Iran, weren't you?
> NORTH: We came to a point in time when we were concerned about that.

A few minutes later, Col. North elaborated on his statement:

> LT. COL. NORTH: I think it is very important for the American people to understand that this is a dangerous world; that we live at risk and that this nation is at risk in a dangerous world. And that they ought not to be led to believe, as a consequence of these hearings, that this nation cannot or should not conduct covert operations. By their very nature, covert operations or special activities are a lie. There is great deceit, deception practiced in the conduct of covert operation[s]. They are at essence a lie. We make every effort to deceive the enemy as to our intent, our conduct and to deny the association of the United States with those activities. The intelligence committees hold hearings on all kinds of activities conducted by our intelligence service. The American people ought not to believe by the way you're asking that question that we intentionally deceived the American people, or had that intent to begin with. The effort to conduct these covert operations was made in such a way that our adversaries would not have knowledge of them or that we could deny American association with it, or the association of this government with those activities. And that is not wrong.[30]

Col. North claimed that he had been granted authority for all of his deceptions: "I sought approval for every one of my actions and it is well documented. I assumed when I had approval to proceed from...Bud McFarlane or Adm. Poindexter, that they had indeed solicited and obtained the approval of the President."[31] Colonel North was supported by Poindexter who testified, "I didn't tell Col. North that I was not going to tell the president."[32] North admitted, however, that following orders is insufficient grounds for breaking the law. Both he and Adm. Poindexter have argued, however, that their activities did not break the law because they did not use money appropriated by the Congress.[33]

Adm. Poindexter's deception was, in many respects, similar to that of Col. North. However, North did not withhold information from his immediate superiors. Adm. Poindexter claims that he deliberately, intentionally failed to inform President Reagan of the diversion of funds to the Contras in an effort to protect the president from responsibility for a politically controversial act. Poindexter argued in his testimony that he was justified in not telling the president for three reasons: the diversion of funds from Iran to the Contras was legal; the diversion was essentially a "detail" of the larger policy of aiding the Contras; and the president would have supported the policy had he known about it:

> My impression was that it was clear to me that these were third country or private-party funds that would result from the arms sale to the Iranians...I felt that it was in terms of supporting and implementing the president's policy, that it was entirely consistent. The president never really changed his policy with regard to supporting the contras since the early decision back in 1981. It seemed that his method of financing was completely consistent with what we had been doing in terms of private parties and third countries. I knew that it would be a controversial issue. I had at that point worked with the president for three of those five-and-a-half years, very directly, meeting with him many times a day, often spending hours every day with him. So I not only clearly understood his policy, but I thought I understood the way he thought about issues. I felt that I had the authority to approve Col. North's request. I also felt that it was, as I said, consistent with the president's policy, and that if I asked him, I felt confident that he would approve it. But because it was controversial, and I obviously knew it would cause a ruckus if it were exposed, I decided to insulate the president from the decision and give him some deniability; and so I decided ...at that point not to tell the president.[34]

As of May 1988, no court has ruled on the legality of either the arms sale or the diversion of funds. However, a grand jury returned a conspiracy indictment against Adm. Poindexter, Col. North, Richard Secord, and Albert Hakim. Also, Col. McFarlane pleaded guilty to four misdemeanor counts.

Col. McFarlane struck a deal with the independent counsel, Lawrence Walsh, in which McFarlane agreed to testify as a witness for the prosecution against Adm. Poindexter and Col. North and to plead guilty to the misdemeanors in exchange for his freedom from felony indictments. After his court appearance, McFarlane told reporters, "I did indeed withhold information from Congress."[35]

The indictment against Poindexter and North included their coverup attempt as illegal activity:

> From August 1985 through November 1986, in order to conceal and cover up their illegal activities and to perpetrate the scheme, the conspirators, including the defendants JOHN M. POINDEXTER and OLIVER L. NORTH, deceived Congress and committees of Congress by making false, fictitious, fraudulent and misleading statements and representations, concerning, among other things, the involvement of officials of the United States, including members of the NSC staff, in support of the military and paramilitary operations in Nicaragua by the Contras at a time when the Boland Amendment was in effect....[36]

Following his indictment, Lt. Col. North resigned from the Marine Corps in order to be in a position to subpoena "testimony and records from the highest-ranking officials of our government" during his trial.[37] This action furthered speculation that President Reagan would pardon North, and possibly Poindexter as well, on the grounds that they had only been following his orders. The *Wall Street Journal* editorial board previously argued in favor of pardons for North and Poindexter for precisely these reasons on November 30, 1987.[38] As of May 1988, President Reagan has neither pardoned nor ruled out the possibility that he would pardon Poindexter and North, who have both pleaded not guilty, but whose trials have not yet begun.

The majority and minority reports of the congressional committees differ in their judgments of the affair and its participants. Almost no aspect of the affair—legal, policy, or moral—commands complete acceptance by the members of Congress or others who have studied the issue. The public also holds varying and changing views. In August, at the height of the hearings, more than half of the American public thought President Reagan had lied and was continuing to lie about the affair. They did not like the way he had handled Iranian policy. The president's job approval rating was in the forty percent range, down from his usual mid-sixties. Nevertheless, as a result of other factors, his personal popularity had returned to high levels by December.

The public did not like Adm. Poindexter, but many praised Col. North, who was as passionate and inspiring on the witness stand as Poindexter was detached and pedantic. Nevertheless, a month after North's testimony was over, a number of polls indicated that most people did not believe North had been justified in deceiving the Congress. Additionally, while public support for aiding the Contras rose dramatically during North's testimony, it dropped equally dramatically in the next two months.[39]

NOTES

1. In the House of Representatives, the Select Committee to Investigate Covert Arms Transactions with Iran was chaired by Representative Lee Hamilton. In the Senate, the Select Committee on Secret Military Assistance to Iran and the Nicaraguan Opposition was chaired by Senator Daniel Inouye. The transcript of the public sessions of Col. North was sold under the title, *Taking the Stand* (New York: Pocket Books). The president appointed a panel to review the affair, known as the Tower Commission, which released a report. Much of the closed testimony by Adm. Poindexter was released in a sanitized version by the Senate committee. The committees released a final report in November 1987 with two titles, S. Rept. No. 100-216 and H. Rept. No. 100-413. This case is based substantially on these sources.

2. John Tower, Edmund Muskie, and Brent Scowcroft, *The Tower Commission Report* (New York: Bantam Books and Times Books, 1987), pp. 55-59, 450-452.

3. *Taking the Stand,* p. 243.

4. *Report of the Congressional Committees Investigating the Iran-Contra Affair,* p. 4.

5. *Poindexter Closed Testimony to the Committees,* May 1987, p. 203. Also see p. 53.

6. *Report of the Congressional Committees Investigating the Iran-Contra Affair,* p. 20.

7. Cited in ibid., p. 123.

8. Ibid., p. 127.

9. *Tower Report,* pp. 527, 536.

10. Cited in *Report of the Congressional Committees Investigating the Iran-Contra Affair,* p. 139.

11. Ibid., p. 331.

12. Ibid., p. 341.

13. *Taking the Stand,* p. 552.

14. *Report of the Congressional Committees,* p. 11.

15. Ibid., p. 141.

16. *Taking the Stand,* p. 245.

17. Ibid., p. 253.

18. Ibid., p. 256.

19. Cited in *Report of the Congressional Committees,* p. 142.

20. *Poindexter Closed Testimony to the Committees,* May 1987, p. 47.

21. This section is based substantially on the *Tower Report.*

22. *Report of the Congressional Committees,* p. 294.

23. Ibid., p. 301.

24. Ibid., p. 298.

25. Ibid., p. 298-300.

26. Ibid., p. 306-7.

27. *Taking the Stand,* p. 362.

28. *Report of the Congressional Committees,* p. 312.

29. *The Chronology* (Warner, 1987), p. 67, compiled by the National Security Archive.

30. *Taking the Stand,* pp. 9, 12.

31. Ibid., p. 13.

32. *Poindexter, Closed Testimony to the Committees,* May 1987, p. 70.

33. *Taking the Stand,* p. 487.

34. *Poindexter Closed Testimony to the Committees,* May 1987, pp. 70-71.

35. *New York Times,* March 12, 1988, p. 1.

36. As reproduced in the *New York Times,* March 17, 1988, p. D26.

37. *New York Times,* March 19, 1988, p. 1.

38. *Wall Street Journal,* Nov. 30, 1987, p. 20.

39. For opinion poll data, I have relied upon an extensive collection of *New York Times*/CBS, Roper, *LA Times, Newsweek, Time* and other polls collected by the Congressional Research Service of the Library of Congress. This data is computerized at the Library of Congress in the "CRS Survey Poll File" under the title "Iran-Contra Affair Polls, October 1986 to Present."

Comment

Although Colonel Muammar el-Qaddafi was the intended victim of the deception described in the 1986 directive signed by President Reagan, journalists (and the public) were also deceived by the campaign of disinformation that ensued. Was the deception of the press and the public necessary to carry out the directive? If so, was the deception justified? More generally, are public officials justified in trying to "manage the news" if necessary to achieve an important, widely shared foreign policy objective? If so, does this case suggest any other conditions that we should place upon public officials before authorizing them to deceive us? Evaluate the defense of deception that is implicit in Secretary of State Shultz's response to reporters. The Senate Select Committee concluded that the administration did not have a formal policy of lying to American reporters. If we accept this conclusion, are there any grounds on which we could still hold the administration morally responsible for the deception of the press and the public?

Unlike most public officials who engage in deception, Admiral John Poindexter and Colonel Oliver North did not deny that they did so. They justified their deception on grounds that their secret actions (1) were necessary to national security, (2) did not violate the letter of the law, and (3) would have been undermined, through leaks and hostile legislation, had they (or anyone else) informed Congress. Consider to what extent their various deceptive statements and actions satisfy their own criteria of justification. What relevant moral considerations are overlooked by their criteria of justified deception? Does North, in his response to the House chief counsel, succeed in reconciling his approval of lying to Congress with a belief in democratic principles? Are there any conditions under which lying to Congress can be reconciled with democratic principles?

Unlike North, Poindexter deliberately withheld information not only from Congress but also from his immediate superiors, thereby doubly avoiding accountability. Assess Poindexter's justification for concealing information about "The Enterprise" from the president's chief of staff, Donald Regan. Did Poindexter's deliberate failure to inform the president about the diversion of funds to the Contras constitute deception? If so, of whom? Assume that Poindexter was correct in believing that the president would not want to know about the diversion of funds: is Poindexter then justified in not informing the president (or, as some have suggested, perhaps even obligated not to inform him)?

One of the most striking features of the deception in "The Iran-Contra Affair" is its pervasiveness. The targets of deception included not only journalists and the American public but also many high-level executive branch officials and congressmen who would normally have been informed about foreign policies of this importance. North and Poindexter seem to have been guided by presumptions favoring deception rather than veracity, and secrecy rather than openness in government. Their testimony provides few if any principled reasons to limit deception and secrecy when public officials act in a cause they believe to be just. What principles could establish a strong presumption in favor of veracity and openness? What political institutions or procedures could guard against unjustified deception by public officials who are motivated either by self-interest or by a passionate dedication to the public interest?

The case and comment are based primarily on information revealed during the congressional hearings. Does information disclosed since then or any subsequent events change your moral assessment of the actions of either North or Poindexter?

The New York City Fiscal Crisis

Jeremy Paul

New York City's budget is the third largest in the nation, exceeded only by the State of California's and the Federal Government's. In the best of times the management of this budget is an awesome responsibility, requiring a clear delineation of priorities and a firm understanding of ethical constraints. It was not the best of times in January 1974, when Abraham Beame was inaugurated as New York's Mayor. The changing social and economic conditions that had plagued New York for at least a decade and the 1973–74 national recession combined to turn budget management from a responsibility into a nightmare. The long-term history of New York City fiscal abuses leading up to this nightmare by itself illustrates government's sometimes unwise tendency to pay for the present by borrowing against the future. Yet a close look at the time period immediately preceding the spring of 1975 collapse of the public market for New York City securities reveals some ethical problems that faced top city officials when suddenly future debts became present ones. These problems concerned the question of deception and full disclosure in government.

Immediately upon taking office, Mayor Beame pointed out that he had inherited a budget deficit for the fiscal year 1973–74 of 500 million dollars and a cumulative deficit of approximately 1.5 billion dollars. The most important problem for City officials and their supporters in the banks was to find some way to keep the City solvent. "The primary responsibility of the Mayor," Mayor Beame said, "is to see that the people of New York get adequate police and fire protection, health care and education."[1] As the City's deficit grew and its case needs increased, these basic services were placed in jeopardy.

Throughout late 1974 and early 1975 the City had also become increasingly dependent for funds upon the public market for short term notes. To maintain the same level of social services, the City needed to continue borrowing money. To meet this need, Beame, Comptroller Goldin, and other city officials worked directly with the major underwriters in an effort to maintain investor confidence. Beame explained his efforts to keep the market open: "No business or government in the world can exist without the ability to borrow."[2]

The Securities and Exchange Commission, in its report on "Transactions in Securities of the City of New York," accuses the City and the banks of not only ethical but also legal violations during the efforts to market City notes. These alleged violations raised the issue of proper disclosure of financial information to investors in New York City securities. The legal issue assumed great importance in 1975 when the City declared a moratorium on short-term City notes. But behind this legal issue lay a broader question of moral and political responsibility: what must public officials disclose about the financial condition of a government at a particular time? In this period, full disclosure, in the view of officials, posed a grave risk of bankruptcy and therefore a threat to the services and jobs of millions of city residents.

The legal requirements concerning proper disclosure of information are described in Rule 10-b-5, a regulation issued by the Securities and Exchange Commission in accord with the Securities and Exchange Act of 1934. Unlike corporate bonds, municipal securities are not subject to the stringent requirements of registration and formal prospectus. The City often made this point in its own defense. Nevertheless, all issuers of securities are subject to the Rule, which states in part, "It shall be unlawful for any person, directly or indirectly. . .to make any untrue statement of a material fact or *to omit to state a material fact* in order to make the statements made, in the light of the circumstances under which they were made, not misleading. . .in connection with the purchase or sale of any security" [emphasis added]. In connection with the sale of New York City securities, the legal question then becomes: What were the material facts concerning the City's finances, and to what extent were they disclosed? To understand the ethical aspects of the problem, these questions must also be addressed but in the context of the broader political circumstances of the fiscal crisis.

The financial circumstances of the New York City fiscal crisis have three separate but related aspects. The first and most important is that for many years prior to Beame's inauguration, New York's growth in expenditures had been outpacing its growth in revenues resulting in an increasing and unwieldy budget deficit. Second, in order to show a balanced budget in the books, as required by the Local Finance Law of the State of New York, the City had for years been resorting to seemingly questionable accounting practices. These practices are the central focus of the disclosure question. Finally, the City relied heavily for its cash needs on the issuance of short-term notes.[3] Whether the City should have issued this debt without a more complete description of its finances, whether the banks should have underwritten these securities, and whether there were really any other workable alternatives were questions that observers raised.

The causes of fiscal strain on municipal treasuries were well known. White emigration from the suburbs, black and Puerto Rican immigration into the cities, and the loss of urban jobs particularly in manufacturing, left New York and other northeastern cities with ever-increasing costs of public assistance and a corresponding diminishing tax base. In the case of New York, the figures are staggering; one study reveals that New York City's expenditures on public assistance payments and purchases of social and medical services grew by almost 800 percent from 1960–61 to 1972–73.[4] At the same time, employment in manufacturing in New York declined by 180,000, a drop of about 18 percent.[5] In addition, since 1970 employment in New York increased only in the public sector placing a further drain on City funds. As these pressures mounted, the City's own report agrees that it was the "repeatedly publicized judgments of Governors, State Legislators, Mayors, and City Councilmen to resort to borrowing instead of fiscal restraint as a means of meeting needs."[6] Thus, as Mayor Beame began his term in office, New York was a city in debt and in trouble.

The exact size of the cumulative budget deficit at fiscal year end 1975 was a subject of much contention. Mayor Beame repeatedly said he had inherited a cumulative deficit of a billion and a half dollars at the end of the fiscal year 1973-74. Although Beame says he began work on reducing the deficit, his efforts were outweighed by the effects of the recession, and the deficit continued to grow. Later, revised figures published on August 29, 1975, by the municipal assistance corporation (a state agency created in June, 1975, to convert three billion dollars of city notes into long-term securities) placed the deficit as of June 30, 1975, at 2.6 billion dollars.[7] Still later revised figures issued by the City Comptroller in October, 1976, which included estimates for accrued pension liabilities, placed the cumulative deficit figure at over 5 billion dollars.[8] The size of any one of these figures is enough to indicate that New York was plagued with severe fiscal problems.

Knowledge of New York City's large cumulative deficit was certainly not withheld from the public since Mayor Beame's statements about it were publicized continually by all of the major media from the time he took office. It is not for concealing this deficit that the Mayor and City officials were accused of inadequate disclosure. Yet there is a discrepancy between the Mayor's figure, repeatedly publicized at the time, and the later figures released by MAC and the City Comptroller. Without trying to resolve these discrepancies, we need to understand how they were an outgrowth of the City's continued use of questionable accounting practices. These legally sanctioned fiscal "gimmicks," which had been used to create the impression of a balanced budget in the years prior to 1974–75, were maintained by the Beame administration. It was chiefly because of these gimmicks that the SEC accused the City of withholding relevant information from the public.

Probably no technique of budget-balancing was more publicized or more heavily criticized than the transfer of funds from the capital budget to the expense budget. Pursuant to the City Charter, the City operates under two budgets, which are prepared for different purposes and are funded from different sources. The expense budget is designed to handle costs of operations such as police, fire, health, and educational services and is financed by Federal and State aid and tax revenues. Significantly, the expense budget is also charged with debt service. The capital budget is designed to pay for construction of capital projects such as schools, parks, bridges, and tunnels. Except for specific grants from the Federal and State governments, this budget is funded by the issuing of long-term debt.[9]

Over the years, the distinction between the two budgets became increasingly blurred. Beginning in 1965, the City embarked upon a steadily increasing and dangerous schedule of issuing debt for the capital budget and using these funds to meet operating expenses. Ironically, this practice had no greater critic than the then Comptroller Beame, whose comments were extensively reported by the press. Yet by the time he had become Mayor, the capitalization of expenses had become an integral part of the City's finances.

This capitalization of expenses moved the City closer and closer toward fiscal disaster as the high interest costs became part of the City's expense obligations, and the capital fund became too depleted to finance needed construction projects. By 1975, Beame's first budget, the expenses funded by the capital budget totalled 722 million dollars up from 195 million just five years earlier![10]

The practice of capitalization of expenses was the most publicized of the City's book-balancing methods. A clear example of such publicity can be found in the *New York Times* editorial of November 4, 1974: "No one knows better than the Mayor the folly of continuing a course in which debt service takes an ever bigger share of the tax dollar while schools, subway lines, parks and other needed municipal facilities go unbuilt because *half of the capital budget is diverted to paying for salaries, pensions, and other day-to-day costs*"[11] [emphasis added]. The practice of using the capital budget to fund operating expenses was also criticized by the Citizens Budget Commission, a public interest group founded in 1932 as a watchdog for City finances. Finally, Comptroller Goldin himself pointed out and criticized the practice in a press release of June 3, 1974.[12] Mayor Beame could not have been expected single-handedly to end the practice although he says he wanted to do so. By the time he became Mayor, the City probably did not have the money for such constructive reforms.

The second kind of fiscal "gimmick" arose from the City's books themselves. Although no statute required municipalities to conform to generally accepted accounting principles, the SEC criticized the shoddy state of New York's accounts. In the words of one observer, the City "not only used every gimmick that had ever been invented but they came up with every gimmick that will ever be invented."[13]

Most important among these accounting practices was the following: the City kept its receivables as a whole on an accrual basis while it charged liabilities only as cash was actually dispensed. In other words, the city would credit a given fiscal year with revenues received in that year as well as all revenues which were estimated to be earned in that year but collectible in later years; at the same time the city charged the fiscal year only with money actually spent in that year. This practice was an effective way of hiding a portion of the City's true cumulative deficit. Examples of accrual basis receivables were the water and sewer charges, and the yearly estimate of accrued sales taxes known as the June accrual. On the liability side, the largest postponed charge was a two-year lag in the City's pension fund contributions; the City recorded its contributions two years later than the liabilities were actually incurred. A final example of this pay-as-you-go accounting strategy was the reliance on one-shot sources of funds as if they were recurring revenues. This last practice, like the capitalization of expenses, was well publicized and highly criticized.[14]

None of these practices explicitly violated any state or Federal law. In fact, the state laws allowing these practices to occur are in many ways responsible for their existence. Over the years, as New York City came to the state asking for aid to help balance the budget, the state would agree to allow fiscal sleight of hand rather than choose to supply additional cash. Beyond legal issues, City officials evidently did not believe they were obliged to adopt accounting methods that would have revealed the underlying deficit. With respect to nonrecurring revenues, Mayor Beame in his testimony before the SEC said that if (in accordance with conservative accounting) he had reserved such revenues instead of using them, he would have been forced to discontinue some needed city service.

The questionable practices evolved as an integral part of city finances over the years, and only a long-term plan of accounting revisions combined with fiscal austerity could have completely solved the problem. The Beame administration could have chosen to begin such a program, but it would have been politically unpopular and the sacrifices might have been great.

Although the poor state of the City's books with regard to the accrual method and the one-shot revenues was certainly not a secret, it contributed to the SEC's charges of a lack of disclosure. The SEC cites the Annual Reports of the Comptroller for 1974 and 1975 which "failed to disclose the City's unusual basis for recording water charges and sewer rent revenues."[15] More importantly, the SEC claims that the Annual Reports for fiscal years 1973 and 1974 "failed to explicitly set forth that the City recognized revenues on an accrual basis and expenditures on a cash basis."[16] Yet the SEC acknowledges that this method of revenue recognition was alluded to in the Annual Reports.

It is generally agreed that the SEC showed that the City's books were chaotic. Even the most trained observer trying to understand these books would have found them confusing. Such obfuscation was allowed to continue partly because independent audits of the City's accounts were not required. Comptroller Goldin tried to institute such audits of his books upon first taking office. In the meantime, his justification for their lack of clarity is summed up in a May 4, 1976, statement: "There was a strong feeling, I believe, that even though the City's accounting and budgeting had been revealed as a kind of Rube Goldberg conception—a system which defied understanding or control—it was better to leave it alone as long as it churned out enough money to meet the bills and pay the debts."[17]

The alleged overstatement of receivables was the most controversial of the practices. To make its case for inadequate disclosure, the SEC depends heavily upon its charges that City officials intentionally withheld information concerning receivables. The Commission states "there was no disclosure of the fact that the City carried disputed receivables on its books, did not reserve against the possibility of noncollection, and borrowed against these receivables by issuing RAN's [Revenue Anticipation Notes]."[18] Likewise, other critics claimed that no one outside the City Government was aware, until after the collapse of the market, that possibly uncollectible receivables were being kept on the books. According to Dr. Herbert Ranschburg, the research director of the Citizens Budget Commission, "the one thing we didn't know and I don't think anybody (outside the City government) knew was that the City was 'kiting' its receivables."[19] Similarly, Jac Friedgut of Citibank, defending his bank's policy of underwriting the March 13 offer of City RAN's, states that he was unaware that the City's Report on Essential Facts (an additional disclosure document) contained "revenue which proved to be phony."[20]

The City's overestimation of receivables has two aspects. First, the City's figures concerning the amount of Federal and State aid it would receive proved to be inflated. Second, the City overestimated its eventual collection of real estate taxes. In 1976 the Office of the City Comptroller attributed 678 million dollars of the City's cumulative deficit to a re-evaluation of aid receivables.[21] And in the summer of 1975 the State Comptroller estimated 408 million dollars or 80 percent of the 502 million dollars of the City's real estate taxes had been overstated.[22] These overstatements were discovered well after the public market for City securities was already closed. They were not highlighted in City documents before this, nor were they emphasized by the Mayor, the Comptroller, or the press during late 1974 or early 1975 when the City was attempting to sell notes. Comptroller Goldin nevertheless stated, "I disclosed everything that I knew."[23]

Overstatements concerning Federal and State aid receivables came about in two ways. First, estimates made by low level City officials of anticipated funds from various Federal and State agencies were placed directly on the books as receivables. This definition of a receivable is explicitly permitted in Section 25 of the State Local Finance Law. These estimates in many cases proved to be too high and thus gave a false and more favorable picture of City finances. Mayor Beame said that he did not check such estimates but merely assumed them to be accurate, and, in his testimony before the SEC, he denied any deliberate overstatement of these receivables.[24] As for Goldin, his office was not responsible for preparing these estimates and was unable to audit them.

More important for the City's overall fiscal position was the continuing practice of leaving disputed receivables on the books.

For example, the Federal government would announce a spending program for some social service such as day care centers. The City would then borrow money against expected revenue, using the loan to begin the service. If the Federal Government then changed its mind and cut back funds, the City would protest, arguing that such a reversal was a violation of an agreement. In the meantime, the City would maintain the expected revenue on the books as a receivable, ignoring the fact that it was disputed. This type of dispute could take years to resolve, and although City officials often received the funds, City books did not indicate the tenuous nature of such receivables.

Deputy Mayor Cavanaugh sought to justify the practice of keeping disputed receivables on the books by arguing that, if they were removed, they would become truly uncollectible. Mayor Beame said he was aware that some receivables on the City books were in dispute, and his actions seem to indicate that he concurred with Cavanaugh's assessment. Comptroller Goldin was made aware of the whole receivables question, and particularly the problems with overstated Medicaid claims, in repeated memos from his adviser Steven Clifford. Goldin maintained, however, that he was unable to check the problem through an audit, and thus could not verify that there were any specific overstatements.

Disclosure of the importance of full collection of all receivables to balance the City's books can be found in the foreword of the Comptroller's Annual Report of 1973–74. Although these receivables are acknowledged to be *unaudited,*[25] the SEC argued that a clear reference to the disputed nature of Federal and State aid receivables should have been made. Critics scored the City's failure to call attention to disputed receivables in its fiscal documents. Some saw Beame's constant reassurance to the financial community that "we are borrowing against firm receivables,"[26] as part of a strategy to emphasize the positive side of City finances in order to keep the public market open, and, not incidentally, to keep the Beame administration politically popular.

The second kind of receivable overstated by the City was the level of expected real estate taxes. This overstatement came about in two ways. First, despite the inevitability that some real estate taxes would prove uncollectible, the City failed to make an allowance for uncollectibles. The City issued TANs (Tax Anticipation Notes) against the full amount of real estate taxes receivable and according to law could roll these notes over for a period of five years before recognizing taxes as definitely uncollectible and writing them off. It was Beame's experience that after the five year period such write-offs had proven to be very small.[27] Yet during the recession, as more and more buildings were abandoned, permanently uncollectible real estate taxes reached higher levels. The SEC states that "there was no disclosure of the fact that a significant portion of the City's real estate tax receivables were uncollectible."[28] Both Beame and Goldin publicly complained about the increase in real estate tax delinquency. Apparently, what the SEC means is that neither Beame nor Goldin admitted publicly in a disclosure document that these taxes would remain uncollectible. Beame, in keeping with his desire to emphasize the positive, preferred to assume that such taxes might be collected.

The other kind of overstatement of the real estate taxes is more difficult to explain. Completely undisclosed was the fact that some 126 million dollars of the City's uncollectible real estate taxes were on *City-owned* property.[29] Beame said that he did not know this taxing was taking place. The recession in New York had caused many landlords to default on real estate taxes so long that the City would foreclose on their property. This property (known as "in rem") became city-owned; yet it took some time for the City to recognize this and stop assessing taxes. The City's position was that this breakdown in communication was responsible for the self-taxation. Nevertheless, Steven Clifford, former special deputy Comptroller and a consultant to Goldin during this period, maintains that any effort made towards removing such City property from the tax rolls would not have been looked upon kindly by those in City Hall.[30]

Another important historical force confronting Beame was the city's increasing dependence upon short-term debt. "The City had dramatically increased its short-term debt six-fold from $747 million to $4.5 billion in the six years from 1969 to June 30, 1975."[31] During the six months from October 1974 to April 1975, the City sold through its underwriters about 4 billion dollars in short-term debt, an extraordinarily high figure in historical terms.[32] In fact, the heavy volume of borrowing alone was a major cause of the eventual collapse of the public market. The financial community simply could not find buyers for the vast quantity of City notes being issued so frequently.

In December 1974, members of the financial community met with top City officials to express their concern about the market for city bonds. In response to this meeting, Comptroller Goldin established a reduced borrowing schedule for the following six months. This schedule, however, still consisted of an average of 550 million dollars in short-term notes each month, the issuance of which was essential to continued operation of the City.

Whatever he said, then, about the City's complete or incomplete disclosure concerning the different specific facts of New York's finances, there is no uncertainty regarding the City's overall strategy. The City continued to issue short-term notes through late 1974 and early 1975, and the top officials worked diligently to make these notes appear attractive. Both Beame and Goldin took the position in numerous public statements that investment in City securities was completely secure. Moreover, the City took direct action to expand the public market to a broader class of investors by reducing the minimum size of New York City's short-term notes from 25,000 to 10,000 dollars in November 1974.[33] Given the large budget deficit and the extremely precarious state of the City's finances, how could City officials justify this strategy? Publicly, the justification came in the form of the repeated distinction between problems in closing the budget gap and problems in paying off securities.

The public position of both Beame and Goldin concerning the sale of notes during this period was clear. While almost daily admitting to very serious budgetary problems, both Beame and Goldin constantly reassured investors of the soundness of City securities. Such reassurances were based primarily on the principle of "first lien." This principle, enunciated in the New York State Constitution, requires that the City use all revenues from taxes and federal and state aid to pay bonds and notes before making any other expenditures. Technically, the principle requires that bond and note holders be paid before police officers and firefighters. City officials maintained that there would always be enough revenue to cover bonds and notes, since the City each year took in many times the amount of its maturing debt. Therefore, no matter how bad things became, Beame and Goldin said City notes were safe (see Appendix).

The SEC questioned whether the principle of "first lien" applied to the principal amounts of City short-term debt. Although the Commission's argument may throw the "first lien" principle into doubt, it does not substantiate the claim that Beame and Goldin were intentionally misleading the public on this count. Both

Beame and Goldin testified that they firmly believed in the constitutional guarantee of "first lien." Goldin argued that, as Comptroller, he was responsible for dispensing New York's money: "As far as I was concerned I was going to pay the bond and note holders first. It was as simple as that."[34] Strong confirmation of the constitutional position of Beame and Goldin came in the November 1976 ruling of the New York State Court of Appeals (New York's highest court), which declared the November 1975 Moratorium on City notes to be unconstitutional.[35] This moratorium was enacted by the state legislature over the objection of City officials. Despite the fact that the principle of "first lien" was upheld by the courts, the security of investing in City notes that may be refundable only if police officers and firefighters are not paid is not "as simple as that."

City officials repeatedly attempted to separate the issue of the City's financial problems from its ability to pay back its debt. Yet these two aspects of the crisis were essentially related. As problems with the budget became more severe, the City depended more and more upon borrowing. This dependence put a greater and greater strain on the City's ability to pay back its debt. If the sources of borrowing were cut off (as they eventually were), the City would be forced immediately to choose between maintaining its essential services and paying off noteholders. In this case, despite the most explicit and emphatic legal requirements to pay the debts first, officials would have been hard pressed to dispense cash to investors while watching the City collapse around them. Yet if they used funds to meet payroll expenses, the ensuing default on City securities would have had disastrous consequences for the entire national money market. To avoid this painful dilemma, city officials believed they had to continue borrowing. Thus, they did not mention the connection between the budget gap and the City's ability to pay its debt. Officials did not publicly question the principle of "first lien" despite the likelihood it would come under pressure. Although the legality of "first lien" was confirmed, short-term City note holders in November 1975 were forced to wait for their money while an unconstitutional moratorium was enforced. This moratorium gave State and Federal officials time to establish a scheme for fiscal recovery.

In addition to stressing the principle of "first lien," Beame made strenuous efforts to present City securities in a positive light. He fought publicly with the financial community about the "outrageous" interest rates being charged for underwriting bids. He was partially correct in publicly attributing these rates to national tight money policy and the weakened credit market caused by the default of the Urban Development Corporation, but these high rates were also attributable to the market's growing perception of the risk inherent in City notes. The Mayor also stressed the rapid repayment schedule for sizable portions of New York City debt while ignoring the fact that the money to meet this schedule would be raised by still further borrowing.[36] Beame and Goldin also stressed, in a letter to the *New York Times*, the large amount of real estate owned by the City although the ability of the City to convert such property into liquid assets was dubious.[37] Although the press was constantly reporting the serious fiscal problems of the City, the Mayor in his public statements spoke as a booster of City notes, ignoring the impact of the various bookkeeping methods on City accounts, and relying on the members of the financial community to "keep the market open." In his words, "I believe the financial community has a selling job to do to make the investing public see the financial strengths of [New York's] obligations."[38]

The financial community, chiefly the major New York banks—Chemical Bank, Manufacturers Hanover Trust Co., The

Chase Manhattan Bank, Morgan Guaranty Trust Co., Bankers Trust Co., and Citibank—played a quasi-public role during the crisis. These banks, responsible for the underwriting and sale of City securities during this time, had access to City books and records. Because of their experience in the field of finance, these banks were knowledgeable participants in the City's efforts to market notes. According to Beame, after the formation of the Financial Community Liaison Group (a group designed to help the City work out its fiscal problems and maintain market access) in January 1975, the bankers were privy to all relevant information.[39] Yet until March of 1975, the last month of successful City note sales, the banks made no more effort than City officials to disclose the City's plight.

The ethical position of the bankers was in some ways even more complex than that of City officials. All of the banks had huge capital investments in New York and stood to lose greatly if the City defaulted. Furthermore, they were making a profit on their underwriting activity. Thus, on the one hand, banks had a large interest in keeping the market for City notes open. On the other hand, they had an obligation to their investors to check the security of the notes they were underwriting. In addition, Section 10-b-5 applied directly to these offerings, and the banks' lawyers warned them of possible questions about "due diligence" arising from an accurate presentation of the City's financial condition. In this respect, the dilemma for the bankers resembled that which faced City officials.

Nevertheless, the bankers were operating in a once-removed position. They could know nothing for sure. Concerning figures on the City's books such as estimates of receivables, the banks had little choice but to accept them as accurate. Furthermore, as Jac Friedgut, a Vice President of Citibank, pointed out, "there was a very thin line between opinion and fact concerning our assessment of the City's financial strength." Friedgut explained, "anything I said concerning the plight of the City might be accepted as fact, and even though it might be expert opinion, it was still only my opinion, and I had to be very careful because anything negative I said could prove to help lead to the close of the market."[40] The truth of this assessment was vividly confirmed after Friedgut's March 18, 1975, testimony before the New York Congressional delegation where he said that unless something gives, the City fiscal situation is not viable; City paper will be suspect regardless of interest rate.[41] Following this statement, Beame telephoned Citibank to complain that they were "bad mouthing" the City.

Other banks said less and thus received less criticism. Yet it is hard to determine exactly what any of them were supposed to say or do. A declaration by any one of the major banks that City notes were unsafe probably would have resulted in an immediate collapse of the public market. A withdrawal by any of the major banks from the underwriting syndicate would have brought about the same result. Furthermore, many of the banks did not have an internal structure that could have helped the officers understand enough about the City to take such drastic steps. The connection between the research (rating) division and the underwriting division in most of the banks was not close.

Besides an adequate understanding of the City's financial position, the banks also lacked control over the spending choices made by the City. Unlike the Mayor, the banks could not decide to cut services in order to increase the security of City notes. The bankers were presented with City notes (take them or leave them), and for a long time, the banks chose to take them. The banks, then, did not break with the Mayor's policy by becoming a principal source of disclosure. The banks did, however, make an attempt to check on the City's accounting in February 1975 by requesting information concerning taxes receivable. When the Comptroller refused to comply with this "unprecedented request," the banks aborted a planned TAN offering. It was later shown that the City had insufficient taxes to make this offering, since the taxes supposedly receivable had been collected in January, 1975. Comptroller Goldin subsequently denied knowing that satisfying the banks' request would have revealed such damaging news.[42]

In addition, the banks were responsible for the March 13, 1975 issuance of "The Report of Essential Facts," a disclosure document that they felt would help keep the market open. This document, prepared with the aid of the City, ignored the major budget "gimmicks" and presented this particular issuance of RANs as being against firm receivables (which it was). The document contained no outright false statements; yet it did not highlight the issue of receivables under dispute. When, despite the release of this document, Citibank ("which felt comfortable with the offering: unaware of the phony receivable issue"[43]) could not sell notes, it was clear that the market for City notes was rapidly closing.

The SEC charged that the banks were "dumping" City securities. The SEC claimed that, because of the information known to the financial community concerning the plight of the City, the banks were selling off their investments in New York while at the same time they were underwriting City notes for the general public. If this charge were sustained, it would place the actions of the bankers in a very different light. It is one thing to continue to underwrite securities that are later shown to be suspect but quite another to underwrite securities that are deemed by a bank safe enough for the public but not safe enough for the bank.

There were important differences among the banks. Chemical, Citibank, and Morgan could most plausibly defend themselves against the charge of "dumping." Chemical's holdings in City securities actually increased during the period September 30, 1974 to April 30, 1975. The same is true of Morgan, although the SEC attributes this to Morgan's holding securities issued in March 1975 when the public market was closing. Citibank had no City securities in its investment account either at the beginning or at the end of the period. Manufacturers's total ownership of City securities declined from 180 million on September 30, 1974 to 163 million dollars on April 30, 1975—apparently not a significant drop, but the SEC again attributes 40 million of the latter holdings to notes that Manufacturers could not market in March of 1975.[44]

The charges against Bankers and Chase are more difficult to answer. Bankers had a total initial position excluding syndicate and manager accounts of 118,670,000 dollars and as of April 30, 1975, its position amounted to approximately 58 million dollars. Of the latter amount, 40 million represented a position in the March BAN and RAN offerings, which apparently reflected an inability to dispose of the notes in the market place. Concerning Chase, the SEC states, "Chase's total September 30 position in City notes was approximately $165 million, and its position as of April 30, 1975 was approximately $59 million. Of this latter amount, approximately $43 million represents holdings in its trading account, apparently as a result of the inability to distribute the March BAN and RAN offerings. An analysis of Chase's investment account reflects the same pattern. As of September 30, its investment account held approximately $74 million in City notes, and as of April 30, its investment account held no City notes."[45]

None of these figures, however, establishes the motives of the different banks. Some of the declines in total holdings were caused by a large amount of maturation taking place during this period rather than a policy of deliberate sales. Likewise, sales of municipal securities can be made for tax reasons and other financial reasons, not only because the securities are deemed a substantial risk.

One aspect of the crisis with which the financial community was more familiar than City officials was the state of the market for City securities. As the market began to close, it was the financial community who became aware of it first. The reaction of the bankers was swift. In December, 1974, they informed City officials of the problem and, as we saw, this resulted in a reduced borrowing schedule. Likewise, the Financial Community Liaison Group worked constantly with the Mayor to try to keep the market open. The SEC heard testimony regarding various meetings between Beame and members of the financial community, and confirmed that the bankers had expressed their concern. In fact, the danger to the credit market was a topic of constant debate between Beame and the bankers. Beame felt the underwriters should take more City notes into their own portfolios and that they should be able to market City notes at lower interest rates. Although Beame may have sincerely believed that the credit market would remain open, there was no doubt that the market was in danger throughout the period in question.

The threat posed by the national recession to New York's ability to sell securities was apparent to all, and indeed was highlighted by Beame and Goldin in public statements. Likewise, the glut caused by the large volume of City borrowings was also a matter of public record. Yet the real possibility that the credit market would close came about only because of a combination of these factors with the poor state of the City's finances. Furthermore, the possible collapse of the credit market was an extremely important fact to investors in City notes. For the City's finances were in such a state that if the City could no longer borrow, it would no longer have enough money to both provide services and pay off maturing debt. The SEC thus concludes that the state of the market was a material fact, and that the City officials had the obligation to make it public.

Although neither Beame nor Goldin ever publicly stated that the market would close, and although they did everything possible to keep it open and to persuade investors that it would remain open, the danger to the market and the risk inherent in City securities should have been apparent to any intelligent investor from simply looking at the interest rate. City tax-free notes paid rates of interest over twice those of similar issues and higher than many taxable notes. Were Beame and Goldin to have actually said that the market for city securities was on the verge of collapse, this could have been a self-fulfilling prophecy. Furthermore, the collapse of the market would (and indeed eventually did) necessitate drastic cuts in City services and a general decline in New York's quality of life. For a mayor whose toughest decision while in office was "the decision to lay off workers,"[46] to accept the collapse of the market without a fight was an untenable solution. Beame saw his primary duty as keeping the market open, not providing full disclosure. He later said that, "anybody who didn't know what was going on was either asleep or had his head in the sand."[47] If any deception actually took place (which Beame never conceded), some observers thought it justified to save the services and jobs for millions of city residents. As the *New York Times* later headlined, "'Deception' May Have Kept the City Solvent."[48]

EPILOGUE

It took the City four years to regain some control over its finances and reestablish its credibility in the securities market. During this time, the City suffered many of the consequences that Beame had feared, and had tried to avoid by his strategy of keeping the market open at all costs. The city was forced to lay off workers. Firefighters staged a work slowdown. Police warned that the streets were not safe. Sanitation workers and the teachers struck. Services were cut, the subway fare increased, and City University had to charge tuition.

To end the crisis, the City had to surrender some political authority to state officials and non-elected businessmen and lawyers. After months of difficult negotiations, the City, the state, the banks, and the unions agreed to establish a semi-permanent control board, which would have authority over the City's finances until the City paid off all its loans from the Municipal Assistance Corporation (MAC) and the federal government, and balanced its budget for three consecutive years. The board insisted that the "gimmicks" in the City budget be eliminated, and that fiscal austerity have priority over politically more popular policies.

The City made substantial progress toward recovery under Beame, though he lost his bid for reelection in 1977, defeated by Ed Koch who had Governor Carey's support. In 1977-78, the city had no short-term debt at all, and entered the market on its own for the first time since 1975. The accounting practices later changed so that actual expenditures could be followed in detail. Aid receipts were not recorded until actually received, and reserve accounts were created to protect against the contingency of uncollectible aid and taxes. The definition of capital projects also was made stricter. Finally, a consortium of outside accountants was established to audit the City's books on a regular basis.

Some observers suggested that subsequent events showed that Beame gained little by his strategy of trying to present the city's finances in the best possible light to the public. The problems had to be confronted eventually anyhow, and he should have publicly faced up to them sooner than he did. Other observers believed, however, that if Beame had been able to continue to work quietly behind the scenes with state and federal officials, instead of in the glare of publicity and in an atmosphere of constant crisis, he could have brought the city out of its financial quagmire sooner and with less harm to the welfare of city workers and city residents. He could, moreover, have brought about a settlement that kept political authority in the hands of elected city officials rather than outside persons who were not primarily accountable to the citizens of New York. On this view, Beame's actions during 1974-75 at least gave city officials more time to strengthen their position vis-a-vis the state and federal government, and therefore put them in a better position to work out a settlement more favorable to the workers and residents of the City.

Whatever one's interpretation of subsequent events, Beame and his colleagues had to make choices in 1974-75 on the basis of limited information and options available to them then. But they could have decided differently than they did. An appraisal of the ethics of their actions and their inactions is therefore possible.

Appendix: Public Statements of Mayor Beame and Comptroller Goldin

NEWS RELEASE, OFFICE OF THE MAYOR, OCTOBER 2, 1974:

The Mayor emphasized that the City's credit position was "solid and strong," even though the national economy is under the stresses of both inflation and recession, and even though these inflationary-recessionary trends are "creating some budget balancing problems for the City."

From SEC Report, Washington, D.C.: Govt. Print. Off., 1977.

The Mayor said, "There is absolutely no question about the City's ability to repay all of its debts on time, and that this ability has improved over the last fifteen years."

LETTER OF THE MAYOR AND COMPTROLLER, PUBLISHED IN THE *NEW YORK TIMES*, NOVEMBER 11, 1974:

Bankruptcy means that liabilities exceed assets or that credit obligations cannot be met—a situation in which the City of New York, even in the darkest days of the Great Depression, never has found itself, nor will it. . . .

It should be clear, in connection with our municipal budget, that the Constitution of the State of New York makes our New York City bonds and notes a first lien on all revenues which include the real estate tax, all other City taxes, fees and permits, all state aid and all Federal aid.

Over and above the constitutional, legal and moral guarantees afforded to investors in New York City notes and bonds is the fact that they are investing in the world's wealthiest and soundest city as far as these obligations are concerned. . . .

This picture should be very reassuring to all city investors.

A recitation of these facts should by no means be construed as complacency in the face of the city's budget difficulties. While we have not always agreed on ways and means to place the budget in balance, we do agree that tough fiscal decisions and reforms, including substantial capital budget reductions, will have to be made in order to cope with runaway inflation, unemployment, business recession and the carryover effects of past fiscal practices. . . .

We will do what needs to be done in the general interest of taxpayers, for the preservation and strengthening of the city's economy and to insure the continuing soundness of the city's obligations as an investment medium.

NEWS RELEASE, OFFICE OF THE COMPTROLLER, DECEMBER 1, 1974:

. . .the budget deficit "should not impair confidence in the essential soundness and safety of the City's obligations."

SPEECH BY THE COMPTROLLER, DECEMBER 20, 1974 (AT THE CITY CLUB OF NEW YORK):

New York's budget problems should be of only marginal interest to investors, who are protected by the State Constitutional guarantee making New York City bonds and notes a first lien on all revenues.

JOINT STATEMENT OF MAYOR AND COMPTROLLER, JANUARY 11, 1975:

This City is not bankrupt, near bankrupt nor will it ever be bankrupt. This City has always repaid all of its obligations on time and it always will.

NEWS RELEASE, OFFICE OF COMPTROLLER, MARCH 4, 1975:

For the truth is that from the time of the Revolutionary War, through the dark days of the Great Depression, and in every era of national economic uncertainty—New York City has compiled an unblemished record of full payment of bond principal and interest without a single default.

Investors in New York City securities are, therefore, absolutely protected.

NEWS RELEASE, OFFICE OF THE COMPTROLLER, MARCH 13, 1975:

We have experienced an insistent drumbeat of publicity on our budget problems, and this publicity has sometimes unfortunately failed to distinguish between balancing a budget, which *is* a problem; and meeting obligations to our creditors, which the City has never failed to do and which, it is my conviction, it never *will* fail to do, barring a complete collapse of our economic system and capital markets....

So the impact on New York of national and international inflation and recession which has affected all cities, is a separate issue, which should be of only marginal interest to investors.

Notes

1. Interview with Mayor Beame—July 11, 1978.
2. Ibid.
3. SEC Report, "Transactions in the Securities of the City of New York," Subcommittee on Economic Stabilization of the Committee on Banking, Finance, and Urban Affairs—House of Representatives, 95th Congress, First Session, August 1977. U.S. Government Printing Office, Washington: 1977, chapter 3, p. 2.
4. City Report to the SEC, Nov. 23, 1976, ch. 2, p. 18.
5. City Report, ch. 2, p. 23.
6. City Report, ch. 2, p. 83.
7. SEC Report, ch. 3, p. 23.
8. Ibid.
9. SEC Report, ch. 2, p. 66.
10. Ibid.
11. *New York Times,* Nov. 4, 1974.
12. Response of the City of New York to the Report of the Staff of the SEC on Transactions in Securities of the City of New York, p. 14.
13. Interview with Dr. Herbert Rauschburg—June 28, 1978.
14. SEC Report, ch. 2, sec. 1, part B, pp. 8 ff.
15. SEC Report, ch. 2, p. 102.
16. SEC Report, ch. 2, p. 104.
17. SEC Report, ch. 3, p. 28.
18. SEC Report, ch. 3, p. 26.
19. Rauschburg Interview—June 28, 1978.
20. Interview with Jac Friedgut—June 15, 1978.
21. SEC Report, ch. 3, p. 23.
22. Ibid.
23. Interview with Harrison Goldin—July 18, 1978.
24. SEC Report, ch. 3, p. 38.
25. Response to the SEC, p. 68.
26. SEC Report, ch. 3, p. 39.
27. Beame Interview—July 11, 1978.
28. SEC Report, ch. 3, p. 27.
29. SEC Report, ch. 3, p. 26.
30. Interview with Steven Clifford—July 31, 1978.
31. SEC Report, Introduction, p. 3.
32. Ibid.
33. SEC Report, Chronology, p. 27.
34. Goldin Interview—July 18, 1978.
35. SEC Report, Chronology, p. 260.
36. SEC Report, ch. 3, p. 123.
37. Ibid., p. 122.
38. SEC Report, Chronology, p. 84.
39. Beame Interview—July 11, 1978.
40. Friedgut Interview—June 15, 1978.
41. Ibid.
42. Goldin Interview—July 18, 1978.
43. Friedgut Interview—June 15, 1978.
44. SEC Report, ch. 4, pp. 32 ff.
45. Ibid.
46. Beame Interview—July 11, 1978.
47. Ibid.
48. *New York Times,* Aug. 27, 1977, p. 1.

Comment

Mayor Beame and other officials denied that they made any false statements and also denied that they should have disclosed more than they did. As Beame said, "Anybody who didn't know what was going on was either asleep or had his head in the sand." Which (if any) officials' statements were so misleading as to constitute deception? Could there have been deceptive practices even if no one intended to deceive the public?

Beame and other officials gave, or could have given, two kinds of arguments to defend deception in this case. The first is, strictly speaking, a justification, and it appeals to the harmful consequences that full disclosure would have had for the city. In the face of such a claim, we should ask: (1) Who would have been harmed by the truth and to what degree? (2) What was the likelihood that disclosure would have actually produced these harmful consequences? If you think you need further information to answer these questions in this case, state precisely what it is and show how it would affect your conclusion about the justifiability of the deception.

The second kind of argument that city officials could give is better understood as an excuse than as a justification, since it concedes that unjustified deception occurred and seeks to eliminate or mitigate the blame that would otherwise fall on the officials. Beame and Goldin claimed that they did not know, or at least did not fully appreciate, the fact that the city counted as expected income real estate taxes on property that the city itself owned. Their claim is plausible, since it usually took a long time for the change of ownership of such property to show up on the books. Moreover, we would normally blame lower-level officials in such cases. But did Beame's actions or omissions discourage lower-level officials from questioning the estimate? And, if so, should Beame (or any other higher-level official) at least share the responsibility for the misleading records?

Some commentators have argued that the issue of deception in this case is only part of the larger question of the political power exercised by the ruling economic elite in the city. They suggest that the collapse of the market was planned by bankers, corporate leaders, and government officials in order to force cuts in services that benefited the poor (for example, the low transit fare, daycare centers, hospitals, and free tuition at city university). What evidence would you need and what theoretical assumptions would you have to make in order to assess this argument?

Recommended Reading

The standard book on the problem of deception is Sissela Bok, *Lying: Moral Choice in Public and Private Life* (New York: Random House, 1979), especially chapters 1, 2, 4, 6 to 8, and 12. The appendix provides substantial excerpts from works by Augustine, Aquinas, Bacon, Grotius, Kant, Sidgwick, Harrod, Bonhoeffer, and Warnock. Bok's analysis of secrecy is also relevant to the problem of deception: *Secrets: On the Ethics of Concealment and Revelation* (New York: Pantheon, 1982), especially chapters 8, 12, 14, 17, and 18. Also, see Hannah Arendt, "Truth and Politics," in P. Laslett and W. G. Runciman (eds.), *Philosophy, Politics and Society,* third series (Oxford: Blackwell, 1967), pp. 104–33; Charles Fried, *Right and Wrong* (Cambridge, Mass.: Harvard University Press, 1978), chapter 3; Robert Goodin, *Manipulatory Politics* (New Haven, Conn.: Yale University Press, 1980), chs. 1, 2, 7; and Christine M. Korsgaard, "The Right to Lie: Kant on Dealing with Evil," *Philosophy & Public Affairs* 15 (Fall 1986), pp. 325–49.

On the fiscal crisis, see Martin Shefter, *Political Crisis, Fiscal Crisis: The Collapse and Renewal of New York City* (New York: Basic Books, 1985) and Dennis Thompson, "Moral Responsibility and the New York City Fiscal Crisis," in J. Fleishman et al. (eds.), *Public Duties* (Cambridge, Mass.: Harvard University Press, 1981), pp. 266–85.

3 Using Citizens as Means and Breaking Promises

Introduction

"Treat man always as an end, never merely as a means." For Kant this was one version of the fundamental principle of morality, a principle that would prohibit absolutely all kinds of immoral actions. But even moral philosophers who are less absolutist recognize the principle as an important one. It expresses respect for the freedom of persons, telling us that we should not use other people only to serve our own purposes.

Notice that the principle does not say people may never be used as means, only that they should not be used *merely* as means. If you agree to let yourself be used for someone else's purposes, you are not being used merely as a means; your consent protects your freedom as an independent moral agent.

The trouble is, however, that some people may agree to be used without being fully aware of what they are agreeing to or without feeling fully free from pressure to agree to it. This is most likely when the agreement is between unequal parties—as when the government deals with individual citizens or small groups of citizens. In such encounters, governmental officials not only have more information and power than private citizens, but also can often claim to be pursuing nobler aims. Because officials serve the whole society (or imagine that they do), they may sometimes be justified and other times tempted to use some citizens as means of furthering projects that benefit other citizens.

Nowhere do these justifications and temptations seem stronger than in social experimentation, in which the government undertakes large-scale studies of proposed programs to see what their effects would be if they were enacted. Such experiments have been much more numerous and extensive than most people realize. With staffs and subjects numbering in the thousands and budgets in the millions, government-sponsored experiments in recent years have studied housing allowances, educational vouchers, educational performance contracts, health insurance plans, and guaranteed income programs. The Denver Income Maintenance Experiment (DIME) was part of the largest of these experiments, and it vividly illustrates most of their ethical problems.

The case is especially instructive because the officials themselves were aware of some of the ethical issues and even wrote memos about them. At the time, the experiment seemed to most to be benign and fully justifiable. But a closer look at it suggests a more complex judgment. Arguably, the subjects were induced to take part in a project that changed their lives in ways they were not told about and in ways some of them did not like. Insofar as the experiment benefited the subjects, citizens who were not given the opportunity to take part might complain, as some did, that the experimenters had been unfair to them. The case forces us to develop criteria for deciding when citizens may be used as means in governmental projects and when citizens may be said to consent to participation in them.

The DIME did not turn out the way officals had planned, and it had to be ended early. Because of the termination, the case raises a second set of issues: when do governments have moral commitments to citizens and under what conditions, if any, may those commitments be overridden? Few moral philosophers claim that commitments or promises may never be broken, but most have insisted that they may be broken only under special conditions. A promise may be overridden, for example, if circumstances have changed in ways that neither party could have foreseen when the promise was made. In politics, circumstances are always changing in unexpected ways, and many well-intentioned projects go awry. We therefore need to be quite careful about invoking "changed circumstances" to justify setting aside a promise the government makes. An assessment of what the government did with families in the DIME at the end of the experiment requires developing criteria for governments to follow when they have to pick up the pieces of projects that turn out badly.

The Denver Income Maintenance Experiment

Dennis Thompson

The Denver Income Maintenance Experiment (DIME) was the last in a series of four government-sponsored studies designed to discover to what extent (if any) recipients of a guaranteed income would change their behavior—chiefly whether they would work less. Policymakers hoped to use the results of the research to assess various income maintenance programs the government might adopt (such as a negative income tax). The experiments constituted the largest, most sophisticated social research on public policy that the government had yet undertaken. Several leading social scientists wrote in 1978 that "the research represents a peak in the present state of the art and will become an important exemplar for future studies."

Some 4,800 families took part in the Seattle-Denver experiment, more than 70 percent in programs that lasted only three years and 25 percent in five-year programs. The rest comprised the DIME twenty-year group, whose characteristics in other respects matched the larger groups. In the twenty-year sample none of the families earned more than $5,000 a year before the experiment and most less than $3,000.

All of the experiments attempted to isolate the effects of income maintenance from the various other factors that might affect the work behavior of families who received the guaranteed income. A predetermined number of families who met the requirements for enrollment for each experiment were randomly selected and assigned to experimental or control groups. The experimental groups received income payments under one of several plans. These plans differed in the amount of income guaranteed to the families (the "basic benefit," which ranged from 50 percent to 135 percent of the poverty line), and in the proportion by which the guaranteed income would be reduced for each dollar of other income the family earned (the "benefit reduction rate," which ranged from 30 percent to 80 percent). Families in the experimental groups reported their income and household composition every month, and were interviewed several times a year. Families in the control groups received no benefit payments from the experiment but remained eligible for any welfare and Food Stamp assistance to which they were entitled. They received a small payment for the information they supplied to interviewers several times a year.

Although the Office of Economic Opportunity initiated the early research, the Department of Health, Education and Welfare administered the later experiments including DIME. Funding for DIME came from the Office of the Assistant Secretary for Planning and Evaluation, under a provision of the Social Security Act that authorized policy research. The Assistant Secretary (or his Deputy) formulated general policy on the experiments and supervised the work of contractors. The primary contractor was the Colorado Department of Social Services, which subcontracted with the Stanford Research Institute (SRI) to design the program and conduct data analysis, and with Mathematica Policy Research (MPR) to collect the data and administer the payments to the families. MPR maintained the only list of the names and addresses of the families enrolled in the program. The President of MPR had earlier demonstrated that he would go to jail rather than relinquish this list. No one at HEW ever knew the identities of the families in DIME (except for one man who sued the government, alleging that his wife had left him because of the independent income the experiment gave her).

The Decision to Initiate the Twenty-year Experiment

Critics of the earlier experiments, as well as some of the researchers conducting them, had suspected that the short duration (three or even five years) could bias the conclusions. If subjects know that the experiment will end in a few years, they may be less likely to quit their jobs, or make other drastic changes in their habits of work, than they would if they expected the income guaranteed to continue indefinitely. Also, in a temporary experiment, especially when increased earnings reduced the benefits, some subjects such as women who worked part-time might try to reduce the amount of time they worked during the experiment, postponing until the experiment ended employment they might otherwise have accepted.

To answer these objections, SRI in 1973 proposed the formation of a new experimental group that would continue for twenty years. They suggested that this twenty-year subsample, when compared with the five-year group, would give a better indication of "the true long-run responses" of families in actual government programs, which (it was assumed) citizens perceive to be relatively permanent. HEW's project director for DIME, Joseph Corbett, tentatively approved the proposal in July 1973 and told SRI to submit for Departmental review a precise description of the procedures they would follow. MPR prepared the description, and SRI forwarded it to Corbett in August, 1973. During the next six months, HEW modified its contract with SRI to include the new research, and HEW officials began reviewing the proposal.

On March 4, 1974, the Assistant Secretary for Planning and Evaluation, William Morrill, wrote to the Undersecretary of HEW, recommending approval of a twenty-year subsample in DIME. He explained the need for such a sample (more or less as the SRI proposal had done) and then he added:

> While we plan to tell the families that the program will continue for 20 years, it is not necessary to run this experiment for the full 20 years to obtain the required information we desire. The true long run response of these families, who will expect the program to last for 20 years, can be observed by comparing their responses over a 5-year period with the responses of families participating in the shorter term experiments, who will expect their guarantee to last only 3-5 years.
>
> Hence, unless we find other compelling research reasons for continuing the families on the program for the full time period, we tentatively plan to terminate this new treatment group at the end of 5 years, giving the families a lump sum payment at that time to compensate them for the early termination of the program.
>
> In order to eliminate any ethical issues relating to the early termination of the 20-year sample, families would be given a choice at that time as to whether to accept the lump sum payment or to continue receiving their regular benefits. A plan for administering the continued benefits would be developed during the course of the experiment.

The Assistant Secretary circulated this memo within the Department and encouraged extensive discussion. Other officials raised three major objections. First, the Undersecretary questioned the assumption that citizens perceive regular welfare programs to be more permanent than income maintenance experiments. To answer this question, the subcontractors conducted a survey in Seattle and Denver, and found that lower-income families have "a very high expectation for long run continuity of government cash transfer programs," whereas they expect experiments to last only a few years. Officials interpreted the survey as confirming the need for the twenty-year experiment, which would create expectations closer to those of citizens in a permanent program of income maintenance.

The Commissioner of Welfare, Robert Carleson, while not objecting to the general plan for a twenty-year experiment, criticized the specific proposal that "the subsample be terminated at five years and that lump sum payments be made." He argued that some of the families would almost certainly find out that the experiment would end in the fifth year, and would therefore adjust their behavior so that they would remain eligible for the monthly payment in that year and thus for the lump-sum payment. Even if officials managed to keep the plan secret, to give a lump-sum payment to those who happened to remain eligible in the fifth year would be arbitrary.

The Administrator for Social and Rehabilitation Service, James Dwight, raised a third objection, more explicitly ethical. On March 20, he wrote to Morrill:

> I continue to have serious reservations about the value of this experiment when contrasted with the ethical issues regarding public policy. The survey which was taken reflects the perception that public programs will exist for 5 to 20 years at least. This leaves unanswered the question of to what extent this perception influences personal behavior. In answering this, as proposed, the involved families may: (1) take on long-range debt

commitments; (2) decide to have more children than they otherwise would; (3) decide on early retirement; or (4) decide to forego savings or life insurance. In some cases the 5-year lump-sum terminations may have traumatic effects and may involve adverse publicity and lawsuits. If, on the other hand, it was emphasized that the transfer payments might be stopped at *any time*, the effect of the experiment would be negated. This issue of how to design this experiment must be viewed in the context of the serious questions raised about the ethics of using people as guinea pigs in research experiments without fully disclosing possible consequences.

After further discussions within the Department, the Assistant Secretary, Morrill, sent an "action memorandum" to the Undersecretary on April 18, again recommending establishing a twenty-year group but this time without a "termination option":

> Under our proposed plan about 100 of the 5,000 families participating in the Seattle/Denver Experiment would be reassigned from a control group status to a new 20-year financial treatment. Because for research purposes we only need to maintain the new subsample for 5 years, we had earlier considered terminating the program at the end of 5 years and giving the families a lump-sum payment at that time to compensate them for the early ending of the program. The early termination with compensation option was proposed since it was thought that it would both satisfy our research needs and lessen our administrative burden and costs. However, in order to eliminate any possible ethical issues that might arise from the early termination option, we have revised our proposal to eliminate the option. Thus, we now propose to continue the program for the full twenty years.
>
> I would also like to respond to the points raised by Bob Carleson and Jim Dwight. . . . Bob had no objection to the proposal except that he recommended that we continue the program for the full twenty years. Jim similarly expressed practical and ethical concerns about the early termination option. Our revision of the proposal to eliminate this option should satisfy their concerns. I hope this revision will also satisfy your concerns about the ethical issues involved in this proposal.

The Undersecretary approved the proposal, subject to some further consultation within the Department, and enrollment of the twenty-year group began in July 1974.

Initially, the experiment included about 110 families. The sample was kept small because of the high cost per family in a twenty-year study, and because SRI believed that even this small sample would reveal any large differences in behavior between the twenty-year group and the three- and five-year groups. However, for two different reasons, the sample soon had to be expanded. First, it turned out that many families in the original sample earned too much to benefit from the income maintenance payments, and that therefore the number of families actually receiving DIME payments would be too small to yield significant experimental results. Consequently, researchers added more families to the sample (evidently about 60). These families had been members of the three-year experimental group (unlike the original sample of 110 who came from the three-year control groups). HEW officials made sure that no family suffered financially as a result of the transfer.

A second reason for the increase in the sample arose out of criticisms Mexican-American activists directed against DIME. The Mexican-American Legal Defense and Education Fund (MALDEF) complained that no Spanish-surnamed families had been invited to participate in the DIME, and charged that this exclusion represented discrimination against Mexican-Americans. Jacob Shockley, DIME project Director for the Colorado Department of Social Services, reported this charge to Corbett in Washington and warned that MALDEF might file a suit or make a complaint to HEW's Office of Civil Rights. Shockley noted that already the Regional Office of HEW had cited his own department for violations of regulations on affirmative action. Robert Williams, project director of DIME for MPR in Denver, wrote to SRI expressing similar worries. R. G. Spiegelman, SRI's project manager, then recommended to Corbett that twenty-five to thirty Mexican-American families be added to the twenty-year sample. Spiegelman's memorandum at one point referred to the "political implications of omitting such a sample," but mostly stressed the research value of including the Mexican-Americans. SRI had originally declined to add a sample of Mexican-Americans because of the additional cost and because the staff believed they could, from the other populations, extrapolate conclusions about Mexican-Americans. Now Spiegelman decided that the extrapolation would be too experimentally "risky" and thought "it would be preferable" to avoid it. Corbett and other HEW officials accepted the recommendation to add the Mexican-Americans to the DIME. By January 1975, the researchers had completed the expansion of the sample, which now totaled 195 families, including both those subjects added from the previous experimental groups and the new Mexican-Americans.

The MPR staff in Denver, supervised by Williams, enrolled the families in the experiment. Nearly all of the staff had experience in administering the earlier experiments, and now received additional training and instructions. The "enrollers" made personal contact with each family, presenting a package of materials, which included a letter inviting the family to join the experiment, and an agreement stipulating the terms of their participation. Shockley had written the letter, at the request of Spiegelman, who believed that the signature of a representative of the State government would enhance the credibility of the invitation and especially of the twenty-year guarantee. That the families believe this guarantee, Spiegelman wrote, is "of crucial importance to the success of the experiment." About the guarantee, Shockley's letter said:

> It is the intent of the Federal government to continue your family's income guarantee for a period of twenty years. Should it be necessary for the government to terminate this program before twenty years have elapsed, the government's plan is to make a cash settlement with your family to help cover the unused portion of your income guarantee period. [For full text, see Appendix I.]

The staff member gave each family a copy of the letter, and explained the experiment and its rules. Enrollers were instructed to:

> . . . explain that it is the intent of the government to run the program for 20 years. In response to questions, enrollers would be able to tell families that the government could cancel the program at any time, as it could do with any program, but that if the program were cancelled, it is the government's intention to compensate them. The amount of such compensation would depend on the size of the grant they are receiving at the time the program is terminated, the length of time the guarantee period has to run, and the availability of government funds.

There is no record of how many (if any) families asked questions about possible termination, nor is there any information about what enrollers actually told the families. The enrollment agreement, which the enrollers asked each head of household to sign, included this provision:

> Finally, I understand that my participation in the program is governed by the provisions of the *Rules of Operation* (a copy of the summary of which had been provided to me) and that while it is the intention of the Government to continue the program for twenty years, both the operation of the program and the duration of the payments are subject to modification as determined by the Secretary of Health, Education and Welfare, or his designee. [For full text, see Appendix II.]

The Decision to Terminate the Experiment

In November 1978, staff from HEW, SRI, the state governments of Washington and Colorado and MPR's Denver office met in Menlo Park, California, to discuss the conclusion of SRI's "Analysis of the Labor Supply Response of the Twenty Year Families in the DIME." The first conclusion seemed innocuous: the study found no statistically significant "labor supply response" by the twenty-year group during the first year of the experiment. More ominous were two other conclusions—both raising the old worry about the size of the sample. The study found that the enlarged sample had not adequately met the problem. The sample was still too small to yield statistically significant comparisons and estimates. But the fatal blow came from the study's conclusion that "the nonrandom assignment of families to the twenty-year program . . . makes it extremely difficult to interpret any responses estimated for this group." Apparently no one had noticed that, among other things, the subjects in the experimental group had worked significantly less in the year before the experiment than had subjects in the control group. Various attempts to correct for this difference proved unsatisfactory. Everyone at the Menlo Park meeting reluctantly but unequivocally agreed that the experiment had no research value.* The participants at the meeting concluded that families should be disenrolled as soon as suitable arrangements could be made, but they left unresolved the question of what compensation should be provided to the families. HEW initiated several further meetings and conversations with nearly all officials and groups involved in the experiment (though not with any of the families or their representatives).

In late January, 1979, Thomas Harper (of MPR's subsidiary, the Council for Grants to Families) in a letter to the families announced some changes in the rules of the program. No longer would interviewers collect data from the families, and no longer would benefits increase when the cost of living rose. New family members could not now join the program as easily as before. The letter also said:

> Although the interviews are ending, the payment program continues under revised Rules of Operation. . . . The DIME has been a successful study which has supplied significant information to the government. This information has already helped the government respond to the welfare needs of families throughout the country. The changes being made in the DIME program will not diminish that success.

Now HEW officials turned to the question of what to do with the families in the DIME. A memorandum from Spiegelman at SRI outlined some of the issues that they considered. Any decision would have to recognize HEW's "obligations to the public": taxpayers could reasonably object to continuation of a program that yielded absolutely no research value. Spiegelman mentioned two kinds of "obligations to the families"—legal and moral. On legal obligations, SRI's attorney wrote: "The use of the words 'intent' and 'plan' in the agreement and the statements to the families indicate the 'good intentions' of the government rather than a legal commitment. Nevertheless, this is a difficult legal question." HEW's legal counsel later concluded that the government had no legal

*The participants relied chiefly on a paper by Philip K. Robins and Gary L. Stieger, "The Labor Supply Response of Twenty-Year Families in the Denver Income Maintenance Experiment," Menlo Park, Calif.: SRI International, 1978. A more recent review confirms the seriousness of the error in the expansion of the sample, but nevertheless draws some conclusions about the effect of income maintenance and suggests that continuing the experiment might have yielded some useful data about single female heads of families. See Robins and Stieger, "An Analysis of the Labor Supply Response of Twenty-Year Families in the D.I.M.E." Menlo Park, Calif.: SRI International, April 1980 (draft).

obligation at all to continue the income payments or even to offer any significant lump sum settlement, though some officials in HEW thought that some of the families, encouraged by welfare rights lawyers, might decide to sue.

The discussion of the moral obligations to the families seemed to take for granted that early termination was justified, and concentrated on the moral criteria that the procedures for termination should satisfy. First, safeguards should be provided to protect the families from exploitation in any negotiations with the government about the amount of a settlement. Later, other officials mentioned this point in arguing against any negotiations at all with the families. They wanted to avoid any direct discussions with the families or their representatives. Now that the government itself had financed and encouraged the growth of welfare rights organizations and legal aid offices, HEW officials felt they had to treat almost any contact with clients as a potential subject of litigation or formal complaint. As one HEW official remarked, "it may be on balance a good thing that citizens can now easily threaten bureaucrats like me with legal action, but it sure does change the way I can deal with the people in our programs. It's much more impersonal and distant."

The second moral criterion in the Spiegelman memo held that any termination settlement should recognize the fact that families may have made choices on the expectation that the program would continue, and would suffer serious losses when the income payments ceased. What recognizing this fact meant became clearer in Spiegelman's analysis of the "multiplier" that would determine the termination payments:

> It is generally agreed that the program has a moral, if not legal, obligation to assure the families that they will be no worse off as a result of DIME participation than if they had not participated at all. The program must, therefore, underwrite the consequences of choices made that place them in jeopardy should the program be cancelled. They may have quit their job, had children, bought a home, moved to some preferred location, etc. Whatever their actions we owe them the time and resources to recover and return to a normal situation. The multiplier is viewed as an expression of the number of months the program is willing to support the family while it adjusts to a non-DIME environment of work and public support.
>
> For some families, who are not dependent on DIME at all, a multiplier of zero months would be adequate to ensure their transition. Other families may never eliminate their dependency on DIME or some other form of public support. For these dependent families, a multiplier of 192 months, reflecting the entire period remaining in the agreement, might seem justified. But the fact of the availability of other public support is a convincing argument against it. Further, the discounted value of such a cash stream, using present bank interest rates indicates that a multiplier of 95 would purchase an equivalent annuity. And, assuming that the families would be eligible for other public support a multiplier of less than 50 would provide an annuity that in combination would give the family the equivalent of the DIME program stipend. If it is argued that the program is really only morally obligated to help the family return to its former status a multiplier as high as 50 cannot be justified. The participants in our first seminar felt, intuitively, that a more appropriate period would be represented by a multiplier in the range of 24-30 months.

By the fall of 1979, Ben W. Heineman, Jr., who was now the Assistant Secretary, had decided against continuing payments to the families for the next fifteen years; he favored providing benefits at most for three years, making each monthly check somewhat smaller than the previous one (as a way of ensuring that families realized the payments would end). Before he could implement the decision, he resigned, and John Palmer, his principal deputy, became Acting Assistant Secretary in November,

1979. Palmer was inclined to agree with his predecessor's decision and prepared a draft memorandum justifying the decision and explaining how it would be implemented. Palmer's argument against continuing the program or offering a larger settlement was that "there is an implicit *quid pro quo* involved in participation in such an experiment and that since there is no longer any benefit to taxpayers and the Federal government in continuing the experiment, there is no reason for taxpayers to continue funding benefit payments that exceed AFDC plus Food Stamps and the added administrative costs."

Palmer also feared that to request from Congress the large appropriation necessary to continue the program or to provide large lump sum payments would create adverse public reaction, and jeopardize possibilities for policy research in the future. Already Senator William Armstrong of Colorado had publicly condemned the experiment as a waste of public funds. Officials in HEW's Legislative Liaison Office talked informally to members of the staff of some of the other Colorado delegations, who usually could be counted on to support HEW's liberal programs, but found little enthusiasm for the additional appropriations that would be necessary to give the DIME families a large settlement. Generally, the mood in Congress, effectively expressed in several unusual budget-cutting resolutions, threatened many of HEW's most important programs. At this point, however, the Liaison Office did not recommend against any settlement that would require Congressional approval. They did not want to seem to be in the position of ruling out the right course of action simply because it was not politically expedient; they presumably hoped Palmer and his staff would reach the conclusion that a smaller settlement was justifiable on the merits.

The President of MPR and some of his staff had argued vigorously with HEW officials, insisting that the government had a moral commitment to continue the program for twenty years, or at least to provide a cash settlement that would be equivalent to what families would have received if the program had continued for twenty years. Like Spiegelman, they pointed out that the families may have relied on the government's promise, perhaps making irreversible decisions such as having another child or retiring early, that they would not have otherwise made. Since it would be impossible to prove that people had not made such decisions on this basis, the government should assume that people had done so, and provide a settlement compatible with this assumption. In his draft memorandum in January, Palmer rejected this line of argument, maintaining that the families were probably made better off by participation in the experiment than they would have been if they had stayed in the regular welfare system. With a reasonable period of notice, they should be able to adjust to pre-experimental life quite easily, at least no worse off than before.

Nevertheless, Palmer still had some doubts. He was not absolutely sure that the government did not have an "inviolable commitment" to these families. He was also troubled by the fact that he himself had been officially, if not actually, responsible for initiating the twenty-year sample in 1974. While serving as Director of Income Security Policy then, he had not paid much attention to the experiment because higher officials, especially Morrill, had taken a personal interest in it and usually dealt directly with officials in Palmer's Office of Research. But now Palmer thought that because of his own previous responsibility (however nominal), he personally might have some special obligation to the families, and that the government's commitment therefore might be stronger than it would have otherwise been. In early 1980, Michael Barth, Palmer's Deputy Assistant Secretary for

Income Security Policy, while preparing the materials to implement the decision expressed in Palmer's draft memo, came to the conclusion that the decision was wrong. He persuaded Palmer at least to delay implementing it until Barth could conduct another review of the "options for termination."

Barth was well placed to help Palmer reach an objective decision. Barth had not held office when the DIME began; nor had he participated in major decisions about the experiment. Moreover, he intended for personal reasons to leave government shortly after Palmer made his decision, and could not be suspected of recommending a course of action mainly because it seemed easier to implement. He also believed that the Department on its own should determine the right course of action, and not pass the buck to Congress. Department officials should neither ask Congress for a larger settlement than they themselves believed justified, nor should they refrain from proposing a larger settlement simply because they thought Congress might reject it. Barth began discussions with other officials in the Department, the contractors' offices and Congress, and then prepared a "background paper" drawing on these discussions and on earlier memoranda in the HEW files on the experiment.

Reviewing the current status of the program, Barth found that income maintenance payments for the families cost $500,000 in 1979. Administrative expenses added $200,000. To continue the program for the next fifteen years, as originally intended, would cost $9.2 million. The number of families had grown from 195 to 237 (adult family members who left their original families, and young adult family members who set up households of their own, had been permitted to remain in the experiment). At the end of 1979, 18 families were receiving $601–900 a month; 52 families, $301–600 a month; 31 families, $21–300 a month; and 125 families the minimum payment of $20 a month.

In his background paper Barth outlined the major "alternate courses of action" that had been discussed within HEW. Those still under serious consideration were:

A. Continue the experiment for the full fifteen years.

1. *Income conditioned payments.* Continue to base payments on reports of income. This would require maintaining a payment apparatus for the families left on DIME. Expected cost: $9.17 million.* (Present discounted value, using an interest rate of 10%: $5.31 million.)

Pros

—Fulfills original stated intent of the Government.

—Fulfills probable expectations of an otherwise disadvantaged and therefore possibly specially vulnerable population.

Cons

—Can be argued to be irresponsible use of public funds appropriated for research purposes, since no further research value is gained.

—Ability to implement is questionable, since either annual appropriations for fourteen years *or* one or more large appropriations for this purpose would have to be sought.

—Requires maintenance of expensive administrative mechanism to process income reports for small number of families for fifteen years.

—May generate substantial adverse publicity, since sample would have little or no research value, and ethical justification would not be widely accepted.

*This figure, as well as those under options that follow, does not take into account the cost of AFDC and Food Stamps for which some families would be eligible if DIME ended. Therefore, the true cost to the taxpayer of any of these options would be somewhat less than the figures given (though by how much it would be difficult to determine).

—Adjustment problems for families when payments end may be substantially worse than under early termination.

2. *Non-income conditioned payments.* Drop income-conditioning and pay fixed monthly payments equal to average in base period until end of enrollment period. Administration by private carrier possible. Cost (as of January 1980): $8.27 million. (Present discounted value: $4.70 million.)

Pros

—Fulfills original stated intent of the Government if non-income-tested payments are accepted as a continuation of the program.

—Fulfills probable expectations of an otherwise disadvantaged and therefore possibly specially vulnerable population.

Cons

—Same as previous option except that administrative mechanism would be much simpler.

—Families would lose "insurance value" of income conditioned payments.

—As families' economic circumstances change over time, some high-income families might receive very large payments, generating adverse publicity and raising questions of responsible use of public funds.

B. Terminate with lump sum payments.

1. *Early termination with compensation for fifteen years of payments.* Terminate program in 1980 and provide lump-sum payments (possibly in quarterly installments) equal to present discounted value of fifteen-year stream of expected payments. Cost: 10% discount rate—$5.38 million; 15% discount rate—$4.48 million; 20% discount rate—$3.86 million.

Pros

—Fully discharges ethical obligation on families if lump-sum payment is viewed as acceptable substitute for monthly income-conditioned payments.

Cons

—Can be argued to be irresponsible use of public funds appropriated for research purposes because, in comparison with lower-cost options, this option gives no additional benefit.

—Ability to implement is questionable, since additional appropriation of $3–4 million in FY 80-81 would be required.

—Lump-sum payments averaging $14,000 to $20,000, and as high as $86,000 to a single family, would generate serious adverse publicity.

—Calculation of expected future payments and selection of discount rate is arbitrary; may be hard to justify and defend in individual cases.

2. *Early termination with two-years' non-income-conditioned payments made in quarterly investments.* Terminate program in 1980, and make four fixed quarterly payments totalling twice the family's payments in the base year, subject to minimum of $500 and maximum of $12,000. Cost: $1.23 million.

Pros

—Clearly provides compensation for early termination.

—Provides fifteen-months lead time for families to adjust to cessation of payments; families know with certainty payments for last twelve months.

—Can be funded with available funds; no risk to families that plan won't be implemented for lack of funds.

Cons

—Does not discharge twenty-year commitment.

—Single payments of up to $3,000 may generate adverse publicity and create budgeting problems for the families.

—Doubling the family's payments during the transition year may make adjustment problems worse, rather than better.

C. Terminate with non-income-conditioned transition payments.

1. *Three-year declining payment options.* Terminate payments in 1980, and provide three years of non-income-conditioned monthly transition payments equal initially to the family's average payment in a recent twelve-month base period. Payments decline 1.25% per month so that the final payment is 65% of the initial transition payment. Optional accelerated payments of up to $500 per month available. Assist families through counseling and other means to move into post-experimental life. Cost: $1.47 million.

Pros

—Fulfills obligation to families as defined in enrollment documents if transition payments are interpreted as compensation for early cessation of NIT payments.

—Provides at least thirty-six months lead time for families to adjust to end of payments.

—Payments are easy to calculate, explain, and administer.

—Can be funded with available funds; no risk to families that plan won't be implemented for lack of funds.

—Monthly payments probably less disruptive to family budgeting than lump sums or quarterly payments.

Cons

—May appear to be termination without compensation, in violation of Enrollment Agreement.

—Decline in transition payments renders recipients less well-off without providing enough stimulus to seek alternative means of support.

2. *Six-month option.* Using the unemployment compensation system as a guide, advise families that the government intends to terminate the program and that benefits will be phased out over a six-month period. Initial month's benefit would be the same as as that in the previous option (i.e., the family's average payment in the prior twelve months). The phase-out might or might not involve a declining payment. Cost: with constant payment—$300,000; with phase-out of 10% per month—$185,000.

Pros

—Gives DIME twenty-year participants the same benefit period as unemployed persons.

Cons

—Does not discharge twenty-year commitment.

—Does not provide families with enough time to consider options and change plans.

Barth presented these options to three outside consultants whom he asked to recommend "the soundest course of action," specifically taking into account "moral/ethical" factors. On May 7, 1980, the consultants presented their recommendations, which ranged from a modified version of C.2 to versions of B.1. Barth reported that officials in Colorado's Department of Social Services and HEW's Regional Office in Denver with whom he had talked favored some version of C.1. So apparently did some staff members of key Congressional delegations. The staff of Senator Gary Hart, who might have been expected to support a more generous settlement for the families, never responded to Barth's inquiries. From Senator Armstrong's previous public statements, HEW officials had inferred that he would disapprove of continuing the payments for more than a few months.

In June 1980, Palmer decided in favor of C.1. In addition, Palmer instituted a program of counseling and support to help the families during the period of transition. On July 11, he sent Secretary Patricia Harris a memorandum informing her of his decision. In September 1980, the department, now the Department of Health and Human Services (HHS), announced the end of the DIME. The families received their first transition payments in October.

Appendix I

State of Colorado
DEPARTMENT OF SOCIAL SERVICES

Dear Family:

You have been asked by a member of the staff of the Council for Grants to Families (a subsidiary of Mathematica, Inc.) to enroll in an experimental national income maintenance program funded by the United States Government through the state of Colorado. Under this program, you will be offered an annual income guarantee. The purpose of the experimental program is to help the government design an income maintenance program that will be best for the country. The experimental program contributes to this purpose by showing how various programs affect families. It is the intent of the Federal government to continue your family's income guarantee for a period of twenty years. Should it be necessary for the government to terminate this program before twenty years have elapsed, the government's plan is to make a cash settlement with your family to help cover the unused portion of your income guarantee period.

Each family asked to join the program has been selected at random from among similar families in Denver and is representative of many other families living in the area. I would like personally to urge you to join the program, as your participation is essential to its success.

If you have any questions concerning this program or your participation in it, please do not hesitate to call me. My number is 892-2556.

Sincerely,

COLORADO DEPARTMENT OF SOCIAL SERVICES

Jacob Shockley, Project Director
Denver Income Maintenance Experiment

Appendix II

COUNCIL FOR GRANTS TO FAMILIES

ENROLLMENT AGREEMENT

I agree to participate in the Denver Income Maintenance Experiment until ____________, 1994. A representative of the Council for Grants to Families has explained the program to me.

I agree to report to the Council every month all the income from all sources received by me and by all members of my family who are included in the program and to report promptly to the Council any change in address or in the number of people living with my family.

I also agree to take periodic interviews as requested by Urban Opinion Surveys, a division of Mathematica, Inc., or its successor, and to provide such other full and truthful information as may be required to conduct the experiment. I understand that any information given by me to Urban Opinion Surveys or the Council for Grants to Families will be used only to evaluate the program, will be held in strict confidence, and will never be released to any person without my written permission except if required by law.

I am aware that my family will not be eligible to receive payments from the Council above the minimum ($20 per month) for any period in which any member of my family is receiving Aid to Families with Dependent Children (AFDC).

I understand that my family will be eligible for a grant payment from the Council each month calculated according to the rules of the program. I also understand that the grant payments paid to my family are ours to use in any way we wish and that, unless we give incorrect information about our income, family size, or residential address, or receive payments in excess of those provided under the rules of the program, we will never be required to return any part of this money.

I understand further that the Council may add to my monthly payments reimbursement for some or all of my federal or state income tax payments (including social security payments), but that the Council may require repayment if it reimburses more than provided under the rules of the program during any calendar year.

Finally, I understand that my participation in the program is governed by the provisions of the Rules of Operation (a copy of the summary of which has been provided to me) and that while it is the intention of the Government to continue the program for twenty years, both the operation of the program and the duration of the payments are subject to modification as determined by the Secretary of Health, Education and Welfare or his designee.

Signed ______________________________ Date ______________________________
Male Head of Household

______________________________ Date ______________________________
Female Head of Household

Approved ______________________________ Date ______________________________
Project Manager

Comment

It is a good idea to separate your analysis of the two parts of this case—the initiation and the termination of the experiment. Otherwise, knowing the experiment turned out badly, you may conclude too quickly that it should never have begun and fail to appreciate the strength of the case in favor of the experiment as officials saw it in 1974. Similarly, if you dwell on the possibility that the problems in terminating the experiment in 1980 could have been avoided if the experiment had been better planned and executed, you may find it more difficult to focus specifically on what Palmer should have done with the families. Palmer faced a dilemma that is common in modern government: what should officials do when others have not done what they should have done?

The first part of this case calls for an analysis of the criteria that officials used in deciding to initiate the DIME. One type of criterion, stipulated in the government's own regulations, is utilitarian: the risks of harm to the participants must be outweighed by the sum of the benefits to the participants and the social importance of the knowledge to be gained from the experiment. What exactly were the risks and benefits to the subjects? What were the benefits to society? Did officials appraise the risks and benefits adequately?

Critics of the utilitarian criterion point out that it leaves participants quite vulnerable, justifying a lot of inconvenience and even harm to them when the social value of the experiment is great or can be described as such (e.g., "eliminating poverty in our time"). Defenders of the criterion argue that the short-term harms to the subjects, which are likely to be more certain than the speculative long-term benefits, will usually have more weight in any proper utilitarian calculation. Also, consider this alternative to the utilitarian criterion (proposed by David Kershaw): the experiment must "restore the *status quo ante*—to assure that...subjects are left after the experiment as if it had never existed."

A second kind of criterion pays more attention to the rights of the participants: people may not be used in experiments without their informed consent. In many experiments, participants cannot be told everything without undermining the purpose of the experiment. Could the participants in DIME have been told more than officials told them without destroying the experiment? To justify using people in experiments, what must officials do to make sure participants understand what they are told?

The standard for consent is not only adequate information but also the absence of undue pressure. Did the payments to the DIME families amount to "undue enticement" and vitiate their free choice? It is generally assumed that the standards for consent in social and medical experiments must be stricter than for ordinary governmental programs even if the risks are no greater. Why or why not is this assumption correct?

The second part of the case concerns the government's commitment to the families. Did the government make a morally binding commitment or promise? Consider (1) the families' expectations—whether they had good reason to rely on the government's commitment, and (2) the harm the families might experience—whether they would actually suffer harm by having relied on the government's apparent promise. If, for practical or moral reasons, the government could not reliably determine what harm the families might suffer (as evidently was true), how does this affect the commitment?

Even if the government had a binding commitment, we still have to ask: Must the government fulfill it? Promises may sometimes be legitimately set aside. Since the experiment no longer served its original purpose, could one rightly claim that the government no longer owed the families anything (Palmer's *quid pro quo* argument)? Could one argue that the government owed the greater duty to all citizens, including taxpayers and citizens on welfare who are less well off than the families in the DIME?

The government should not be viewed as a monolithic moral agent in this case. Part of the problem here is whether administrators should on their own authority settle with families or turn the matter over to Congress (whose support was necessary for any larger settlement than the one Palmer chose). Is the belief that going to Congress would jeopardize other important programs in HEW a legitimate moral reason not to attempt any larger settlement? What if, by going to Congress, officials risked getting less for the families than the settlement HEW could provide out of its own budget?

Recommended Reading

Kant explains and defends his principle of treating persons as ends in the second section of the *Metaphysical Foundations of Morals* (Indianapolis: Bobbs-Merrill, 1959). An excellent exposition of Kant's moral theory as applied to politics is Jeffrie Murphy, *Kant: The Philosophy of Right* (London: Macmillan, 1970). On the utilitarian criterion, see the Recommended Reading in the Introduction.

Two useful collections on the ethics of social experimentation are: Alice Rivlin and P. Michael Timpane (eds.), *Ethical and Legal Issues of Social Experimentation* (Washington, D.C.: Brookings, 1975); and Gordon Bermant et al. (eds.), *The Ethics of Social Intervention* (Washington, D.C.: Hemisphere Pub., 1978). On the DIME, see Dennis F. Thompson, *Political Ethics and Public Office* (Cambridge, Mass.: Harvard University Press, 1987), chapter 7.

The criterion of informed consent may be illuminated by consulting some theoretical writings on political consent: see Hanna Pitkin, "Obligation and Consent—II," *American Political Science Review,* 60 (March 1966), pp. 39–52; Michael Walzer, *Obligations* (New York: Simon and Schuster, 1971); and A. John Simmons, *Moral Principles and Political Obligations* (Princeton, N.J.: Princeton University Press, 1979). Also, see Ruth R. Faden and Tom L. Beauchamp, *A History of Informed Consent* (New York: Oxford University Press, 1986).

For recent philosophical discussions of promises, see P. S. Atiyah, *Promises, Morals and Law* (New York: Oxford University Press, 1981); Charles Fried, *Contract as Promise* (Cambridge, Mass.: Harvard University Press, 1981); H. A. Prichard, "The Obligation to Keep a Promise," in *Moral Obligation* (Oxford: Clarendon Press, 1949), pp. 169–79; John Rawls, *A Theory of Justice* (Cambridge, Mass.: Harvard University Press, 1971), pp. 344–48; and Henry Sidgwick, *Methods of Ethics* (London: Macmillan, 1962), pp. 303–11.

4 Official Disobedience

Introduction

What should public officials do when they disagree with governmental policy? For nonelected officials this question poses a particularly difficult dilemma. They are bound to carry out the orders of others, yet they should not act contrary to their own moral convictions. Their duty to carry out policy rests in part on the requirements of the democratic process. We do not want officials whom we cannot hold accountable to impose their own views on us, overriding the policies determined by the democratic process. We may assume, furthermore, that officials consent to the terms of office. They know in advance what is expected of them, and they should not hold office if they cannot accept a policy once it is formulated. On this view, the moral responsibilities of the nonelected public official are completely captured by the injunction, "obey or resign."

Critics of this view argue, first, that it underestimates the discretion that administrators exercise in modern governments. Neither the law nor their superiors can determine all their decisions, and they must use their own judgment in many matters. Second, if all public officials followed this injunction, public offices would soon be populated only by people who never had any inclination to disagree with anything the government decided to do. Men and women of strong moral conviction would always resign. Third, officials have broader obligations to the public—not merely obligations to their own conscience or to their superiors. "Obey or resign" presents too limited a menu of moral options. Officials may be warranted in staying in office and expressing their opposition in various ways—for example, by internal opposition, public protest, refusal to carry out the policy personally, supporting outside opponents of the policy, or direct obstruction.

The methods that seem the most difficult to accept are those that are illegal or violate governmental procedures and lawful orders of superiors. The justification for such tactics resembles in part the rationale for civil disobedience by citizens. A democratic society benefits from permitting moral dissent. Extreme measures are sometimes necessary to force democratic majorities and governments to recognize that they have made a serious mistake, and sometimes officials are the only people in a position to bring such a mistake to public attention. But since it is an extreme measure, civil disobedience is generally thought to be justified only under certain conditions. Those who disobey must: (1) act publicly; (2) act nonviolently; (3) appeal to principles shared by other citizens; (4) direct their challenge against a substantial injustice; and (5) exhaust all normal channels of protest.

The cases in this chapter—three instances of disobedience, one of a successful threat to resign, and one of strong criticism stopping short of disobedience—can help you understand whether official disobedience is justified, if so under what conditions, and whether the alternatives are better. The first case—a protest by attorneys in the Justice Department against their superiors' decision to delay school desegregation—seems the easiest to justify under the traditional criteria of civil disobedience, but some critics of the attorneys believed that their protest went too far and others suggested that it did not go far enough. The case also raises the question of the moral responsibility not only of lawyers but of all professionals who hold public office—for example, doctors, engineers, journalists, and teachers.

The second and third selections in this chapter invite a comparison of two instances of unauthorized disclosure (otherwise known as leaks). Otto Otepka, a State Department official, passed classified information to a congressional staff member in an effort to undermine the department's policy on security clearance, which he believed endangered national security. Daniel Ellsberg gave the classified Pentagon Papers to the *New York Times* to encourage opposition to the Vietnam War. Unlike the attorneys in "Revolt at Justice," Otepka and Ellsberg acted alone and in secret.

George Schultz acted alone but openly when he threatened to resign over a directive that would require polygraph testing of all federal officials with access to sensitive information. The case suggests an addition to the injunction "obey or resign"—officials may also "threaten to resign." In the case of the space shuttle *Challenger,* nobody involved in the decision-making process that culminated in its disastrous launching threatened to resign or publicly protested. Yet two senior engineers protested as strongly as they believed possible, short of disobeying or threatening to resign. Evaluating their actions can help clarify both the moral advantages and limitations of lawful dissent.

Revolt at Justice

Gary J. Greenberg

When a lawyer is admitted to the bar, he takes an oath to support the Constitution of the United States. When a lawyer joins the Department of Justice, he takes another oath—the same one that is taken by the Attorney General and, in fact, by all federal employees.

That oath reads:

From *Inside the System,* edited by Charles Peters and Timothy J. Adams. Copyright © 1970 by The Washington Monthly Corp. Reprinted by permission of Holt, Rinehart and Winston, CBS College Publ.

> I solemnly swear (or affirm) that I will support and defend the Constitution of the United States against all enemies, foreign and domestic, that I will bear true faith and allegiance to the same; that I take this obligation freely, and without any mental reservation or purpose of evasion; and that I will well and faithfully discharge the duties of the office on which I am about to enter. So help me God.

It was largely because of this oath—and the pressures we were under to violate it—that a majority of the attorneys from the Civil Rights Division of the Department of Justice gathered in a Washington apartment in August of 1969. We wanted to ascertain whether, under the Constitution, there was any legal argument that might conceivably support the Nixon Administration's request in a Mississippi courtroom, for a delay in implementing desegregation in thirty-three of that state's school districts. The assembled lawyers concluded that there was not. Thus was born the reluctant movement that the press was to call "the revolt" in the Civil Rights Division.

August 19, 1969, was a historic date in the field of civil rights. It was on that day that Robert H. Finch, the Secretary of Health, Education, and Welfare, in letters to the U.S. District Judges for the Southern District of Mississippi and to the Chief Judge of the U.S. Fifth Circuit Court of Appeals, sought to withdraw school desegregation plans that his department had filed in the district court a week earlier. It marked the first time—since the Supreme Court's 1954 decision in *Brown v. Board of Education*—that the United States had broken faith with the black children of Mississippi and aligned itself with the forces of delay on the issue of school desegregation.

Less than a week later—on August 25—Attorney General John N. Mitchell placed the Department of Justice imprimatur on Finch's actions when Jerris Leonard, the Assistant Attorney General in charge of the Civil Rights Division, joined local officials in a Mississippi district court to argue for a delay.

The same day, in Washington, some of my colleagues in the Civil Rights Division and I prepared and distributed a memorandum inviting the Division's attorneys to a meeting the next evening to discuss these and other recent events that had, in the words of the memo, cast ominous shadows over "the future course of law enforcement in civil rights." The meeting's purpose was "to determine whether we have a common position and what action, if any, would be appropriate to take."

The forty who attended the meeting that next night first heard detailed factual accounts from those lawyers with firsthand knowledge of the government's actions in school desegregation cases in Mississippi, Louisiana, and South Carolina. We discussed the legal principles at length. We could find, as lawyers, no grounds for these actions that did not run cross-grain to the Constitution. We concluded that the request for delay in Mississippi was not only politically motivated but unsupportable under the law we were sworn to uphold. I then asked whether the attorneys in the Civil Rights Division should protest the actions of Messrs. Mitchell, Finch, and Leonard. Much to my astonishment, the answer was an unhesitating, unequivocal, and unanimous call for action.

But how? The group's immediate, though probably unattainable, goal was a reversal of the Justice Department's actions in Mississippi. Beyond that, however, we wanted to ensure that future Mississippi-type decisions would not be made; we wanted guarantees that the Administration would, in the future, take the actions that were required by law, without reference to the political exigencies. We hoped that the protest could serve as a deterrent to future political accommodation. We agreed to write a dignified and reasonable statement of protest that would make our views known and demonstrate our unity and resolve. We chose a committee of six to draft the document.

Two evenings later, on August 28, we held another meeting to review the draft submitted by the committee. The fifty attorneys in attendance discussed the draft, modified it somewhat, and then adopted it unanimously. (It was later signed by sixty-five of the seventy-four nonsupervisory attorneys in the Civil Rights Division, some of whom had missed one or both of the meetings because they were out of town.)

The four-paragraph, 400-word document expressed, in painstaking language, the continuing concerns, motivations, and goals of the signatories. The last two paragraphs said:

> It is our fear that a policy which dictates that clear legal mandates are to be sacrificed to other considerations will seriously impair the ability of the Civil Rights Division, and ultimately the Judiciary, to attend to the faithful execution of the federal civil-rights statutes. Such an impairment, by eroding public faith in our Constitutional institutions, is likely to damage the capacity of those institutions to accommodate conflicting interests and ensure the full enjoyment of fundamental rights for all.
>
> We recognize that, as members of the Department of Justice, we have an obligation to follow the directives of our departmental superiors. However, we are compelled, in conscience, to urge that henceforth the enforcement policies of this Division be predicated solely upon relevant legal principles. We further request that this Department vigorously enforce those laws protecting human dignity and equal rights for all persons and by its actions promptly assure concerned citizens that the objectives of those laws will be pursued.

Why did the consciences of sixty-five federal employees compel them to protest a government law-enforcement decision? Why did sixty-five members of a profession that generally attracts the conservative and circumspect to its ranks—and reinforces those characteristics in three years of academic training—launch the first "revolt" within the federal bureaucracy?

Part of the answer lies in the fact that the new Administration was elected largely by voters who expected—and, from the rhetoric of the campaign, had every reason to expect—a slowdown in federal civil rights enforcement efforts. Those political debts ran counter to the devotion and commitment of the attorneys in the Civil Rights Division. They had labored long and hard in civil rights law enforcement, and had come to realize by experience that only unremitting pressure could bring about compliance with the civil rights statutes and the Fourteenth Amendment. Yet this conflict of commitments did not of itself lead to the revolt. There was no inevitability in the situation.

Certain other irritants played a part in creating an attitude among the attorneys which made "revolt" possible. There was Leonard himself, a politician from Wisconsin with no background in civil rights and, indeed, very little as a lawyer. He was insensitive to the problems of black citizens and other minority-group victims of discrimination. Almost from the beginning, he distrusted the attorneys he found in the Division. He demonstrated that distrust by isolating himself from the line attorneys. Still another element was the shock of his ineptitude as a lawyer. In marked contrast to the distinguished lawyers who had preceded him in his job, Leonard lacked the intellectual equipment to deal with the legal problems that came across his desk.

His handling of the Mississippi case enlarged this mood of irritation and frustration. Secretary Finch's letter—drafted in part, and approved in full, by Leonard—said that the HEW plans were certain to produce "a catastrophic educational setback" for the school children involved. Yet the Office of Education personnel who prepared the plans and Dr. Gregory Anrig, who supervised their work, and the Civil Rights Division attorneys, who were preparing to defend them in court, had found no major flaws. Indeed, Dr. Anrig, in transmitting the plans to the district court on August 11, wrote that in his judgment "each of the enclosed plans is educationally and administratively sound, both in terms of substance and in terms of timing." It was not until the afternoon of August 20, only hours before the attorneys were to defend the plans in court, that Leonard called them in Mississippi to inform them of the Administration's decision. Finally, in justifying the government's actions to his own supervisory attorneys—and in arranging that they, and not he, would inform the line attorneys of the reasons for the requested delay—Leonard could be no more candid than to say that the chief educator in the country had made an educational decision and that the Department of Justice had to back him up.

But, again, these superficial signs of malaise were not what led to the lawyers' widespread revolt. Discontent only created the atmosphere for it.

The revolt occurred for one paramount reason: the sixty-five attorneys had obligations to their profession and to the public interest. As lawyers, we are bound by the Canons of Professional Ethics and by our oaths upon admission to the bar; as officers of the United States, we were bound by our oaths of office.

Membership in the bar entails much more than a license to practice law. One becomes an officer of the courts, duty-bound to support the judiciary and to aid in every way in the administration of justice. The scope of this duty was nicely summarized by U.S. District Judge George M. Bourquin in the case of *In re Kelly* in 1917, when he wrote:

> Counsel must remember that they, too, are officers of the courts, administrators of justice, oath-bound servants of society; that their first duty is not to their clients, as many suppose, but is to the administration of justice; that to this their clients' success is wholly subordinate; that their conduct ought to and must be scrupulously observant of law and ethics; and to the extent that they fail therein, they injure themselves, wrong their brothers at the bar, bring reproach upon an honorable profession, betray the courts, and defeat justice.

The Canons of Ethics command that an attorney "obey his own conscience" (Canon 15) and strive to improve the administration of justice (Canon 29). The Canons go on to echo Judge Bourquin's words:

> No...cause, civil or political, however important, is entitled to receive, nor should any lawyer render, any service or advice involving disloyalty to the law whose ministers we are, or disrespect of the judicial office, which we are bound to uphold. ...When rendering any such improper service...the lawyer invites and merits stern and just condemnation....Above all a lawyer will find his highest honor in a deserved reputation for fidelity to...public duty, as an honest man and as a patriotic and loyal citizen. [Canon 32]

Bearing these obligations in mind, examine for a moment the situation confronting the attorneys as a result of the decision to seek delay in Mississippi.

In May 1954, the Supreme Court declared that "in the field of public education the doctrine of 'separate but equal' has no place. Separate educational facilities are inherently unequal." One year later, the Court decreed that school officials would be required to make a "prompt and reasonable start" toward achieving the Constitutional goal with "all deliberate speed." Tragically, a decade went by and little was accomplished; that was the era of "massive resistance." In 1964, the Supreme Court ruled that "the time for mere 'deliberate speed' has run out." In 1968, the Court held that school officials were under a Constitutional obligation to come forward with desegregation plans that worked, and to do so "*now*." The Fifth Circuit Court of Appeals interpreted that edict, in the summer of 1968, to mean that the dual school system, with its racially identifiable schools, had to be eliminated in all of the states within its jurisdiction by September, 1969. (Mississippi is one of those states.)

Secretary Finch's letter, besides suggesting the possibility of a catastrophic educational setback if desegregation were effected at once, spoke of the certainty of chaos and confusion in the school districts if delay were not allowed. That allegation was based upon the uncontestable existence of hostility to desegregation within the local communities. While there was a danger of chaos and confusion in the desegregation of public schools in Mississippi, the Supreme Court had ruled again and again that neither opposition to Constitutional rights nor the likelihood of a confrontation with those opposed to the Constitutional imperative may legally stand as a bar to the immediate vindication of those rights.*

Thus, while pledged by our oaths to support and defend the Constitution and bound by duty to follow our consciences and adhere to the law, we faced a situation in which the Administration had proposed to act in violation of the law. We knew that we could not remain silent, for silence, particularly in this Administration, is interpreted as support or acquiescence. Only through some form of protest could we live up to our obligations as lawyers and as officers of the United States. The form that this protest should take emerged so clearly that it then became a matter of inevitability, rather than a choice made from among several alternatives.

*On October 29, of course, the Supreme Court unanimously rejected the Administration's efforts at delay by enunciating the rule that the Constitution requires desegregation "at once." That ruling is not a part of this narrative except as it demonstrated anew that the position we had taken on the law was unassailable.

For the duty to serve the law, to promote the administration of justice, to support and defend the Constitution is more than a negative command; it is more than a "thou shalt not." It is an affirmative duty to act in a manner that would best serve and promote those interests. Thus, at the first group meeting, we immediately and unanimously rejected the notion of mass resignation because it would have served no positive purpose. It would only have removed us from association with the supporters of delay; it would not have fulfilled our obligation to act affirmatively to ensure that Constitutional rights would be protected and that the civil rights laws would be vigorously enforced.

Many of the attorneys thought that our obligation could not be met by merely drafting, signing, and delivering a protest statement. If delay for the purpose of mollifying a hostile community did not comport with the Constitution—thus impelling us to raise our voices in protest—then we were likewise duty-bound not to support the Mitchell-Finch-Leonard position through any of our official actions. The bureaucratic concept of "loyalty" notwithstanding, some of us concluded that we could not, for example, defend the government's position in court.

The question arises as to whether the action taken by the group met the burden imposed upon us by our obligations to the law and to the public interest. Did our fidelity to these obligations demand more than the soft and lofty importunings of the protest statement? Should all of the attorneys have explicitly refused to defend in court the action taken in the Mississippi case? Should the attorneys have embarked on a more direct course of action to block the government's efforts to win a year's delay for school desegregation in Mississippi?

To begin with, we were hard pressed to come up with some appropriate alternative to the protest statement as a vehicle to make the views of sixty-five people known. But beyond that, it was vitally important to preserve the appearance of dignity and professionalism if our protest were not to be dismissed as the puerile rantings of a group of unresurrected idealists who, except for their attire, bore a close resemblance to the "Weathermen" and the "Crazies." To generate the public support we thought vital to the success of the protest, we had to act in a responsible and statesmanlike manner. Furthermore, it seemed to us that the presentation of any statement signed by nearly all of the attorneys in the Division would be a remarkable feat and that a demonstration of commitment was more important than the words actually used. In our view, the soft language implied everything that a blunter statement might have said. It also had the virtue of not putting the Administration up against a wall, which might have forced it to respond with a hard-line position of its own.

Though duty and conscience compelled a protest, reason dictated the nature of that protest. We did not merely seek an opportunity for catharsis; we sought to devise a course of action that had a chance to reap a harvest of practical results. This being the overriding consideration, the attorneys chose the course of a mildly worded group statement. Other overt manifestations of disagreement were left open for individuals to pursue as they saw fit.

The group action we took—that is, the drafting and signing of the statement—was a "protest," if by that we mean a dissent from the actions of one's administrative superiors. The language of the statement did not move into the area of "revolt," if by that we mean an explicit refusal to obey the orders of one's superiors—although the statement was intended to imply that "revolt" was in the air.

Compelled by what they felt to be their obligations to the law, individual attorneys took a number of actions on their own, most of them in that murky area where there is a confluence of protest and revolt.

Even before the first group meeting, the Division lawyers assigned to Mississippi expressed their disinclination to present the government's case for delay in the district court. As a consequence, Leonard made his first appearance in a federal district court as Assistant Attorney General and argued the motion for delay himself. In mid-September, two Division attorneys (the author being one) appeared in federal courts in other school desegregation cases. When pressed by those courts to reconcile the government's "desegregate-now" position in those cases with Leonard's position in Mississippi, both attorneys said they could not defend the government's action in Mississippi.* Some of the Division's attorneys went a step further; they passed information along to lawyers for the NAACP Legal Defense Fund in order to aid their Mississippi court battle against the delay requested by the Administration. Others spoke with the press to ensure that the public was fully aware of the role political pressures had played in the decision to seek delay.

*In my situation, I was in St. Louis before the Eighth Circuit Court of Appeals, sitting *en banc* (i.e., the full seven judges of the court were present), arguing that a delay granted by the district court to an Arkansas school district for the desegregation of its high schools should be reversed. One of the judges asked whether I could assure the court that the Attorney General would not "come along and pull the rug out from under" them if they ordered instant integration. I was pressed to reconcile my request for immediate integration in Arkansas with the position taken in the Mississippi case. After the court listened to my attempts to distinguish between the two cases, one judge said it appeared to the court that the practical effect of the government's posture was that Mississippi was being given special treatment. At this point, a number of judges called upon me to state my personal views on the contradictory positions taken by the government. I responded by saying I assumed that the court knew from the press accounts of the "revolt" what the feelings were in the Division. I indicated that, as a signatory of the protest statement, I could not be expected to defend the government's action in Mississippi.

These actions, while neither authorized nor approved by the group as a whole, were individual responses to the same crisis of conscience that had led to the protest statement itself. One may have reservations as to the propriety of some or all of these acts of defiance. (Indeed, I have doubts as to whether it was proper for a Division attorney to furnish information to the NAACP after the government's action transformed the NAACP into an opposing party.) But it is important to recognize that the demands of conscience compelled more than just the signing of a piece of paper, and, in this sense, the protest was, realistically, a "revolt."

When the storm clouds first began to gather within the Civil Rights Division, the hierarchy of the Department of Justice, including the Attorney General and Leonard, reacted with a professed sense of surprise and even shock. Despite this, however, the Administration's actions were, at the outset, nothing short of accommodating.

The supervisory attorneys in the Division took the position that we had a perfect right, under the First Amendment, to meet and discuss matters of mutual concern. Prior to our second meeting, Leonard Garment, President Nixon's special consultant for youth and minority problems, let it be known through an intermediary that the Administration was likely to respond favorably to a reasonable and responsible protest. Indeed, Garment and the Deputy Attorney General, Richard G. Kleindienst, facilitated the protest by allowing us to hold our second meeting behind closed doors in the Department of Justice.

But later, when the Administration came to a fuller appreciation of the depth and unanimity of the protest, this attitude began to change.

On September 18, Leonard responded to the attorneys' statement for the Administration. We were informed that his reply was a final articulation of policy; in other words, if we did not like what we read, we should resign. The reply was curiously unresponsive. Whereas the attorneys' statement was carefully limited to questions concerning the intrusion of political influences into areas of law enforcement where only considerations of law belong, Leonard's reply outlined how the Administration would go about desegregating public schools. To this extent, the reply completely missed, or avoided, the point of the protest. We had never challenged the discretionary authority of the Attorney General and the President to determine the method by which the Constitutional imperative would be achieved. In matters where discretion is vested in the Attorney General to choose among policy alternatives, the attorneys have no business challenging his right to make the choice. But in the matter of enforcing Constitutionally required school desegregation in Mississippi, the Attorney General had no discretion. He was bound to uphold the dictates of the law, an obligation that could not be squared with the decision to seek delay.

Aside from its nonresponsiveness to the questions we had raised, Leonard's reply was disturbing on two other counts. First, it conceded, with delayed candor, that political pressures had played a role in the Mississippi decision. Second, it announced a new touchstone for civil rights law-enforcement policies: future actions would be taken on the basis of "soundness," rather than on the basis of the law. Thus, when defense appropriations are thrown into the balance, a decision to seek delay of school desegregation in Mississippi in return for the continued support of Senator John Stennis (D-Miss.) on the ABM can presumably be certified as "sound," notwithstanding its inconsistency with clear legal mandates.

The attorneys decided that we would neither accept the response nor resign. But the situation demanded further action, and we chose to reiterate our commitment to the law. On September 25, we delivered a new statement to the Attorney General and Leonard. It expressed our view that Leonard's reply "indicates an intention to continue with the policy of civil rights law enforcement toward which our August 29 statement was directed, a policy which, in our view, is inconsistent with clearly defined legal mandates."

The Attorney General's patience was wearing thin. The next day he told the press that "policy is going to be made by the Justice Department, not by a group of lawyers in the Civil Rights Division." At a news conference three days later, Leonard said that he thought the position taken by the attorneys was wrong. He warned that the revolt would have to end as of that date.

On October 1, Leonard called me to his office. He told me that he considered it to be the obligation of all of his attorneys to defend the government's Mississippi action in court. He asked whether I would be able to do so in the future. I said that I could not and would not. Our obligation was to represent the Attorney General, he said, and John Mitchell had decided that delay was the appropriate course to follow in Mississippi. I countered by explaining that I was obliged to represent the public interest in court and that my responsibility was to enforce the law. Leonard then made his attitude on the meaning of law enforcement very clear. "Around here the Attorney General is the law," he said. The difference of opinion was irreconcilable, and I was told to resign or be fired. I said I would forthwith submit a letter of resignation, and did—effective immediately. Leonard concluded the meeting by heaping effusive praise upon my abilities as a lawyer and offering to write a glowing letter of recommendation if I requested one. I did not.

Later that day, Leonard issued a memorandum that banned any "further unauthorized statement. . . regarding our work and our policies." He directed the attorneys to keep all "decisions of our work and policies within this Department."

Thus, the Administration's official attitude boiled down to an absolute ban on any further protest activity. The public was to be kept in the dark as a matter of policy. Law-enforcement decisions were to be made by John Mitchell, and the test for those decisions was to be soundness, including the relevant political considerations. The attorney's job was to articulate and defend the Attorney General's decisions in court, and this duty would apply without reference to one's individual oath of office and the dictates of conscience.

As attorneys, I and my former colleagues who still remain in the Civil Rights Division cannot accept this point of view. The Justice Department lawyer's primary obligation must be to the Constitution. That should hold true whether the attorney is John Mitchell, Jerris Leonard, or Gary Greenberg. In his role as an officer of the United States, the Justice Department lawyer represents the public interest. While Jerris Leonard equates that obligation with obedience to the President and the Attorney General, I and my former colleagues could not. The Justice Department lawyer is not hired to represent John Mitchell in court. He is hired to represent the United States.

The ban on future protest by attorneys was unreal. Indeed, it would have been self-deception for John Mitchell or Jerris Leonard to assume that the "massive resistance" in the Civil Rights Division was over. The revolt may have been driven underground, but the attorneys remain within the system. They retain their voice and their ability to influence policy from within. They continue to adhere to their view of the law, and they see their obligation to the public, and to their oath of office, as paramount. The attorneys remain a potent and organized deterrent, ready to act should there be another Mississippi.

Whether or not the revolt achieved its long-range objectives, one cannot yet judge. There are indications that in the area of civil rights, as in other matters, the Attorney General is either unaware or contemptuous of the forces that conflict with the politics of the Southern Strategy. The attorneys in the Civil Rights Division continue to take a hard line in individual cases. They assume this posture every day in the pleadings and briefs they present to the Attorney General and Leonard for approval. So long as the Administration is kept in the position of having to say no—an attitude adopted so far only in those few cases in which the political pressures were intense—it is not likely that it can effect the wholesale retreat on enforcement of the civil rights laws which it seems ready to trade for public support. But while it is vital that the revolutionaries remain within the Division, and while their presence within the system may deter future Mississippi-type decisions, there is some question whether their determination will sustain them for the balance of this Administration. If not, the prospects for even the grudging enforcement of civil rights laws are bleak indeed.

A NOTE ON THE LITIGATION*

On July 3, 1969, the Fifth Circuit Court of Appeals ordered desegregation plans submitted and put into effect by that fall in thirty-three Mississippi school districts. The Justice Department and the Mississippi Attorney General asked for a delay, arguing that the time was too short and administrative problems too difficult to accomplish an orderly implementation of the plans before September. Both the District Court and the Court of Appeals accepted this argument, and on August 28, the Court of Appeals suspended its July 3 order and postponed the date for submission of new plans until December 1. Plaintiffs in fourteen of these districts appealed to the U.S. Supreme Court. On September 5, Justice Black, as Circuit Justice, denied their request for an immediate suspension of the postponement even though he personally believed the postponement was unjustified. [*Alexander et al.* v. *Holmes County Board of Education,* 396 US 19 (1969)]. Black wrote in part:

> . . .when an individual justice is asked to grant special relief, such as a stay, he must consider in light of past decisions and other factors what action the entire Court might possibly take. . . .Although Green [*Green* v. *County School Board of New Kent* 391 US 430 (1968)] reiterated that the time for all deliberate speed had passed, there is language in that opinion which might be interpreted as approving a "transition period" during which federal courts would continue to supervise the passage of the Southern schools from dual to unitary systems. Although I feel there is a strong possibility that the full Court would agree with my views, I cannot say definitely that they would, and therefore I am compelled to consider the factors relied upon in the courts below for postponing the effective date of the original desegregation order. . . .The District Court found as a matter of fact that the time was too short, and the Court of Appeals held that these findings were supported by the evidence. I am unable to say that these findings are not supported. Therefore, deplorable as it is to me, I must uphold the court's order which both sides indicate could have the effect of delaying total desegregation of these schools for as long as a year.

When the full court heard the case on October 23, Assistant Attorney General Leonard and the Solicitor General argued again for delay. Although they insisted that the government was fully dedicated to ending segregated schools, they maintained

*Prepared with the assistance of Mike Comiskey.

that the best means of achieving this goal was to follow the Court of Appeals' order so that the school boards would have time to develop reasonable plans for desegregation. They argued that the views of the lower courts should be respected because of their "close familiarity with these cases and distinguished experience in the field." In a *per curiam* opinion decided on October 29, the Supreme Court rejected these arguments and vacated the Court of Appeals' suspension order. A unanimous Supreme Court held that all motions for additional time should have been denied. Continued operation of segregated schools under a standard of allowing "all deliberate speed" was no longer constitutionally permissible, and every school district was obligated to terminate dual school systems at once and to operate only unitary schools.

Comment

Although the initial protest was seen as an exercise of free speech, further opposition became disobedience once Leonard ordered the attorneys to cease their public protest or resign. Was Greenberg right to resign at this point? The attorneys who remained in office (carrying out their duties but still publicly opposing the policy) engaged in a kind of civil disobedience in office. Does their action meet the traditional test of justifiable civil disobedience? In what respects (if any) should that test be revised to deal with disobedience by officials?

Evaluate the actions of the attorneys whose protest went beyond signing the petition by (1) expressing opposition to the government's case in Mississippi while representing the government in another desegregation case in another district; (2) refusing to present the government's case for delay in any district; (3) giving the press inside information that might fuel public opposition to the attorney general's policy; and (4) passing information to lawyers for the opponents of the government's case. Would any other means of protest have been better?

To what extent does the justifiability of disobedience depend on assuming that the attorney general's position was against the law? Suppose (contrary to Greenberg) that the attorney general was acting within his lawful discretion but against the moral rights of some Mississippi citizens. On what basis could you defend the protest or other forms of opposition?

If you accept some part of the "revolt," ask yourself to what extent your acceptance depends on your agreement with the policy the attorneys favored. Reverse some of the facts in the case and see if your conclusions change. Consider, for example, whether (and why or why not) your judgment would change if the protest had been organized by lawyers who opposed an attorney general's effort to speed up school desegregation beyond what was required by law.

The Odd Couple

Taylor Branch

The public reaction to two whistle-blowers, Otto F. Otepka and Daniel Ellsberg, clearly illustrates the disorienting spells cast upon fervent observers by the spectacle and drama of disclosures that involve national security. Otepka violated our national security by slipping classified documents to veteran Red-hunter Julien G. Sourwine, counsel to the Senate Internal Security Subcommittee. He was fired for his transgressions in 1963, lost his position as chief of the State Department's security-evaluation division, became a martyr of the right wing, and is considered by some to be the first whistle-blower in the modern period. Ellsberg violated our national security by slipping classified documents, later to be called the Pentagon Papers, to numerous senators and newspapers. He was indicted for his transgressions in 1971, lost his security clearance at the RAND Corporation, became a martyr of the left wing, and is often considered the capstone whistle-blower of recent years.

While these two men are ideological opposites, there are unmistakable similarities between their respective exploits, viewed on a suitably high plane of reflection after all the human juices and interesting particulars have been drained away to leave the arid generalities in which lawyers earn their keep. Like colliding planets, Ellsberg and Otepka still operate by the same laws of motion in some ways, following their higher instincts regarding the public interest as they see it, exposing treachery in places of power regarding questions of life and death. These similarities suggest that anyone who wants to fight institutional rigor mortis by encouraging people to speak out from within the government is obliged by honesty and consistency to take his Otepkas with his Ellsbergs, and vice versa—to take a man like Otepka, who thought his bosses were ruining the country by being too sweet to communists everywhere, with one like Ellsberg, who thought his former colleagues were ruining the country by killing numerous people and lying about the whole affair. Regardless of who is right on the lofty world-view questions, the comments on the two men by prestigious newspapers and politicians suggest a strange kinship that bears some examination.

Otepka had been in the government for twenty-seven years and in the Office of Security for ten years when he was fired on November 5, 1963, on charges of "conduct unbecoming an officer of the Department of State." President Kennedy, setting a precedent for dealing with criticism from the right, assuaged a Calley-like tide by announcing that "I will examine the matter myself when it comes time," but he was killed before the review process got underway. It seems that Otepka, described by *Reader's Digest* as a "tall, quiet, darkly handsome man," by *Newsweek* as "a sad-eyed, introverted man," and by the *New York Times* only as "stocky," (descriptions indicative of the impact of political position on the eye), had been running afoul of important people in the Kennedy Administration for some time.

In 1955, for example, he had refused to dispense with the formalities of the security clearance procedure for Walt W. Rostow, when Secretary of State Dulles wanted Rostow on State's Committee on Operations. Subjecting Rostow to a full-dress examination of his character was considered an affront to his dignity. When President Kennedy wanted Rostow on the

---

team in 1961, Otepka again refused to waive security proceedings, which, some say, is why Rostow ended up in the White House while Otepka was at State, rather than going through the State security mill. (Apparently Otepka was a bit troubled by the internationalist leanings of Rostow's writings on economic development, hesitant to be taken in by possible ruses like Rostow's "non-Communist Manifesto," *The Stages of Economic Growth.* Also, as a professor, Rostow's commitment against communism was suspect a priori. Although subsequent events and the Pentagon Papers were to show that Otepka was dead wrong in his doubts about Rostow, some beneficiaries of hindsight have wished that he had possessed more clout in his efforts to keep Rostow out of the government.)

In addition to the Rostow rebuke, Otepka had nettled the new administration by locating and firing the State Department employee who had leaked a secret survey of U.S. prestige abroad to the Kennedy campaign forces in 1960. The survey, showing a dip in America's international esteem, was used with telling effect by John Kennedy in the campaign to show that the Republicans were blowing things in foreign policy, partly by following what seemed to be a deliberate path toward national weakness. Otepka had also been critical of the lax security procedures for the Cuba desk officers at the State Department, one of whom, William Wieland, was considered by the Republican Party almost single-handedly responsible for delivering Cuba into the enemy camp. Otepka testified before a Senate committee that he had dissented from the decision to clear Wieland without further study of his inner proclivities, and so much stir was created over Wieland that President Kennedy was forced to defend him publicly in a press conference.

Finally, Otepka had refused to waive security investigations for six men of decorum whom Secretary Rusk wanted in 1962 for the Advisory Committee on Management Improvement to the Assistant Secretary of State for International Organization Affairs. The six, which included Harding Bancroft, Sol Linowitz, and Andrew Cordier, were chosen to that august and rather useless body to study whether or not American employees of international organizations should be required to pass U.S. security investigations. The issue itself was one of some controversy, spurred on by a letter to the *New York Times* on July 30, 1962, that attacked the security regulations as a dangerous legacy of the McCarthy era. The letter came from Leonard Boudin, who is now the chief attorney for Daniel Ellsberg. In any case, Otepka refused to waive security clearances for men who were going to study the need for security clearances, and that kind of zeal to check out the private leanings of prestigious people had long since aggrieved the Kennedy Administration.

John F. Reilly, Assistant Secretary of State for Security, was so intent upon getting rid of his anachronistic subordinate, the John Wayne rough rider on the New Frontier, that he bugged Otepka's telephone and set up an elaborate system of surveillance to catch him in an act of shame that would stand up as evidence for doing him in. Reilly's sleuths scoured Otepka's "burn bag," a receptacle used to mark for instant destruction items like doodle pads and carbon paper and other parts of the afterbirth of state secrets that might leave telltale signs, and finally scored one day when they found classification stamps which Otepka had clipped from classified documents. Thus declassified informally, the documents were being sent by Otto over to old J. G. Sourwine at the Senate Internal Security Subcommittee, where they were used to help surprise and embarrass Otto's bosses regarding how lightly they took the red menace right here at home. The burn bag also contained a used typewriter ribbon, an instant replay of which revealed that Otepka had worked up a primer of questions for Sourwine that he could use to catch State Department officials in factual errors regarding the communist question.

Otto's Highest Loyalty

When the State Department used the burn bag evidence to fire Otepka, the fireworks and orations began. The *Chicago Tribune* skipped over the classified document problem to define the issue as a test of the principle of patriotism: "There can be no doubt that this case reflects an intention by the Kennedy Administration to conduct a purge of patriots." The Charleston, South Carolina, *News & Courier* agreed: "To reprimand a U.S. citizen for doing his duty would be a shame and an outrage." *Reader's Digest* later published an article called "The Ordeal of Otto Otepka," subtitled, "Why have State Department employees been using tactics of a police state to oust a dedicated security officer whose only sin seems to be loyalty to his country?", which pretty well summed up the conservative presentation of the problem. The police state argument reflects the tactical guideline that it is easier to attack the process by which the opponent operates than the substance of what he says. However, it also bore some risk of the "corner problem," by which people paint themselves into a corner through the hasty use of principles whose future application might haunt them. In this case, the *Digest*'s forthright position against a police state was quite risky. It not only made it tougher to argue in subsequent tirades that the State Department was undisciplined and namby-pamby, but it also would require a redefinition of the issues when the wiretapping and surveillance of J. Edgar Hoover came to the fore. Most conservative journals ignored the classification question and the he-broke-a-rule point of view, except perhaps to note in passing that classification was nonsense in general and that Otepka's leakage of secret material did not hurt the national interest anyway, but rather struck another blow against the pinkos in the State Department.

Meanwhile, in the Senate, members surveyed the Otepka affair and concluded that the main issue at stake was, as is so often the case, the dignity of the U.S. Senate. Conservative Senator Williams of Delaware remarked that, "In this instance, all that Mr. Otepka was guilty of was cooperating with a congressional committee." Senator Dominick of Colorado thanked Senator Dodd for having "pointed out the very difficult position Senate committees would find themselves in if it continued to be held that the executive branch could prevent any of its employees from coming before Senate committees, either by threatening them with dismissal or by verbally preventing them from testifying under that threat." Dodd, a foreign policy buff, defined the question in terms of national survival: "If those forces bent on destroying Otepka and the no-nonsense security approach he represents are successful, who knows how many more Chinas or Cubas we may lose?" But Dodd, too, was anxious about the powers of himself and his colleagues, and he entered a long discourse with Senators Strom Thurmond and Frank Lausche on November 5, the day Otepka's dismissal was consummated, which Thurmond climaxed by declaring that the Kennedy Administration's action would "nullify our system of government by tending to destroy the constitutional system of checks and balances." There was no commander-in-chief talk on that day, no talk about how the President's powers were essential to survive in a hostile international environment. The conservatives were safe from the corner problem, however, because the war in Vietnam had not yet begun. The doves in the Senate would not really discover the checks and balances principle until about 1968, leaving the conservatives ample time to switch over to the commander-in-chief line without undue embarrassment.

"Orderly Procedures Are Essential"

The liberals in the Senate were exceedingly mousy about Otepka as the supporters of the Kennedy Administration sought to ride out the storm in public silence. This does not necessarily mean that they were apathetic, for some Otepka supporters claim that there was great pressure to let the Otepka fervor die out like the groundswell for General MacArthur. Clark Mollenhoff, a straightforward, very conservative reporter for the *Des Moines Register,* made a speech about the obstacles to coverage of the case:

> I realize the broad range of direct and indirect pressures brought to discourage a defense of Otepka, for I met most of them at some stage from my friends in the Kennedy Administration. One put it crudely: "What are you lining up with Otepka and all those far-right nuts for? Do you want to destroy yourself?"
>
> There were also hints that I could be cut off from the White House contacts and other high Administration contacts if I continued to push for the facts in the Otepka case.

Liberal newspapers made slightly more noise in the dispute than their compatriot senators, and their editorial writers swept aside all the chaff about higher loyalty and patriotism and the dignity of Congress to focus on the principles at stake, with a fixity that is born of discipline. The *Washington Post,* for example, zeroed in on the law and order question, following the rule that it is always best to attack on matters of procedure: "For all of Senator Dodd's sputtering, he must know that what Otto Otepka did was not only unlawful but unconscionable as well. Mr. Otepka certainly knew this himself—which is no doubt why he did it covertly instead of candidly. He gave classified information to someone not authorized to receive it." The *New York Times* took a similar line, with slightly greater emphasis on propriety: "The disturbing aspect of this case is that both Mr. Otepka and members of the Senate subcommittee have defended their actions on grounds of 'higher loyalty'.... Orderly procedures are essential if the vital division of powers between the legislative and executive branches is not to be undermined. The use of 'underground' methods to obtain classified documents from lower level officials is a dangerous departure from such orderly procedures."

The liberal press also used words like "controversial," "McCarthyism," "tattle," and "infidelity" as often as possible in connection with Otepka's name. This strategy, following from the rule that it is often useful to adopt your opponent's principles and turn them back on him in verbal counterinsurgency, amounted to McCarthyism turned on its head, as Marx did to Hegel, or guilt by association with McCarthy. Thus, when Otepka defended himself by citing the government employees' Code of Ethics (which charges employees to place loyalty to conscience, country, and the "highest moral principles" above "loyalty to persons, party or government department"), the *Washington Post* news story stated that "the last time that issue was raised with public prominence, it was raised by Senator McCarthy in sweeping form. . . ." A *New York Times* story by Neil Sheehan in 1969 continued this theme of the beat-them-at-their-own-game campaign: "The enthusiastic pursuit of 'subversive elements' in the government loosed by the late Senator Joseph McCarthy slowed to a desultory walk in later years, but Mr. Otepka. . .did not change."

"His Trained Jackal, Jack Anderson"

Otepka returned to the public light in 1969, when President Nixon made good on his campaign promise to review the case "with a view to seeing that justice is accorded this man who served his country so long and well." The Subversive Activities Control Board seemed like an appropriate resting spot for a seasoned personnel sniffer, who could spend the rest of his days perusing political groups for loyalty blemishes. Actually, the SACB was a secondary choice for Otepka, who really wanted to go back to the State Department but was frustrated in his desire by Secretary of State Rogers, who did not want him. Senator Dirksen, claiming Otepka as a constituent and an ideological brother, suggested the SACB spot and went to work with the other conservative senators to give the board and its $36,000-a-year members something to do. They knew that Otepka would be an additional burden in the annual battle with the liberals over the fact that the SACB members are so inert that they appear strikingly like welfare recipients, at ten times the poverty standard.

The task of selling Otepka himself was undertaken with the old principles of patriotism and higher loyalty. In the Senate, the four hoariest members of the Judiciary Committee—Eastland, McClellan, Dirksen, and Hruska—assembled for a confirmation hearing to pay homage to the SACB nominee. "You have been punished because you attempted to protect your country," said Chairman Eastland to Otto, and the four senators respectfully declined to ask the witness anything other than his name.

And Senator Dodd, now deceased, led the fight on the floor of the Senate and helped organize Otepka Day, on which patriots around the nation celebrated his resurrection. Every time Senator Dodd took the floor to wax eloquent about Otepka's higher mission against international communism, he represented the largest collection of loyalty contradictions ever assembled in one place—a veritable one-man intersection of passions on the morality of exposure. For since Dodd had first praised Otepka for exposing the State Department with pilfered documents and denounced the State Department for firing the higher patriotism of Otepka, Dodd himself had been exposed for pocketing campaign contributions and other financial misdealings. While Dodd praised the patriot who exposed corruption in the State Department, he fired the infidel who exposed corruption in himself—his administrative assistant of twelve years, James Boyd. Boyd's medium of exposure, the Drew Pearson/Jack Anderson column, decided to switch in the Otepka affair—exposing the exposer, Otepka, because of his leanings to the right. In this vortex of half-hero, it was not surprising that Dodd would resort to arguments tinged with the *ad hominem,* "The press campaign against Otto Otepka has been spearheaded by Drew Pearson, the lying character assassin and his trained jackal, Jack Anderson."

In the end, however, Dodd regained the lofty, joined by the honey tongue of Senator Dirksen—who read to the Senate a moving letter from Mrs. Otepka, describing the hardships the family had faced since Otto had been demoted in 1967, while his dismissal was still being appealed, to a $15,000-a-year job that was so "demeaning" that Otto protested by taking a leave without pay and forced her to go to work to support him. What is $36,000 for a patriot, asked Dirksen and Dodd of their fellow senators, and the two crusaders went to their graves knowing that the world would be better with Otepka on the SACB. Otepka, for his part, called the Senate confirmation "my vindication," and a well-deserved one to boot, because as he later wrote, "I have disagreed only with those who quarrel with the truth. I shall continue to disagree."

Nailing Down the Case

The vindication did not come easily, for during the period when Senate confirmation was pending, the *New York Times* practiced an enthusiastic brand of beat-them-at-their-own-gamism. Reporter Neil Sheehan was dispatched to check up on Otepka's acquaintances, and began his April 4, 1969, story as follows: "A fund with John Birch Society ties has paid about 80 percent of the $26,500 in legal costs incurred by Otto F. Otepka in his four-year fight to win reinstatement as the State Department's chief security evaluator." The story went on to pin down Otepka's "ties" to the Birchers by declaring that "last summer he attended the four-day annual God, Family, and Country rally in Boston, organized by Birch Society leaders." Sheehan also tracked down James M. Stewart, chief fund-raiser of the American Defense Fund, which channeled money to Otepka's lawyers. Stewart looked and acted like a Bircher, although Sheehan wrote triumphantly that he "would neither affirm nor deny whether he was a member of the Birch Society," saying, like Pete Seeger, "I am not answering that question because it is irrelevant." Beyond such waffling on the affiliation question, Stewart further hanged himself with his reading material, because Sheehan found out, after a hardnosed inquiry, that "he does subscribe to a number of Birch Society publications."

Having established that Otepka's legal defense was being solicited by a man who might as well have been a Bircher, if he were not in fact a bona fide one, and that Otepka himself was hanging around in right wing crowds, the editorial board of the *New York Times* concluded that Otto was ineligible for membership on the SACB. According to the April 8, 1969, editorial, "The disclosure that Otto Otepka received $22,000 from a fund with extreme right-wing associations should be enough to kill his nomination to the Subversive Activities Control Board. After this, senators of conscience cannot vote to confirm Mr. Otepka in a $36,000-a-year job, where his work, if any, will be to judge the loyalty of American citizens and organizations."

Rather than taking the political view that the whole SACB concept is unconstitutional and therefore should not be supported—or the resigned view that the SACB is a useless bit of welfare, doing nothing, but that it was a shame for the President to use his discretion to appoint, in the *Times'* view, a schmuck like Otto—the editorial rested its case on the assertion that Otto was too tainted to do the job right as a subversive-hunter, and that a neutral mainstreamer would be more efficient. The *Times* thus ventured onto the turf of subversive-hunting and declared Otepka ineligible by the very standards the SACB uses to ferret out dangerous organizations.

An average newspaper might have rested its case there, but fortunately the *Times* is not an average newspaper and therefore was possessed of a "wait a minute" person on the board—the long view of responsibility. Apparently, such a person noticed that the Otepka editorial might look like McCarthyism to some readers, and told his colleagues that such an impression, left uncorrected, would be detrimental to the *Times'* historical commitment against Joe McCarthy's methods. So the argument was sealed with the addition of the following mop-up paragraph:

> The far right doubtless will cry "guilt by association," the charge made long ago by civil libertarians against the likes of Mr. Otepka, but there is a crucial difference here. Mr. Otepka's link to Birchites is no youthful indiscretion of many years ago but an activity carried on as recently as last summer.

Thus, the editorial board took the precautionary measure of protecting its flank against charges of McCarthyism by recalling the best case against old Senator Joe—the telling point about the unfairness of using "youthful indiscretions" that the *Times* itself had once made—and beating it down. This done, the *Times* had at least as strong an indictment against Otepka as McCarthy would have had against his victims if he had not ruined it all by rummaging through their old college notebooks.

The fact that Otto's sins did not fall in the "youthful indiscretion" category probably did carry some weight with a liberal readership—with people who remembered going to the verbal barricades for Alger Hiss and others like him over whether their doings on the left were permanent blemishes of character or merely the wanderings of callow youth. Those people who (perhaps for tactical reasons) had said that what was really wrong with Joe McCarthy was his reliance on outdated evidence, his once-a-subversive-always-a-subversive line, would be relieved to learn that Otepka, unlike Hiss, was still at it. "As recently as last summer," concluded the *Times,* in an apparent reference to the God, Family, and Country rally that Sheehan had uncovered. (Some sources suggest that the freshness of Otto's blight could have been established also by the subscription dates on James Stewart's magazines.) Anyone who bought all of McCarthyism except for the Senator's attacks on people for what they did in the past would be sympathetic to disqualifying Otto from the SACB for associations that persisted well into his maturity.

"His Peculiar Infidelity"

After Sheehan wrote another story for the Sunday *Times* on April 20, emphasizing Otepka's right-wing associations and his likeness to a bureaucratic version of Joe McCarthy, Senator Strom Thurmond strode to Otto's battlements by declaring on the Senate floor that the *Times* had deliberately smeared Otepka. He charged that *Times* executive editor Harding Bancroft had commissioned the Sheehan investigation in order to get even with Otto for vexations caused back in 1962, when Bancroft was examined for loyalty before going on the Advisory Committee on Management Improvement to the Assistant Secretary of State for International Organization Affairs, or ACMIASSIOA. The *Times* had no comment on this counter-smear, holding to its position that its interest in Otepka sprang from the logical force of the youthful indiscretion editorial.

Whatever the motivation behind the Sheehan articles, their spirit caught on in the Senate, culminating in Senator Stephen Young's speech against the Otepka nomination on June 24, minutes before the vote. Senator Young avowed that James Stewart, who raised money to give to Otepka's lawyer to use in Otepka's defense, had, on June 16, 1969 "attended a fund-raising party at the home of Julius W. Butler. . .an admitted fund-raiser for the John Birch Society and active in several John Birch front organizations. . . .The guests at Mr. Butler's home last week included Robert Welch, founder and head of the John Birch Society, who spoke at length spewing forth the usual John Birch lunatic obsessions. Mr. and Mrs. James Stewart, I am told, were in charge of the refreshments that were served at the meeting and were introduced to the crowd and received with applause."

All this failed, and the Senate confirmed Otepka by a vote of 61 to 28. The *Washington Post* emphasized the fidelity question in its editorial lament: "Otto Otepka's long and unfaithful service to the State Department certainly entitled him to some reward from those on Capitol Hill who were the beneficiaries of his peculiar form of infidelity." The *New York Times,* as is its custom, focused on the who-are-you question to bewail Otto as a "living symbol of some of the worst days of the McCarthy-McCarran era."

The Ellsberg Reverse

Two years after his investigation of Otepka, Neil Sheehan was ensconced in a New York hideaway as head of a *New York Times* writing team that prepared stories based on the top-secret Pentagon Papers—

slipped to the *Times*, the *Washington Post*, and other parties by Daniel Ellsberg. Rather than investigating the left wing associations of Ellsberg (such demented pariahs as Noam Chomsky, SDS leaders, the staff of the *Harvard Crimson*, and the editors of the *Washington Monthly*), or noting the glazed-eyed, Martin Lutherish manner in which Ellsberg had been starting speeches by confessing himself as a war criminal, Sheehan stuck to the material at hand and exposed the deceptions perpetrated by Ellsberg's former bosses. It is possible that Sheehan's views on classified material had changed over the two years since 1969, as had his views on the war in Vietnam. As late as 1967 Sheehan had described himself as only half way along the path from war support to war opposition in a *Times* magazine article entitled "No Longer a Hawk, But Not Yet a Dove." By 1971, he had progressed far enough to write a piece in the *Times* speculating on the possible criminality of people behind him on the path, and this progress helped both Sheehan and Ellsberg decide that the classified document issue paled in significance compared with the overriding injustice of the war.

Of course, the decisions regarding publication of the Pentagon Papers were not made by Sheehan, but by the management of the *Times* and the other papers involved. By 1971, the editors of the *Times* had decided that the real issue involved in the exposure of classified documents was not orderly procedures, but the people's right to know as embodied in the freedom of the press. A June 15 editorial in the *Times* stated that the paper felt it had an obligation to publish the Pentagon Papers "once these materials fell into our hands." The *Times*, almost as disposed to see conflicts in light of its own powers as the Senate is likely to see them turning on Senate dignity, defined its position so narrowly that it left Dan Ellsberg out in the cold. Rather than presenting the Pentagon Papers as a joint venture between Ellsberg and the newspaper, the *Times* argued that retribution for "declassifying" the Pentagon Papers was a matter between Ellsberg and the government. The *Times* took responsibility for the papers only when they fell on its doorstep out of nowhere, after which their news value required publication. (There is considerable circumstantial evidence that the *Times* was not as passive in the matter as it implies.)

The *Times*' forthright exposition of press duties in matters hot enough to be classified must have convinced Otto Otepka that *he* could in the future slip classified documents to the *New York Times* and expect to see them published. He must have been heartened by the *Times*' objectivity—by the fact that the editors took no overt political or moral position regarding why the war papers should be read in spite of their classifications, and that there was no editorial at all on the war series until the government stupidly tried to suppress it and introduced the freedom of the press question. The editors then said that the people should have a chance to read the papers, that neither the government nor the press should stand in the way of such fireside enlightenment, and that no one but the people can really tell what they mean. Otto must have reasoned that the people could also decide what his documents meant—that they could supply the political judgment if the press would only give them the chance, as the *Times* said it should.

Of course, Otto is no fool at $36,000-a-year, and he might have concluded that the *Times*' opinion on the war really did have something to do with its willingness to publish the Pentagon Papers, despite appearances and circumstantial evidence to the contrary. He might have guessed that the *Times* would not have published material like the Pentagon Papers in 1961, 1968, or even in 1969 when he joined the SACB. Even so, the newspaper's changing views on the war would also help get Otto exposure. His previous efforts to sully the reputations and political judgment of war criminals like Walt Rostow and McGeorge Bundy had not been appreciated at all, but the *Times* seemed to have come around enough on the war that it would go for a batch of documents on such men now. Both the *Times*' increasing readiness to examine the doings of war criminals and its agnosticism about the actual meaning of the Pentagon Papers should logically work in Otto's favor—and get his documents at least in the back pages. Nevertheless Otepka must fear lest the strictures about orderly procedures reappear, rising ever above the freedom of the press to leave him out in the cold again.

Despite apparent abandonment by the *New York Times,* the need for orderly procedures was identified as the central issue in the Pentagon Papers controversy by such newspapers as the Richmond *Times-Dispatch.* This journal, which had been all courage and patriotism and Paul Revere when Otto was riding, might well have dipped into the *Washington Post*'s clipping file on Otepka for its editorial on Ellsberg: "If each clerk, administrative assistant, or under secretary could ignore departmental policy and decide for himself how information should be classified, nothing would be safe." Senator Gordon Allot, a supporter of Otto, chimed in with his attention similarly focused on the rules, as he felt they should apply to the *New York Times:* "The point is that the *Times* has neither the right nor the duty to decide which classified documents should be classified in which way."

The State Department has been one of the few bastions of consistency in the Otepka and Ellsberg matters, opposing both men on the procedural grounds of loyalty and classification rules. But while the State Department has seen both the Ellsberg and Otepka cases through a monocle, most of the rest of us have been so wall-eyed on the matter that we have seen no parallel between them at all. When columnist Carl Rowan suggested that Otepka was "a sort of Daniel Ellsberg in reverse," most of his readers were shocked at the connection proposed, even a reverse one. One reader, Otto Otepka, scoffed at such a kinship in an interview with UPI reporter Marguerite Davis, who wrote that "Otepka said he gave no classified documents to newspapers but merely provided senators, at their request, with information to support his own sworn testimony." Thus, even Otto—convicted by the *New York Times* on a technicality—distinguishes himself from Dan Ellsberg on a technicality, and a misleading one at that since part of the "information" he gave the senators was a batch of classified documents.

Fiddling over Rules

It is highly ironic that the cases of these two men, whose purposes are so far apart ideologically that it is dangerous to suggest a similarity at any level, have been argued on virtually interchangeable principles. None of them—the Senate's right to know, the people's right to know, freedom of the press, orderly procedures, or national security—went to the heart of the matter. Both men made an essentially moral choice, much like the civil rights sit-ins, to take a specifically illegal step in order to dramatize an injustice that they felt transcended the classification system. Otepka thought the classification system was important, but that the Administration's spinelessness in the Cold War was more important. Ellsberg thought the classification system was important (which is why his decision produced such personal anguish), but that the history of the Vietnam war was more important in its lessons about the past and the nature of the war. Both men made their decisions in the midst of ethical conflict, and any evaluation of them demands that you take a position on why that stand is or is not worthy of support. In other words, given that it is possible for something to be important enough to transcend the classification regulations, you have to make a political judgment about the purposes of Otepka and Ellsberg.

It is well for those of us who support what Ellsberg did—because the Pentagon Papers changed some minds on the war—to keep the Otepka episode in mind. Thinking of his arguments and the furor around him should keep people from being opportunists in debate—from latching on to the arbitrary rules that pop up here and there, like prairie dogs, around any such controversy. These rules, and the sonorous platitudes that editorial writers and politicians trumpet in their names, providc ludicrously poor guidance in evaluating as serious and complex a matter as the Pentagon Papers. By themselves, the rules make an ungrounded compass, each one pointing east for Ellsberg and west for Otepka, in a spectacle that is nearly comic in the conviction people work up over principles like orderly procedures.

Arguing in support of Dan Ellsberg on the basis of the obvious weaknesses in the classification system is shaky because it runs headlong into opposite impulses regarding Otepka. But more importantly, such an argument misses the point. It is like speaking out for a sit-in because of improprieties in the disturbing-the-peace laws, when the real issue is race. Whatever positive force there is in what Ellsberg did comes from the nature of the war and what the Pentagon Papers say about the war—from political and moral issues that have no simple ground rules. When the debate strays from that central question, it loses both its passion and its logic, leaving a dusty bag of rules that Otto Otepka can use just as well. When the discussion centers on personalities and sideline skirmishes, it makes fewer converts for the antiwar message of the Pentagon Papers and Ellsberg, and thus detracts from what he is trying to accomplish.

Daniel Ellsberg and the Pentagon Papers

Fred Leebron

In 1959, Daniel Ellsberg became a defense researcher at the Rand Corporation, a California think tank largely funded by the Air Force. While at Rand, Ellsberg focused on nuclear strategy, especially the "missile gap," thought to exist after the Soviet Sputnik launch. Ellsberg possessed a top-secret security clearance and was an advisor to the Kennedy Administration during the 1962 Cuban Missile Crisis.

Ellsberg moved to the Defense Department in 1964, as special assistant in the Department of International Security Affairs (ISA). He represented the Defense Department's views at college teach-ins, where the expanding war in Vietnam was being debated.

Soon after, Ellsberg volunteered for duty in Vietnam, working with controversial Major General Edward G. Lansdale on "counterinsurgency"—the attempt to combat Viet Cong guerrillas. At first, Ellsberg was an enthusiastic participant. Yet, as he witnessed the war first-hand, he became increasingly critical. By July 1967, when he returned to the United States after a bout with hepatitis, Ellsberg "felt we were destroying the society [Vietnam] and the war must be stopped."[1]

THE PENTAGON PAPERS

During this period, the Defense Department also began to take a harder look at U.S. decision making. In summer 1967, an internal task force under the direction of Morton Halperin, Deputy Assistant Secretary of Defense for ISA, and Halperin's assistant, Leslie Gelb, launched a massive study of U.S. policies towards Indochina.

This study, later known as the Pentagon Papers, involved thirty-six scholars from the government, Rand, and several universities. It eventually produced three thousand pages of detailed analysis and history, along with thousands of highly classified documents describing U.S. intentions and policies.[2] Ellsberg himself played a key role in the project before a relapse of hepatitis forced him to play a more passive role.[3]

In December 1968, the study was finished and was sent to the Rand Corporation for storage. Although the documents were held under tight security, Ellsberg was able to gain access as part of a research project he was completing for Rand, "Lessons of Vietnam."[4]

By the following fall, Ellsberg had carefully read the 7,000-page document. His reaction:

> . . . I was in a state of mind [prior to the reading] that thought: This is terrible. The President isn't getting the truth. I had this impression "If only the Czar knew." . . . But reading 7,000 pages of the Pentagon Papers has shown me that the President of the United States is part of the problem.[5]

Ellsberg considered the study "the best we have—a good starting point for a real understanding of the war, the U.S. equivalent of the Nuremburg war crime documents."[6] He decided that leading government decision-makers needed to read the papers, to understand where the war had gone astray. He also hoped that the papers' findings would increase political pressure to end the war. With the help of his friend Anthony Russo, Ellsberg illegally made his own photocopy of the Pentagon study.

Ellsberg first contacted a leading congressional opponent of the Vietnam war, J. W. Fulbright, chairman of the Senate Foreign Relations Committee. Ellsberg informed Fulbright of the existence of the Pentagon Papers, and he gave the Senator a section dealing with the 1964 Tonkin Gulf incident.* Ellsberg asked Fulbright to make the papers public, "perhaps through full congressional release of their contents."[7]

But Fulbright hesitated. He was concerned that a controversy over the procedure of releasing classified information might overshadow debate over the content of the Pentagon study. There was also the possibility that any breach of security might be used as a basis to deny Fulbright classified information in the future.[8]

Instead of releasing the information, Fulbright put the Tonkin Gulf documents into the committee safe, and two days later petitioned Defense Secretary Melvin Laird for an official copy. After months of delay, Laird refused the Senator's request. Although frustrated, Fulbright chose not to illegally divulge the Pentagon study.[9]

Ellsberg had no better luck with two other Senate opponents of the war: George

*The controversial incident, which precipitated direct U.S. military action, occurred when North Vietnamese patrol boats apparently fired on U.S. destroyers. Within days, the Senate passed the Tonkin Gulf Resolution, which granted President Johnson broad support "to take all necessary measures to repel any armed attack against the forces of the United States and to repel aggression." Fulbright was quite bitter about Tonkin Gulf, because he believed he had been lied to and manipulated by the President.

McGovern and Charles Goodell. He even attempted, without success, to interest National Security Advisor Henry Kissinger.[10]

The Decision to Go Public

By the end of 1970, Ellsberg came to view attempts to work through government channels as futile. He felt that he needed to act more assertively on his own. First, he resigned from Rand:

> . . . In order to be able to speak freely, in a way that seemed impossible to do at Rand . . . because every time I criticized the war I caused great apprehension among my colleagues that they were about to lose their contract, and hence their jobs.[11]

Ellsberg began to consider more radical strategies. He approached several lawyers, in order to initiate "civil suits or injunctions claiming the unconstitutionality of the war," Ellsberg hoped that such court actions would provide a public forum to reveal the papers' findings. No lawyers emerged to meet Ellsberg's challenge.[12]

With all legal channels exhausted, Ellsberg turned to the extralegal alternative: direct public release of the classified documents. Ellsberg learned that an acquaintance, reporter Neil Sheehan, was preparing an article on thirty-three antiwar books for the *New York Times Book Review.* Like Ellsberg, Sheehan was a disillusioned hawk, deeply opposed to continued U.S. military involvement in Vietnam.

In March 1971, Ellsberg contacted Sheehan. Within days Sheehan traveled to Cambridge to pick up the documents. On June 13, 1971, under the headline "Vietnam Archive: Pentagon Study Traces 3 Decades of Growing U.S. Involvement," the *Times* began publishing excerpts from the Pentagon Papers.

The *Times* articles chronicled the long history of American diplomatic and military involvement in Indochina. By reproducing actual memoranda, cablegrams, and other government documents, and by including narrative analyses by the government's own historians, the *Times* revealed that four administrations had committed the United States to defending South Vietnam to a much greater extent than their public statements had indicated. The Pentagon Papers contained few conclusions that critics of the war had not already reached, but they did give official support to many of these conclusions and provided the detailed information that made these conclusions more striking.

The Reaction

Within a week, the FBI discovered that Ellsberg was the source of the leak. On June 28, 1971, a federal grand jury charged Ellsberg with "unauthorized possession of . . . documents and writings related to the national defense." The indictment also charged Ellsberg with a violation of the Espionage Act, which asserted that he had "reason to believe" that the information he leaked "could be used to the injury of the United States or to the advantage of any foreign nation."[13]

President Nixon and his advisors responded angrily to the papers' publication. They feared that Ellsberg had more damaging information to release and that Ellsberg's disclosures might inspire others to release classified materials. Perhaps more important, Nixon and Kissinger worried that the papers would undermine world confidence in the United States' ability to keep secrets: intelligence sources would be more reluctant to share information; nations would be less willing to engage in sensitive negotiations with the United States, for fear that they would read about these dealings in the morning papers. Finally, there was concern that conservatives within the government might adopt similar disclosure tactics in order to sabotage secret diplomatic overtures to the Soviets and the Chinese.[14] The White

House tightened control over classified information, enlisting a group of self-styled "plumbers" to fix "the leaks."

Ellsberg acknowledged that leaking the papers was illegal. Yet he denied that his actions undermined American security. He pointed out that he had deliberately withheld from the *Times* several sensitive documents about secret negotiations among Washington, Hanoi, and Moscow. "Obviously," Ellsberg said, "I didn't think there was a single page...that would do grave damage to the national interest, or I wouldn't have released them." Ellsberg defended his actions as "nonviolent civil disobedience...a dramatic statement of conscience."[15]

Many friends and associates offered different interpretations of his motives. Journalist Peter Schrag, for example, argued that Ellsberg was trying to establish his credibility with the antiwar movement. Others asserted it was ego that led Ellsberg to leak the Pentagon Papers. Said one friend, "One morning, Dan woke up, and saw he was forty years old and not famous yet. Turning forty does something to people, and Dan always thought he was bigger than other men."[16]

Ellsberg's former colleagues at Rand felt especially betrayed. As one bitter analyst put it, "It's just unbelievably disloyal to do what he did, an arrogant, egotistical act by a guy with a martyr complex." Rand lost control to the Air Force of all its top secret documents. Ellsberg's best friend, Henry Rowen, was forced to resign his post as Rand's president. Ellsberg defended himself against the charge that he had betrayed his friends: "After all, there were thousands of very real people—among them some of my friends—who would also be deeply affected—even killed—by a continuation of the war."

Ellsberg himself eventually escaped legal penalties for his leaking of the Pentagon Papers. All charges were dropped in 1973, when word reached a federal judge that the White House Plumbers unit had broken into the offices of Dr. Henry Fielding, Ellsberg's psychiatrist, in an effort to gather personal information about the researcher. During the 1970s and 1980s, Ellsberg continued his role as a peace activist, first against the Vietnam war and later against the development of nuclear weapons.

In September 1971, Daniel Ellsberg received the Employee of the Year Award at a dinner of Federal Employees for Peace. Inscribed on the award was the code of ethics of government service: "Put loyalty to higher moral principle and to country above loyalty to persons, party, or government department." Many scholars, government officials, and fellow citizens felt that Ellsberg had served that code well. Others believed equally strongly that he had not.

Notes

1. Frank Rich, "Q: Do the Claims of Conscience Outweigh the Duties of Citizenship, Testimony of the Witness, Daniel Ellsberg," *Esquire,* Dec. 1971, p. 293.

2. Peter Schrag, *Test of Loyalty* (New York: Simon and Schuster, 1974), p. 35.

3. Rich, p. 294.

4. Schrag, pp. 37–38.

5. J. Anthony Lukas, "After the Pentagon Papers—A Day in the New Life of Daniel Ellsberg," *New York Times Magazine,* Dec. 12, 1971, p. 98.

6. "The Suspect: A Hawk Who Turned Dove," *Newsweek,* June 28, 1971, p. 16.

7. Sanford J. Ungar, *The Papers and the Papers* (New York: E.P. Dutton, 1972), pp. 67–68.

8. Ibid, p. 68.

9. Ibid, p. 72.

10. "The Suspect," p. 16.

11. Studs Terkel, "Servants of the State," *Harpers,* 244, p. 56.

12. J. Robert Moskin, "Ellsberg Talks," *Look,* Oct. 5, 1971, p. 32.

13. "The Man Who Started It All," *Newsweek,* July 12, 1971, p. 20.

14. J. Anthony Lukas, *Nightmare* (New York: Viking Press, 1976), p. 71.

15. Moskin, p. 41.

16. Rich, p. 302.

Comment

Do you agree that "anyone who wishes to justify civil disobedience by officials must take his Otepkas with his Ellsbergs"? Both Otepka and Ellsberg broke the law and acted alone in secret and in the service of what they believed to be an important public interest. The obvious way of distinguishing the two acts of disobedience is to say that one sought the right end and the other did not. But this evades the problem of what means are justifiable when society disagrees about the ends. Consider whether these differences in the means make any moral difference: (1) releasing information to the press/to a congressional staffer; (2) extensive efforts to appeal to other officials/few such efforts; (3) some/no likelihood that release of information could endanger national security; (4) status as a private citizen/public official at the time of the act.

The State Department's view about such disobedience would treat Otepka and Ellsberg alike: both were wrong. Evaluate the best argument you can construct for this view. An alternative position that also treats Otepka and Ellsberg alike would conclude that both were justified. One difficulty with this conclusion is that neither acted publicly, as the traditional theory of civil disobedience requires. Should official disobedience always have to be public to be legitimate? Does the comparison of Ellsberg and Otepka suggest any revisions in the traditional criteria of civil disobedience if they are applied to public officials?

The Space Shuttle *Challenger*

Nicholas Carter

January 28, 1986. The space shuttle had already successfully flown twenty-four times and would that day attempt its twenty-fifth flight. To the outside observer, it seemed that NASA had, after more than a decade's work, successfully built a "space truck." After so many apparently flawless flights, there was little interest in this launch. For the first time, none of the networks was planning to show it live, despite the fact that this flight would mark the first time a civilian went to space.

At 11:30 A.M., the final countdown for liftoff had begun. It was a clear, crisp day. For those who had come to Cape Canaveral to watch, it looked like a beautiful day for flying. Many people were present but most conspicuous among the crowd gathered were the astronauts' families surrounded by photographers and NASA escorts. The astronauts' families were excited, yet nervous as well. They knew that, although the shuttle had successfully flown many times before, there were still dangers. After all, this launch had already been delayed three times. The adults had butterflies. The children, however, were full of enthusiasm. They were getting special treatment, and they knew that something very special was about to occur.[1]

In Brigham, Utah, in the shadows of the Wasatch Mountains, the engineers at Morton Thiokol who had designed the solid rocket boosters (SRBs) that lift the

Challenger into orbit gathered around a monitor to watch the lift-off. Bob Ebeling, one of the engineers, settled into his chair as Roger Boisjoly (pronounced "bo-zho-lay") walked by. Boisjoly was Morton Thiokol Inc.'s (MTI) most senior engineer on the SRB project. Ebeling went after his friend and asked him to come and watch. But Boisjoly had decided earlier he would not watch this launch attempt. In the last two days, it had grown unusually cold at Cape Canaveral. The freezing temperatures had alarmed Boisjoly and Arnie Thompson, one of the other senior Thiokol engineers. They felt that the O-rings might not be able to seal in such cold weather.

The O-rings are the bands designed to prevent pressure, heat, and flames from escaping through the SRB joints. (The SRB—there are two—provides the power to lift the Shuttle into orbit.) Upon ignition, the internal pressure in the SRB forces the walls to balloon out causing "joint rotation," and the gap the O-rings are supposed to fill becomes wider. It only takes a split second for this gap to grow too large for the O-rings to fill. After ignition, therefore, the O-rings must seal instantaneously (within the first three-fifths of a second). Otherwise, the O-rings do not seal properly, creating the likelihood of a shuttle explosion or crash.

Because the O-rings are rubber, the cold makes them less resilient and impairs their ability to move into the joints and fill them. One temperature test had been undertaken in March 1985 at Morton Thiokol to examine the effects of cold on the O-rings. Boisjoly conducted the tests which involved compressing the O-rings with a metal plate and then drawing the metal plate away slightly to see how resilient the O-rings were at varying temperatures. At 100 degrees F., the O-rings never lost contact. At 75 degrees F., they lost contact for 2.4 seconds. And at 50 degrees F. the seals never regained contact. During ten minutes at 50 degrees F., the O-rings were unable to retake their original form. For Boisjoly, this was damning evidence that the O-rings were unreliable at low temperatures.[2]

The night before the launch, Boisjoly and Thompson had strenuously argued against launching. They believed it was too risky given the cold weather at the Cape. However, they had failed to convince either NASA or their own management at Thiokol. Angry and concerned, Boisjoly did not want to watch the take-off. But Ebeling was persistent, and Boisjoly finally relented.

Ebeling returned to his chair. Boisjoly found a place on the floor in front of Ebeling. On the screen was the gleaming Space Shuttle Challenger, cocked and ready for flight. Boisjoly hoped the flight would be successful. He hoped that the O-rings would seal. But he also hoped that when NASA recovered the SRB's they would find that the first of the two seals had failed.[3] This had happened before. He also hoped that the secondary seal would show more erosion than ever before. Then perhaps someone with authority would stop the launches until the O-ring problem was solved.[4]

The final seconds elapsed. The engines ignited. The mechanized arms holding the rockets upright moved away. The shuttle rose powerfully. Smoke and dust billowed out from underneath, creating enormous rolling clouds. The shuttle kept driving toward the sky. The critical stage for the O-rings had passed. The engineers breathed a sigh of relief. Ebeling turned to Boisjoly and told him that during the lift-off he had been praying that everything would go all right. The first minute of flight passed and everything looked good. Boisjoly kept watching. Suddenly an eruption of smoke engulfed the *Challenger.* And the rocket came apart. No one, not even NASA officials, knew what had happened. Back at Cape Canaveral, the crowd was bewildered. The families drew together.

The children cried uncontrollably. There was no hope that the seven astronauts had survived.

Without a word, Boisjoly got up and went back to his office to be alone. He spent the rest of the day unable to do anything. At one point, two engineers stopped in to see if he was O.K. Boisjoly could not speak. He just nodded that he was all right. After a long moment of silence, they left. Boisjoly knew what had gone wrong. His O-rings.[5]

* * *

The day before the *Challenger* disaster, a cold front had swept down the East Coast. The temperature hovered around 31 degrees F. Through tests NASA had determined that below 31 degrees F. the shuttle would not work.[6] The launch was scheduled for the next morning and a decision had to be made in time to start the twelve hour countdown. The cold weather had not been a factor in the previous launch delays, but the temperature was dropping now and was beginning to cause concerns, especially among Thiokol's engineers in Utah. Temperatures would be below freezing that night, and the engineers estimated that the temperature at the joint where the O-rings operated would be between 27 and 30 degrees F. by late morning the next day. The temperature in the air might be 31 degrees, passable by NASA rules but alarming to the Thiokol engineers. The coldest it had ever been for a launch, in January 1985, was 53 degrees F. During that launch, Flight 41-C, one of the SRB joints experienced the worst case of blow-by in the shuttle's brief history. (Blow-by occurs when the SRB's scalding gases have "blown by" the O-ring before it has sealed, burning the grease that dresses the O-rings.) Another flight later in 1985 (Flight 41-B) also gave the Thiokol engineers pause. On the day of that flight's launch, the temperature had been in the upper 50s. But the primary O-ring at one of the nozzle joints never sealed. Fortunately, the back-up seal did, but among Thiokol's engineers there was a growing suspicion that cold weather impaired the O-rings' sealing function.

These experiences of blow-by in cold weather led Thiokol to undertake tests to determine whether cold temperatures actually affected the O-rings. The O-rings are "activated" (i.e., pushed into the gap of the joint where they seal) by the initial pressure of the hot gases inside the SRB. When the force of the gas hits the O-ring it is so powerful that the O-ring is squashed. How long it stays squashed depends on its resiliency, its ability to bounce back and resume its original shape. And, in turn, the resiliency of the O-rings depends on the temperature. The tests showed that the O-rings, which are made of hard rubber (Viton), became less resilient when cold. The hot gases blowing past the O-ring will have enough time to burn away so much of it that it will lose its ability to seal altogether.

Tests and experience were revealing that cold definitely slowed the O-rings' sealing speed. Actual launch experience showed only that the O-rings worked at 53 degrees F., and even at that temperature there had been significant blow-by. No one knew how much colder it could be before the O-rings failed. In 1985, Thiokol began running tests on the joint design but they were proceeding slowly. Other than launch experience, there was no data to prove the O-rings' resistance to cold. The one temperature test that had been run showed that cold temperature *slowed* the sealing speed.

Even though the data base was small, it was the only evidence with which to make a decision. The Thiokol engineers did not feel it was safe to fly. On January 27, they communicated their concern to NASA officials at the Marshall Space Flight Center. Marshall was the NASA center responsible for the development of the SRBs; when Thiokiol communicated with NASA, it was always through Marshall. They arranged to discuss the problem over a teleconference which they scheduled for that evening at 5:45 P.M. At this first teleconference, Thiokol engineers told Stanley Reinartz, manager of the Shuttle Projects Office at Marshall, and Judson Lovingood, his deputy, that they did not recommend launching until noon or later in the afternoon of the next day, the 28th. In order that Thiokol could "telefax" its data to Marshall officials at Marshall and at the Kennedy Space Center at Cape Canaveral, and in order to include other, responsible officials, they agreed to a second teleconference at 8:45 P.M.

At 8:45 P.M., the second teleconference began. The senior officials and key participants included, at Morton Thiokol, Utah: (1) Jerald Mason, senior vice president, Wasatch Operations; (2) Calvin Wiggins, vice president and general manager, Space Division, Wasatch; (3) Joe Kilminster, vice president, Space Booster Programs, Wasatch; (4) Bob Lund, vice president, Engineering; (5) Roger Boisjoly, member, Seal Task Force; and (6) Arnie Thompson, supervisor, Rocket Motor Cases; at Kennedy, Stanley Reinartz, and Lawrence Mulloy, manager, SRB Project (both Marshall officials); also at Kennedy, Allan McDonald, director of the Solid Rocket Motor (SRM) Project for Morton Thiokol; at Marshall, George Hardy, deputy director, Science and Engineering, and Judson Lovingood.

Essentially, there were three groups participating in the teleconference: NASA, the Thiokol management, and the Thiokol engineers. Reinartz was the senior NASA official at the teleconference. At this meeting, he had the ultimate say about whether or not to launch. He did have his superior at Marshall, the director, Dr. William Lucas. But NASA rules did not require Dr. Lucas to be present at this meeting. At Thiokol, the senior representative was Mason.

The teleconference began with Thiokol engineers explaining why they believed it unsafe to fly the next day. Their argument hinged on the evidence that the functioning of the O-rings was adversely affected by the cold. By the time preparations for the *Challenger* launch were underway, there had been several incidences of blow-by but not one on a launch where the temperature had been 67 degrees F. or higher. Boisjoly and his colleague, Arnie Thompson, presented this data and recommended not launching until the ambient temperature had reached at least 53 degrees F.

However, NASA officials challenged Thiokol's engineers and the connection they were making between O-ring failure and cold weather. Someone at NASA (and it is not known who) brought up Flight 61-A. That flight had experienced blow-by past the primary O-ring and it had been launched at *75 degrees F.* NASA could not square this evidence with that of Thiokol. Here after all was an instance where there had been an O-ring problem when it had been *warm.*

Boisjoly's explanation was that the blow-by on 61-A had been much less serious than on the colder flights. Moreover, although 61A may have seemed an anomaly, compared to the total shuttle flight history it fit a pattern. Out of twenty flights at 66 degrees F. or higher only three showed evidence of O-ring malfunction. However, all four flights launched at temperatures below 66 degrees F. showed signs of O-ring malfunction.

Nevertheless, NASA's Marshall officials disagreed with the conclusions the Thiokol engineers were drawing. When asked by Stan Reinartz for his reaction to Thiokol's recommendation not to launch, George Hardy said he was "appalled" but that if that were their recommendation, he could not override it. As for Mulloy, NASA's SRB expert at Marshall, he stated that Thiokol's data was "inconclusive" and objected to the suggestion of Thiokol's engineers that all launches be postponed until the ambient temperature reached 53 degrees F. He pointedly asked, "My God, Thiokol, when do you want me to launch, next April?" This pressure on Thiokol to reconsider the engineers' recommendation was due to NASA's preflight review process that required, as a first step, contractor approval of Shuttle readiness.

Since its first days, NASA had had a staff that made safety a priority, and the new willingness to launch at risk to human life surprised many of those who participated in the teleconference. The attitude at NASA had always required proof that it was safe to fly, until January 27, when NASA officials were demanding rock-solid proof that it was *not* safe to fly. NASA's new attitude astounded Boisjoly. It had the same effect on Thiokol's vice president of engineering, Bob Lund, who reported to the presidential commission on the shuttle accident (the Rogers Commission), "I had never heard those kinds of things (i.e., the pressure to launch) come from people at Marshall."[7] Even some NASA officials were taken aback by the unprecedented relaxation of safety standards. Wilbur Riehl, a veteran NASA engineer involved in the teleconference, wrote a note to a colleague, "Did you ever expect to see MSFC [Marshall Space Flight Center] want to fly when MTI-Wasatch didn't?"[8]

After Boisjoly and Thompson had presented their view and Hardy and Mulloy had responded, Joe Kilminster, one of the four Thiokol managers involved in the teleconference, asked for a five minute "caucus" for Thiokol to discuss the situation among themselves. All agreed, and Thiokol went off the line. Mason, the senior vice president who had said nothing up to this point, took charge in the Thiokol-only discussion. Before anyone else spoke, he said in a soft voice, intending only the managers to hear, "We have to make a management decision."[9]

Boisjoly was furious. He and Thompson were sitting at the table with the managers and had overheard Mason's comment. They knew what Mason was driving at. By speaking of "a management decision," he meant overruling the engineers. Boisjoly and Thompson, alarmed, got to their feet and tried once again to show why Thiokol must uphold the recommendation not to launch. The mood was tense as they again presented their arguments and the data. Everyone knew what NASA wanted to hear: they wanted Thiokol to give them the go-ahead. As the two engineers struggled to convince the managers, Mason looked at them threateningly.[10] It did not take long before Boisjoly and Thompson recognized that the other managers were now impervious to their appeals. They sat down. Again, Mason said in a soft voice, "We have to make a management decision," then turned to Lund. Of the four managers present, Lund had the best understanding of the O-ring problem, since he had worked most closely with the engineers in designing and developing the SRB. That afternoon, when the engineers first heard about the projected cold weather for the next day's launch, they had gone to him and explained why they felt it was unsafe to fly. In the end, they had convinced him, and he in turn had supported their conclusion in the teleconference with NASA. Perhaps more than the engineers, the pressure was on him. Now, Mason turned to him and said, in words that became famous during the Rogers Commission hearings, "It's time to take off your engineer's cap and put on your manager's cap."[11] By the end of the managers' discussion, Lund had changed his mind. He would support the managers' conclusion that, though conditions for launching were not desirable, they were acceptable.[12]

Thiokol resumed its teleconference with NASA and told NASA officials of its final decision. As was required, Mulloy asked

Kilminster to put in writing this recommendation to launch, sign it, and "telefax" it to NASA.

* * *

In the early 1970s, the Shuttle program was sold to the president and Congress in a way that led inexorably to the arm-twisting in the teleconference and the shuttle disaster the following day. On January 27, only a few individuals, particularly Mulloy at NASA and Mason at Thiokol, were responsible for the reckless decision to launch. However, blame should not be restricted to them. A brief review of NASA's history shows that Nixon's space policy and his NASA administrator, Dr. James Fletcher, were responsible for developing the shuttle despite inadequate funding. It was a disastrous course on which to set NASA for the future.

Under President Kennedy, NASA had the political and financial support to work at a safe pace, never compelled to risk astronauts' lives. Kennedy saw the exploration of space as an important race between the United States and the Soviets. He ordered Vice President Johnson to determine how the United States could beat the Soviets in space. In his report, Johnson captures the Kennedy administration's attitude toward space. He writes, "In the crucial aspects of our Cold War world, in the eyes of the world, first in space is first, period. Second in space is second in everything." [13]

With a feeling that this was perhaps the most important undertaking of his administration, Kennedy poured money and support into space exploration. There would be no cutting corners. Things were going to be done right. Most importantly, safety was made a top priority, even at the expense of losing out to the Soviets in the short run. For example, in 1961, James Webb, NASA's administrator under Kennedy (and Johnson), was under tremendous pressure to attempt to send the first human being into suborbital flight. The Soviets were on the verge of accomplishing the feat themselves, and America was ready. But Webb, like T. Keith Glennan before him, knew that safety had to come first. There was still more testing necessary to guarantee the safety of the astronaut. Not only were these NASA officials deeply concerned for the safety of the astronauts, but they also realized that NASA's long-term interests would be best served by a safe space program. NASA could survive being beaten by the Soviets but could not if it killed astronauts. The essential tests were carried out, and the Soviets did beat the Americans in the race to launch a man into space, with the flight of Maj. Yuri Alexseyevich Gagarin on April 12, 1961. But the United States followed suit thirteen days later with the launching of Alan Shepard.

The Soviet successes continued, yet NASA officials proceeded only when they knew they were ready. In August 1961, the Soviets successfully completed a manned seventeen-orbit mission. Six months later, John Glenn became the first American to orbit Earth. With Kennedy's wholehearted support, NASA embarked on plans for a manned lunar mission.

With testing and the oversight of contractors' work a top priority, the moon mission proceeded cautiously. On Sunday, July 20, 1969, the lunar race ended when the United States successfully landed Apollo XI on the moon, thereby fulfilling Kennedy's promise of landing a man on the moon within the decade. Though the Apollo program spent more years under Johnson's watchful eye than under Kennedy's and the moon landing actually occurred under President Nixon, everyone knew that NASA belonged to JFK. It had been his leadership and support that had created the lunar attempt.

Nixon, more than anyone else, understood that NASA was still Kennedy's agency. Realizing he would get very little political mileage from another space program and recognizing that after the lunar landing the public's interest in space had at least been temporarily satisfied, Nixon did very little for the space agency.[14]

Three options were presented to his administration concerning America's future in space. Option A was presented by a team of NASA scientists perhaps most responsible for the success of the lunar landing. They wanted to develop (1) an economical shuttle to ferry people to and from (2) a space station from which (3) manned and unmanned flights to Mars would proceed. Option A would have cost about $10 billion a year. The idea of a manned flight to Mars appealed to many, and Spiro Agnew actually predicted that Nixon would opt for it. Option B called for an end to manned spaceflight by 1974 and provided a paltry $3 billion for research into possibilities for future manned or unmanned programs. Option C, presented by NASA Administrator Thomas Paine, was an enormous and totally reusable system. To develop this version of the shuttle would cost about $10-$12 billion. In the end, Nixon chose Option B. It was the least he could get away with politically without killing manned spaceflight completely. Paine resigned when he realized that he would not be able to win from Nixon the kind of financial support he felt NASA should have.[15]

In response to the same budgetary constraints, George Low, acting as NASA administrator until another could be named, forwarded a cheaper plan than Paine's. Because Low cared so strongly about keeping the manned spaceflight programs alive, he went to all lengths to sell the shuttle to the Nixon administration. Though Paine's team had estimated that the cheapest shuttle system that could be developed was $10-$15 billion, Low said it could be done for $8 billion.[16]

Dr. James Fletcher was appointed NASA administrator in 1971. An ambitious man, Fletcher wanted another big, Apollo-like project for NASA to which he could attach his name. Option B did not give Fletcher the funds necessary to develop a manned space shuttle, but he decided to develop the shuttle anyway. Where former NASA administrators demanded the best, Fletcher was willing to proceed with whatever he could get. He continued to prune the shuttle budget, cutting costs that eroded safety margins.[17] Because it was less expensive, NASA agreed to use solid fuel rockets, not previously used by NASA in manned flight because, once ignited, they cannot be shut down. Thus in an emergency they leave the astronauts helpless. Another cost compromise was the elimination of an escape system for the astronauts.

In the end, Fletcher pared the shuttle cost projections down from $8 billion to $5.5 billion plus $1 billion for contingencies. The aggressive Office of Management and Budget (OMB), under the leadership of George Schultz, forced Fletcher back down to the $5.5 billion level.

But some former and current NASA officials recognized immediately the impossibility of putting the shuttle together on Fletcher's budget. John Naugle, who had been at NASA under Webb and was there under Fletcher, knew that the shuttle could never be self-financing as Fletcher predicted. He felt Fletcher was deceiving the public, and he believed that Fletcher should have told Nixon that the shuttle should operate as a purely public, R & D program and assume great costs, or that the United States should get out of manned spaceflight altogether.[18] Dr. Seamans, one of the top three NASA officials under Kennedy and secretary of the Air Force under Nixon, knew that NASA needed much more than Fletcher was projecting to develop the shuttle properly. He sensed that Fletcher was distorting the figures because he had a personal stake in the shuttle, wanting to oversee his own great space program.[19]

Fletcher sold the shuttle to Congress based on the idea that it would be "operational," that it would cover its costs by trucking satellites into space for the military and others. The promises he made in the early 70s were so unrealistic that the shuttle never approached being truly "operational." Much of Fletcher's sales pitch came from a study by Mathematica, a research firm commissioned by NASA to study the shuttle's cost effectiveness. Fletcher used the study to argue that the shuttle could pay for itself if it flew at least thirty times a year.[20] At that launch rate, Fletcher predicted that a pound of payload would only cost $100 and would be commercially competitive. But cost overruns were tremendous. According to the Congressional Budget Office, the cost per pound of payload, adjusted for inflation, is now $5,264 if all the development costs are included. If only the current per flight operational costs are considered, then the price per pound is $2,849.[21]

According to the General Accounting Office, Dr. Fletcher gave "misleading" and "overly optimistic" accounts of projected costs. He had predicted that the cost per launch would be $10.45 million. Not including all the construction costs, the cost today (adjusted for inflation) is $151 million ($279 million including construction costs).[22] Launch operations cost almost fifteen times more than originally predicted.

Boosting the launch rate was an ongoing demand at NASA. Officials at NASA understood that only a higher launch rate would quiet their critics in Congress and the Pentagon, and only a higher launch rate would enable the shuttle to compete with the unmanned Ariane, a French rocket able to send commercial satellites into space cheaply. In March 1985, James Beggs, administrator of NASA, said, "The next eighteen months are very critical for the shuttle. If we are going to prove our mettle and demonstrate our capability, we have got to fly out that [flight] manifest."[23] The goal for 1986 was awesome, if not crazy—twenty-four flights.

The impossible promises that Fletcher made in the early 70s thoroughly affected NASA and the shuttle program. NASA had agreed to let economics be the measure of success. If it could produce a cost-efficient space craft, then and only then would the critics on Capitol Hill be silenced. Technological achievements like sending human beings to the moon or building a reusable "space truck" were no longer enough to satisfy politicians or the public.

In order to succeed, the shuttle had to stay within budget, which meant that many corners had to be cut. Where money was saved, safety was spent. NASA cut back on the shuttle's design. In awarding contracts, NASA gave first priority to cost, not quality. For example, in choosing among design proposals for the SRB, NASA's Source Evaluation Board passed over the monolithic, unsegmented aerojet design that was judged to be safest. The monolithic SRB avoided the problems of joints where pressure and hot gas might escape, but it was too costly.

Moreover, there were cutbacks in testing and NASA oversight of contractors. Between 1974 and 1977, at least five studies found that NASA was shirking its responsibility to test shuttle parts under construction. One study, conducted by thirty-five aeronautical and space experts, found that testing was being "highly compressed"—from sixteen months to three—and called for more testing.[24] But NASA said that more testing would not be "cost effective." Over the course of the shuttle's development, more than half a billion dollars were cut from testing. Furthermore, the number of NASA officials responsible for checking the work of the contractors declined precipitously. NASA oversight of contractors practically stopped altogether. During the Apollo era, the Johnson Space Flight Center had twenty-eight contract monitors, whereas in 1980 it only had two.[25] Dangerously flawed parts went unnoticed. At one point, it was discovered that JetAir, a subcontractor of Rockwell, had doctored X-rays revealing cracks and faulty welding in the Orbiter.[26] Many hands were involved in putting the shuttle together, and NASA had lost control of them and the quality of their work.

Given the lack of funds, did NASA have any alternative to compromising its safety standards? Yes, NASA could have exited from manned spaceflight altogether or at least not committed to a completely manned space program like the shuttle. Except for the publicity that manned spaceflight receives and, consequently, the financial support that accrues to NASA from that favorable coverage, there is apparently very little that people can do in space that could not be done for much less by unmanned programs. Important groups outside NASA were, in fact, making this argument when the shuttle was still on the drawing board. Dr. Seamans, secretary of the Air Force at the time, did not support the idea of a manned shuttle. In his mind, it was unnecessary to have people aboard with all the requisite life support systems just to put satellites into orbit.[27] Even Mars and deeper space can be explored without human beings. Currently, in fact, the Voyager, an unmanned space vehicle, has far surpassed the shuttle in important discoveries.

But NASA officials, especially Fletcher and Low, wanted manned flight. And there were signs that the public wanted it too. Nixon apparently agreed to the shuttle idea primarily because he did not want to be remembered as the president who killed manned spaceflight. Therefore, it was political obstacles and ambitions among NASA Administrators that brought about the decision to man the shuttle.

* * *

With all the cost overruns and the shuttle delays, the pressure to live up to that "manifest" to which James Beggs had referred became intense. It was this pressure, constantly in the minds of every NASA manager, that led to risk-taking. With the goal set for twenty-four flights in 1986, the pressure had reached a new high. Even if no one talked explicitly about it, everyone felt it. The contractors, like Thiokol, knew that NASA did not want to hear the recommendations that a launch be delayed, especially if the delay were indefinite as it probably should have been with the O-rings.[28] And NASA managers knew that their superiors did not want to hear that recommendation from them either. In this kind of cover-your-eyes-and-go-for-it setting, loss of life was almost inevitable.

Because Fletcher had accepted an inadequate budget for the shuttle, he deserves much of the blame for risks taken later. However, he is not culpable alone. There were outside observers who were aware of potential dangers but remained silent. The General Accounting Office, a congressional watchdog agency, openly warned of safety compromises that NASA was allowing. But because of the success of the Apollo program, neither Congress nor the press paid much attention.[29] There were also NASA insiders who had access to reports disclosing mechanical flaws in the shuttle. At one time or another, engineers at NASA and at Morton Thiokol urgently warned about weaknesses in the O-rings' design. For several years, NASA engineers at Marshall expressed their concern over the O-ring design. In 1978, John Q. Miller, Marshall's chief of the SRB project, wrote George Hardy that the O-ring design might allow hot gas leaks that could result in "catastrophic failure." But Hardy did not respond to these warnings. He did not question Miller or the other engineers about their concerns, nor did he press

Thiokol to address the design problems.[30] By 1981, NASA's engineers had stopped raising concerns about the O-rings even though no design changes were ever made.

And at Morton Thiokol, after flight 41-C where there had been substantial blow-by on one of the primary O-rings, the engineers began seriously to express their fears about the O-ring design. In the year preceding the *Challenger* disaster, the engineers' worries continued to escalate. A task force was established by Thiokol to improve the O-ring design. By mid-summer 1985, some of Thiokol's engineers were deeply concerned. The management had been dragging its feet on the redesign effort and not assigning as many people to the task force as were needed. The engineers stopped mincing words. In one memo to the management, Bob Ebeling, one of the task force engineers, expressed how urgent it was that the task force become Thiokol's first priority. He wrote, "HELP! The seal task force is constantly being delayed by every possible means. We wish we could get action by verbal request [they had been frequently going to one of the managers, Joe Kilminster], but such is not the case. This is a red flag."[31]

Roger Boisjoly also wrote a memo: "This letter is written to insure that management is fully aware of the seriousness of the current O-ring erosion problem in the SRM joints from an engineering standpoint.... The mistakenly accepted position on the joint problem was to fly without fear of failure and to run a series of design evaluations which would ultimately lead to a solution or at least a significant reduction of the erosion problem. This position is now drastically changed as a result of the SRM 16A nozzle joint erosion [Flight 41-B] which eroded a secondary O-ring with the primary O-ring never sealing. If the same scenario should occur in a field joint (and it could), then it is a jump ball as to the success or failure of the joint because the secondary O-ring cannot respond to the clevis opening rate and may not be capable of pressurization. *The result would be a catastrophe of the highest order—loss of human life.*"[32]

Despite the engineers' appeal to Thiokol's management, the seal redesign effort continued to be neglected. After the accident, the redesign effort was finally made first priority at Thiokol. It went on day and night, and in two and a half months a solution had been found. Before the accident, only eight people out of an employee pool of two thousand had been assigned to the SRB redesign task force. With such a small task force, it would have taken two and a half years to come up with the same solution they found in two months of aggressive research.[33]

Knowledge of the dangers did exist. Still, the pressures to make the shuttle "operational" were such that both Marshall officials and Thiokol managers continued to recommend launching. Everyone knew that the lives of the astronauts and their families were being jeopardized, but the men in power pressed on willing to take the risks. The end result was a tragedy that could have been avoided.

EPILOGUE

The official Rogers Commission report blamed NASA's system of communication for the shuttle accident. It concluded that sufficient information about the O-ring problem existed before the accident to have prompted an indefinite launch delay.[34] That the launches continued was due, the commission found, to mid-level NASA managers deciding independently that continuing the flights would not endanger the lives of the astronauts. Despite serious questions raised by Thiokol's engineers, these managers (such as Mulloy and Reinartz) never informed their superiors of the gravity of the engineer's concerns. The commission was "troubled by what appears to be a propensity of management at Marshall to contain potentially serious problems and to attempt to resolve them internally rather than communicate them forward."[35] The commission also concluded that NASA had made it clear that they did not welcome shuttle delays, thereby pressuring contractors to override internal dissent and approve flight readiness.[36]

However, due to the candid testimony of two Thiokol employees, Boisjoly and Allan McDonald, certain individuals were blamed, unofficially at least, for the accident. Mulloy seemed particularly responsible, especially after letting Morton Thiokol know how he was unhappy with the engineers' recommendation not to launch. He appeared to have pressured Thiokol into reversing that recommendation. Though NASA offered to continue his employ, he went into early retirement.[37] At Thiokol, the CEO blamed Mason for having "risked the company."[38] Mason also retired early. Kilminster was transferred out of all space programs but continued his job at Thiokol.

Boisjoly and McDonald were demoted for publicly speaking against the company's pro-launch decision. After Boisjoly testified before the Rogers Commission, a senior Thiokol official chastised him for having aired the company's dirty laundry. Sure, tell the truth, he was told, but put the company in a favorable light too.[39] Boisjoly was kept on the payroll but was stripped of any responsibility in the SRB redesign effort.

After Chairman William Rogers vigorously protested the demotion of the two whistle-blowers, Thiokol quickly responded and promoted McDonald to head the SRB redesign effort. Boisjoly, however, was so stricken by a sense of responsibility for the lives of the astronauts that he could not continue to work and took a leave of absence. For months following the accident, he could not sleep and began to take medication. Finally, a year after the accident, he was well enough to speak publicly about his experience, which he has been doing now for over a year. He states that for personal reasons he will never be able to work on the shuttle again.

Four out of seven of the astronauts' families settled with the U.S. government for, unofficially, more than $750,000. Two of the families have filed suits against NASA, one for $15 million. A third filed suit against Thiokol. As of August 1987, none of these suits had been settled.

Notes

1. Malcolm McConnell, *Challenger: A Major Malfunction* (Garden City, N.Y.: Doubleday, 1987), 207–49.
2. Roger Boisjoly, "Company Loyalty and Whistleblowing: Ethical Decisions and the Space Shuttle Disaster" (videotape), Jan. 7, 1987.
3. Each joint had a primary and a secondary seal.
4. Interview with Boisjoly, Fall 1987
5. Boisjoly video and Boisjoly interview.
6. McConnell, 165.
7. *Report of the Presidential Commission on the Space Shuttle Challenger Accident* (Washington, DC, June 6, 1986), Vol. I, p. 94.
8. McConnell, 198.
9. Boisjoly interview, and McConnell, 199.
10. Boisjoly interview.
11. *Report of the Presidential Commission,* Vol. I, 94.
12. *Report of the Presidential Commission,* Vol. I, 97; and McConnell, 200.
13. Joseph J. Trento, *A Prescription for Disaster* (New York: Crown, 1987), 36.
14. Trento, 84–87.
15. Ibid., 93–94.
16. Ibid., 102–3.
17. Fletcher's soft stand on safety is a point Trento makes throughout *Prescription for Disaster.*
18. Trento, 118–21.
19. Ibid., 112–13.
20. McConnell, 41.
21. Stuart Diamond, "NASA Wasted Billions, Federal Audits Disclose," *New York Times,* 12 April 1987, 1, 1:1.
22. Ibid.
23. McConnell, 62.
24. Ibid.
25. Ibid.
26. Ibid.
27. Trento, 112.

28. "The [Rogers] Commission concluded that the Thiokol management reversed its position and recommended the launch of 51-L [the *Challenger*], at the urging of Marshall and contrary to the views of its engineers in order to accommodate a major customer." *Report of the Presidential Commission,* Vol. I, 104.

29. McConnell, Ch. 6, "The Spellbound Press."

30. *Report of the Presidential Commission,* Vol. I, 123–24.

31. McConnell, 180.

32. *Report,* Vol. I, 139 (emphasis added).

33. Boisjoly interview.

34. *Report,* Vol. I, 148.

35. Ibid., 104.

36. Ibid.

37. The Associated Press, "Ex-Shuttle Rocket Chief Quits Space Agency," *New York Times*, 17 July 1986, V, 19:1.

38. Boisjoly interview.

39. Boisjoly video.

George Shultz and the Polygraph Test

Don Lippincott

On December 19, 1985, Secretary of State George Shultz, widely considered to be a politically discreet team player (unlike his predecessor, Alexander Haig), stung the administration when he publicly threatened to resign. This action was not based on a substantive disagreement over foreign policy. Rather, Shultz was demonstrating—in no uncertain terms—his strong opposition to an administration plan to require polygraph (lie detector) tests for all government officials with access to "highly classified information." Roughly 182,000 government employees—including some agency heads like Shultz—were to be affected by this plan, including about 4,500 members of the State Department. In remarks to reporters in the department, Shultz proclaimed that his first lie detector test would be his last, adding, "The minute in this government I am told that I'm not trusted is the day I leave."[1] (See Exhibit 1.)

BACKGROUND: THE REAGAN ADMINISTRATION AND THE POLYGRAPH

From the outset, the Reagan Administration has been strongly interested in crushing espionage activities within the U.S. government. While the problem has plagued governments since time immemorial, a rash of recent revelations about spying in the United States has alarmed many Reagan officials as well as much of the public. Among the recent examples of espionage within the government was the late 1983 arrest of a California engineer accused of selling secret defense papers to the Poles. (The engineer's wife, who worked for a California company doing military research, had security clearance.) At the end of 1984, an ex-CIA employee was arrested on the charge of spying for Czechoslovakia. Then, in what the *Washington Post* termed "the year of the spy," 1985 witnessed an unprecedented wave of spying accusations within the U.S. government. In June, the FBI nabbed three members of the Arthur Walker family, who had apparently been passing important naval intelligence information to the Soviets for years. According to one administration official, these arrests were only "the tip of the iceberg."[2] This claim was substantiated in late November when arrests of four alleged spies in five days grabbed the nation's attention.

Former Ambassador to the United Nations Jeane Kirkpatrick offered her views on the problem of espionage in an editorial in the *Washington Post*:

> Whether the spy works for money (as the Walker ring apparently did) or for love of another country or ideology (as the Rosenbergs did), spying can seriously damage national security. The Walkers, for example, have apparently compromised our communication system and endangered aspects of our defenses.
>
> That the Soviet Union encourages such betrayals of national security is beyond reasonable doubt. They also rely on spying to promote development. Documents captured when the French government broke a major spy ring two years ago (and expelled 47 Soviet officials) confirmed that the Soviets rely heavily on planned theft and stolen technology and field large networks of spies to steal the desired technology.
>
> Spying is big, serious, dirty business and does us real harm. Recent disclosures suggest, moreover, that it may be increasing.[3]

Whether spying has been increasing or whether there is simply better counter-espionage today is a debatable issue. What's clear is that the wave of spying revelations has whetted the appetite of certain administration officials—such as CIA Director William Casey—for tighter security controls. The polygraph has been one of his favorite tools. The CIA and National Security Agency use the device to screen the backgrounds of all prospective employees, with random examinations given subsequently. The State Department does neither.

On another front, the administration has proposed on more than one occasion that polygraphs be used to help prevent leaks from government employees to the press. Ex-Ambassador Kirkpatrick offers her views on how leaks have affected the Reagan Administration:

> For five years leaks—of information and disinformation—have plagued the Reagan Administration, embarrassing the government, complicating policy-making and creating international problems. Leaks have been used at high, high levels of government to undermine policy rivals and advance personal ambitions. They have caused real damage to policies and policymakers. They have undermined our government's dignity. They have called into question the president's competence.[4]

Throughout the Reagan years, Congress has been decidedly more hesitant about supporting government use of polygraphs (although it did authorize a pilot Defense Department polygraph clearance program—for 3,500 employees and contractors in 1986 and twice that number in 1987—in the summer of 1985). For instance, when President Reagan sought approval of an order to require government employees to submit to the polygraph during investigations of leaks to the media, Congress blocked the move. Moreover, during the 99th Congress, Congress was also "seriously considering a [bill] to ban the use of polygraphs in the private sector."[5]

While admitting the seriousness of the threat to national security posed by espionage, polygraph opponents argue that the tests are an invasion of privacy as well as a form of harassment. Opponents also contend that the polygraph is hardly an infallible instrument. They have argued that not only do polygraphs often "miss" known spies—such as Larry Wu-Tai Chin, an ex-CIA employee who spied for China for more than thirty years—but they also intimidate and run the risk of jeopardizing the careers of innocent people, who are not trained to react with the icy calm (or feigned emotions) that CIA and KGB "spooks" utilize to beat the system. They also point out that the results of polygraphs "are not used as evidence in Federal court... because of the[ir] notorious unreliability."[6] An article in the *National Journal* entitled "To Tell the Truth," discussed some competing views concerning the reliability of polygraph tests for pre-employment screening:

Use of the test for [employment] screenings raises the loudest objections from civil libertarians. One objection is that "there is little research or scientific evidence to establish polygraph test validity in screening situations," as the congressional Office of Technology Assessment (OTA) concluded in 1983. The CIA and NSA, though, say that despite its limitations in actually finding liars, the test often compels confessions.[7]

DEJA VU

The Reagan administration had discussed instituting more widespread use of polygraphs, prior to issuing its new directive in late 1985. On at least one occasion, newsleaks had been the major impetus for the discussion. The *Washington Post* sketched an interesting vignette of the earlier episode:

Shortly before noon on Sept. 14, 1983, [White House aide Michael] Deaver entered the Oval Office to find Edwin Meese III (then White House counselor) and William P. Clark (then national security affairs adviser) in an intense and apparently confidential conversation with Reagan about a paper they wanted him to sign. The paper, Deaver discovered, would have authorized the FBI to use polygraphs to investigate top officials who were privy to highly classified decision-making about Lebanon.

Two days earlier, NBC News had reported that Reagan was secretly considering air strikes against Syrian positions in Lebanon where Marines were being shelled heavily. Meese and Clark were furious at the leak and determined to identify the culprit.

Deaver described the Oval Office scene he had encountered to James A. Baker III (then White House chief of staff) while the two were driving to lunch. According to a later account, Baker was so alarmed that he ordered the car back to the White House, where Baker and Deaver barged into a luncheon meeting of Reagan with Shultz and Vice President Bush.

Shultz and Bush were startled to learn of the plan and like Deaver and Baker, they criticized any requirement that top officials submit to polygraphs. If asked to prove his veracity with a polygraph, Shultz declared, "Here's a secretary of state who isn't going to stay."[8]

The Meese-Clark paper ultimately went unsigned by the president.

AUGUST 1985: DIRECTIVE 196

The most recent directive emerged from the administration's National Security Planning Group (NSPG), a small National Security Council (NSC) committee chaired by National Security Adviser Robert McFarlane and including Shultz, CIA Director William Casey and Defense Secretary Caspar Weinberger. In an August committee meeting about possible countermeasures to spying, Casey had been the chief advocate of employing the polygraph tests, which were already in wide use at the CIA and National Security Agency. Casey apparently claimed that it was vital for national security to monitor all agency personnel handling highly classified information. According to the *Washington Post*, at this meeting:

Shultz reportedly expressed his deeply felt view that what he termed "so-called lie detector tests" are misleading and ineffective, and that their imposition on public servants in non-secret jobs carries the message that their loyalty and character is in question."[9]

The meeting apparently produced no decision on the Casey recommendation. A subsequent article reported that the defense secretary had experienced a change of heart after learning of Shultz's position:

Weinberger was "no big fan" of lie detectors, but when he discovered Shultz's opposition, the defense secretary "fell in love with polygraphs," one involved official sa[id].[10]

THE PRESIDENT SIGNS

On November 1, President Reagan signed National Security Decision Directive 196, affirming the NSC committee recommendation that:

the U.S. government adopt, in principle, the use of aperiodic non-lifestyle, CI (counter-

> intelligence)-type polygraph examinations for all individuals with access to U.S. government sensitive compartmented information (SCI), communications security information (COMSEC) and other special access program classified information.

Though a member of the committee, Shultz only learned of the decision when the White House mailed him a copy of the five-page directive shortly after it was signed. He was not pleased. According to one aide, who informed the secretary that certain State Department officials would threaten to resign if they were forced to submit to the polygraph, Shultz tersely replied, "And I'm one of them."[11]

George Shultz

An economist by trade, the sixty-five-year-old Shultz left the deanship of the University of Chicago's School of Business to join the ranks of government service as Nixon's secretary of labor in 1969. Subsequently, Shultz served as the budget director (1970-72)* and secretary of the treasury (1972-74). When Shultz returned to government in 1982 to replace the resigning secretary of state, Alexander Haig, he was president of Bechtel, Inc., a San Francisco-based engineering firm. He was also teaching part-time at Stanford University.

In addition to having a reputation as a consummate team player, George Shultz is widely regarded as a man of high integrity with a "deep sense of personal rectitude."[12] A significant portion of this assessment is based on Treasury Secretary Shultz's much-publicized refusal to provide President Nixon with information on the tax returns of certain individuals on Nixon's enemies' list.

As far as President Reagan was concerned, the generally even-tempered Shultz was a welcome relief from the combative, ambitious Alexander Haig. Ex-White House aide Michael Deaver described the president's behavior during an Oval Office meeting with Shultz several months before he joined the Reagan team:

> As I watched, the president just visibly relaxed with Shultz. He has a marvelous staff style that appeals to Reagan, and he is a tough guy, a good interlocutor and a consummate government official. It was clear the president was very comfortable with Shultz![13]

On substantive matters, Shultz's record as Reagan's secretary of state had been relatively smooth up to the end of 1985—the only major foreign policy failure being Lebanon and especially the terrorist killing of 245 U.S. marines there in 1983. At the same time, critics claimed that his tenure had no major foreign policy successes—e.g., no breakthroughs in the Middle East or Latin America or with the Soviet Union. Former Undersecretary for Political Affairs Lawrence Eagleburger compared him to some highly respected predecessors: "There is a bit of the moralism of [John Foster] Dulles in Shultz. And he is solid and steady with a style reminiscent in some ways of [Dean] Rusk.... It's possible to say someone was a good secretary of state because he took events and prevented them from making things worse." Another government official added: "Shultz is very self-possessed. He likes power, he likes to run things and he likes to have his own way."[14]

Reagan Plan Revealed

Information about the new polygraph requirement was shielded from the public until the *Los Angeles Times* broke the story about the directive on December 11, a week before Shultz's outburst. The *Times* revealed that the president's directive would require thousands of federal employees and contractor personnel with access to highly classified information to submit to lie detector tests on an irregular and random basis. The White House responded to the

*Shultz's deputy at the budget bureau was Caspar Weinberger, a long-time competitor if not adversary.

story the next day through press spokesman Larry Speakes, who announced that the president was attempting to address espionage and unauthorized information disclosures (leaks). While the directive was designed to target "a selective number of individuals who have highest levels of access" to secret information, according to Speakes, he denied that the action was related to recent and highly publicized revelations about spy activity within the U.S. government. Speakes also emphasized that "the new directive would be used mainly for counterespionage rather than for trying to identify officials who help journalists."[15] When asked by reporters for copies of the directive, Speakes claimed he could not provide it because the directive was itself a classified document. As the *New York Times* reported, "[T]his produced a round of laughter..., since news of the directive had already appeared in the *Los Angeles Times*."[16]

While these revelations were coming out in the national press, George Shultz was in Europe visiting several heads of state and foreign ministers. When reporters there questioned him about his opinion on the White House directive, Shultz refused to discuss the matter on the grounds that it was a domestic policy issue and should only be discussed when he returned to the United States.

Shultz Returns

Only hours after his return to Washington from Europe on December 18, Shultz requested—and got—a private meeting with President Reagan. Apparently this meeting neither changed the nature of the directive nor mollified Shultz. The next day Shultz went public with what amounted to his ultimatum. After the secretary made clear his "grave reservations," one senior White House official told the *New York Times* that it was nonetheless unlikely that Shultz would resign, adding, however, that, "This is one thing that sends him through the roof. It touches a nerve."[17]

Reacting only hours after Shultz's strong criticism of the polygraph, the CIA issued a statement claiming that "selective, careful use" of polygraph tests was essential for those "branches of government" (i.e., the State Department) that received classified information. (See Exhibit 2.) The CIA spokesman also pointed out that CIA Director "Casey and all his predecessors had voluntarily taken polygraph tests" to set an example for their employees. In an interview on television, Caspar Weinberger said that taking the test "wouldn't bother me a bit."[18]

The White House Retreats

The following afternoon, after another meeting between the secretary and President Reagan, the White House issued a statement which said that the president believed polygraph tests to be "a limited, though sometimes useful tool when used in conjunction with other investigative and security procedures in espionage cases." The statement added that the secretary "fully shares the president's view of the seriousness of espionage cases and agrees with the need to use all legal means in the investigation of such cases."[19] In effect, the White House was backing down from its earlier position, expressed in NSDD 196, that increased and widespread use of polygraphs was necessary and should be implemented. Nonetheless, CIA Director Casey and other secret agency heads could still use the tests as a screening test for employment.

After his meeting with Shultz, the president, when asked if the secretary would have to take a lie detector test, responded, "Neither one of us are going to," adding, "I just explained to him that what he read in the press in Europe was not true."[20] A State Department official told the *New York Times* that the White House statement indicated that the president and Shultz agreed that such "tests should be limited to cases of suspected espionage," adding that the secretary "believed his public comments had helped modify the president's position."[21]

Postscript

Three days later, the Christmas Eve edition of the *Washington Post* ran a front-page article under the headline, "President Said to Be Unaware of Sweep of Polygraph Order." In this article, "administration sources" claimed that the president "was not fully aware of the sweeping nature" of the directive in question, nor were several other key administration figures, including Chief White House Counsel Fred Fielding and Treasury Secretary (and ex-Chief of Staff) James Baker.[22] The Christmas edition of the *Post* contained an article in which Larry Speakes denied the claim about Reagan, asserting that the president had been "fully aware of the scope" of the directive.[23]

Exhibit 1.

Secretary of State George Shultz's remarks to the press (December 19) concerning his views on polygraph testing

Personally, I have grave reservations about so-called lie detector tests because the experience with them that I have read about—I don't claim to be an expert—it's hardly a scientific instrument.

It tends to identify quite a few people who are innocent as guilty, and it misses at least some fraction of people who are guilty of lying, and it is, I think, pretty well demonstrated that a professional, let us say, a professional spy or a professional leaker, can probably train himself or herself not to be caught by the test.

So the use of it as a broad-gauged condition of employment, you might say, seems to me to be questionable. That's my viewpoint.... The minute in this government I am told that I'm not trusted is the day that I leave.

Exhibit 2.

CIA written statement (Issued December 19)

Thousands of people in the intelligence community submit to polygraph examinations in recognition of the need to protect the nation's secrets and because of the proved usefulness of the polygraph as an investigative tool.

They understand that the government, in granting access to the nation's secrets, also bestows a special trust as well as a shared responsibility for protecting those secrets. The number of leaks of sensitive, classified information in recent years makes clear that a growing number of those given special trust have not lived up to their obligations. The reality is that the loss of classified information is severely damaging our foreign policy and our intelligence capabilities.

The use of polygraphing in the intelligence community has proven to be the best deterrent to the misuse of sensitive information. There is an acute need to extend its selective, careful use to branches of government that receive that information.

The director of Central Intelligence and his predecessors voluntarily have been polygraphed, believing in the importance of setting an example in that all those with access must do what they can to protect our secrets and to cooperate in identifying those who do not.

Notes

1. *New York Times*, Dec. 20, 1985, p. 30.
2. Ibid., June 7, 1985, p. 1.
3. *Washington Post*, Dec. 29, 1985, p. 29.
4. Ibid.
5. *National Journal*, Jan. 18, 1986, p. 184.
6. *New York Times*, Dec. 20, 1985, p. 30.
7. *National Journal*, Jan. 18, 1986, p. 184.
8. *Washington Post National Weekly Edition*, Feb. 17, 1986, p. 8.
9. *Washington Post*, Dec. 21, 1985, p. A8.

10. *Washington Post National Weekly Edition,* Feb. 17, 1986, pp. 6–8.
11. Ibid.
12. Ibid.
13. Ibid.
14. *National Journal,* Feb. 15, 1986, p. 377.
15. *New York Times,* Dec. 12, 1985, p. A19.
16. Ibid.
17. *New York Times,* Dec. 20, 1985, p. 1.
18. Ibid.
19. Ibid., Dec. 21, 1985.
20. Ibid.
21. Ibid.
22. *Washington Post,* Dec. 24, 1985, p. 1.
23. Ibid., Dec. 25, p. A16.

Comment

Had George Shultz followed the injunction "obey or resign," he would have quietly left office. By publicly threatening to resign, Shultz succeeded in changing a governmental policy. Should our judgment of Shultz's actions depend on whether he was acting according to his own conscience, whether his position on polygraph testing was morally correct, or both? If you agree with Shultz's position on polygraph testing, consider whether your judgment would change had Shultz threatened to resign over a White House directive of which you approve. Are there any other issues over which Shultz or someone in a similar role should have threatened to resign (for example, trading of arms for hostages during the Iran-Contra Affair)?

Is a sincere appeal to personal conscience sufficient to justify resignation or the threat to resign? Consider whether public officials who, like Shultz, threaten to resign should have to give moral reasons that are widely shared. Evaluate the reasons that Shultz publicly offered. Because resignation is less extreme than disobedience, should the conditions for threatening to resign be less strict than those for official disobedience? For example, must the policy that prompts the threat constitute a substantial injustice? Did polygraph testing (or any other policy Shultz opposed during his term of office) constitute such an injustice?

The Shultz case demonstrates that measures less extreme than official disobedience are sometimes effective in changing policies. But the success of Shultz's threat to resign no doubt depended on his reputation and prominence, which relatively few public officials enjoy. In the *Challenger* case, Roger Boisjoly and Arnie Thompson argued long and hard, but failed to convince the managers of Morton Thiokol to recommend against launching the shuttle. We are not told whether Boisjoly and Thompson thought about threatening to resign or publicly protesting in other ways. But if so, they might understandably have rejected public protest, expecting that it would lead to their dismissal and would leave no high-level defenders of safety standards at Thiokol or NASA. In judging whether Boisjoly and Thompson should have done more (or less), keep in mind that they had to decide their own course of action estimating only the probabilities of a successful or disastrous launch. Also, by remaining on the job, their subsequent action (including their testimony) in defense of improved safety standards may have been more effective. However, it can be argued that, had they publicly protested or threatened to resign before the launch, they stood a good chance of actually stopping the launch and preventing the disaster.

Many discussions of official disobedience emphasize how much trouble officials get into by publicly protesting, leaking information, or otherwise employing unauthorized tactics in pursuit of a just cause. The *Challenger* case, in contrast, demonstrates how much trouble officials can get into simply by doing their jobs well, even if they do not disobey their superiors or violate any procedures. The case also suggests the need to look beyond the immediate decisions and decision makers to those policies and policymakers who create the conditions that lead to bad decisions. What practices at Thiokol and NASA hindered people like Boisjoly and Thompson from doing their jobs well? Who was responsible for those practices? How might the practices be changed so as to make official disobedience less necessary and to render internal criticism more effective?

Recommended Reading

An excellent statement of the theory of civil disobedience is John Rawls, *A Theory of Justice* (Cambridge, Mass.: Harvard University Press, 1971), pp. 363–91. A useful collection on the subject is Jeffrie Murphy (ed.), *Civil Disobedience and Violence* (Belmont, Calif.: Wadsworth, 1971).

General discussions of the concept of obligation that relate to civil disobedience are Michael Walzer, *Obligations* (New York: Simon and Schuster, 1971), chapters 1 and 2, and A. John Simmons, *Moral Principles and Political Obligations* (Princeton, N.J.: Princeton University Press, 1979). Also, see R. Kent Greenawalt, *Conflicts of Law and Morality* (New York: Oxford University Press, 1987), especially Parts III–IV.

On dissident officials, see Sissela Bok, *Secrets* (New York: Pantheon, 1982), chapter 14, "Whistleblowing and Leaking," pp. 210–29, and Myron P. Glazer and Penina M. Glazer, *The Whistleblowers: Exposing Corruption in Government and Industry* (New York: Basic Books, 1989). The practical and theoretical aspects of resignation are discussed in Edward Weisband and Thomas Franck, *Resignation in Protest* (New York: Penguin, 1975), and Albert Hirschman, *Exit, Voice and Loyalty* (Cambridge, Mass.: Harvard University Press, 1970).

Part Two

The Ethics of Policy

5 Policy Analysis

Introduction

The question of means and ends—the focus of the first part of this book—speaks to only part of the moral world of politics. No less important is the question of the ends themselves: how should we choose among competing goals of policy? The most common framework for answering this question is some version of policy analysis, including cost-benefit, cost-effective, and risk-benefit analysis.

All of these approaches rest on the moral foundation of utilitarianism (insofar as they have any moral foundation at all). They assume (1) that the ends or values of policies can be compared by a common measure of expected utility (also called happiness, satisfaction, or welfare) and (2) that the best policy or set of policies is that which maximizes the total expected utility. The great appeal of this approach is that it appears to resolve conflicts among competing ends and seems to do so in a neutral way by simply adding up all the preferences of all citizens. It also appears democratic since it purports to give the most people as much as possible of whatever they want.

Critics of policy analysis attack both of its assumptions. First, they point to problems of aggregation—the way the policy analyst adds preferences to arrive at total utility. Among criticisms of this kind are charges: (1) that individual utilities cannot be compared (How can we say whether cheaper fuel for me is worth a slight risk of nuclear contamination to you?); (2) that ultimate values cannot be traded off against other goods (How can we put a price on life itself?); and (3) that individual preferences cannot be taken as given (How can we assume that participation in the political process will not change people's perception of risks?).

The second set of criticisms concerns problems of distribution. Critics challenge the maximization principle because it ignores how utility is allocated among individuals. They object that for the sake of maximizing general utility, policy analysts will sacrifice (1) the rights of disadvantaged citizens in their own society; (2) the welfare of poorer nations; and (3) the welfare of future generations. Policy analysts try to take account of such groups, but the problem of distributive justice remains the most formidable obstacle to the acceptance of their method.

The issue of nuclear power, like many technological questions, lends itself to the techniques of policy analysis. To choose the best energy policy, we have to compare many different values, each with different probabilities attached to it and each subject to technical interpretation. Of the many analyses of nuclear power, the best known is the Reactor Safety Study (also called the Rasmussen Report), commissioned by the U.S. Atomic Energy Commission in 1975. Since then, techniques of analysis have become more sophisticated, and the focus of the policy debate has shifted to the safety of reactors used for military purposes. But study of the Rasmussen Report still offers one of the best ways to probe the moral strengths and weaknesses of policy analysis.

The report used a kind of policy analysis called "fault tree analysis" to estimate the risks from accidents in nuclear power plants. Such an estimate, of course, is only part of the broader analysis that would be necessary to determine the role nuclear power should play in meeting the energy and defense needs of society. But, as a first step in assigning utility to policy options, a systematic assessment of risks can help dispel some of the confusion and fear that stand in the way of developing morally acceptable policies for the use of nuclear power. Even the analysis of risk, however, is likely to be controversial. The critics cited in the Report of the House Subcommittee on Energy and the Environment challenge the Rasmussen Report seemingly on technical grounds. But, as in other scientific disputes, the technical disagreements reflect ethical differences about such questions as what risks people should accept and who should decide what are acceptable levels of risk. Beyond the problem of adding up the risks, the problem of distributing them—within a society and to future generations—receives little notice in either the Rasmussen Report or the subcommittee's report. Although neither report claims to deal with all the issues in the controversy over nuclear power, we must read them with as much attention to what they omit as to what they include.

The problem of environmental pollution, like that of nuclear power, is often the object of policy analysis. But William Ruckelshaus, responsible for setting emissions standards in the Asarco case, was as sensitive to the weaknesses of policy analysis as to its strengths. Ruckelshaus held a series of public meetings to discuss, with the people who would be most directly affected by his decision, both the technical and moral dimensions of setting emissions standards for the Asarco smelting company. Many observers criticized Ruckelshaus for abdicating his responsibility to make policy on the basis of his own best technical and moral judgment. Others praised him for trying to educate the public on the difficulties in making decisions on the basis of imperfect and incomplete knowledge. The Asarco case does not provide a solution to the philosophical problems of how to aggregate preferences to arrive at total utility and how to distribute risks among people. Instead, it suggests a political process by which the resolution of these problems may be more fairly and fully considered.

The Reactor Safety Study

Norman C. Rasmussen et al.

Section 1. Introduction and Results

The Reactor Safety Study was sponsored by the U.S. Atomic Energy Commission to estimate the public risks that could be involved in potential accidents in commercial nuclear power plants of the type now in use. It was performed under the independent direction of Professor Norman C. Rasmussen of the Massachusetts Institute of Technology. The risks had to be estimated, rather than measured, because although there are about 50 such plants now operating, there have been no nuclear accidents to date resulting in significant releases of radioactivity in U.S. commercial nuclear power plants. Many of the methods used to develop these estimates are based on those that were developed by the Department of Defense and the National Aeronautics and Space Administration in the last 10 years and are coming into increasing use in recent years.

The objective of the study was to make a realistic estimate of these risks and, to provide perspective, to compare them with non-nuclear risks to which our society and its individuals are already exposed. This information may be of help in determining the future reliance by society on nuclear power as a source of electricity.

The results from this study suggest that the risks to the public from potential accidents in nuclear power plants are comparatively small. This is based on the following considerations:

a. The possible consequences of potential reactor accidents are predicted to be no larger, and in many cases much smaller, than those of non-nuclear accidents. The consequences are predicted to be smaller than people have been led to believe by previous studies which deliberately maximized estimates of these consequences.

b. The likelihood of reactor accidents is much smaller than that of many non-nuclear accidents having similar consequences. All non-nuclear accidents examined in this study, including fires, explosions, toxic chemical releases, dam failures, airplane crashes, earthquakes, hurricanes and tornadoes, are much more likely to occur and can have consequences comparable to, or larger than, those of nuclear accidents.

Figures 1, 2, and 3 compare the nuclear reactor accident risks predicted for the 100 plants expected to be operating by about 1980 with risks from other man-caused and natural events to which society is generally already exposed. The following information is contained in the figures:

a. Figures 1 and 2 show the likelihood and number of fatalities from both nuclear and a variety of non-nuclear accidents. These figures indicate that non-nuclear events are about 10,000 times more likely to produce large numbers of fatalities than nuclear plants.*

b. Figure 3 shows the likelihood and dollar value of property damage associated with nuclear and non-nuclear accidents.

Published by the U.S. Nuclear Regulatory Commission, October 1975.

*The fatalities shown in Figs. 1 and 2 for the 100 nuclear plants are those that would be predicted to occur within a short period of time after the potential reactor accident. This was done to provide a consistent comparison to the non-nuclear events which also cause fatalities in the same time frame. As in potential nuclear accidents, there also exist possibilities for injuries and longer term health effects from non-nuclear accidents. Data or predictions of this type are not available for non-nuclear events and so comparisons cannot easily be made.

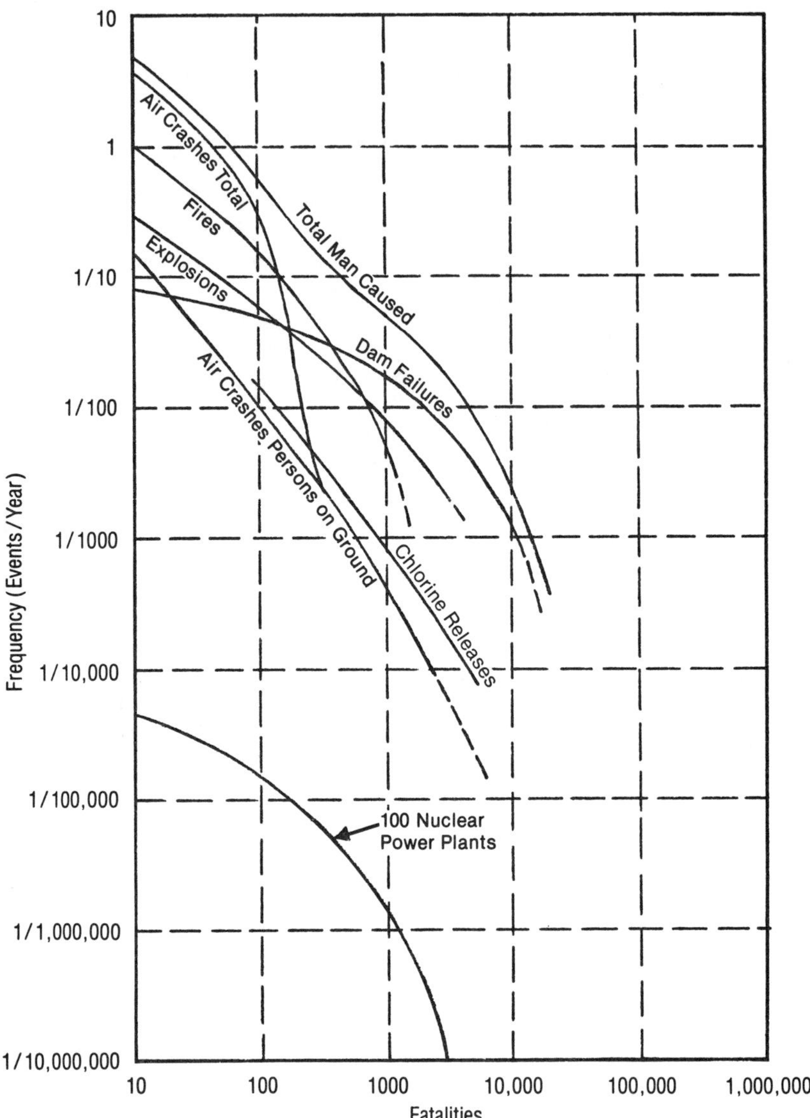

FIGURE 1. FREQUENCY OF FATALITIES DUE TO MAN-CAUSED EVENTS

Notes:

1. Fatalities due to auto accidents are not shown because data are not available. Auto accidents cause about 50,000 fatalities per year.
2. Approximate uncertainties for nuclear events are estimated to be represented by factors of 1/4 and 4 on consequence magnitudes and by factors of 1/5 and 5 on probabilities.
3. For natural and man caused occurrences the uncertainty in probability of largest recorded consequence magnitude is estimated to be represented by factors of 1/20 and 5. Smaller magnitudes have less uncertainty.

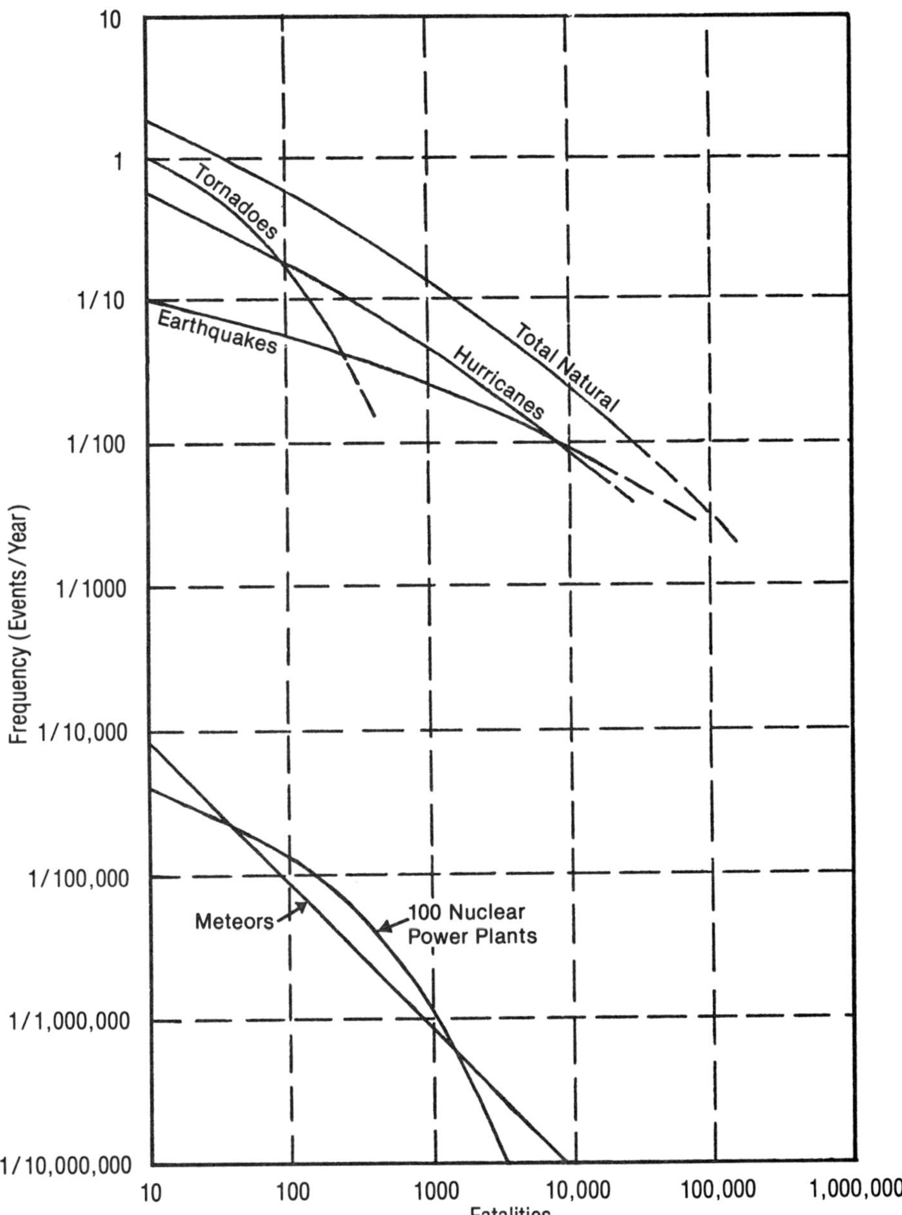

FIGURE 2. FREQUENCY OF FATALITIES DUE TO NATURAL EVENTS

Notes:

1. For natural and man caused occurrences the uncertainty in probability of largest recorded consequence magnitude is estimated to be represented by factors of 1/20 and 5. Smaller magnitudes have less uncertainty.
2. Approximate uncertainties for nuclear events are estimated to be represented by factors of 1/4 and 4 on consequence magnitudes and by factors of 1/5 and 5 on probabilities.

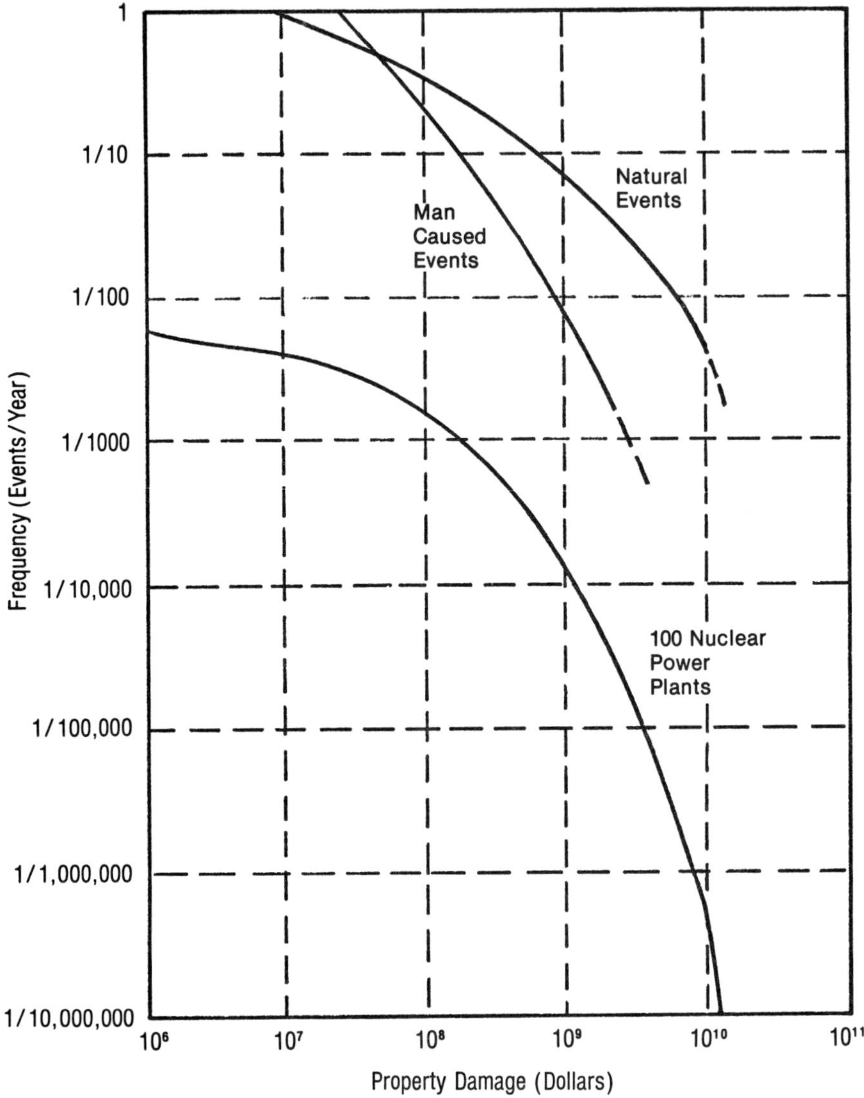

FIGURE 3. FREQUENCY OF PROPERTY DAMAGE DUE TO NATURAL AND MAN-CAUSED EVENTS

Notes:

1. Property damage due to auto accidents is not included because data are not available for low probability events. Auto accidents cause about $15 billion damage each year.
2. Approximate uncertainties for nuclear events are estimated to be represented by factors of 1/5 and 2 on consequence magnitudes and by factors of 1/5 and 5 on probabilities.
3. For natural and man caused occurrences the uncertainty in probability of largest recorded consequence magnitude is estimated to be represented by factors of 1/20 and 5. Smaller magnitudes have less uncertainty.

Nuclear plants are about 1000 times less likely to cause comparable large dollar value accidents than other sources. Property damage is associated with three effects:

1. the cost of relocating people away from contaminated areas,
2. the decontamination of land to avoid overexposing people to radioactivity,
3. the cost of ensuring that people are not exposed to potential sources of radioactivity in food and water supplies.

In addition to the overall risk information in Figs. 1 through 3, it is useful to consider the risk to individuals of being fatally injured by various types of accidents. The bulk of the information shown in Table 1 is taken from the 1973 *Statistical Abstracts of the U.S.* and applies to the year 1969, the latest year for which these data were tabulated when this study was performed. The predicted nuclear accident risks are very small compared to other possible causes of fatal injuries.

In addition to fatalities and property damage, a number of other health effects could be caused by nuclear accidents. These include injuries and long-term health effects such as cancers, genetic effects, and thyroid gland illness. The early illness expected in potential accidents would be about 10 times as large as the fatalities shown in Figs. 1 and 2; for comparison there are 8 million injuries caused annually by other accidents. The number of cases of genetic effects and long-term cancer fatalities is predicted to be smaller than the normal incidence rate of these diseases. Even for a large accident, the small increases in these diseases would be difficult to detect from the normal incidence rate.

Thyroid illnesses that might result from a large accident are mainly the formation of nodules on the thyroid gland; these can be treated by medical procedures and rarely lead to serious consequences. For most accidents, the number of nodules caused would be small compared to their normal incidence rate. The number that might be produced in very unlikely accidents would be about equal to their normal occurrence in the exposed population. These would be observed during a period of 10 to 40 years following the accident.

While the study has presented the estimated risks from nuclear power plant

TABLE 1. AVERAGE RISK OF FATALITY BY VARIOUS CAUSES

Accident Type	*Total Number*	*Individual Chance per Year*
Motor Vehicle	55,791	1 in 4,000
Falls	17,827	1 in 10,000
Fires and Hot Substances	7,451	1 in 25,000
Drowning	6,181	1 in 30,000
Firearms	2,309	1 in 100,000
Air Travel	1,778	1 in 100,000
Falling Objects	1,271	1 in 160,000
Electrocution	1,148	1 in 160,000
Lightning	160	1 in 2,000,000
Tornadoes	91	1 in 2,500,000
Hurricanes	93	1 in 2,500,000
All Accidents	111,992	1 in 1,600
Nuclear Reactor Accidents (100 plants)		1 in 5,000,000,000

accidents and compared them with other risks that exist in our society, it has made no judgment on the acceptability of nuclear risks. The judgment as to what level of risk is acceptable should be made by a broader segment of society than that involved in this study.

SECTION 2. QUESTIONS AND ANSWERS ABOUT THE STUDY

This section of the summary presents more information about the details of the study than was covered in the introduction. It is presented in question and answer format for ease of reference.

2.1 WHO DID THIS STUDY AND HOW MUCH EFFORT WAS INVOLVED?

The study was done principally at the Atomic Energy Commission headquarters by a group of scientists and engineers who had the skills needed to carry out the study's tasks. They came from a variety of organizations, including the AEC, the national laboratories, private laboratories, and universities. About 10 people were AEC employees. The Director of the study was Professor Norman C. Rasmussen of the Department of Nuclear Engineering of the Massachusetts Institute of Technology, who served as an AEC consultant during the course of the study. The Staff Director who had the day-to-day responsibility for the project was Mr. Saul Levine of the AEC. The study was started in the summer of 1972 and took three years to complete. A total of 60 people, various consultants, 70 man-years of effort, and about four million dollars were involved.

2.2 WHAT KIND OF NUCLEAR POWER PLANTS ARE COVERED BY THE STUDY?

The study considered large power reactors of the pressurized water and boiling water type being used in the U.S. today. Reactors of the present generation are all water cooled, and therefore the study limited itself to this type. Although high temperature gas cooled and liquid metal fast breeder reactor designs are now under development, reactors of this type are not expected to have any significant role in U.S. electric power production in this decade; thus they were not considered.

Nuclear power plants produce electricity by the fissioning (or splitting) of uranium atoms. The nuclear reactor fuel in which the uranium atoms fission is in a large steel vessel. The reactor fuel consists of about 100 tons of uranium. The uranium is inside metal rods about 1/2 inch in diameter and about 12 feet long. These rods are formed into fuel bundles of about 50-200 rods each. Each reactor contains several hundred bundles. The vessel is filled with water, which is needed both to cool the fuel and to maintain the fission chain reaction.

The heat released in the uranium by the fission process heats the water and forms steam; the steam turns a turbine to generate electricity. Similarly, coal and oil plants generate electricity using fossil fuel to boil water.

Today's nuclear power plants are very large. A typical plant has an electrical capacity of 1,000,000 kilowatts, or 1,000 megawatts. This is enough electricity for a city of about five hundred thousand people.

2.3 CAN A NUCLEAR POWER PLANT EXPLODE LIKE AN ATOM BOMB?

No. It is impossible for nuclear power plants to explode like a nuclear weapon. The laws of physics do not permit this because the fuel contains only a small fraction (3-5%) of the special type of uranium (called uranium-235) that must be used in weapons.

2.4 HOW IS RISK DEFINED?

The idea of risk involves both the likelihood and consequences of an event. Thus, to estimate the risk involved in driving an automobile, one would need to know the likelihood of an accident in which, for example, an individual could be 1) injured or 2) killed. Thus there are two different consequences, injury or fatality, each with its own likelihood. For injury, an individual's chance per year is about one in 130 and for fatality, it is about one in 4000. This type of data concerns the risk to individuals and can affect attitudes and habits that individuals have toward driving.

However, from an overall societal viewpoint, different types of data are of interest. Here, 1.5 million injuries per year and 55,000 fatalities per year due to automobile accidents represent the kind of information that might be of use in making decisions on highway and automobile safety.

The same type of logic applies to reactors. From the viewpoint of a person living in the general vicinity of a reactor, the likelihood of being killed in any one year in a reactor accident is one chance in 5 billion, and the likelihood of being injured in any one year in a reactor accident is one chance in 75,000,000.

2.5 WHAT CAUSES THE RISKS ASSOCIATED WITH NUCLEAR POWER PLANT ACCIDENTS?

The risks from nuclear power plants are due to the radioactivity formed by the fission process. In normal operation nuclear power plants release minute amounts of this radioactivity under controlled conditions. In the event of highly unlikely accidents, larger amounts of radioactivity could be released and could cause significant risks.

The fragments of the uranium atom that remain after it fissions are radioactive. These radioactive atoms are called fission products. They disintegrate further with the release of nuclear radiations. Many of them decay away quickly, in a matter of minutes or hours, to nonradioactive forms. Others decay away more slowly and require months, and in a few cases, many years to decay. The fission products accumulating in the fuel rods include both gases and solids. Included are iodine, gases like krypton and xenon, and solids like cesium and strontium.

2.6 HOW CAN RADIOACTIVITY BE RELEASED?

The only way that potentially large amounts of radioactivity could be released is by melting the fuel in the reactor core. The fuel that is removed from a reactor after use and stored at the plant site also contains considerable amounts of radioactivity. However, accidental releases from such used fuel were found to be quite unlikely and small compared to potential releases of radioactivity from the fuel in the reactor core.

The safety design of reactors includes a series of systems to prevent the overheating of fuel and to control potential releases of radioactivity from the fuel. Thus, for a potential accidental release of radioactivity to the environment to occur, there must be a series of sequential failures that would cause the fuel to overheat and release its radioactivity. There would also have to be failures in the systems designed to remove and contain the radioactivity.

The study has examined a very large number of potential paths by which potential radioactive releases might occur and has identified those that determine the risks. This involved defining the ways in which the fuel in the core could melt and the ways in which systems to control the release of radioactivity could fail.

2.7 HOW MIGHT A CORE MELT ACCIDENT OCCUR?

It is significant that in some 200 reactor-years of commercial operation of reactors of the type considered in the report there have been no fuel melting accidents. To melt the fuel requires a failure in the cooling system or the occurrence of a heat imbalance that would allow the fuel to heat up to its melting point, about 5,000°F.

To those unfamiliar with the characteristics of reactors, it might seem that all that is required to prevent fuel from overheating is a system to promptly stop, or shut down, the fission process at the first sign of trouble. Although reactors have such systems, they alone are not enough since the radioactive decay of fission fragments in the fuel continues to generate heat (called decay heat) that must be removed even after the fission process stops. Thus, redundant decay heat removal systems are also provided in reactors. In addition, emergency core cooling systems (ECCS) are provided to cope with a series of potential but unlikely accidents, caused by ruptures in, and loss of coolant from, the normal cooling system.

The Reactor Safety Study has defined two broad types of situations that might potentially lead to a melting of the reactor core: the loss-of-coolant accident (LOCA) and transients. In the event of a potential loss of coolant, the normal cooling water would be lost from the cooling systems and core melting would be prevented by the use of the emergency core cooling system (ECCS). However, melting could occur in a loss of coolant if the ECCS were to fail to operate.

The term "transient" refers to any one of a number of conditions which could occur in a plant and would require the reactor to be shut down. Following shutdown, the decay heat removal systems would operate to keep the core from overheating. Certain failures in either the shutdown or the decay heat removal systems also have the potential to cause melting of the core.

2.8 WHAT FEATURES ARE PROVIDED IN REACTORS TO COPE WITH A CORE MELT ACCIDENT?

Nuclear power plants have numerous systems designed to prevent core melting. Furthermore, there are inherent physical processes and additional features that come into play to remove and contain the radioactivity released from the molten fuel should core melting occur. Although there are features provided to keep the containment building from being damaged for some time after the core melts, the containment would ultimately fail, causing a release of radioactivity.

An essentially leaktight containment building is provided to prevent the initial dispersion of the airborne radioactivity into the environment. Although the containment would fail in time if the core were to melt, until that time, the radioactivity released from the fuel would be deposited by natural processes on the surfaces inside the containment. In addition, plants are provided with systems to contain and trap the radioactivity released within the containment building. These systems include such things as water sprays and pools to wash radioactivity out of the building atmosphere and filters to trap radioactive particles prior to their release. Since the containment building is made essentially leaktight, the radioactivity is contained as long as the building remains intact. Even if the building were to have sizable leaks, large amounts of the radioactivity would likely be removed by the systems provided for that purpose or would be deposited on interior surfaces of the building by natural processes.

Even though the containment building would be expected to remain intact for some time following a core melt, eventually the molten mass would be expected to eat its way through the concrete floor into the ground below. Following this, much of the radioactive material would be trapped in the soil; however, a small amount would escape to the surface and be released. Almost all of the non-gaseous radioactivity would be trapped in the soil.

It is possible to postulate core melt accidents in which the containment building would fail by overpressurization or by missiles created by the accident. Such accidents are less likely but could release a larger amount of airborne radioactivity and have more serious consequences. The consequences of these less likely accidents have been included in the study's results shown in Figs. 1 through 3.

2.9 HOW MIGHT THE LOSS-OF-COOLANT ACCIDENT LEAD TO A CORE MELT?

Loss of coolant accidents are postulated to result from failures in the normal reactor cooling water system, and plants are designed to cope with such failures. The water in the reactor cooling systems is at a very high pressure (between 50 to 100 times the pressure in a car tire) and if a rupture were to occur in the pipes, pumps, valves, or vessels that contain it, then a "blowout" would happen. In this case some of the water would flash to steam and blow out of the hole. This could be serious since the fuel could melt if additional cooling were not supplied in a rather short time.

The loss of normal cooling in the event of a LOCA would stop the chain reaction, so that the amount of heat produced would drop very rapidly to a few percent of its operating level. However, after this sudden drop the amount of heat being produced would decrease much more slowly and would be controlled by the decay of the radioactivity in the fuel. Although this decrease in heat generation is helpful, it would not be enough to prevent the fuel from melting unless additional cooling were supplied. To deal with this situation, reactors have emergency core cooling systems (ECCS) whose function is to provide cooling for just such events. These systems have pumps, pipes, valves, and water supplies which are capable of dealing with breaks of various sizes. They are also designed to be redundant so that if some components fail to operate, the core can still be cooled.

The study has examined a large number of potential sequences of events following LOCAs of various sizes. In almost all of the cases, the LOCA must be followed by failures in the emergency core cooling system for the core to melt. The principal exception to this is the massive failure of the large pressure vessel that contains the core. However, the accumulated experience with pressure vessels indicates that the chance of such a failure is small. In fact the study found that the likelihood of pressure vessel failure was so small that it did not contribute to the overall risk from reactor accidents.

2.10 HOW MIGHT A REACTOR TRANSIENT LEAD TO A CORE MELT?

The term "reactor transient" refers to a number of events that require the reactor to be shut down. These range from normal shutdown for such things as refueling to such unplanned but expected events as loss of power to the plant from the utility transmission lines. The reactor is designed to cope with unplanned transients by automatically shutting down. Following shutdown, cooling systems would be operated to remove the heat produced by the radioactivity in the fuel. There are several different cooling systems capable of removing this heat, but if they all should fail, the heat being produced would be sufficient to eventually boil away all the cooling water and melt the core.

In addition to the above pathway to core melt, it is also possible to postulate core melt resulting from the failure of the reactor shutdown systems following a transient event. In this case it would be possible for the amounts of heat generated to be such that the available cooling systems might not cope with it and core melt could result.

2.11 HOW LIKELY IS A CORE MELT ACCIDENT?

The Reactor Safety Study carefully examined the various paths leading to core melt. Using methods developed in recent years for estimating the likelihood of such accidents, a probability of occurrence was determined for each core melt accident identified. These probabilities were combined to obtain the total probability of melting the core. The value obtained was about one in 20,000 per reactor per year. With 100 reactors operating, as is anticipated for the U.S. by about 1980, this means that the chance for one such accident is one in 200 per year.

2.12 WHAT IS THE NATURE OF THE HEALTH EFFECTS THAT A CORE MELT ACCIDENT MIGHT PRODUCE?

It is possible for a potential core melt accident to release enough radioactivity so that some fatalities might occur within a short time (about one year) after the accident. Other people may be exposed to radiation levels which would produce observable effects which would require medical attention but from which they would recover. In addition, some people may receive even lower exposures, which would produce no noticeable effects but might increase the incidence of certain diseases over a period of many years. The observable effects which occur shortly after the accident are called early, or acute, effects.

The delayed, or latent, effects of radiation exposure could cause some increase in the incidence of diseases such as cancer, genetic effects, and thyroid gland illnesses in the exposed population. In general these effects would appear as an increase in these diseases over a 10 to 50 year period following the exposure. Such effects may be difficult to notice because the increase is expected to be small compared to the normal incidence rate of these diseases.

The study has estimated the increased incidence of potentially fatal cancers over the 50 years following an accident. The number of latent cancer fatalities are predicted to be relatively small compared to their normal incidence. Thyroid illness refers mainly to small lumps, or nodules, on the thyroid gland. The nodules are treated by medical procedures that sometimes involve simple surgery, and these are unlikely to lead to serious consequences. Medication may also be needed to supplement the gland function.

Radiation is recognized as one of the factors that can produce genetic effects which appear as defects in a subsequent generation. From the total population exposure caused by the accident, the expected increase in genetic effects in subsequent generations can be estimated. These effects are predicted to be small compared to their normal incidence rate.

2.13 WHAT ARE THE MOST LIKELY CONSEQUENCES OF A CORE MELT ACCIDENT?

As stated, the probability of a core melt accident is on the average one in 20,000 per reactor per year. The most likely consequences of such an accident are given [in Table 2].

2.14 HOW DOES THE AVERAGE ANNUAL RISK FROM NUCLEAR ACCIDENTS COMPARE TO OTHER COMMON RISKS?

Considering the 15 million people who live within 25 miles of current or planned U.S. reactor sites, and based on current accident rates in the U.S., the annual numbers of fatalities and injuries expected from various sources are shown in [Table 3].

TABLE 2. MOST LIKELY CONSEQUENCES OF A CORE MELT ACCIDENT

	Consequences
Fatalities	<1
Injuries	<1
Latent Fatalities per year	<1
Thyroid Nodules per year	<1
Genetic Defects per year	<1
Property Damage[(a)]	<$1,000,000

(a) This does not include damage that might occur to the plant or costs for replacing the power generation lost by such damage.

TABLE 3. ANNUAL FATALITIES AND INJURIES EXPECTED AMONG THE 15 MILLION PEOPLE LIVING WITHIN 25 MILES OF U.S. REACTOR SITES

Accident Type	*Fatalities*	*Injuries*
Automobile	4,200	375,000
Falls	1,500	75,000
Fire	560	22,000
Electrocution	90	–
Lightning	8	–
Reactors (100 plants)		

2.15 WHAT IS THE NUMBER OF FATALITIES AND INJURIES EXPECTED AS A RESULT OF A CORE MELT ACCIDENT?

A core melt accident is similar to many other types of major accidents such as fires, explosions, dam failures, etc., in that a wide range of consequences is possible depending on the exact conditions under which the accident occurs. In the case of a core melt, the consequences would depend mainly on three factors: the amount of radioactivity released, the way it is dispersed by the prevailing weather conditions, and the number of people exposed to the radiation. With these three factors known, it is possible to make a reasonable estimate of the consequences.

The study calculated the health effects and the probability of occurrence for 140,000 possible combinations of radioactive release magnitude, weather type, and population exposed. The probability of a given release was determined from careful examination of the probability of various reactor system failures. The probability of various weather conditions was obtained from weather data collected at many reactor sites. The probability of various numbers of people being exposed was obtained from U.S. census data for current and planned U.S. reactor sites. These thousands of computations were carried out with the aid of a large digital computer.

These results showed that the probability of an accident resulting in 10 or more fatalities is predicted to be about 1 in 3,000,000 per plant per year. The probability of 100 or more fatalities is predicted to be about 1 in 10,000,000 and for 1000 or more, 1 in 100,000,000. The largest value reported in the study was 3300 fatalities, with a probability of about one in a billion.

The above estimates are derived from a consequence model which includes statistical calculations to describe evacuations of people out of the path of airborne radioactivity. This evacuation model was developed from data describing evacuations that have been performed during non-nuclear events.

If a group of 100 similar plants are considered, then the chance of an accident causing 10 or more fatalities is 1 in 30,000 per year. For accidents involving 1000 or more fatalities the number is 1 in 1,000,000 per year. Interestingly, this value coincides with the probability that a meteor would strike a U.S. population center and cause 1000 fatalities.

[Table 4] can be used to compare the likelihood of a nuclear accident to non-nuclear accidents that could cause the same consequences.

TABLE 4. AVERAGE PROBABILITY OF MAJOR MAN-CAUSED AND NATURAL EVENTS

Type of Event	*Probability of 100 or More Fatalities*	*Probability of 1,000 or More Fatalities*
Man-Caused		
Airplane Crash	1 in 2 years	1 in 2,000 years
Fire	1 in 7 years	1 in 200 years
Explosion	1 in 16 years	1 in 120 years
Toxic Gas	1 in 100 years	1 in 1,000 years
Natural		
Tornado	1 in 5 years	very small
Hurricane	1 in 5 years	1 in 25 years
Earthquake	1 in 20 years	1 in 50 years
Meteorite Impact	1 in 100,000 years	1 in 1,000,000 years
Reactors		
100 plants	1 in 100,000 years	1 in 1,000,000 years

These include man-caused as well as natural events. Many of these probabilities are obtained from historical records, but others are so small that no such event has ever been observed. In the latter cases the probability has been calculated using techniques similar to those used for the nuclear plant.

In regard to injuries from potential nuclear power plant accidents, the number of injuries that would require medical attention shortly after an accident is about 10 times larger than the number of fatalities predicted.

2.16 WHAT IS THE MAGNITUDE OF THE LATENT, OR LONG-TERM, HEALTH EFFECTS?

As with the short-term effects, the incidence of latent cancers, treatable latent thyroid illness, and genetic effects would vary with the exact accident conditions. [Table 5] below illustrates the potential size of such events. The first column shows the consequences that would be produced by core melt accidents, the most likely of which has one chance in 20,000 per reactor per year of occurring. The second column shows the consequences for an accident that has a chance of one in a million of occurring. The third column shows the normal incidence rate.

In these accidents, only the induction of thyroid nodules would be observable, and this only in the case of larger, less likely accidents. These nodules are easily diagnosed and treatable by medical or surgical procedures. The incidence of other effects would be low and should not be discernible in view of the high normal incidence of these two diseases. [See Table 5.]

TABLE 5. INCIDENCE PER YEAR OF LATENT HEALTH EFFECTS FOLLOWING A POTENTIAL REACTOR ACCIDENT

Health Effect (per year)	*Chance per Reactor per Year*		*Normal[b] Incidence Rate in Exposed Population (per year)*
	One in 20,000[a]	*One in 1,000,000[a]*	
Latent Cancers	<1	170	17,000
Thyroid Illness	<1	1,400	8,000
Genetic Effects	<1	25	8,000

(a) The rates due to reactor accidents are temporary and would decrease with time. The bulk of the cancers and thyroid modules would occur over a few decades and the genetic effects would be significantly reduced in five generations.

(b) This is the normal incidence that would be expected for a population of 10,000,000 people who might receive some exposure in a very large accident over the time period that the potential reactor accident effects might occur.

2.17 WHAT TYPE OF PROPERTY DAMAGE MIGHT A CORE MELT ACCIDENT PRODUCE?

A nuclear accident would cause no physical damage to property beyond the plant site but may contaminate it with radioactivity. At high levels of contamination, people would have to be relocated from their homes until decontamination procedures permitted their return. At levels lower than this, but involving a larger area, decontamination procedures would also be required, but people would be able to continue to live in the area. The area requiring decontamination would involve a few hundred to a few thousand square miles. The principal concern in this larger area would be to monitor farm produce to keep the amount of radioactivity ingested through the food chain small. Farms in this area would have their produce monitored, and any produce above a safe level could not be used.

The core melt accident having a likelihood of 1 in 20,000 per plant per year would most likely result in little or no contamination. The probability of an accident that requires relocation of 20 square miles is 1 in 100,000 per reactor per year. Eighty per cent of all core melt accidents would be expected to be less severe than this. The largest accident might require relocation from 290 square miles. In an accident such as this, agricultural products, particularly milk, would have to be monitored for a month or two over an area about 50 times larger until the iodine decayed away. After that, the area requiring monitoring would be very much smaller.

2.18 WHAT WOULD BE THE COST OF THE CONSEQUENCES OF A CORE MELT ACCIDENT?

As with the other consequences, the cost would depend upon the exact circumstances of the accident. The cost calculated by the Reactor Safety Study included the cost of moving and housing the people that were relocated, the cost caused by denial of land use and the cost associated with the denial of use of reproducible assets such as dwellings and factories, and costs associated with the cleanup of contaminated property. The core melt accident having a likelihood of 1 in 20,000 per reactor per year would most likely cause property damage of less than $1,000,000. The chance of an accident causing $150,000,000 damage would be about 1 in 100,000 per reactor per year. The probability would be about 1 in 1,000,000 per plant per year of causing damage of about 1 billion dollars. The maximum value would be predicted to be about 14 billion dollars, with a probability of about 1 in 1,000,000,000 per plant per year.

This property damage risk from nuclear accidents can be compared to other risks in several ways. The largest man-caused events that have occurred are fires. In recent years there have been an average of three fires with damage in excess of 10 million dollars every year. About once every two years there is a fire with damage in the 50 to 100 million dollar range. There have been four hurricanes in the last 10 years which caused damage in the range of 0.5 to 5 billion dollars. Recent earthquake estimates suggest that a 1 billion dollar earthquake can be expected in the U.S. about once every 50 years.

A comparison of the preceding costs shows that, although a severe reactor accident would be very costly, the costs would be within the range of other serious accidents experienced by society and the probability of such a nuclear accident is estimated to be smaller than that of the other events.

2.19 WHAT WILL BE THE CHANCE OF A REACTOR MELTDOWN IN THE YEAR 2000 IF WE HAVE 1000 REACTORS OPERATING?

One might be tempted to take the per plant probability of a particular reactor accident and multiply it by 1000 to estimate the chance of an accident in the year 2000. This is not a valid calculation, however, because it assumes that the reactors to be built during the next 25 years will be the same as those being built today. Experience with other technologies, such as automobiles and aircraft for example, generally shows that, as more units are built and more experience is gained, the overall safety record improves in terms of fewer accidents occurring per unit. There are changes in plants now being constructed that appear to be improved as compared to the plants analyzed in the study.

2.20 HOW DO WE KNOW THAT THE STUDY HAS INCLUDED ALL ACCIDENTS IN THE ANALYSIS?

The study devoted a large amount of its effort to ensuring that it covered those potential accidents of importance to determining the public risk. It relied heavily on over 20 years of experience that exists in the identification and analysis of potential reactor accidents. It also went considerably beyond earlier analyses that have been performed by considering a large number of potential failures that had never before been analyzed. For example, the failure of reactor systems that can lead to core melt and the failure of systems that affect the consequences of core melt have been analyzed. The consequences of the failure of the massive steel reactor vessel and of the containment were considered for the first time. The likelihood that various external forces such as earthquakes, floods, and tornadoes could cause accidents was also analyzed.

In addition there are further factors that give a high degree of confidence that the important and significant accidents affecting risk have been included. These are: (1) the identification of all significant sources of radioactivity located at nuclear power plants, (2) the fact that a large release of radioactivity can occur only if the reactor fuel were to melt, and (3) knowledge of the physical phenomena which can cause fuel to melt. This type of approach led to the screening of thousands of potential accident paths to identify those that would essentially determine the public risk.

While there is no way of proving that all possible accident sequences which contribute to public risk have been considered in the study, the systematic approach used in identifying possible accident sequences makes it unlikely that an accident was overlooked which would significantly change the overall risk.

2.21 WHAT TECHNIQUES WERE USED IN PERFORMING THE STUDY?

Methodologies developed over the past 10 years by the Department of Defense and the National Aeronautics and Space Administration were used in the study. As used in this study, these techniques, called event trees and fault trees, helped to define potential accident paths and their likelihood of occurrence.

An event tree defines an initial failure within the plant. It then examines the course of events which follow as determined by the operation or failure of various systems that are provided to prevent the core from melting and to prevent the release of radioactivity to the environment. Event trees were used in this study to define thousands of potential accident paths which were examined to determine their likelihood of occurrence and the amount of radioactivity that they might release.

Fault trees were used to determine the likelihood of failure of the various systems identified in the event tree accident paths. A fault tree starts with the definition of an undesired event, such as the failure of a system to operate, and then determines, using engineering and mathematical logic, the ways in which the system can fail. Using data covering (1) the failure of components such as pumps, pipes and valves, (2) the likelihood of operator errors, and (3) the likelihood of maintenance errors, it is possible to estimate the likelihood of system failure, even where no data on total system failure exist.

The likelihood and the size of radioactive releases from potential accident paths were used in combination with the likelihood of various weather conditions and population distributions in the vicinity of the reactor to calculate the consequences of the various potential accidents.

Observations on the Reactor Safety Study

U.S. House, Subcommittee on Energy and the Environment

The subcommittee received a wide range of commentary, pro and con, concerning the Reactor Safety Study. In addition to testimony presented at the hearing, the hearing record includes eleven responses to Chairman Udall's request for comments upon a series of issues around which discussion of the Study has centered.

Published by the U.S. Government Printing Office, Washington, D.C., January 1977.

Typical of generally favorable summary comments are the following:

> To my mind the most important finding of NUREG 75/014 (Reactor Safety Study) is that the probability of a meltdown in a PWR [Pressurized Water Reactor] reactor is about 1 in 20,000 per reactor per year, and that 9 out of 10 times in such an accident the aboveground containment would not be breached. (Letter from Dr. Alvin Weinberg, Oak Ridge Associated Universities, to Chairman Udall, June 21, 1976.)

> I conclude that the analysis was appropriate and adequate, probably within a factor of about 10. Beyond that, I cannot be specific. Nevertheless, that puts the likelihood of low-probability, high-consequence events into the class of very rare phenomena, and the actuarial damage to be expected from them is very low. (Letter from Dr. David Rose, Massachusetts Institute of Technology, to subcommittee Chairman Udall: June 18, 1976.)

> My opinion is that the Reactor Safety Study is highly relevant, satisfactory and a workmanlike job....
>
> On the whole, I believe that the Rasmussen Report leans to the conservative side and reactors are, in fact, even less likely to malfunction than as stated in WASH-1400 (NUREG 75/014) [Reactor Safety Study]. (Letter from Dr. Edward Teller, Lawrence Livermore Laboratory, to Chairman Udall, August 16, 1976.)

Major areas of critical comment concern: (A) the method of presentation of the Study's results and conclusions; (B) the Study's emphasis of short-term effects vis-a-vis those which will occur over the decades following the accident; (C) the treatment of uncertainty in discussion of the risk associated with low-probability, high-consequence events; (D) the failure to discuss the substantial accident consequence variability that might result from some reactors being located much closer than others to population centers; (E) an obtuseness of presentation which made the report difficult to analyze; and (F) failure to compare risks of nuclear energy with those associated with other energy options.

A. Presentation of Results and Conclusions

The Study was presented in a manner which can readily give the impression that hazards associated with nuclear powers are "acceptably low." This impression is conveyed in spite of a disclaimer which appears as the final paragraph in Section I of the Study's Executive Summary:

> While the Study has presented the estimated risks from nuclear powerplant accidents and compared them with other risks that exist in our society, it has made no judgment on the acceptability of nuclear risks. The judgment as to what level of risk is acceptable should be made by a broader segment of society than that involved in this Study.

The misleading impression (namely that the risk is "acceptably low") results from the contents of Section I of the Study's Executive Summary which consists primarily of comparisons of various kinds of risks. According to the material presented in Section I the probability of a person dying as a result of a nuclear powerplant accident is exceedingly small in comparison to the probability of death from other accidental causes such as motor vehicle accidents, falls, or fires. The data presented indicates that the risk of death from a nuclear accident approximates the risk of death from a falling meteor.

However, Section I of the Executive Summary provides little indication that the significance of the results presented therein is subject to a wide ranging debate. The data in Section I are criticized (as the following discussion indicates) on grounds of gross understatement of uncertainty; incomplete fatality estimates; inadequate discussion of variability of consequences; and absence of the most relevant risk comparisons, namely, comparison of nuclear risks with those associated with other energy technologies.

Thus although the NRC says, on the one hand, that the Reactor Safety Study makes no judgment concerning the "acceptability" of nuclear risks, an NRC environmental impact statement prepared in relation to the Diablo Canyon nuclear generating stations, states:

> The risk of accidental radiation exposure has been addressed in depth in the Commission's Reactor Safety Study and found to be acceptably low.

Representative Bingham's view of the study's presentation of the data was:

> I myself, as a fairly careful lay student of these matters, was enormously impressed by these photographs [i.e., Executive Summary, Figures 1-1, 1-2, and 1-3]. If somebody had asked me a week afterward what was the main impact of the Rasmussen Study, I would have referred to these photographs. The print, even though it is there, simply doesn't catch up to the impact of the photographs.

In his testimony at the subcommittee's hearings, Dr. Frank von Hippel, who was the organizer and a member of the American Physical Society Study on Light Water Reactor Safety, noted the misleading nature of the presentation; he said:

> Indeed, it appears that even the Chairman of the Nuclear Regulatory Commission has been misled in this connection. Only last month, he told the Pacific Coast Electrical Association that the risks from potential nuclear accidents would be comparable to those from meteorites.

The risk comparisons, without qualifications, have, in fact, been widely quoted. One example appears on the first page of a Middle South Utilities brochure presenting arguments in favor of nuclear power.

B. LONG-TERM VERSUS SHORT-TERM EFFECTS OF NUCLEAR ACCIDENTS

A pervasive criticism of the Reactor Safety Study is its failure to emphasize that the greatest health hazard associated with nuclear powerplant accidents would be in the long-term effects.

Page 2 of the Executive Summary contains graphs which compare nuclear accident probabilities and consequences with those associated with other commercial activities and with natural events.

For example, Executive Summary, Figure 1-2 of the Reactor Safety Study indicates that with 100 nuclear powerplants in operation, there would be 1 chance in 10,000 per year of an accident at 1 of these reactors resulting in 10 or more fatalities. Figure 1-2 suggests as many people will be killed by meteor impact as by nuclear powerplant accidents. The caption associated with the figure does not indicate, however, that it refers to "early" fatalities and that over a thirty- or forty-year period there would be a much larger number of deaths due to latent cancers caused by radiation exposure resulting from the accident. Figure 5-12 which appears on page 97 of the Study's main report indicates that the 1 in 10,000 accident which caused ten "early" deaths also would cause approximately 200 latent deaths per year; the text on page 74 says that such deaths might be expected to occur over a period of ten to forty years following the accident. Therefore, the same accident which caused approximately ten "early" deaths would also cause approximately 6,000 "latent" but fatal cancers.

While the second section of the Study's Executive Summary does contain a table on page 10 indicating that the number of latent cancer deaths is far in excess of the "early" deaths, the data are difficult to compare with the figures showing "early" fatalities on page 2 of the Study's Executive Summary. Moreover, the caption does not make clear that the latent deaths will occur over a thirty-year period and that, therefore, the 170 deaths expected each year should be multiplied by 30 to obtain the total number.

Also of interest is that the table on page 10 presents data in terms of "probability per reactor year" rather than in terms of "probability per 100 reactor years" which is the basis for the figures on page 2. Therefore, the 1 in 1,000,000 probability indicated on page 10 corresponds to the 1 in 10,000 probability shown on page 2. The switch from presenting data on the basis of 100 reactor year probabilities to individual reactor year probabilities tends to further downplay the total accident risk.

Mr. Saul Levine, Deputy Director of the NRC's Office of Nuclear Regulatory Research, explained in the hearings that the data were presented in this fashion because there were insufficient data concerning latent deaths associated with other types of accidents. This explanation is not readily reconcilable with the fact that the above noted table on page 10 did contain a comparison of nuclear-accident related cancers with those that would occur normally. Dr. Rasmussen said the page 10 comparison was significant because "the large majority of the normally occurring incidence of cancer fatalities are related to man-caused environmental factors." The implication is that the number of cancers caused by nuclear accidents is small in comparison to that arising from other industrial activities.

Mr. Levine further justified the overall method of presentation by noting all the relevant data were included in the report. He implied that critics had not taken proper account of the difficulty in summarizing a 2,300-page report in ten or fifteen pages.

In addressing this matter, Dr. Wolfgang Panofsky (who was Chairman of the Committee that prepared the review of the American Physical Society Study on Light Water Reactor Safety) stated at the hearing:

> I am referring to the latent effect matter. I do take a slightly less benign view of that presentation. The reason is that in terms of total fatalities caused by a potential accident, the latent effects potentially can cause several hundred times or so more deaths than the prompt effects.
>
> Therefore, they do deserve a more prominent display in comparison to other events which are within the realm of human experience than is apparent from the summary.
>
> Now it is indeed true that latent effects from an accident are of a very different nature. They essentially increase the likelihood of disease and death in the affected population.
>
> There are no good data of a comparable nature for other incidents. However, there are some data. As Mr. Levine himself said, there are data of increased morbidity and risk to life of coal-fired plants.
>
> So there are bases of judgment where one could compare the latent deaths from potential reactor accidents with those of other manmade experiences, other experiences of man.
>
> I feel it is not constructive to avoid displaying explicitly that one consequence of nuclear accidents which predominates by a substantial factor over the other causes.

C. Treatment of Uncertainty and Low Probability Events

Several reviewers were critical of the Study's seeming confidence in its presentation of conclusions concerning the likelihood and effects of low-probability, high-consequence events. Dr. Henry Kendall, professor of physics at the Massachusetts Institute of Technology and founding member of the Union of Concerned Scientists, enumerated in his testimony at the June 11 hearing what he believed to be weaknesses in the Study's approach with regard to its ability to identify all important accident sequences, its ability to take account of equipment design inadequacies, its assumptions concerning human error as a contribution to accidents, and its assumptions concerning the interdependence of reactor components wherein one failure leads to another or wherein multiple failures occur as a consequence of the same external event (common mode failures). Dr. Kendall said:

1. I regard it as impossible that RSS [Reactor Safety Study] was able to identify all of the important accident sequences. There are far too many damaging examples of serious accident chains in complex technologies—including in the nuclear experience—to support the RSS view of success in this area.

2. The RSS methodology does not include the design adequacy of equipment. This can introduce serious errors. Fault tree methodology poorly treats design adequacy considerations.

3. Human error can make major contributions to accidents. It is the least tractable source of failure in a fault tree analysis and was not treated adequately in RSS.

4. Fault tree analysis can reflect the dependency of one component failure on another if the dependency is known. However, in the vast majority of cases studied in RSS, components are assumed to fail independently. Subtle but crucially important dependencies can arise from physical proximity, unexpected component response to the abnormal circumstance of an accident or design error. Experiences with reactor accidents show this to be an important consideration as such dependencies have badly aggravated otherwise innocuous events. RSS made unsubstantiated assumptions about this dependency.

5. RSS significantly understates the role of common mode failures. Common mode failures are relatively uncommon unscheduled events in which redundant and presumably independent systems are nevertheless simultaneously disabled through some common cause. Such events do occur. For example, multiple redundant reactor shutdown mechanisms have been found to be wholly inoperative. This is a very critical issue and RSS has made an apparently sincere effort to assess it by adopting certain analytical assumptions, concluding that such failures do not contribute importantly to reactor risk. However, the same assumptions applied to combinations of common mode failures that have actually occurred assess them to be virtually impossible, indicating that this is a more important source of risk than recognized by RSS. I doubt that it is, in principle, possible to locate all such potential failures.

Dr. von Hippel was also critical of the failures to emphasize uncertainties inherent in the analysis:

> Consider now the question of accident probabilities. No uncertainties are shown on the figure where the Rasmussen group displays their computed results—yet, when you examine the calculation by which these predictions were obtained, you find enormous uncertainties. Whole categories of accident-initiating events such as earthquakes and fires were dismissed with handwaving arguments; sabotage was explicitly not considered; it was assumed without substantial analysis that the performance of emergency systems would not be degraded by accident conditions when the reactor building would be filled with superheated steam and water; the design of only two reactors was looked at in detail and the results would therefore be vitiated if there were a real "lemon" out there somewhere; and, when crucial numbers were not available, they were simply guessed—although different investigators might have guessed values 10 to 100 times larger or smaller. It was for such reasons that the American Physical Society Reactor Safety Study concluded that "based on our experience with problems of this nature involving very low probabilities, we do not now have confidence in the presently calculated absolute values of the probabilities."

Dr. Panofsky was asked by subcommittee member Representative John Seiberling to comment upon the question of understatement of risk:

> My testimony mainly addressed itself to the fact that the uncertainty of the risk assessment in my view is a great deal larger than that given in the Rasmussen report.
>
> The reason for that statement is that even though the fault tree analysis method presents a heroic effort to deal with an extraordinarily difficult situation, it cannot be any better than the information which you put into it, and this is particularly important in the case of common mode failures.
>
> You are dealing with a situation where the range of probability estimates which you have

to span as you go from what one calls "independent failures" and "dependent failures" is so large that when averaging over the two, you cannot help but obtain an estimate which will be very uncertain, because you do not have enough physical information.

The power of mathematics and probabilities are limited if you don't have sufficient physical information.

Therefore, you can have underestimates and you can have overestimates. Obviously underestimates of risks are the ones of greatest concern to everyone. However, I have no way to say whether I am criticizing the report on the basis of either underestimates or overestimates.

I am just criticizing it in reference to exaggerated statements of certainty.

In discussing EPA's assessment of the Study, Dr. William Rowe, EPA Deputy Assistant Administrator for Radiation Programs testified:

> It is not possible to combine these uncertainties directly to obtain an overall corrective risk value because they address different aspects of probabilities and consequences and because the most likely values within these ranges cannot be derived from the information in the Reactor Safety Study report. However, we believe that the Study has understated the risk based on underestimated health effects, evacuation doses, and probabilities of releases. The range is believed to be between a value of one and a value of several hundred.
>
> As a footnote, I should indicate that over the past several days we have been talking with the NRC staff and they have provided us with information which is not quite apparent from the Study, and it is most likely we are probably talking about the lower end of that range.

Related to the criticism that the Study understated uncertainty in its conclusions, are doubts concerning the Study's ability to develop estimates of the likelihood of improbable events. Thus there is the question of the impact of the Browns Ferry fire* and its consequences upon the credibility of the Study's conclusions.

Mr. Levine indicated in his testimony that, assuming occurrence of the control system damage created by the fire, there was still only a probability of approximately 0.5 percent that a core meltdown would result. The basis for this estimate is discussed at length in appendix XI of the Study; the assertion is that although several control systems were not operating as a consequence of control cables having been destroyed in the fire, there was a substantial probability that redundant safety systems were in working order, and that these could be used, as indeed they were, to prevent development of a situation in which there might be a core meltdown. The NRC's overall conclusion is:

> . . .the potential for a core melt accident as a result of the Browns Ferry fire is about 20 percent of that obtained from all other causes analyzed by the Reactor Safety Study and is within uncertainty bounds of the predictions.

Countering NRC's contention that the Browns Ferry fire gave no reason for significantly revising the Study's conclusions, are claims that it was fortuitous that the fire did not eliminate redundancy to the point where there would be a meltdown of the reactor core. For example, Dr. Kendall stated:

> It is my belief based on the study my colleagues and I have carried out so far and on private talks with engineers from TVA that

*The fire occurred on Mar. 22, 1975 at TVA's Browns Ferry nuclear powerplant in Alabama. On that date, two of the plant's 1,067-megawatt boiling water reactors were operating and a third was under construction. The fire started when a candle flame, used to test for air leaks at a point where cables passed through a wall, ignited a polyurethane sealant. The resulting fire damaged approximately 1,600 cables, causing many electrical short circuits. Following the accident, the two reactors were shut down for approximately 18 months while repairs and modifications were made. Losses suffered by TVA, as a result of the plants not operating for this period, were in excess of $200 million.

the absence of core melting in the Browns Ferry fire was a matter of considerable good luck. We can all be grateful that in the actual event a melting accident was avoided. In my view the accident was *a close call*. It was not, as RSS and NRC assert, an accident at all times under adequate control, with safety reserves, and with negligible risk of uncontrolled development toward melting. This is simply not the case.

The NRC's Advisory Committee on Reactor Safeguards (ACRS) commented as follows on the adequacy of the Study's analysis to take account of multiple, correlated errors in procedures, design, judgment, and construction such as those leading to the Browns Ferry fire:

> The ACRS believes that the methodology of NUREG 75/014 [the Study] is useful in accounting for that portion of the risk resulting from identifiable potential common mode or dependent failures, and can be used to search out the possibility of multiple correlated errors. *However, the methodology cannot guarantee that all major contributors to risk will be identified, and a considerable element of subjective judgment is involved in assigning many of the quantitative input parameters.* Both for nuclear and non-nuclear applications, for complex systems, where multiple, correlated failures or common cause failures may be significant, the record shows that investigators working independently will frequently make estimates of system unreliability which differ from one another by a large factor. *At this stage of its review, the ACRS believes that a substantial effort may be required to develop and apply dependable methods for quantitatively accounting for the very large number of multiple correlated or dependent failure paths and to obtain the necessary failure rate data bases.* [Emphasis added.]
>
> Whether multiple correlated errors will dominate the overall risk, however, is subject to question, particularly if simpler postulated accident sequences are generally the dominant contributors to the likelihood of system failure. . . .

D. Variability in Accident Consequences

In a paper which appears in the spring 1976 issue of the *Bell Journal of Economics* and submitted for the hearing record, Dr. Joel Yellin (Associate Professor of Social Sciences at MIT) states that the Study's usefulness as an aid to policymakers is diminished by virtue of the analysis having averaged risks over 68 reactor sites, rather than indicating specifically the wide variation among individual sites. Dr. Yellin notes that risks associated with particular sites vary by a factor of 1,000; e.g., between the Maine Yankee plant located in Wiscasset, Maine and the Zion plant in Illinois. The Yellin analysis infers that the Study's conclusions concerning prompt fatalities are heavily dominated by accidents at plants located near large populations.

E. Obtuse and Incomplete Presentation

Several reviewers commented that the Study was organized in a manner such that it was difficult to determine the validity of the analysis.

Dr. Panofsky testified:

> It is almost impossible to make an overall thorough critical review of the report for a number of reasons: One is the sheer length of the report and the second is that the method of presentation of the report leaves much to be desired in terms of clarity and exact statement as to origin of data and procedures actually used. Most people have read only the summary report, or the brief executive summary. However, these versions do not do justice to the main body of the report, and in some crucial instances seriously misrepresent the conclusions of the main report.

Dr. Rowe said the EPA reviewers had found the Study incomplete with regard to its discussion of accident consequences:

> Because the description of the formulation of the estimate was incomplete, EPA was not able to evaluate the assessment in terms of the range of uncertainties. We have found, however, that what we consider more reasonable assumptions in health effects, emergency actions, and estimates of probabilities of releases, would cause modifications of the overall risk analysis.

Dr. von Hippel was also critical of the presentation. He said:

> The report itself, in all its 2400 pages of detail, is virtually impenetrable to all but the professional reader. Indeed, I am not even sure about the professional reader.

F. Nuclear Risk vis-a-vis Risks Associated with Other Energy Options

The Study presented comparisons of nuclear risks with those associated with various natural phenomena and man-caused events. The Study did not compare nuclear risks with those arising from the use of other energy technologies. There are, for example, little data to indicate the health consequences arising from the use of coal for electric generation. Dr. Panofsky said the following in regard to this omission:

> The Rasmussen Report compares nuclear reactor risks with those associated with totally unrelated natural or manmade accidents. While such comparisons are of interest, it is more important from an energy policy point of view to compare the risk to public health produced by a growing reactor industry with those hazards posed by competing means of generating electrical energy. The Rasmussen Report does not deal with this question, although it is crucial in judging "acceptability" of risk. There is little question that the matter of reactor safety has been subjected to considerably more searching inquiry than the public health dangers of competing technologies. The health and environmental hazards of the only feasible immediate alternative to a growing nuclear industry, namely, increased coal production, are receiving increased attention; without going into detail here I can say that such comparisons tend to lead to the conclusion that expanded coal production imposes a larger social burden in regard to occupational and public health and adverse environmental consequences than does nuclear energy. I do not have to remind members of this committee that the current direct financial burden on the Federal Government stemming from payments to coal mineworkers and their families to compensate for occupational respiratory disease has been above $1 billion per year.

G. Applicability of Study Results to Many Reactors

The Study's conclusions are intended to apply to the first 100 large nuclear generating stations to be constructed in the United States. The analysis itself is based on the actual design of two operating reactors: the 788-megawatt Surry unit I, a pressurized water reactor; and the 1,065-megawatt Peach Bottom unit II, a boiling water reactor. Some comments on the Study concerned whether the analysis based on two reactors can be used to reach conclusions concerning ninety-eight other plants.

The Study itself addressed this question and concluded that the analysis when applied to other reactors will tend to overstate the risk.... The basis for this conclusion was, in effect, that reactor safety research and actual experience in design and operations will lead to a level of risk lower than that perceived today.

Some concern has been expressed that unique design features of particular reactors may lead to much more serious accidents than would be indicated by the analysis applied to Surry and Peach Bottom. In appearing before the Advisory Committee on Reactor Safeguards on January 4, 1977, Dr. Rowe said:

> A point which deserves stress is that those performing further work in assessment of

nuclear powerplant accident risks should not ignore any deficiency [indicated] in the Reactor Safety Study simply because it has been concluded that refinement in that specific case would not make a significant change in the overall results published in WASH-1400. With another nuclear powerplant design, having a different set of safety systems, the same deficiency may be important.

Comment

As these reports illustrate, policy analysis often seems inaccessible to citizens because of its technical vocabulary and quantitative techniques. Yet citizens should be able to evaluate such analyses in general terms by considering whether they address the right questions. Examine the Rasmussen Report in this spirit by asking: Are the basic assumptions plausible? Are any ethical issues treated as merely technical questions? What important ethical factors are ignored?

"Who. . .could have guessed," Robert Goodin asks, "that technicians would plug a leaky coolant pipe with a basketball or connect a radioactive waste storage tank to the plant's drinking water system or carry a lighted candle into electrical cable housing at Browns Ferry?" Can the "human factor" be adequately taken into account in risk analysis? If so, how? If not, does this render the analysis ethically and politically useless?

The authors of the Rasmussen Report say that they "made no judgment on the acceptability of nuclear risks." That judgment, they write, "should be made by a broader segment of society." Is the report completely neutral on the question of the acceptability of risks?

On what principles should we decide whether society should accept new risks? For example, is a risk acceptable if it is no greater than the ones we already live with? By what process should government decide whether risks are acceptable? Who should be included in the "broader segment of society" that decides the acceptability of risk—people living near a power plant or everyone who will benefit from the energy?

The waste from nuclear power plants exposes future generations to severe dangers from radioactivity. The assumptions of policy analysis tend to discount these dangers because they are so remote. People in the distant future, it is suggested, are likely to have ways of coping with such waste. In any case, they will be better off in many other ways than we are, because they will be enjoying the fruits of the investments made by earlier generations. To what extent and in what ways should we consider the welfare of distant future generations when we choose among energy policies?

The conventional decision-making rule in policy analysis says "choose the policy that maximizes the total expected utility." (The total expected utility is the sum of the benefits minus the harms, discounting for the uncertainty of each.) Some critics of conventional policy analysis suggest that because the risks of nuclear energy are so uncertain and potential harm so great we should adopt more cautious decision-making rules. Assess the moral implications of the following rules: (1) Keep the options open (reject irreversible policies). (2) Protect the vulnerable (give special weight to future generations). (3) Maximize minimum payoff (make sure the worst outcome is as good as possible). (4) Avoid harm (give more weight to causing harms than to failing to produce benefits of the same size). Under what circumstances would these rules lead us to prefer energy sources such as solar and fossil fuel over nuclear power? How would you justify each of the rules?

The Risks of Asarco

Esther Scott

On July 12, 1983, William Ruckelshaus, administrator of the Environmental Protection Agency (EPA), announced in Washington proposed standards that would regulate arsenic emissions from copper smelting and glass manufacturing plants in the United States. Arsenic had increasingly been regarded as a dangerous air pollutant and as such fell within the purview of EPA. Issuing standards for pollutants was nothing new at the agency, but this announcement attracted more than usual interest: Ruckelshaus was proposing to involve the public in helping him decide just how stringent those regulations should be.

The arsenic standards were expected to have their greatest impact on Tacoma, Washington, because of its proximity to a copper smelter owned by the American Smelting and Refining Company (Asarco) —the only smelter in the nation that used ore with high arsenic content and a major source of arsenic emissions. The proposed standards applied the best available technology to reduce emissions; but even so, there would remain a residual risk factor that might, according to EPA calculations, result in roughly one additional cancer death per year among Tacoma area residents. However, imposing further requirements to eliminate that risk could drive up the plant's costs and make it uneconomical to run. The smelter employed more than five hundred people, in a state that was experiencing over 11 percent unemployment. "My view," Ruckelshaus later told a *Los Angeles Times* reporter, "is that these are the kinds of tough, balancing questions that we're involved in here in this country in trying to regulate all kinds of hazardous substances. I don't like these questions either, but the societal issue is what risks are we willing to take and for what benefits?" To get answers to that question, Ruckelshaus announced EPA's intention of actively soliciting the views and wishes of the people most affected by the proposed regulations: the residents who lived and worked near the Asarco smelter. "For me to sit here in Washington," Ruckelshaus told the assembled press, "and tell the people of Tacoma what is an acceptable risk would be at best arrogant and at worst inexcusable."

Ruckelshaus at EPA

At the time the proposed arsenic regulations were announced, Ruckelshaus had only recently returned to the agency he had

---

Reprinted by permission of the Case Program, Kennedy School of Government, Harvard University.

first headed in 1970, the year EPA was established. During the brief tenure of his predecessor, Anne Burford (formerly Gorsuch), EPA had become mired in scandal and controversy, and was frequently attacked for failure to enforce environmental laws and to carry out the agency's mission. The appointment of Ruckelshaus, who was highly regarded for his integrity and admired for his work as EPA's first administrator, had done much to restore credibility to the agency, but mistrust of the Reagan administration's commitment to environmental issues lingered in the public mind.

In Ruckelshaus' view, moreover, there were other troubling uncertainties facing his second EPA administration. In the 1980s, scientists were no longer assuming the existence of a threshold of safety from carcinogens: in theory, at least, adverse effects could occur from exposure to even one molecule of a carcinogenic substance. Ruckelshaus, in a June 1983 address to the National Academy of Sciences (NAS), put it this way: "[W]e must assume that life now takes place in a minefield of risks from hundreds, perhaps thousands, of substances. No more can we tell the public: You are home free with an adequate margin of safety." In this starker world, Ruckelshaus told the assembled scientists,

> We need more research on the health effects of the substances we regulate.... Given the necessity of acting in the face of enormous scientific uncertainties, it is more important than ever that our scientific analysis be rigorous and the quality of our data be high. We must take great pains not to mislead people regarding the risks to their health. We can help avoid confusion both by the quality of our science and the clarity of our language in exploring the hazards.

THE ASARCO SMELTER

The Asarco copper smelting plant on the edge of Tacoma was a model of the kind of wrenching choices the EPA administrator often faced in proposing regulations. Built in 1890, the Asarco smelter, whose 571-foot smokestack dominated the landscape around it, processed high arsenic content copper ore and produced commercial arsenic as a by-product from its smelter. (Arsenic is present as an impurity in certain ores, such as copper and lead, and can be produced either as a waste or as a by-product in the smelting of these ores. The arsenic was used in the manufacture of glass, herbicides, insecticides, and other products.) The Asarco plant—the only one in the nation that used high arsenic content ore—was also the only domestic producer of industrial arsenic, providing approximately one-third of the U.S. supply of arsenic.

In recent times, the smelter had been in shaky financial condition. World prices for copper had plummeted from $1.45/lb. in 1980 to $.60/lb. in 1982, and U.S. copper processors were facing intense competition from Japan. At the Asarco plant, the cost of producing copper was $.82/lb. The plant had for awhile been able to make a profit largely due to sales of residual metals—chiefly gold—from the copper smelting process; but as the price of gold dropped, so too did the plant's earnings and, according to Asarco officials, it had been losing money for several years.

For generations, the Asarco smelter had provided a livelihood to the families of Ruston, a small company town (population 636) that had sprung up around the big smokestack, and the surrounding area. In 1983, it employed roughly 575 workers on an annual payroll of about $23 million. (According to company estimates, it could cost the state of Washington as much as $5.5 million in unemployment benefits if the plant shut down.) The smelter also contributed to the economy of the area by spending approximately $12 million locally on supplies, indirectly supporting $13 million of auxiliary business, and paying $3 million in state and local taxes. Seventy-year-old Owen Gallagher, a former mayor of Ruston and an employee of Asarco for forty-three years, spoke for many town residents when he told reporters from the *Chicago Tribune*:

> I've worked in the plant all my life. So have my brothers, and so have my neighbors. We're not sick. This town was built around that plant. People came here looking for fire and smoke in the 1900s to find work. Now the government's complaining about that same smoke and trying to take our children's livelihood away.

But the fact was that Asarco had long been regarded as one of the major polluters in the Northwest, and held what one report called "the dubious distinction of being the worst arsenic polluter in the United States."[1] Commencement Bay, Tacoma's industrial harbor, had been designated a Superfund hazardous waste clean-up site partially because of accumulated arsenic both in the soil around the plant and in the bottom sand of the bay. Asarco was also one of the two major emitters of sulfur dioxide (SO_2, a by-product of burning carbon fuel) in the state of Washington.[2]

Area residents affected by this pollution made no bones about their feelings. Bill Tobin, a lawyer and resident of Vashon Island—a semi-rural, middle-income community two miles offshore from Ruston—pointed out that, because of the high smokestack and prevailing wind directions, "we are the dumping grounds for these pollutants without any benefits such as jobs or Asarco tax payments." Island residents were particularly concerned over high levels of arsenic found in urine samples of their children and in soil from local gardens. "I'm not for the loss of jobs," one homeowner told the *Tacoma News Tribune*; but he added, "Numerous people who staked their life savings on a place and a home are finding they can't enjoy the land because of the emissions of the Asarco plant." Vashon Island was by no means the only reluctant host to emissions from the smelter. Neighboring Tacoma received tons of air pollution from the plant, and little by way of taxes from the smelter to compensate. One member of the Tacoma city council described the effects of the smelter as "somebody standing on the other side of the city line with a thirty-ought-six and firing it into Tacoma."

Over the years, efforts to control pollution from the Asarco smelter came primarily from the regional level.[3] Since 1970, the Puget Sound Air Pollution Control Agency (PSAPCA), a regional air pollution authority, had issued a variety of orders aimed at reducing both SO_2 and arsenic emissions; but Asarco had either failed to comply and paid the relatively small penalties, or delayed action through litigation and variance proceedings.

However, despite the court battles and delays, PSAPCA had made some headway in getting Asarco to comply with its orders. As Asarco officials were quick to point out, the company had spent about $40 million over a ten-year period in equipment and practices designed to reduce pollution; it had also agreed to curtail operations when meteorological conditions would cause high ambient SO_2 levels. In the late 1970s, Asarco and PSAPCA negotiated a compromise agreement covering both SO_2 and arsenic emissions. For the latter, Asarco agreed to install, by 1984, secondary converter hoods, which would reduce "fugitive" arsenic emissions that were not funnelled up the smokestack (and were considered more dangerous because they were less likely to disperse before reaching the public).[4] According to later EPA estimates, the cost of the converters would run to roughly $3.5 million in capital outlay (Asarco put the figure at $4.5 million), along with an estimated $1.5 million per year in operating and maintenance expenses. These costs were expected to result in an estimated product price increase of 0.5 to 0.8 percent.

While these local efforts were ongoing, EPA had been, more or less, out of the picture. Under the provisions of the Clean Air Act, the federal agency was required to identify, list, and promulgate National Emission Standards for Hazardous Air Pollutants (NESHAPs) for substances believed to be detrimental to human health. EPA had listed inorganic arsenic as a hazardous air pollutant in June 1980, but had decided the following year not to issue a NESHAP for it. This decision chagrined PSAPCA officials, who felt that a ruling from EPA would give them another tool to use in their dealings with Asarco. But, as it turned out, EPA was soon forced to take a stronger hand in the matter. In late 1982, the state of New York, concerned about arsenic emissions from a Corning Glass manufacturing plant in New Jersey, took EPA to court. The U.S. District Court subsequently ruled that the agency must publish proposed national standards by July 11, 1983, six months later. Thus was the stage set for Ruckelshaus' experiment in risk management.

Taking It to the Public

the risk assessment.

On July 12, 1983—the same day that Ruckelshaus announced the proposed regulations on arsenic emissions[5]—Ernesta Barnes, administrator of EPA's northwest regional office, appeared before the press in Tacoma. "We ask the public's help to consider the very difficult issues raised by arsenic air emissions," Barnes told the assembled reporters. "Together we must determine 'What is an "acceptable" or "reasonable" risk to public health from arsenic emissions.'" To aid in that process, she announced public hearings in Tacoma on August 30 and 31, to be preceded by "public workshops and other activities to inform you of the many technical issues involved."

The hearings—wherein the public had an opportunity to present testimony—would have been held anyway, because the proposed standards for the Tacoma smelter were part of a national rulemaking process. What was different, says Ernesta Barnes, was the workshops. The "underlying theory," she explains, was that the decision-makers had a "moral responsibility" to provide "adequate information" and opportunity for discussion in advance of the hearings, "so that when the actual public hearing was held, those that had chosen to become especially well informed would have not only their own values on which to base their testimony, but also better information about what the facts actually were."

At the press conference, Barnes provided a brief sketch of some of the technical issues the workshops would cover, outlining the risk assessment EPA had performed as part of the standard-setting process. EPA analysts had used a dispersion model to calculate concentrations of arsenic at over one hundred locations within approximately twelve miles of the smelter, and combined those figures with "unit risk numbers"[6] derived from previous epidemiological studies of workers exposed to arsenic. The results of EPA's analyses yielded an estimate of some 310 tons of arsenic emissions spewed out each year by the Asarco smelter, and the risk of up to four related cancer deaths per year within twelve miles of the smelter.

Because EPA considered inorganic arsenic a non-threshold pollutant—i.e., even the most minute trace of it could not definitely be said to be harmless—it determined that the arsenic emissions from the Asarco smelter should be, in the language of the proposed standards, "controlled at least to the level that reflects best available technology (BAT), and to a more stringent level if, in the judgment of the administrator, it is necessary to prevent unreasonable risks." The appropriate BAT, Barnes explained at the press conference, was the converter hoods Asarco had already agreed to (and had in fact begun installing) in its negotiations with PSAPCA.[7] The hoods would, she said, reduce arsenic emissions from the smelter to 189 tons per year. "The number of related cancer cases within a twelve-mile radius of the plant," she added, "would drop from four per year to one a year."

Ruckelshaus was free to impose on his own a "more stringent level" of emission control. He could, for instance, set emissions standards that would require Asarco to use a lower arsenic content ore[8] or to convert to electric smelting. However, Asarco maintained that the added cost of shipping the low arsenic ore would force the company to close the smelter. Similarly, the expense of switching to electric smelting would amount to $150 million in capital outlays, and could also precipitate a shutdown. It was to consider such options and their implications that Ruckelshaus sought public involvement. "Should we interpret the legislative intent of the Clean Air Act to mandate a total shutdown to produce zero risk to public health?" Barnes asked at the Tacoma press conference. "...Or is there a level of risk that is acceptable to the community and consistent with the law?"

REACTION.

The workshops were not scheduled to start until mid-August, but debate on the issue began as soon as Barnes' press conference was over. Ruckelshaus' proposal to involve the public in the final decisionmaking received, not surprisingly, intense coverage in the local media, but it was widely reported in the national press as well. Many of the headlines depicted Tacomans as facing a stark choice: "Smelter workers have choice: Keep their jobs or their health" (*Chicago Tribune*); "What Cost a Life? EPA Asks Tacoma" (*Los Angeles Times*); "Tacoma Gets Choice: Cancer Risk or Lost Jobs" (*New York Times*). Most articles quoted Tacoma area citizens who stood on opposite sides of the fence on the issue, citing their fears of ill health or unemployment. "I'm concerned about getting lung cancer," one resident told the *New York Times*, while the head of the local union representing the workers at the smelter countered, "Simply dying from cancer is not different from a man losing his job and then committing suicide."

Many observers were critical of Ruckelshaus for what one area resident called "copping out." "It is up to the EPA to protect public health," said Ruth Weiner, head of the Cascade Chapter of the Sierra Club, in an interview with the *New York Times*, "not to ask the public what it is willing to sacrifice not to die from cancer." Another local citizen told a *Los Angeles Times* reporter, "EPA came in recently and found that our drinking water was contaminated and just cleaned it up, saying they'd find out why later. Now, why aren't they just cleaning this mess up instead of asking people how much cancer they would like to have?"

On the day he announced the proposed regulations, Ruckelshaus had told the press that he was not seeking a referendum from the people, only seeing if a consensus emerged from the public meetings; however, he added, in a remark that was widely quoted, "I don't know what we'll do if there is a 50-50 split." Perhaps in part because of that remark, the notion persisted among the public and some of the press that Ruckelshaus was in fact taking a vote. This idea received its harshest expression in a July 16 *New York Times* editorial, titled "Mr. Ruckelshaus as Caesar," that compared the EPA administrator with a Roman emperor "who would ask the amphitheater crowd to signal with thumbs up or down whether a defeated gladiator should live or die." For Ruckelshaus to "impose such an impossible choice on Tacomans," the editorial stated, was "inexcusable."

Ruckelshaus responded to the editorial in a July 23 letter to the *Times* insisting that "no poll of Tacoma's citizens will be taken." The people of Tacoma were being asked for their "informed opinion," not a decision, he continued. "They know that the right to be heard is not the same thing as the right to be heeded. The final decision is mine." Ruckelshaus continued to defend his position despite the criticism. "Listen," he told the *Los Angeles Times,* "I know people don't like these kinds of decisions. Welcome to the world of regulation. People have demanded to be involved and now I have involved them and they say: 'Don't ask that question.' What's the alternative? Don't involve them? Then you're accused of doing something nefarious."

CONTROVERSY OVER NUMBERS.

Disagreements with EPA over the proposed arsenic regulations were not limited to how the agency was handling the process. Even before the official round of workshops and hearings began, EPA's risk calculations were being called into question. Just days after Ruckelshaus announced the proposed regulations, Asarco officials noted that their own figures on arsenic concentrations in the vicinity of the smelter—based on routine monitoring on the site—were significantly lower than the estimates—based on a computer model—provided by EPA; in a letter to EPA (later published in the *New York Times*), Asarco asserted that the agency had "overpredict[ed] maximum ambient concentrations of arsenic by a factor of 10." It soon turned up that EPA's model had some serious flaws—most notably the assumption that the smelter was on flat land, when in reality it was on the side of a steep hill. EPA quickly announced its intention of revising its estimates; and when they were published, the agency's new figures for overall arsenic emissions were indeed lower: 115 tons per year (instead of 310), to be lowered to 85 tons (instead of 189) with the installation of the converter hoods.[9] However, these new estimates were not available until late October—too late for the workshops but in time for the public hearings; in the meantime, there was uncertainty about what were the right figures and whom to trust. One leaflet distributed by the union at the time of the workshops asserted that the "figures used for the computer model were from 410% to 2267% higher than the actual figures."

Other questions about EPA's calculations arose around the time the workshops were to begin. Dr. Samuel Milham, Jr., of the Washington State Department of Social and Health Services, told the *Los Angeles Times* that EPA's projections of possible lung cancers were "baloney." Milham, who had conducted studies in the Tacoma area, found elevated lung cancer rates among retired Asarco workers, but, he added, "we have been looking for extra lung cancers in the community (among those who do not work at the smelter) and we haven't found them. Nothing."

THE WORKSHOPS

Against this backdrop of well-publicized controversy, the northwest EPA office (Region 10) began conducting its workshops, aimed at acquainting residents with the details of the proposed regulations in preparation for the upcoming hearings. The first workshop was held on Vashon Island on August 10, 1983, followed soon after by two more in Tacoma itself. All three workshops (which were covered by local and national TV) were well attended, particularly the two in Tacoma, which drew environmental groups, local citizen organizations, and a large number of smelter workers, who had come at the urging of their union representative. (The importance of stacking the aisles with large numbers of supporters, one observer noted, might have stemmed from a lingering feeling that Ruckelshaus was going to make the decision by counting heads.)

The format of all three workshops was basically the same: after a formal presentation by EPA staff, the audience divided into smaller groups in order to encourage dialogue and permit more individual response to specific questions. EPA national headquarters sent two key policymakers—Robert Ajax, chief of the Standards Development Branch, and Betty Anderson, director of the Office of Health and Environmental Assessment—to assist in the process. They, along with Ernesta Barnes, rotated among the groups, answering questions. Each group had a "facilitator" (hired by EPA for the occasion), a recorder, and three EPA staff from the regional office. "Every comment [from the public] was recorded...and [later] typed up," says Barnes. To accompany discussion, staff from the Region 10 office prepared and distributed a number of handouts for the workshop, including illustrations of how hooding helped control emissions, excerpts from Ruckelshaus' NAS speech, and fact sheets on arsenic controls and risk calculations.

EPA had come prepared to discuss risk assessment figures and dispersion models and present graphs and charts, yet many of the questions they encountered had little to do with verifiable "facts." "The personal nature of the complaints and questions made a striking counterpoint to the presentations of meteorological models and health effect extrapolations," wrote Gilbert Omenn, dean of the School of Public Health at the University of Washington, in a letter to Ernesta Barnes. (Omenn had been hired by EPA to observe and help evaluate the workshops.) People asked about the symptoms of arsenic poisoning, about other health effects from arsenic, about the advisability of eating produce from Vashon Island gardens. One person asked whether it would be necessary to remove a foot of dirt from her garden to make it safe (and who would pay for it); another wanted to know what effect arsenic emissions would have on animals. Ruckelshaus, who had received a personal report on the Vashon Island workshop, later recounted that, after EPA health experts finished their presentation, "A woman got up in the audience and said, 'Last week, my dog ate some spinach and dropped over dead. Did he die of arsenic?'" There were more sobering moments as well, Ruckelshaus noted, as when "another woman got up and said, 'Will my child die of cancer?'"

Nevertheless, technical matters such as the risk figures and epidemiological studies formed the basis for the majority of questions. Several inquiries focused on EPA's dispersion model and the reliability of the proposed control equipment. One resident wanted to know if any studies had been done on birth defects or miscarriages in the area; another asked whether the risk posed by emissions from the smelter was greater than the risk from ambient carbon monoxide from cars. This last question highlighted EPA's difficulties in explaining adequately the risk numbers in a relative context. Although EPA had prepared a table illustrating comparative risk, it was described as "cluttered" and needing fuller explanation. One critic commented, "How can they expect a relatively unsophisticated public to understand what these risk figures mean when the environmental establishment in this state doesn't even understand them?"

Several questions betrayed a lingering hostility toward EPA for not resolving the issue on its own. "Seems like EPA is leaving the interpretation of the law up to the public," one resident commented. "Why has Asarco continued to obtain variances from complying with the law? What authority does EPA have to do this?" Another resident asked, "At this point in time is Asarco in violation of any clean air requirements? If so, why are they allowed to operate? Why is EPA spending taxpayers' money for this process if Asarco is not violating any laws?" "We elected people to run our government, we don't expect them to turn around and ask us to run it for them," said still another. "These issues are very complex and the public is not sophisticated enough to make these decisions. This is not to say that EPA doesn't have an obligation to inform the public, but information is one thing—defaulting its legal mandate is another."

In the end, the workshops got mixed, but generally favorable notices. "Many of the questioners were impressively well informed," Gilbert Omenn wrote. "I expect that some rethinking of elements of the *Federal Register* notice and the presentation of certain assumptions and facts will result from [the workshop]." "We also got educated," agrees Randy Smith, an EPA analyst from Region 10. "The questions raised at the workshops sent some people back to the drawing board."

Closing Arguments: The Hearings

At the conclusion of the workshops, several groups asked EPA to postpone the formal hearing, slated for late August, to allow them more time to prepare the testimony. The agency agreed, and the hearings were rescheduled for early November. In the meantime, EPA participated in a few more workshops run by others—the city of Tacoma and the Steelworkers Union, where the comments and questions bordered on the openly hostile. ("I have seen studies which show that stress is the main source of cancer," one worker told an EPA representative. "The EPA is one main cause of stress.") By the end of the summer, all the interested parties were gearing up to present their arguments at the public hearing.

The hearings began on November 2, 1983. A panel of EPA officials (made up of representatives from the regional office, EPA headquarters, and EPA's research facility in North Carolina) presided over a three-day period, as roughly 150 people representing a variety of groups or just individual concerns offered their views on the proposed arsenic regulations. Their testimony ran the gamut from sophisticated technical arguments for more controls to anxious complaints that EPA was asking Tacoma residents to vote on a death sentence for one of their fellow citizens![10]

PSAPCA's testimony.

Harvey Poll, chairman of PSAPCA, was first to speak at the hearings. The PSAPCA board had evaluated EPA's proposed standard, Poll told the hearing panel, and concluded that it had some serious shortcomings. The board's primary objection was that the proposal did not establish arsenic ambient air quality standards. (EPA was, however, constrained by statutory requirements, which directed the administrator to set technology-based, not ambient air, standards in issuing NESHAPS.) PSAPCA was also concerned that because the new hooding would reduce SO_2 emissions, Asarco would be able to operate the smelter more often (instead of curtailing operations during adverse meteorological conditions), thereby actually increasing the total volume of plant-wide arsenic emissions. PSAPCA wanted EPA to consider requiring Asarco to install a flue gas desulfurization system (at a cost several times higher than the $3.5 million for secondary hooding) or, more drastically, to force the company to convert to a new smelting technology at a projected cost of roughly $130-$150 million. PSAPCA had already issued a compliance order forcing the company to choose one of these options by 1987 in order to reduce SO_2 emissions (and, of necessity, arsenic emissions) by 90 percent.

Asarco's testimony.

Next to testify was Asarco, which had hired the public relations firm of Hill and Knowlton to organize and present its case at the hearings. In addition to Armand L. Labbe, an Asarco vice president and former manager of the Tacoma smelter, the company employed five expert witnesses to refute EPA's numbers and modeling assumptions and to assert that "there *now* exists an ample margin of safety" from arsenic emissions from the smelter [emphasis in original]. Most of the experts were affiliated with universities, and each boasted an impressive curriculum vitae with relevant experience.

"Epidemiological studies demonstrate that arsenic emissions from the Asarco Tacoma smelter are not at levels that pose a health risk to the public living in the vicinity of the plant," Labbe flatly stated. Tom Downs, a professor of biology at the University of Texas, disputed EPA's extrapolations of health effects: "[EPA's assumptions about exposure to arsenic] is like saying that the effects of taking five aspirin tablets a day for a lifetime are the same as the effects of taking 500 aspirin tablets every day for 1 percent of a lifetime."

Despite its assertion that, in the words of Asarco attorney C. John Newlands, "the Tacoma Smelter is now in compliance with Section 112 of the Federal Clean Air Act," the company stated its support for EPA's proposed arsenic standards—and at the same time outlined its opposition to ambient standards or to efforts to reduce emissions further. Asarco also detailed the projects—some of them voluntary—the firm had undertaken over the years to control SO_2 and arsenic pollution. Summing up the firm's position, Labbe reminded his listeners that a prolonged depression in the copper industry had hurt the Tacoma plant's ability to compete, and that the smelter had lost money in recent years. He concluded: "We are unable to commit additional expenditures beyond installation of BAT under present conditions."

ENVIRONMENTAL GROUPS.

A host of environmental groups appeared at the hearings—ranging from long-established organizations like the American Lung Association of Washington (which, according to staff member Janet Chalupnick, played a key role in coordinating a coalition of clean air groups) to more recently formed groups like Tacomans for a Healthy Environment.[11] For the most part, the environmentalists' testimony was critical of EPA—arguing that its proposed regulation did not go far enough—and supportive of PSAPCA's more comprehensive recommendations. Several environmental organizations opposed EPA's "best available technology" approach, asserting that it effectively discouraged the development of new technology to improve emissions control. "By allowing a company to only install the available technology it says is affordable, the EPA is creating a situation in which the company is still allowed to emit substantial amounts of toxic substances but may be inclined for financial reasons to resist development of improved control technologies," said Brian Baird of Tacomans for a Healthy Environment. "If BAT standards are regularly used," he continued, "It seems reasonable to anticipate that the pace of technological development of all types of pollution control will be substantially slowed, because the market for Better Available Technologies will not only have been removed, it will have been significantly undermined."

In its testimony, the National Audubon Society reiterated Baird's point: ". . . If EPA finds zero emissions of a pollutant to be impossible, they should set the standards at the lowest levels possible rather than at the levels achievable through pollution control technologies easily affordable by the polluting industries. In order to protect [the public] health, standards must be used to force technological innovation in pollution control rather than to simply reinforce the status quo." Similarly, Nancy Ellison of the Washington Environmental Council chided EPA for proposing only the "absolute minimum" in regulation; nor did the council agree, she told the panel, "that the only choices available are hood installation or smelter shutdown. This is not a jobs-versus-the-environment issue."

THE SMELTER WORKERS.

As Ellison's remark indicated, environmentalists in the area had been making an effort to reverse the longstanding pattern of labor vs. environmental interests, and to find common ground with the workers in resolving arsenic emissions problems. Further evidence of a fragile alliance between the two groups was observable in the testimony of Michael Wright, an industrial hygienist for the United Steelworkers union. "No one has to convince our union that arsenic at high levels is risky," said Wright. "We know what arsenic has done to many of our union brothers and sisters in the Tacoma Smelter and other copper smelters. It was the death of our members which provided the conclusive evidence that arsenic causes lung cancer." Wright went on to urge EPA to encourage the development of technology which would make the plant safer for workers and community residents by reducing pollution.[12] He supported the installation of secondary hooding and research to determine if further controls would be useful and economically feasible.

Not surprisingly, the union spoke out against requiring control equipment that was too costly, and would therefore force the plant to close. Referring to a study which he used to estimate the health risk of forcing the smelter to close, Wright claimed that the stress resulting from unemployment could cause eighty-four deaths in Pierce County over a six year period. "That," he asserted, "is a considerably greater risk of death than what EPA predicts from arsenic after the installation of secondary hooding."

Following Wright's testimony, individual smelter workers spoke before the panel. In what was often emotional testimony, several members of the "twenty-five year club"—people who had worked at the plant for more than a quarter of a century—made their case. "I'm eighty-eight years old and I ain't dead yet. I'm still breathing," said Ross Bridges. The workers reflected on the good life the smelter had made possible for them and their families. If the smelter closed, they maintained, it would leave them jobless. "No high-tech industry moving into Tacoma is going to hire me," one man lamented. "The smelter is all I've got."

VASHON ISLAND RESIDENTS.

Residents of Vashon Island (which, except for Tacoma's North End, received the majority of emissions from Asarco) provided equally emotional testimony of the trauma they had experienced as a result of the arsenic pollution. One man came to the hearing sporting a gas mask, several were clad in hospital patient garb, and some carried young children to the podium to make their point. One woman, who claimed to have been diagnosed by her doctor as ultra-sensitive to arsenic, tearfully told the panel that she and her husband had been forced to sell their small farm for a fraction of its worth—due to depressed real estate prices on the island—and leave the area. Michael Bradley, chairman of a group named Island Residents Against Toxic Emissions (IRATE), made note of a recent cautionary statement issued by a local health agency warning against eating vegetables grown in the arsenic-laced soil on the island. "If Asarco cannot clean up their act and prevent this kind of pollution then they should be forced to close," he stated angrily.

POSTMORTEMS

After three days of testimony, the hearings came to an end. Ruckelshaus was not expected to make a decision on the final standards for arsenic emissions until

February or March of 1984. In the meanwhile, some assessment, at least of the process, had already begun. From an administrative point of view, the brunt of managing the tasks of informing and involving the public had fallen on Ernesta Barnes and EPA's Region 10 office. According to one source, roughly thirty people from the regional office had worked full-time for four months on the Asarco case. Randy Smith of the Region 10 office told one reporter that the "process proved terrifically costly and time-consuming."[13]

But the regional office did feel that there had been an internal payoff for them in a greater appreciation by EPA headquarters of what it meant to be "on the front lines." The regional staff felt that because of their frequent contact with area groups, they were better able to engage the public's participation. "After a while," remarked one regional staff member, "we realized we couldn't let [headquarters staff] do the spiel [in the public workshops]. The people from headquarters were just not enough in touch with the local level.... They were too scientific." Another regional office commented:

> At headquarters [in Washington, DC] they thought we were a bunch of bozos out here in the region. They could not understand why we were scrambling and bending over backwards to organize the workshops and put out easily digestible information for the public. When they arrived in Tacoma, however, and found themselves face-to-face with a well-informed and often angry public, they began to appreciate our problem a little better.

The process also proved beneficial to the regional office from the standpoint of image and public trust. A number of witnesses and observers agreed with Nancy Ellison of the Washington Environmental Council, who complimented the Region 10 office for its "openness and willingness to share information during this process." The office's cooperation and outreach efforts had, she continued, "gone a long way toward restoring trust and confidence in the agency here in the region."

Even Ruckelshaus' decision to involve the public received gentler treatment at some hands. Ruth Weiner of the Sierra Club, who had earlier criticized the EPA administrator for "copping out," stated at the conclusion of her testimony that the Clean Air Act "requires public involvement." She continued, "Moreover, in becoming involved, the public begins to appreciate the difficulty attendant on making regulatory decisions, the ease with which EPA can be made a scapegoat because the agency's blunders are so readily magnified, and the inadequacy of simply identifying 'heroes' and 'villains' in environmental protection. It may have been hard work and a headache for all of us, but the public involvement is most certainly worth it."

Ruckelshaus himself was largely in agreement with this last sentiment. Back in June, in his speech before the National Academy of Sciences, he had told his audience that, in managing risk, "we must seek new ways to involve the public in the decision-making process." He continued, "It is clear to me that in a society in which democratic principles so dominate, the perceptions of the public must be weighed." Later, as he looked back on the process he had kicked off when he announced the proposed arsenic regulations for the Asarco smelter, he found validation for these views. Ruckelshaus felt that local citizens had shown they were "capable of understanding [the problem of the smelter] in its complexities and dealing with it and coming back to us with rather sensible suggestions." In fact, he added, "the public—the non-technical, unschooled public—came back with some very good suggestions as to how they could reduce the emissions of arsenic in the plant [and still keep it open]." But, perhaps, the final proof of the success of the venture would be in the decision that—as he had often repeated—Ruckelshaus alone would make. It was still an open question as to how Asarco might respond to citizens' suggestions, and whether it would feel as sanguine as Ruckelshaus about remaining open. While he pondered his decision on the final standards, the debate on his risk management techniques continued.

NOTES

1. Barnett N. Kalikow, "Environmental Risk: Power to the People," *Technology Review* 87 (October 1984), p. 55. As a result of studies of workers exposed to arsenic in copper smelting and arsenic manufacturing plants, a number of widely respected groups, including the National Academy of Sciences and the National Cancer Institute, concluded that inorganic arsenic was carcinogenic in humans. It has been linked to skin and lung cancer.

2. The other was a coal power plant in western Washington.

3. Under the provisions of the Clean Air Act, EPA routinely delegates many of its powers to regulate and enforce to the states, which in turn can delegate their powers to regional authorities.

4. The actual order from PSAPCA to install the hoods was not issued until 1981.

5. The standards actually comprised three sets of regulations—for copper smelters processing high arsenic content ore, for copper smelters processing low arsenic content ore, and for glass manufacturing plants. The Asarco smelter in Ruston was the only facility in the U.S. that fell into the first category. The risk assessment (and resulting standards) for high arsenic content copper smelters thus applied only to that one plant.

6. In its proposed regulations, EPA defined a unit risk number as its estimate of the lifetime cancer risk occurring in a hypothetical population which is exposed throughout their lifetime to a concentration of one microgram (1/28 millionths of an ounce) of a pollutant per cubic meter of air.

7. In fact, some critics felt that EPA's (albeit involuntary) entry into the regulatory scene delayed installation of the hoods, while Asarco waited to learn what EPA would propose as best available technology.

8. Asarco-Tacoma used ore that contained 4 percent arsenic; the remaining fourteen smelters in the US used ores with 0.7 percent or lower arsenic content.

9. In announcing these lower figures on October 20, 1983, Ernesta Barnes did note that the amount of fugitive emissions released near ground level was higher than originally estimated.

10. According to one observer, a number of witnesses at the hearing were confused about the meaning of the term "risk," assuming that the risk of one additional cancer death meant the certainty of the fatality—not the worst-case probability.

11. Tacoma is the Indian name for Mt. Rainier.

12. The Occupational Safety and Health Administration—not EPA—was responsible for setting safety standards in the workplace itself. According to Ernesta Barnes, OSHA had already issued regulations requiring workers to wear respirators in the smelter.

13. Kalikow, p. 61.

Comment

William Ruckelshaus recognized that even the technically best policy analysis could not yield an answer to the question of what cancer risk should be borne by the residents of the Tacoma area, especially when a lower risk was likely to create higher unemployment. As an alternative or supplement to policy analysis, Ruckelshaus solicited the views of the people most affected by the proposed regulations. But he seemed to be uncertain about how best to use the results of this participatory process in making his final decision. In announcing his plan to hold public meetings, Ruckelshaus implied that he would let the people of Tacoma determine his decision: "For me to sit here in Washington and tell the people of Tacoma what is an acceptable risk would be at best arrogant and at worst inexcusable." Yet, in response to the *New York Times*'s charge that to impose such a choice on the citizens of Tacoma would itself be "inexcusable," Ruckelshaus said that he would not simply follow the opinion of the majority of Tacoma's citizens, but would make his own decision, presumably on the basis of his own best judgment after taking into account the views expressed by the citizens of Tacoma. Is this a morally consistent position for the head of EPA to take? Is Ruckelshaus abdicating his official responsibility in giving (or appearing to give) so much weight to current public opinion? In spending public funds on workshops rather than directly on environmental regulation? In raising levels of social stress among people who do not want to know the environmental risks under which they live?

Evaluate these reasons for involving the public in making regulatory decisions that require technical expertise: participation can (1) help restore (or create) confidence in a regulatory agency; (2) enable the public better "to appreciate the difficulty attendant on making regulatory decisions"; and (3) make the final decision fairer and wiser. Suppose that the workshops generated more criticism of the EPA and left the citizens of Tacoma more dissatisfied with Ruckelshaus' final decision than they otherwise would have been. How (if at all) would this outcome affect your judgment of whether the public should be included in the decision-making process?

Apart from the opinions of the citizens of Tacoma, what should Ruckelshaus take into account in making his final decision, and what importance should he accord to each relevant consideration? Consider how the following factors should be weighed in determining the regulatory standard: Asarco's competitive situation and rate of profit; Asarco's level of wages and employment; cost to consumers of increased prices of Asarco products as a result of regulation; cost to the EPA of various levels of regulation; scientific uncertainty concerning cancer risk associated with various emission levels; best available technology (BAT); views of citizens who are not residents of the Tacoma area; harms and benefits to future generations; the imputed value of life.

On the basis of information provided in the case, can you determine what Ruckelshaus' final decision should be? If not, what additional information does Ruckelshaus need in order to decide?

Recommended Reading

An excellent introduction to how advocates of policy analysis intend it to be used is Edith Stokey and Richard Zeckhauser, *A Primer for Policy Analysis* (New York: Norton, 1978). For a flavor of the ethical controversy over policy analysis, see Alasdair MacIntyre, "Utilitarianism and Cost/Benefit Analysis," in Tom Beauchamp and Norman Bowie (eds.), *Ethical Theory and Business* (Englewood Cliffs, N.J.: Prentice-Hall, 1979), pp. 266–76; and Tom Beauchamp, "A Reply to MacIntyre," in Beauchamp and Bowie, pp. 276–82. Also see James T. Campen, *Benefit, Cost, and Beyond: The Political Economy of Benefit-Cost Analysis* (Cambridge, Mass.: Ballinger, 1986), and Rosemary Tong, *Ethics in Policy Analysis*

(Englewood Cliffs, N.J.: Prentice-Hall, 1986). On the question of evaluating risks, see Douglas MacLean (ed.), *Values at Risk* (Totowa, N.J.: Rowman and Allanheld, 1986), and the review by Elizabeth Anderson, "Values, Risks and Market Norms," *Philosophy & Public Affairs* 17 (Winter 1988), pp. 54–65. More generally on utilitarianism and its problems, see the Recommended Reading in the Introduction.

A critical review of studies of nuclear power from a philosophical perspective is Robert Goodin, *Political Theory and Public Policy* (Chicago: University of Chicago Press, 1982), chapter 10.

On the question of the value of life in public policy, see Steven Rhoads (ed.), *Valuing Life: Public Policy Dilemmas* (Boulder, Colo.: Westview Press, 1980); and Charles Fried, *Anatomy of Values* (Cambridge, Mass.: Harvard University Press, 1970), chapter 12.

6 Distributive Justice

Introduction

On what principles should government control the distribution of goods to citizens? Utilitarians and their progeny (discussed in the previous chapter) do not believe that any special theory of justice is necessary. The right distribution is simply the one that maximizes the total welfare of most citizens. While utilitarianism is widely criticized for ignoring claims of individuals that even the welfare of the whole society should not override, the critics do not agree on what theory of justice to put in its place.

Libertarians argue that governments should secure only liberty, not distribute goods. Goods come into the world attached to specific people who have earned, inherited, or received them by free exchange, and for the state to redistribute their property without their consent is a violation of their fundamental right to liberty. Because "taxation is on a par with forced labor" (Robert Nozick), even a democratic government may not tax the rich to provide welfare for the poor. Nor may it protect the rich from competition by sheltering their industries or licensing their professions. Individual liberty, understood as noninterference, trumps social welfare and democracy.

Egalitarian critics argue that, just as utilitarianism can be faulted for submerging individuals beneath all social purposes, so libertarianism can be criticized for elevating them above all social responsibility. For egalitarians, our social interdependence creates certain duties of mutual aid.

Most egalitarian theories of distributive justice also give priority to basic liberty over social welfare. But their list of basic liberties differs from that of libertarians. It includes political liberty, freedom of religion, speech, and assembly, and the right to hold personal property. But it does not include an absolute right to commercial property or unqualified freedom of contract. According to egalitarians, although liberty has priority it is not the only good that governments should distribute. Other primary goods include income and wealth, the distributions of which are just (according to John Rawls' difference principle) only if they maximize the welfare of the least advantaged citizens.

Egalitarians are commonly criticized for subordinating individual liberty to equality. This criticism is compelling only if one accepts the libertarian understanding of liberty and its absolute value. A more general problem is that the maximization of some primary goods (such as health care) might require an egalitarian government to neglect other primary goods, since there is virtually no limit to the resources that can be spent on making people healthy.

Democratic theories of distributive justice build upon this criticism. The people, constituted by democratic majorities at various levels of government, should have the right to determine priorities among goods according to what they deem most important to their collective ways of life. Most democratic theorists recognize that majorities should have this right only when the procedures by which they make decisions are fair. But the requirements of this standard of procedural fairness are controversial. Some democrats argue that it requires governments only to secure certain basic liberties, such as freedom of speech, association, and the right to vote. Others claim that it also requires governments to guarantee the distribution of a higher level of welfare—education, food, housing, and health care—for all citizens. The first position has been criticized for permitting majority tyranny over disadvantaged minorities, the second, for smuggling egalitarian values into democratic theory and thereby encroaching on the rights of democratic majorities who may not favor so much equality.

The political controversy over the distribution of health care in the United States is an instructive problem in distributive justice. Good health care is necessary for pursuing most other things in life. Yet equal access to health care would require the government not only to redistribute resources from the rich and healthy to the poor and infirm, but also to restrict the freedom of doctors and other health care providers. Such redistributions and restrictions may be warranted, but on what principles and to what extent? The first case—the Arizona state legislature's decision in 1987 to eliminate funding for most organ transplants—is part of this continuing controversy over whether government has a right or a responsibility to provide citizens with the preconditions of a good life. The second case, which describes the controversy over AIDS testing by insurance companies in the District of Columbia, highlights the less direct but no less powerful role of government in regulating access to health care. By evaluating these political decisions that in different ways both affect the distribution of medical care, we can refine our understanding of the relative strengths and weaknesses of competing theories of distributive justice.

Defunding Organ Transplants in Arizona

Pamela Varley

Dianna Brown, who will be buried this morning in Yuma, was the first person to die under Arizona's newest death penalty law. She was forty-three years old. She had committed no murder. No conspiracy. No theft. No parking violation. No crime. Dianna Brown's only offense was to be poor and sick. Under Arizona law, that's now punishable by death.

E.J. Montini, *Arizona Republic*
September 18, 1987

In the spring of 1987, the Arizona state legislature voted to eliminate funding for most organ transplants from the state's health care program for the indigent, the Arizona Health Care Cost Containment System (AHCCCS—pronounced "access"). At the same time, however, the legislature voted to increase other kinds of health coverage provided by AHCCCS. The most controversial item was the extension of basic health service to pregnant women and to children between the ages of six and thirteen[1] in the so-called "notch group"—families that earn too much to qualify for AHCCCS automatically, but still earn less than the federal poverty level.[2]

Although the decision to extend health coverage to these women and children was debated extensively, the decision to defund organ transplants slipped through the legislature with relatively little notice or attention. A few months later, however, the legislators had to confront the effect of their decision in the person of forty-three-year-old Dianna Brown, a Yuma woman suffering from terminal liver disease. In accordance with the new state policy, AHCCCS denied Brown's request for a liver transplant in August 1987. A few weeks later, she died. In the flurry of news coverage attending her death, several legislators publicly questioned their decision to defund the transplants and called for reconsideration of the matter in the 1988 legislative session.

Background

In a brief characterization of Arizona's political landscape, the 1988 *Almanac of American Politics* states, "Arizona citizens face squarely first questions—government or free enterprise, development or environment, regulation or freedom—and tend to come out squarely on one side or the other." More often than not, the Almanac adds, they come out squarely on the conservative side. Arizona is the only state to have voted Republican in every presidential election since 1948, and Republicans heavily dominate both chambers of the state legislature. The Grand Canyon State also prides itself on a certain independent spirit. For instance, Arizona is the only one of the forty-eight contiguous states to have steadfastly resisted the convention of daylight savings time.[3] It was the last state to develop a state park system. And from 1972 to 1981, it was the only state in the country which had not accepted the federal Medicaid program.

Although the Dianna Brown case may have taken the public and even some legislators by surprise, it did not spring from nowhere. It grew out of a several-year struggle within AHCCCS to establish and enforce an organ transplant policy. More broadly, the case arose in the context of longstanding controversy over the type and cost of health care provided to Arizona's poor.

The Birth of AHCCCS

Medicaid was created at the national level in 1966 as an optional program: if a state met the federal standards established for health care of the poor, the federal government would pay a share of the costs (the percentage varied depending on the relative wealth of the state). Many states were quick to sign on, but Arizona legislators steered clear of the program. "State policymakers feared intrusive federal intervention, as well as the potential for fraud and abuse and the uncontrolled cost to the state," according to a June 1987 report on the program prepared by the federal Health Care Financing Administration (HCFA).[4] For the next fifteen years, each county in Arizona continued to provide some measure of health care to the poor with its own dollars. Over time, however, the county system resulted in "unequal eligibility, uneven services [across the state], and, most important, an increasing cost burden on the counties," according to the HCFA report. In the seventies, as elsewhere in the country, health care costs began escalating dramatically in Arizona—from $49 million in 1974 to $106 million in 1979—until they consumed, on average, a quarter of each county's annual revenues, drawn primarily from property taxes. In 1980, when Arizonans passed a referendum limiting the property tax levy, the counties' budget squeeze became a flat-out crisis: "The counties faced the possibility of a complete fiscal breakdown in 1981," HCFA wrote.

It was under this kind of financial pressure that the state legislature began to talk of ushering in a Medicaid program as a way to tap into federal funds. But many legislators remained reluctant, and during the summer of 1981, they bargained with HCFA to set up a program significantly different from a conventional Medicaid system. The Arizona program would be "experimental," designed "to contain cost by encouraging cost competition among prepaid plans and discouraging overutilization of health care," according to HCFA. In each county, different health maintenance organizations (HMOs) would bid to provide an agreed-upon health care package to AHCCCS-eligible residents in return for a fixed payment per person per month from AHCCCS.[5] The goal was to create within each HMO an incentive to keep medical costs low for routine health care. Similarly, the federal government would pay a fixed "capitation rate" per month to the state for each Medicaid-eligible person in the program (a departure from the usual method of reimbursement: paying a share of the actual medical costs incurred.[6]) For this reason, the state had an incentive to keep its own costs low and to push for low bids from HMOs.

The set-up of the AHCCCS program was also to be different from conventional Medicaid in several respects. For one thing, the entire program was to be administered by a private firm. For another, AHCCCS would not cover the full array of Medicaid services (the state received a special waiver so that it would not have to provide skilled nursing facilities for long-term care,[7] home health care, family planning, or nurse midwife services). Within the state, the program was never even called "Medicaid." In fact, according to AHCCCS Deputy Director David Lowenberg:

> When we submit a budget [to the legislature], or make presentations, or talk about policy issues, it's in terms of "AHCCCS" or—the closest we'll get is "Title IX programs." I've been asked not to put the word "Medicaid" in, because Medicaid brings up all the bad that [the legislators] have either heard personally or read about in other states. There is a high level of concern of the abuse, the fraud. They did not want to be a party to such a system in this state.

The legislature and governor approved the creation of AHCCCS in November of 1981, and the program took effect eleven months later. In retrospect, health care professionals tend to think this speedy implementation allowed too little time for program planning and development. In any event, in its first eighteen months, AHCCCS was "beset with administrative and budgetary problems," according to the HCFA report. The agency was criticized by the public for the lengthy, cumbersome process for determining eligibility. (In some cases, people reportedly died for lack of medical treatment before their eligibility was determined.) Due to financial irregularities, the legislature decided to shift administrative control of AHCCCS from the private firm to the state in March of 1984, and hired Dr. Donald F. Schaller to head the program. Schaller had had extensive administrative experience with health maintenance organizations ever since 1972, when he had left fifteen years of work in private practice to co-found the Arizona Health Plan—one of the oldest HMOs in the state. When he came to AHCCCS, Schaller had also spent a year as senior vice president and medical director of the CIGNA Healthplan, and a year as consultant to a consortium of four HMOs working with AHCCCS.

Although AHCCCS remained controversial within the state under Schaller's leadership, he is widely credited with bringing the agency under fiscal and administrative control. By early 1987, 200,469 people were covered by AHCCCS,[8] and the program had a year-long budget of $294 million. More than two-thirds of Arizona's licensed physicians participated in the program directly or through an HMO, and fourteen different private HMOs were contracted to provide health care for the program.

During its first shaky year and a half of operation, AHCCCS had no policy about funding transplants per se, partly because the agency received few transplant requests. Before his arrival, Schaller says, "I'm not sure how many transplants were paid for or what happened. There may have been one or two."

THE STATE OF THE ART IN TRANSPLANTATION

The practice of transplanting organs to treat patients began to emerge in the United States in the late 1950s and early 1960s—initially with dismal survival rates, which steadily improved. During the 1980s, transplantation became a more viable method of treatment, and was used for an increasing number of organs. By 1987, the simplest and most routine transplants available were cornea and bone transplants, followed by kidney transplants. Heart, liver, and bone marrow transplants were increasingly common, and pancreas, heart-and-lung, and other organ combinations, while rarer, were actively being developed.

But there was no question that these organ transplants were costly. According to a 1984 study,[9] the fully-allocated one-year cost of a liver transplant averaged between $230,000 and $340,000, and of a heart transplant, between $170,000 and $200,000. "This is in the range of four to ten times the cost of the other most expensive currently employed medical technologies," the task force reported:

> The costs of doing the transplant operation itself are relatively minor, whether the operation lasts three hours or twenty-three hours. The real costs come from the post-operative hospitalization and the frequent need to re-hospitalize transplant patients to treat various complications. These are very common (averaging more than one per case in most reports on the literature). They include rejection episodes, complications from the operation itself, and infections that develop because such patients take drugs to suppress their immune systems to fight organ rejection, making them more vulnerable to other infections. There are also significant costs in pre-operative work-ups, routine post-operative hospitalization, organ procurement, etc.

THE HISTORY OF TRANSPLANT FUNDING IN ARIZONA

Arizona was home to one of the pioneers of the heart transplant field—a much-celebrated young surgeon named Jack Copeland, who built a nationally recognized heart transplant program at the University of Arizona Medical Center in Tucson. Dr. Timothy Icenogle, a surgeon on Copeland's team, says that progress in the heart transplant arena was swift and dramatic in the 1980s. "Back in 1981, there were very dark days and nights of trying to take care of transplants. Survivorship wasn't very good back then. It was back in the days when there were just a few brave souls venturing into this."

It was also back in the days when transplants were covered by virtually no private insurers. "What happened back in 1981, before anyone was paying for this, [the patients] all had to go out and fundraise. And if they had the money, or were able to fundraise enough money, then they came to the 'active' list."[10] If they couldn't come up with the money, he adds, "they died fundraising." By 1986, however, Icenogle said that "almost all private insurers paid for it and if they didn't want to pay for it, we [encouraged the patient] to sue them, [with] nearly 100 percent success."[11]

> Really, the insurers don't have a choice, because heart transplantation now is not experimental. It is an accepted therapeutic modality, and it is the treatment of choice. It is just as therapeutic as getting penicillin for your pneumonia.

Icenogle adds that some companies—especially HMOs competing for business—have been persuaded that the "public embarrassment" of a protracted battle over payment of a transplant is not worth the fight. "One of them we coerced into paying for a patient, because they realized that the fallout from the lawsuit—and having to go in front of the television cameras and say what schmucks they were—was going to cost them a great deal of money."

"We play a sort of an advocacy role," Icenogle adds. "I think society demands something more from physicians than [to be] just a glob of bureaucrats, and I think we have to take a stand now and then. Our role, essentially, as patient advocate, is to tell them, well, just because the insurance company says they're not going to pay, that is not the end of all the resources. We can help show them other resources that are available."

IN THE CONTEXT OF DEREGULATION

The increasing number of organ transplants, and the growing costs associated with them, coincided with another development in the state's health care system: the deregulation of medical facilities in March 1985. Before deregulation, hospitals were required to seek permission to make capital investments in their facilities. Regulation proponents argued that without such a process, hospitals would begin to perform more and more glamorous high tech, high-dollar medical procedures—like transplants—and that costs would escalate while quality of care would decline.[12] Says Rep. Cindy Resnick (D-Tucson), a member of the House Health Committee, the transplant units "get a great deal of PR and they get a great deal of money."

> It is a money-making system. If it was just pure concern about the [medical] needs out there, we'd have far more burn units than we have transplant units. The reality is they make money on those units. You can bring in anywhere from a million to three million dollars on that service alone to a hospital a year.

"There's also a prestige factor," adds Phil Lopes, a regional director of the regulatory Health Systems Agency before it was dismantled. "You do all these fancy high tech things with somebody's ticker, and there's something sexy about that. Everybody wants to have one of those, wants to have that service. You're in the Big Time."

DON SCHALLER'S VIEW

Right from the start, Schaller was uncomfortable about AHCCCS funding of transplants for several reasons. For one, he questioned whether a program with tight resources should be spending its money on high-dollar, high-risk procedures. After all, AHCCCS was intended as a general health program for the genuinely poor. By contrast, many of AHCCCS' transplant recipients did not start out poor enough to qualify for the program, but—due to their illnesses or to the failure of their private insurance companies to cover their medical expenses—they had "spent down" their assets and become AHCCCS-eligible. Schaller worried that AHCCCS might, *de facto*, be swallowed up by such heavy dollar expenses and turn into a catastrophic health program for the general public. AHCCCS should provide "basic health care to poor people, not just cater to people who have real expensive health problems," he said in an interview aired May 29, 1986, on KAET-TV's "Horizon" program.

Schaller also had several fundamental concerns about the ethics and equity of the complex organ transplant system. For one, he questioned the fairness of the system by which scarce organs were allocated—namely, to those with money, media-appeal, or political support. For another, he objected to the high rates doctors and hospitals were charging for the procedures. When an organ was rejected, for instance, the doctors might re-transplant, substantially increasing the patient's cost: "The way things are set up, when the doctor re-operates, guess what? He gets another fee."

> The charges, I think, are excessive. Most of the funding for these procedures goes to private individuals that charge full bore and excessive fees. I would have less objection if the money went to the University of Arizona, and the University of Arizona had on its staff a physician that got only a salary for performing procedures, not a fee for each service. You could almost say that, since the surgeons charge a fee for service, they might even have a financial incentive to do more and more procedures.

Does Schaller think organ transplants have become a racket? "It's not a racket," he says, "but the financial part of it has come close to that."

Surgeons disagree with Schaller's characterization of the costs. In a September 15, 1987, television interview during KAET-TV's "Horizon" program, Dr. Lawrence Koep, a liver transplant surgeon in Phoenix, said:

> The vast majority of the cost is hospital-incurred cost. Personnel, drugs, beds, those are where we spend the lion's share of the money. Time in the operating room—these are long operations—that's horribly expensive. The kind of technology available, particularly in the OR [operating room] and the intensive care unit, is just mind-boggling.

According to Icenogle, the University of Arizona actually provides one of the least expensive heart transplants in the country, but the basic truth, he says, is that "some health care is just more expensive than other health care."

> If penicillin were more expensive, then the state legislature would not approve penicillin for pneumonias. Outpatient health care is less expensive than inpatient health care. But what it really comes down to is—is the health care proven, effective, and therapeutic?

In a few rare instances, he says, the University Medical Center has waived costs for patients, but he adds,

> I don't think the University Medical Center can make it a policy to absorb the state's responsibility to take on transplantation. Those kind of dollars do not exist. The hospital is a small hospital, it's only three hundred beds. This place does not have money to throw away.

AHCCCS' Transplant Policy under Schaller

When Schaller came on board, there was an established procedure for handling organ transplant requests. The patient would submit a request to AHCCCS which would eventually end up on the director's desk. The director would make the final decision either to grant or deny the request. Such decisions had been so infrequent before the mid-1980s that they had not caused much consternation within AHCCCS. But when Schaller became director, the number of transplants—and the amount of money spent on them—began to climb.

In 1984, AHCCCS paid for one heart, one liver, and four kidney transplants. In 1985, the program paid for two heart and sixteen liver transplants. The following year, it was one heart, one liver, seven bone marrow, and twelve kidney transplants.[13] Aggregate costs for heart, liver, bone marrow, and kidney transplants rose from $451,012 in 1984 to $1,060,954 in 1985 to $2,141,663 in 1986. In addition, transplant patients' medical expenses after surgery—even when successful—were chronically high as they needed to take immunosuppressant drugs, at an average cost of $500 per month, for the rest of their lives.

Schaller began to take a hard look at the transplant requests coming to AHCCCS, and to consider the merits of each. Rep. Resnick recalls:

> [There was] one instance—perhaps a rumor—that one of our patients, who ultimately had a liver transplant, needed a new liver because they'd used up the last one with alcohol. And they're quickly on the road to using up the second one. That's difficult for physicians in Dr. Schaller's position to see. First, the transplant is imposed on him, and then he's paying for something [and] perhaps—as he said before—the money could have been used much more wisely someplace else.

Schaller soon discovered, however, that he did not always have clear authority to make decisions about transplant requests. "You've got the legislature pushing on one end, the governor says something else, then you've got a judge that says, 'You've got to do this,' says Schaller. "You know, we tried to have a policy, but it was hard to implement a single policy and apply it the same across every case." The reality was that AHCCCS made its decisions on a case-by-case basis. Before the state legislature took action on the matter—and before the Dianna Brown case surfaced—AHCCCS confronted several controversial transplant cases. Two, in particular, contributed to the development of the legislature's policy.

SHARON BRIERLEY: A CASE OF POLITICAL PRESSURE

Whenever he did deny a transplant request, Schaller found himself engulfed in a whirlwind of political pressure, sometimes from the legislature, sometimes from the governor, and sometimes even from the White House. In 1984, for example, Schaller ran into trouble when he initially refused the request of forty-one-year-old Sharon Brierley for a liver transplant. Brierley had moved to Tucson four years earlier from Vermont after an unhappy marriage, and before she had established a new career, she began to suffer from cirrhosis of the liver, reportedly caused by a previous bout with hepatitis. When Brierley learned she needed a liver transplant, she appealed to AHCCCS. After reviewing the particulars of her case, Schaller refused Brierley's request. (In the interest of patient confidentiality, Schaller declined to talk about any specific transplant decisions.) Two state legislators intervened on Brierley's behalf. At first Schaller stood firm, but in the end, after "much wrangling and political intercession from the State House to the White House," Brierley's transplant costs were shared by the hospital, AHCCCS, and the federal government.[14]

After the Brierley case, Schaller decided to formalize his transplant policy. Following the lead of the Medicare system,[15] Schaller decided that AHCCCS—again, using its own administrative discretion to determine appropriateness—would cover heart and bone marrow transplants, but would cover liver transplants only for patients under the age of eighteen, for whom survival rates were higher. For patients eighteen and older, Schaller argued, liver transplants were still "experimental" procedures, and thus AHCCCS was under no obligation to provide them.

BARBARA BRILLO: A CASE OF JUDICIAL PRESSURE

This policy soon received a legal challenge, however. Barbara Brillo, a forty-six-year-old woman, requested a liver transplant early in 1986 and was denied by AHCCCS on grounds that she was too old. Brillo's husband, Jerome, frantically tried to reverse the decision—an effort which ended with several state legislators and a White House aide exerting pressure on AHCCCS. At the same time, he tried to fundraise for his wife. By April, still without the requisite $50,000 needed for preliminary tests at the liver transplant center at Phoenix's Good Samaritan Hospital, and with Barbara Brillo's life expectancy down to one or two months, Jerome Brillo arranged for his wife to travel to a Pittsburg center. "Down deep, I really thought they would come through for us eventually," he told the *Arizona Star* (April 11, 1986). "But, as the weeks went by, my hopes got dimmer. Yes, I'm bitter, because you know what? This could happen to anyone. And believe me, if you don't have the $50,000 (down payment), you're nowhere."

Schaller continued to defend his decision, and to feel the heat for it. In a July 7, 1986, interview on KAET-TV's "Horizon" program, Brillo's attorney, Howard Baldwin, asked, "Why should we pay $110,000 for Don Schaller's salary when we could use that money to provide medical care? Or why should we have a PR man for AHCCCS? It always troubles me to find people fighting for principles over other people's bodies."

After a rancorous court battle, Brillo won her case in the summer of 1986 on grounds that the surgery was medically necessary and was not properly considered experimental. AHCCCS was forced to fund her liver transplant, which had been carried out in Pittsburg in the interim. Within AHCCCS, "the [Brillo] court decision really precipitated a lot of discussion," says Lowenberg.

> I think what that did is showed us how vulnerable we were going to be to make policy on what's covered and not—and just from the real practical standpoint, as an agency—how do you budget that? What you soon learn is that you really don't have control, because [if you deny patients], they're going to take it to court, and you don't know how the judge is going to rule. In this case, we lost.

In fact, as AHCCCS would write in a report to the legislature the following spring:

> Although the courts, including the Supreme Court, have stated that the states have wide discretion in determining the scope of benefits that they will provide under Medicaid,[16] several courts have held that a particular organ transplant must be covered, since it was determined to be medically necessary under the circumstances.

The report also stated that although no state policy would be "foolproof in the absence of federal law," AHCCCS's counsel advised that at the least, "a statutory amendment will be required to effectively exclude coverage of organ transplants for medically needy persons, indigent persons, and eligible children." Thus, AHCCCS decided to ask the legislature to enact a state transplant policy into law. The next question: exactly what kind of law did AHCCCS want to recommend to the legislature?

Creating the New Policy

During the summer of 1986, Schaller and a group of his top administrators began to discuss various policy options. These discussions were fairly freewheeling, according to Lowenberg, with administrators tossing out a number of possibilities. He recalls:

> We started to get into [ideas like], "Well, we'll cover *one* heart transplant, but we won't cover *two* heart transplants"—in other words, if the [first transplant fails and the] person needs another one. [But] what's the rationale for drawing the line [there]?

So early on, the AHCCCS team began to consider a blanket policy: no transplants, period, a position also favored initially by the governor's staff. But, Lowenberg says, the AHCCCS administrators soon convinced themselves that this approach did not really make any sense either:

> Initially it was—either you have transplants or you don't—because when you start making exceptions, then it becomes more and more difficult to draw the line.... Then, of course, we began to look at the kidney and say, "Well, wait a minute, that doesn't make sense for the kidney or the cornea."

So Schaller and the AHCCCS team began to consider a policy to fund kidney, cornea, and bone transplants, but no other kind of organ transplants. This, they argued, was easily defensible, because kidney, cornea, and bone transplants were significantly different medically and economically from transplant of heart, liver, and bone marrow. In the case of corneas and bone transplants, the procedures were simple, there was no issue of tissue match, and they could be performed at many health care establishments.

In addition, these procedures seemed to meet the "cost-benefit" test: "For the eye implant, it was [a question:] do we allow the person to be on [the] SSI Disabled [list]? Is that in the best interests of the public, that the person becomes blind and cannot work and must be supported by either the state or the federal government?" says Lowenberg.

Kidneys were different from other major organs in that they did not require the donor's death, and were, in fact, often donated by relatives of the patients. Questions of speed, timing, and tissue match were therefore removed from the equation. What's more, though not cheap, kidney transplants were less expensive over time than the alternative—dialysis treatment. AHCCCS discovered that on average, dialysis cost $2500 per month while the average kidney transplant cost $68,000. Thus, "the 'break-even point' economically justifying kidney transplants may be after two years and three months," AHCCCS wrote in a report to the legislature. Heart, liver, and bone marrow transplants were in a whole different league, however, in terms of cost and complexity as were new transplant procedures for the pancreas or heart-and-lung.

After some consideration, AHCCCS did recommend, in the form of its budget request, that the legislature fund only kidney, cornea, and bone transplants—but, cautions Lowenberg, "I think it's real important to understand that we didn't present necessarily a 'policy.' We presented [that] this is an issue that you at the legislature and governor's office need to decide."

Leonard Kirschner's View

Schaller left AHCCCS to become a private consultant in January of 1987 and was succeeded the following month by Leonard Kirschner, a physician who, most recently, had served as the medical director of an HMO in Phoenix that treated AHCCCS patients.

Although Kirschner came to AHCCCS after the agency had already submitted a recommendation to the legislature, he quickly got behind the proposal: "Philosophically, I was already in agreement with them," he says. Kirschner's reasoning about the issue, however, was somewhat different from Schaller's. To the incoming director, "aggregate costs" were the major concern, and spending dollars where they would do the most good. A physician with twenty-two years of service in the military, Kirschner believed that—like the triage practiced on the battlefield—a public program with limited resources must establish clear priorities for treatment. Thus, he favored broad-based health care for the poor over organ transplant coverage. "You take a high risk population that gets no prenatal care—the teenage pregnancy out of the barrio, doesn't want anybody to know she's pregnant, doesn't take care of herself, is on alcohol, and tobacco, or maybe drugs—the risk of low birth weight is up to about 18 percent," he says.

> What's the cost to society for that bad baby? Neonatal intensive care unit costs for that baby are probably going to be in the range of $40,000. And to boot, what you are met with on the outside as that child grows up frequently is residual damage from that premature birth: low IQ, low lifetime learning expectancy, won't be able to function,

> mental retardation, seizures—all the bad things that happen from low birth weight.
>
> So where do you want to spend your money? Do I want to spend my money on doing eight heart transplants at a million and a half dollars? Or go out and get more of these poor people who are not getting prenatal care, and give them some prenatal care? That's about $2000 a case. What's $2000 into a million five? 700 cases? What about 700 deliveries for eight heart transplants?

"This is probably going to make me sound like Attila the Hun," Kirschner adds, but "when I have limited resources, it's women and children first. The *Titanic* concept of medicine."

More broadly, Kirschner believes that the trend toward high-tech medicine is a bad one, not just from a financial point of view but also from a human one. "A young man I was peripherally involved with a year ago had a bone marrow transplant and then went into bone marrow rejection, which is a horrible experience. He died a horrible death," he says. "Obviously spending all those resources and causing him a death far worse than he would have had from the disease makes one sit there and say, 'Well, why in the world did I do that to that person?"

> Every time we bring a new person into the world, we accept the fact that that person's going to die, and we're almost reaching the point in society where we want to repeal that biological fact.
>
> Now if there's an individual who does have those resources and wants to purchase that, we live in a capitalist society. So be it. But in a public program, that has the widest range of responsibilities, and limited resources to handle those responsibilities, I think it's unacceptable to use those limited resources in a way that really doesn't further the public good.

Legislative Action in the Spring of 1987

The legislature—which meets in regular session for only one hundred days a year in Arizona—confronted major budget difficulties during its 1987 session. Conservative Republican Governor Evan Mecham had just taken office and had come to the legislature with an extremely lean budget. At the same time, the state was dealing with a budget overrun from the preceding year, and the legislature was making some mid-year corrections to make up the difference. "So agencies, including ourselves, had to accept serious cutbacks," says AHCCCS's Lowenberg.

What's more, the legislature had to make a number of major budgetary decisions about the AHCCCS program in 1987. The whole program, enacted for five years as a "demonstration," was scheduled to end in October unless the legislature voted to extend it. In addition, the legislature was considering proposals to add services to AHCCCS, including long-term health care, provided at that time by county governments, and service to pregnant women and children between the ages of six and thirteen in the notch group—at that time, not offered at all.

Health care committees in both the House and Senate came up with versions of the omnibus AHCCCS bill. In the Senate discussion, the chair of the Health and Welfare Committee—Senator Greg Lunn (R-Tucson)—played a significant role. Lunn was a moderate young Republican, especially interested in environmental matters, who had come to office in 1981 from a career in broadcast journalism. He was known as an articulate rising young star whose district included the University of Arizona and its Medical Center. Upon learning that the legislature might defund organ transplants, the Medical Center urged its state senator to preserve funding for heart transplants. Lunn found the university's arguments convincing, and, likewise, convinced his colleagues in the Senate to include funding for heart transplants—but not for liver or bone marrow transplants—in the AHCCCS budget.

His reason, he says, was "basically twofold":

> I thought that relative to the other major categories of transplantation that we were, in essence, precluding payment for in the future—liver transplants and bone marrow transplants—that heart had shown a greater rate of success in terms of the success of the procedure itself, longevity, and the quality of life associated after a successful procedure was done.[17] Additionally, I was certainly persuaded by the fact that I believe we have one of the pre-eminent centers for heart transplantation here in the state at the University of Arizona Medical Center, and I thought it was in the interests of that facility and the research they were doing that AHCCCS continue to be a payer.

When the bill moved to the House Health Committee, the question of organ transplants received little consideration, however, and the committee opted for the recommendation of AHCCCS's administration. The two versions of the AHCCCS bill, with assorted differences, then went to the House-Senate conference committee on health care, also chaired by Lunn, for final negotiations.

THE CONFERENCE COMMITTEE RESOLUTION

When the AHCCCS bills reached the conference committee, the Senate bill included coverage for heart transplantation and also for psychotropic drugs, another expensive item. The House bill included neither of these items, but did include a significant expansion of coverage for the notch group.[18] "As in any conference committee procedure, you end up assuming that those elements that are consistent are in the bill, and then you argue about the differences," says Lunn. Within the conference committee, therefore, the transplant debate was narrowed to the question of whether or not to fund heart transplants.

Dr. Jack Copeland, the head of the U of A's heart transplant center, weighed in with a letter to the committee. The U of A had performed a total of 125 heart transplants, he wrote. During the past three years, AHCCCS had funded five heart transplants and one artificial heart ("bridge-to-transplant") procedure. "Five of these patients are doing well and living a high quality of life, and the bridge-to-transplant patient has returned to full-time employment. We currently have two AHCCCS patients needing heart transplants who are being evaluated and we project there will be five or six AHCCCS patients per year." Copeland then offered some economic arguments for funding heart transplants:

> For most of our patients (married males, less than fifty years of age with pre-school or teenage children), the major reasons for undergoing cardiac transplantation were to maintain some semblance of family stability and to resume competitive employment. Our patients are generally referred for vocational rehabilitation and one third have returned to work within six months of transplantation.

Copeland argued that even if AHCCCS refused a patient a transplant, it would have to continue to provide some health care to the person while s/he continued to deteriorate and die. Heart transplants were only performed in dire cases—where the patient's life expectancy was less than twelve months—but those health care costs could still run quite high. He wrote that on average, "according to the National Heart Transplant Study, the cost difference between a patient who is transplanted and one who is not is approximately $6,100"—not much money in the scheme of things. Copeland added:

> Should the nontransplanted patient die leaving a wife and three children (aged five, ten, and fifteen), the family becomes eligible for monthly social security benefits approximating $1036 which payments continue until the youngest child reaches the age of eighteen or until age twenty-one for all three children should they pursue college educations.

Copeland also included cost estimates for heart transplants ($65,000 to $80,000) in his letter, and mentioned that his center was likely to become one of ten approved transplant centers across the country designated by Medicare and therefore approved treatment facilities for Medicare patients.

These last two points aroused the anger and concern of AHCCCS administrators. For one, they felt Copeland had vastly underestimated the true cost of an average heart transplant (which they calculated to be $165,000).[19] In addition, they saw the emergence of the U of A as a nationally recognized transplant center to be a double-edged sword: in increasing numbers, patients would move to the state to receive medical treatment, and if they established residency and were income eligible, AHCCCS would have to pay for them. Already, two such patients had surfaced, according to Schaller, who appeared before the conference committee as a consultant to the committee:

> We're finding ourselves as a state paying for patients who move in from Idaho and California with no ability to go back to those states and collect from their Medicaid agencies our costs. That's one of the reasons I don't think we ought to pay for this, because if we're going to be attracting people from all over the country who are so impressed with Dr. Copeland's ability, I'm wondering who's going to pay for 'em. If he wants to be a regional center, let him go out and collect his money from everybody in the region—not AHCCCS.

Furthermore, AHCCCS warned that if the program began to cover each transplant requested, "it would not be long before most health insurance carriers would cease to consider transplants as a covered benefit on the theory that AHCCCS (and the taxpayers) is the paying alternative."

AHCCCS also confronted the committee with another problem: the Health Care Financing Administration. While HCFA had been willing in the past to provide extra funding for transplants on a case-by-case basis, the federal agency decided in 1986 that this arrangement was not in keeping with the spirit or groundrules of the AHCCCS-Medicaid experiment. Thus, HCFA wanted the costs of the transplants to be covered the way any other medical costs were covered—out of the basic capitation rate given to the state. In a letter to AHCCCS dated October 17, 1986, HCFA wrote that "the state will include all organ transplant costs in the base computations used to determine capitation rates for categorically eligible AHCCCS recipients, and HCFA will not provide a regular federal match based on actual organ transplant costs for these procedures on an individual basis." Paul Lichtenstein, federal project officer for AHCCCS under HCFA's Office of Research and Development, says that HCFA would have been more than willing to increase the capitation rate to reflect the cost of transplants for Medicaid-eligible people. But according to Lowenberg, it is not reasonable to try to work such changeable and erratic costs into a standard formula: "It's our viewpoint that with such a low-volume, high price type of incident, i.e., transplant, it doesn't make sense to attempt to include it in a capitation. . . . Capitation is never going to cover all the costs. Never."

This legislative tug-of-war over funding for heart transplants ended with a decision that heart transplants *might* be funded in part, but only if HCFA relented and agreed to share the costs on a case-by-case basis. Says Lunn:

> It ended in a compromise. A lot of people would have just as soon not had [heart transplants] in there at all. I would have just as soon had [them] in there [unconditionally] as an AHCCCS-covered service. So—just tire people out, that's the way—we never finished the bill. When we *abandoned* the bill, that's what it looked like.
>
> Ultimately, everything [in dispute between House and Senate committees] went in the

> bill, but modified. The way hearts got modified was squirrelly language about "if HCFA agrees to paying for it the way we would like them to participate, then we'll go ahead and do it." Psychotropics got modified by saying, "subject to legislative appropriation," so it wasn't an entitlement—it was, we'll fight that out when we come to the Appropriations Committee next year. And the notch group stuff was modified by putting it off a year, to a later effective date. It was like trying to fit an elephant through a keyhole. You had to push it in different places to get it to fit.
>
> My recollection is that [the heart transplant compromise] was proposed by AHCCCS itself. I think they probably were much more aware than I at the time of the chances of convincing Health Care Financing Administration to go along on that basis were pretty damned small, because that seems to be the case now. So I think, in retrospect, I may have been snookered.

Another member of the conference committee—Rep. Resnick—characterizes the legislature's negotiations over AHCCCS as "raw politics," primarily focused on the question of funding for pregnant women and children in the notch group. Resnick, who had been in the legislature since 1983, was a liberal Democrat from Tucson who had become active in health policy matters in 1980, when she joined a coalition working to bring Medicaid to Arizona. Like most Democrats, Resnick had initially opposed establishment of AHCCCS in favor of a more comprehensive, conventional Medicaid program. Once the AHCCCS program was in place, however, she and other Democrats had worked to make it as comprehensive as possible. During the 1987 session, the Democrats drew a line in the sand: without the notch group extension, they would vote against extending AHCCCS beyond October. The strategy, says Resnick, ultimately worked; the notch group expansion was included.

The legislative vote on the final omnibus AHCCCS bill—including both the notch group coverage and the transplant policy—was overwhelming: 44 to 6, with 10 not voting in the House; 23 to 2 with 5 not voting in the Senate. But, with so much emphasis on the notch group coverage and the general extension of AHCCCS, this vote did not reflect legislative opinion on the transplant issue per se, according to Resnick:

> There is such a select group in the legislature that actually dealt with the AHCCCS issues—there were probably eight of us at the most, and then probably only three to four of us who were intimately involved with the discussion. I don't think [the others] considered [transplants one way or the other.] In the broad scheme of things, the bill looked okay.

In any event, under the terms of the AHCCCS bill, the new transplant policy took effect August 18, 1987. Within the month, the case of Dianna Brown surfaced.

DIANNA BROWN'S STORY

Dianna Brown, forty-three, was a woman from the city of Yuma with lupoid hepatitis, an ailment which had shrunk her liver so that she could not process liquids properly. She had been nearly incapacitated since January of 1985, when her illness forced her to quit her job as manager of a doughnut shop. "I noticed I couldn't pick up anything from counters," she told the *Arizona Republic.*[20] At one point, she remembers, "I nearly fell into the fryer."

"I said, 'I'm going to have to take a leave of absence until I get better.' But then I never got better. I only got worse."

Born in Texas, Brown had quit school at a young age to support her family, and by the summer of 1987, virtually everyone in her immediate family had serious health problems. Her mother was living in a nursing home. Brown had been caring for her niece's two children ever since her niece had suffered brain damage in a car accident. Her sister had recently suffered a heart attack.

"If a transplant isn't necessary, I don't want it," Brown told the *Arizona Republic* in an interview printed September 7, 1987. "But if it is the only solution, I would like a chance for a chance." She said that she hoped "to work again": "That is a dream off in the future. Surely there is something I can do. I might not be able to work with my hands like I used to, but I'm sure I still could do something.

"I can understand that you have to look at the overall picture. I always try to understand. I can't say I always do—Lord knows I don't—but I try."

Four days later, the *Republic* reported that the husband of a woman who had undergone a successful liver transplant had started a transplant fund for Brown with $35,000 left over from their family's fund-raising effort. A radio talk-show host joined the effort, and within a few days had increased the sum to $37,000. But it was too little too late. On September 11, Brown's kidneys began to fail, preventing her body from eliminating toxins. This led to brain damage, coma, and eventual liver failure. On September 14, she died. "I don't think her death was unreasonably painful or prolonged," her personal physician, Dr. George Burdick, told the *Republic* the next day, "but in my mind it was unnecessary."

Brown's family did not even have enough money for her funeral.

The Aftermath of Dianna Brown's Death

When Dianna Brown died, the press began to reconstruct the legislature's policy decision of the previous spring, and in general, reporters and some legislators characterized it as a conscious "tradeoff" between transplants and the notch group expansion. Some observers and participants, however, believe this represents a rewriting of history. "That argument is just a whitewash," says Icenogle. "What we're talking about here is a legislature that just doesn't want to come up with the money, period. And this is their way of trying to defuse the issue."

Rep. Resnick agrees that the legislature was not really trading services. "That's how the press perceived it, and maybe they were not totally wrong, but from my perspective, we weren't making a trade." Instead, she says, dropping funding for transplants was a quick way to respond to Schaller's concern "that the thing was out of control." Other legislators agreed that they relied heavily on AHCCCS's recommendation in making their transplant policy. Says Lunn, "You try to listen to medical experts in terms of what is reasonable and what is cost-effective and what makes sense from a medical standpoint."

"Our legislative session is only one hundred days," adds Resnick, "so it's difficult to say, 'Let's talk about it during the session.' It was easier just to say, 'Let's drop authority for AHCCCS to provide these transplants and then let's re-look at the issue.' No one ever thought that we would just drop it and never deal with transplants."

Resnick saw the transplant debate as part of a larger set of issues. Rather than make an "up" or "down" decision on funding organ transplants under AHCCCS, she believed the legislature should stand back, take a broader view, and "deal with the issue of catastrophic health care."

> We ought to make the health system responsive to those kinds of needs, but it isn't necessarily the AHCCCS system. It isn't necessarily a program for the poor that ought to be responding to that.
>
> What I don't want to see is that we change state policy, allowing more flexibility in the AHCCCS program, without addressing all the other issues related to that decision, without discussing the ramifications of having too many hospitals doing heart transplants, without discussing ramifications related to the insurance industry, which will—if there's somebody out there who's going to pay for these services—back down real quick in providing those for their own

> clients. So my preference would be that we discuss it all at the same time. Otherwise you get a really bad decision.

Other legislators focused primarily on the financial aspect of the question, and the issue of fairness to individuals in need of transplants. AHCCCS's refusal to fund Brown's transplant was "asinine," "grossly discriminating," and "embarrassing," according to Rep. Earl Wilcox (D-Phoenix), a member of the House Health Committee. "If we don't make taking care of this problem a priority in our next session, we'll be remiss as legislators."[21]

"It's not a comfortable decision that we had to make," says Senate Minority Leader Alan Stephens (D-Phoenix). "Unfortunately, you have to look at it in the context of Arizona state government."

> It's been a battle in this state, in a conservative era, to increase services. And we do it on a piecemeal basis. If you want to look at people's deaths, and the case of Mrs. Brown obviously comes to mind in this situation, but if you went back, I'm sure you could find a lot of people that died in this state as a result of not getting care that's routinely given in other states, because we didn't provide the service that other states provide.

But other legislators stood by their decision. "None of us can live forever," said Sen. Doug Todd (R-Tempe). "I think it was a decision that was made by the legislative body to benefit the most residents of the state of Arizona."[22]

"The public generally is not willing to, say, double the taxes in this state to insure that everyone got the maximum possible health care—the public isn't willing to accept that," stated Rep. Bill English (R-Sierra Vista) in an interview aired September 15, 1987 on KAET-TV's "Horizon" program. While he defended the legislature's decision to defund transplants, however, he left open the possibility of changing the decision in the future:

> I'm going to say that next year, the decision may very appropriately be a different decision, with progress in the state of the art [of transplantation]. What is the right decision for today may not be the right decision for tomorrow.

EXHIBIT 1. ARIZONA HEALTH CARE COST CONTAINMENT SYSTEM ADMINISTRATION

Human Organ Transplants	*Fiscal 1986-1987*[a]			*Program Change*			*Fiscal 1987-1988 Request*		
	Number	*Cost Per*	*Amount*	*Number*	*Cost Per*	*Amount*	*Number*	*Cost Per*	*Amount*
Heart Transplants	0	0	0	8	164,000	1,312,000	8	164,000	1,312,000
Liver Transplants	1	134,000	134,000	5	134,000	670,000	6	268,000	804,000
Bone Marrow Transplants	1	230,000	230,000	7	230,000	1,610,000	8	460,000	1,840,000
Totals	2		364,000	20		3,592,000	22		3,956,000

a. For fiscal 1986-1987, transplants are paid as inpatient hospital in the Fee-for-Service category. Number and costs are estimated as transplant bills have not been submitted at the date of this budget request.

EXHIBIT 2. ARIZONA HEALTH CARE COST CONTAINMENT SYSTEM

MEMORANDUM

TO: Leonard J. Kirchner, M.S., M.P.H.
Director

FROM: Bill Merrick, Assistant Director
Division of Financial Management

SUBJECT: Expansion of the Children's Program to Include Age Six (6) through Thirteen (13)

DATE: March 23, 1987

Before going on to the numbers, I calculated the fiscal impact for nine (9) months beginning October 1, 1987, and six (6) months beginning on January 1, 1988. These breaks logically follow our contracting cycle. In my opinion, it would not be cost effective to start the program on July 1, 1987 as AHCCCS would need to bid this population for the period July 1, 1987 to September 30, 1987.

Now the numbers:

	Number of Children	*Total*	*State*	*Federal*
Nine (9) months beginning October 1, 1987	27,000	$10,304,400	$8,449,800	$1,854,600
Six (6) months beginning January 1, 1988	26,200	$ 6,800,500	$5,576,400	$1,224,100

For the purpose of comparison, I also calculated the fiscal impact of just adding the six (6) year olds by the nine (9) and six (6) month breaks.

	Number of Children	*Total*	*State*	*Federal*
Nine (9) months beginning October 1, 1987	4,250	$ 1,708,628	$1,401,075	$ 307,553
Six (6) months beginning January 1, 1988	4,023	$ 1,078,155	$ 895,009	$ 183,146

Should you have any questions, just give me a buzz.

NOTES

1. The legislature had already voted to cover notch group children under age six the year before.

2. In January 1987, AHCCCS's income eligibility cut-off for a family of four was $5,354, while the federal poverty level for a family of four was $13,750. Advocates for the poor estimated that fully two-thirds of Arizona's poor were not eligible for the AHCCCS program.

3. More recently, parts of Indiana have also chosen to exempt themselves from the law.

4. *Evaluation of the Arizona Health Care Cost Containment System,* by Nelda McCall, project director, and Paul Lichtenstein, federal project officer, Office of Research and Demonstrations, HCFA, Department of Health and Human Services, June 1987.

5. HMOs were not expected to finance catastrophic health care, however; thus the relatively exorbitant costs were assumed by AHCCCS. For instance, if any individual's costs exceeded a set amount per year—typically $20,000—then the HMO would be responsible for only a small percentage of the excess; the bulk of the cost would be paid by AHCCCS.

6. This "capitation rate" was to be 95 percent of what HCFA projected it would have paid the state under a conventional Medicaid program (which would have

been 60 percent of costs for all Medicaid-eligible residents).

7. Long-term care was still to be provided county-by-county.

8. Of those people, 127,983 were either AFDC or SSI recipients, and thus automatically eligible for federal reimbursement. Another 51,770 were in roughly the same income range, but were not AFDC or SSI recipients; these people were not eligible for federal reimbursement. In addition, 20,716 AHCCCS recipients were children under age six from notch group families.

9. *Report of the Massachusetts Task Force on Organ Transplantation,* presented to the Massachusetts Commissioner of Public Health and the state's Secretary of Human Services in October 1984.

10. Those waiting in line for a suitable donor organ and ready for surgery at any time.

11. AHCCCS did its own informal survey of some twelve HMOs and insurance companies in the state, and found that while many offered some kind of coverage for transplants, they sometimes imposed limits on them as well. For instance, eight of the companies surveyed offered coverage for heart transplants, but one of the eight had a "cap" on the total amount it would spend and one said its decisions would be based on its own assessment of the individual's case. Thus, in reality, half the companies offered unlimited coverage and half offered limited coverage or none at all.

12. By fall of 1987, no one had traced the impact of deregulation on transplants per se, but a *Phoenix Gazette* reporter, Brad Patten, did a survey of hospitals performing by-pass surgery published on August 26, 1987, and found that: ten hospitals had begun performing by-pass surgery since deregulation; the number of open heart surgeries was up 36 percent from 1983 to 1986, but the number performed per hospital was down 85 percent; hospitals performing a relatively low volume of by-pass operations had a death rate twice that of hospitals performing a high volume of such procedures; and that overall, the death rate for Medicaid patients in by-pass procedures had increased 35 percent in Arizona between 1984 and 1986.

13. Of the forty-five patients to receive these transplants between 1984 and 1986, nine died within a few months of surgery.

14. *Arizona Daily Star,* May 29, 1986.

15. Medicare tends to be a standard-bearer for states in determining which procedures are considered "experimental" and which are regarded as standard medical care. Health care providers and insurers are under no obligation to provide "experimental" care to patients.

16. AHCCCS administrators found that, by 1986, thirty-three states were paying for liver transplants, twenty-four for hearts, thirteen for hearts-and-lungs, and three for pancreases.

17. This view of transplants was not uniformly held. Leonard Kirschner, for instance, argued that on purely medical grounds, he found liver and bone marrow transplants for children to be the most successful and defensible procedures.

18. According to Bill Merrick, assistant director of AHCCCS's Division of Financial Management, health care for some 26,200 notch group children under six between January 1, 1987, and June 30, 1987, was expected to total $6.8 million (with HCFA paying $1.2 million). He estimated that to serve 27,000 children aged six to thirteen from October 1, 1987, to June 30, 1988, would cost $10 million—with HCFA picking up about $1.9 million. (See Exhibit 1.)

19. In fact, the AHCCCS administrators showed the committee that in another context, the university itself had estimated the cost of a heart transplant at $153 million. That cost-estimate included hospitalization as well as twenty-four months of drugs and follow-up care, however.

20. "Patient doomed by policy; AHCCCS refuses to fund transplant," by Martin Van Der Werf, *Arizona Republic,* September 7, 1987.

21. *Arizona Republic,* Sept. 16, 1987.

22. Ibid.

AIDS Testing in the D.C.

Leslie Brunetta

In November 1985, District of Columbia councilmember John Ray (D-at large) introduced a bill that would have imposed a five-year moratorium on all kinds of applicant AIDS-testing in the district by health, life, and disability insurers. Ray wrote the bill (entitled the Prohibition of Discrimination in the Provision of Insurance Act) after learning that insurers were testing for antibodies to the AIDS virus in order to predict who would come down with the fatal disease. He believed insurers had panicked, and were using a test whose accuracy and predictive value hadn't yet been properly established—the test had been FDA-approved just the previous March, and exclusively for blood bank screening and research at that. Ray thought that use of such unproven tests constituted civil rights discrimination against applicants because it didn't conform to standard insurance underwriting practices.

Five years, Ray figured, would allow time for the tests to be refined and for solid actuarial data to be collected. At that point, insurers would be able to make reasonable predictions about applicants' future health and to decide fairly whether to charge increased premiums when a test indicated infection with the AIDS virus. In the meantime, insurers would be allowed to deny insurance coverage to applicants actually diagnosed as suffering full-blown AIDS, just as they were allowed to deny coverage to applicants diagnosed as suffering from cancer, heart disease, or diabetes.

If the council passed Ray's bill, the district would become the only jurisdiction in the United States to outlaw all kinds of AIDS-testing by insurers.

The AIDS Epidemic

Representatives from the district's gay rights groups were the ones first to tell John Ray about AIDS testing by insurance companies in the district. They had reason to be concerned: the burden of the AIDS epidemic had so far fallen heaviest on gay men. Of the 13,611 AIDS cases reported to the United States Centers for Disease Control (CDC) by October 1985, 78 percent had been homosexual or bisexual men.

Acquired immune deficiency syndrome (AIDS) was generally believed to be caused by infection with the human immunodeficiency virus (HIV), which had been shown to destroy white blood cells known as T-lymphocytes in laboratory tests. The destruction of these cells severely damaged a person's immune system, making him or her susceptible to infections and cancers normally vanquished by a healthy immune system. These opportunistic infections or neurological disorders caused by HIV were what usually killed AIDS patients, most often within two years of AIDS diagnosis. Although there were treatments that could help some AIDS patients overcome bouts of *Pneumocystis carinii* pneumonia and slow the progress of Kaposi's sarcoma (two of the otherwise-rare diseases commonly attacking AIDS sufferers), there was no cure for AIDS itself.

HIV passed from one person to another via blood or semen—through anal, vaginal, or perhaps oral sex, the sharing of needles by intravenous drug users, or transfusions of contaminated blood or blood products. HIV infection affected different people in different ways. Many people infected with the virus showed no symptoms. Some had swollen lymph nodes but felt fine. Others suffered from AIDS-related complex (ARC)—they had fevers, diarrhea, and swollen lymph nodes, but didn't meet the clinical criteria for AIDS diagnosis. Researchers didn't know whether these conditions were just way stations along an ineluctable drive ending in full-blown AIDS, but many suspected that this was true. (In fact, some people died of ARC without ever having met the criteria for AIDS diagnosis.)

As of mid-1986, there were 1 million to 1.5 million people in the United States infected with HIV, according to US Public Health Service (PHS) estimates. How many of those people would eventually be diagnosed as suffering from AIDS was a matter of some uncertainty in 1986: the PHS anticipated that 20 to 30 percent of infected people would go on to develop the syndrome within five years, while the

Institute of Medicine and National Academy of Sciences Epidemiology Working Group estimated that 25 to 50 percent would be diagnosed as suffering from AIDS within five to ten years. Other experts made even higher estimates, predicting that in the long run the fatality rate might approach 100 percent.

Further PHS estimates were similarly disheartening. By the end of 1991, less than a decade after the disease was first defined, 270,000 people in the US would have suffered from full-blown AIDS, they predicted. Of that total, 174,000 would be alive and in need of some kind of care during 1991. By the end of that year, the US would have had a cumulative total of more than 179,000 deaths, with 54,000 of those occurring during the year.

By the time John Ray's bill was making its way through council committee hearings, the district had already begun to feel the impact of the AIDS epidemic. The district's Commission of Public Health had counted 349 diagnosed AIDS cases from September 1980 through March 1986, and 191 of those people had died. The CDC calculated that the district, along with California, Florida, New York, and Texas, had one of the five highest rates of HIV infection in the country.

AIDS exacted not only a heavy human toll but also a heavy financial one. Estimates current in 1986 were that total hospital costs for each AIDS patient from diagnosis to death ranged from $50,000 to $150,000. These figures were considered likely to change significantly with the advent of new treatments (which could increase life expectancy and hence costs) and with the institution of lower cost hospice or community care for patients well enough to avoid hospitalization.

The question of who actually paid these costs generated immense speculation. The medical and general press reported various estimates of who was picking up the tab. Some experts said commercial insurers were paying 70 percent of the bill and Medicaid 20 percent, others that commercial insurers were paying 20 percent and Medicaid 70 percent, and others floated every other ratio in between. The true figures were nearly impossible to determine because there was no universal system for either billing or reporting AIDS costs.

Testing

The AIDS screening tests used by insurers employed relatively new knowledge and techniques gained from the fields of biochemistry and biotechnology. Because the virus itself was difficult to detect, they tested for the presence in the blood of antibody to HIV. The tests involved a series of steps requiring the conscientious attention of lab technicians. And their results were open to divergent interpretation.

The Food and Drug Administration had approved the ELISA (enzyme-linked immunosorbent assay) technique in March 1985 for blood bank screening use. It was relatively easy to use, relatively inexpensive, and quite accurate. But it was not entirely reliable. Blood samples testing positive with the ELISA were therefore routinely retested. If the result was again positive, the blood sample was retested again using the more elaborate Western blot procedure. This test was labor intensive and relatively expensive and no standard interpretation of its results existed. Scientific opinion on how the test's results should be interpreted shifted with some frequency.

Both the ELISA and the Western blot were often described as being about 99 percent accurate. But in reality, judging their performance was more complicated than pinpointing a single accuracy figure. Medical screening tests were generally evaluated on their "sensitivity" and "specificity." "Sensitivity" was the probability that a test would give a positive result for a person who was actually positive. Test specificity was the probability that a test would give a negative result for a person who was actually negative. Subtracting the specificity rate from 100 percent gave the "false positive rate"—the rate at which people who were truly negative tested positive.

Determining sensitivity and specificity ratings for the ELISA and the Western blot proved a demanding, and often contentious, occupation. The lack of a "gold standard" against which to judge the tests' results presented the greatest obstacle. It was often difficult to isolate actual HIV in AIDS patients, so that it was impossible to independently verify positive ELISAs or Western blots. In practice, sensitivity was calculated by finding the number of positive test results among diagnosed AIDS patients. Specificity was found by counting the number of negative test results among a group of random blood donors who were assumed not to have been infected with HIV. At the time the FDA granted it a license, the most widely used ELISA had a published sensitivity of 93.4 percent and specificity of 99.78 percent. The latter indicated a false positive rate of about two in 1000. (ELISA sensitivity and specificity were found by the accepted protocol of repeating the test on any blood sample initially found positive; that is, a positive test was one that had tested positive twice.) The Western blot, a technique rather than a packaged device like the ELISA, didn't require an FDA license for use, so it had no published ratings. Trials conducted by the College of American Pathologists found Western blot sensitivity of 90.7 percent and specificity of 95.3 percent.

TESTING CONCERNS

So long as the ELISA and the Western blot were being used just to screen blood donations, not a great deal of controversy about either their employment or accuracy arose. Because false negative results could lead to the use of infected blood, they were all but eliminated by sliding the ELISA cutpoint in the direction of heightened sensitivity. The increased false positive rate meant only that some blood donations were needlessly, but prudently, discarded.

But questions surfaced when life and health insurers began to predict which applicants were likely to sustain substantial medical costs or to die before their premiums had paid for their benefits. From the insurance industry's standpoint, testing for the HIV-antibody was no different from testing already done to determine which insurance applicants were prone to heart disease, diabetes, or other life-threatening and expensive disorders.

The district's gay community, and gay rights organizations across the country, reacted strongly. Fearful of increased discrimination, they saw testing as part of a larger social tendency to "blame the victims" of the epidemic, and thereby to isolate and stigmatize them. "A positive test result, if disseminated, is like being branded with a yellow star," Mark Senak, legal director of Gay Men's Health Crisis, told the *New York Times*, when asked about his objections to AIDS testing anywhere in the nation. "It not only marks an individual as uninsurable, but can have a devastating impact on that person's ability to obtain housing, employment, and financial services."

Dissemination of results seemed a real possibility to gay advocates. Insurance companies shared information such as medical examination results through the Medical Information Bureau, a central clearinghouse designed to combat applicant fraud. The bureau's records could be subpoenaed by government agencies. Advocates also worried that insurance agents might divulge test results, particularly to employers, who would have an interest in positive results, especially if they shared responsibility for paying employees' medical benefits.

Gay advocates believed that, ever since insurance companies had become aware of the AIDS epidemic, they had been denying insurance coverage to certain kinds of male applicants in some neighborhoods in order to avoid taking on homosexual policy holders. Such practices were called "red-lining" after some banks' practice of not issuing mortgages in poor black neighborhoods which had been literally outlined in red on lending officers' maps. In testimony given to the district's council, Steve Smith, a member of the DC Committee on AIDS Issues, said that insurance industry sources had leaked information concerning such practices: "Some companies will attempt specifically to exclude gay men by examining a number of factors, including marital status, relationship to beneficiary, and the observations of sales agents. Some companies propose redlining larger demographic groups in which AIDS cases occur, such as unmarried men aged twenty to fifty living in certain zip code areas."

The insurance industry denied such practices, and argued that, in any case, antibody testing would eliminate even the temptation to redline: testing all applicants offered a much more accurate and fair method of predicting who was at risk. Here, epidemiologists and other medical experts joined the fray. Even though the ELISA and Western blot were very accurate tests, false positive results would always be a possibility. And the proportion of apparent positives who were false positives would rise when testing a population having a relatively low true positive rate—for instance, the population applying for insurance policies. Some experts calculated that in a population having the same infection prevalence rate as that estimated for American blood donors, as many as 22 percent of confirmed positive results would be false positives. Testing opponents asked whether such a false positive rate—and the loss of insurance coverage and possible fear, loss of security, and discrimination resulting from false positive results—could be justified by insurers' desire to eliminate AIDS from their risk pools.

But testing opponents' primary worries were not with the side effects of testing, but with its intended effect, namely to make an entire group of people uninsurable. Those who tested positive would have no health insurance to cover their costs. And without life insurance, they would not only be unable to provide for their dependents in case of death, but also unable to obtain mortgages or make other long-term financial commitments requiring insurance coverage as security. Furthermore, advocates argued, because many, indeed most, of those who were antibody-positive would not develop AIDS during the period of an insurance contact, healthy people were being unfairly denied coverage. In contrast, they claimed, other tests used by the insurance industry sought to find actual disease—such as the presence of heart disease, diabetes, or cancer. The HIV screens, they argued, showed only that a person might be at risk.

At root, this argument was a debate over who should pay for the costs of AIDS treatment in a system without national health insurance. Gay activists believed that somehow profitable insurance companies could and should bear that burden. In contrast, the industry felt that it was a public responsibility. Further, they argued, companies didn't pay, policy holders did and by not testing you enforced cross subsidy from some policy holders to others. In a competitive market, they continued, that pattern simply could not be sustained.

Some AIDS patients of course did have commercial insurance coverage, usually through their employers, although once sickness forced them to leave work, their coverage usually lapsed after a period of time. For those without commercial coverage, Medicare was little help because few AIDS patients survived the twenty-four-month waiting period that program required. The federal government had, however, designated AIDS a "listed impairment" so that qualified AIDS patients could have their costs paid by Medicaid without having to endure a waiting period. But "qualified" meant "poor." Before AIDS patients could receive Medicaid payments, they had to spend down their assets, that is, use all of their savings, other equity, and assets until they reached the qualification limit. In the district, Medicaid patients could own no more than $2500 in assets including all savings, life insurance policies, stocks and bonds, and possessions and have less than $377 monthly income.

The district government was concerned because, under this system, it wound up bearing a significant share of the costs. Because many private hospitals were reluctant to admit AIDS patients, especially those without commercial insurance coverage, many of these individuals found their way to DC General Hospital, the city hospital funded by the district. As the epidemic grew, it began to batter the hospital's—and therefore the district's—budget. Between 1981 and the beginning of 1986, DC General had spent over $1 million on inpatient AIDS care, very little of which had been reimbursed. It wasn't fair, testing opponents argued, for commercial insurers to take profits from healthy policy holders while forcing AIDS patients to spend themselves into poverty before dumping them on the public health care sector. How large a fraction of the district's AIDS patients (many of whom were drug abusers) would ever acquire health insurance even if it were available, was a different matter.

THE INSURERS' ARGUMENT

Insurers argued with almost all these points. In fact, insurers asserted, testing opponents had turned the debates concerning coverage of AIDS costs upside-down. Testing opponents were the ones who were discriminating—by asking other insurance policy holders to subsidize AIDS patients, and by asking that AIDS sufferers be given more favorable access to benefits than those people suffering from cancer, heart disease, diabetes and other maladies disqualifying them from regular coverage.

"Stripping insurance companies of the ability to assess risk literally rips out the foundations of insurance and marks a very dangerous precedent that could ultimately destroy the industry," Karen Clifford, counsel for the industry trade group Health Insurance Association of America, told the *New York Times.* The companies argued that in order to meet their obligations to policy holders (and make a normal rate of profit), incoming premiums had to, over time, amount to more than outgoing claims settlements plus operations costs. Even though some policy holders would turn out to have better luck than others, at the time the policy was written, each one had to be assigned to a "risk pool" of people with equivalent risk. Then those in that pool could be charged a rate so that on average their premiums would cover the payout for which the insurer was liable.

In both the health and the life insurance markets, companies sold both group and individual policies. About 85 percent of the people in the district who had health care insurance had group coverage obtained through their employers. Everybody in the group paid the same premium based upon the last year's health and mortality experience of the group as a whole. So long as an applicant signed on for coverage upon employment or during regular enrollment periods, and had no known preexisting health problems, no physical examination was required. In keeping with this practice, insurers so far had not been testing group applicants for HIV-antibody.

The problem was in the area of individual policies. To assign applicants to the appropriate "risk pool," insurers typically used age, height, weight, occupation, past health experience, personal habits (such as smoking, drinking, drug use, exercise), and upon the results of a physical examination, including tests for diabetes, cholesterol levels, blood and other disorders. This data was used to calculate expected payouts and hence premium rates. Because groups of employees tended to be in better health than those who applied to individual coverage, group rates were much lower. Indeed, long before AIDS, insurers worried that some who applied for coverage did so because they knew they were sick (adverse selection). Given their inability to predict costs perfectly, insurers rarely gave individual coverage to anyone determined to have five times more than the standard risk of death. For this reason, many applicants suffering from diabetes or heart disease, or having a past history of cancer, were denied coverage.

To insurers, the HIV-antibody tests seemed a natural part of this risk assessment process: If there were a way to find out which otherwise-healthy applicants were at increased risk for coming down with the deadly disease, it was ridiculous to treat them unlike any other group and to assign them to inappropriate risk pools and charge them premiums that did not cover the costs of their health or life policies. Of course, insurers argued, the tests predicted risks imperfectly, but so did all other data companies used. Even if actuarial calculations were based upon the PHS's low mortality estimate (that 20 percent of those testing positive would die of AIDS within seven years) the risks were unacceptable—a thirty-four-year-old man testing positive was 26.6 times more likely to die within seven years than a thirty-four-year-old man in standard health. The epidemic's demographics only aggravated the situation: men between the ages of twenty and fifty had historically been expected to make least use of health care resources and to pay premiums over many years.

Insurers predicted dire consequences if they were not allowed to test for the HIV-antibody. They already anticipated losses from those AIDS-related health care costs and deaths that they were contractually committed to cover under existing group and individual policies. Based upon PHS estimates that the annual cost of treating AIDS patients could reach $16 billion by 1991, insurance industry estimates were that perhaps more than $10 billion of that sum would fall on insurers' shoulders, not counting death benefits. The only way to stem the tide, and to ensure that the insurance industry could fulfill its obligations to other policy- and stockholders was to make sure that more high-risk policies weren't taken on.

By refusing to allow insurers to test for HIV-antibodies, the District Council would guarantee that the industry would sustain even greater losses than currently predicted, according to industry representatives. Those at high risk would be foolish not to apply for both a health insurance and a large life insurance policy when they knew they would only have to pay artificially low premiums for a short time. This would force up the rates in the individual insurance market, hurting those who could not get into groups or else forcing them out entirely because they couldn't afford premiums. Since the healthiest would be the first to go uninsured, the pool would become sicker, premiums skyrocket and the cycle reinforce itself. Without new infusions of cash, insurers would soon be unable to pay out on already contracted policies. Individual life insurance policies and risk pools were structured similarly; the life insurance market would also be destroyed.

Insurance industry representatives said that they sympathized with the plight of AIDS victims. And, they said, they would uphold their commitments to those AIDS patients who already held insurance policies. But AIDS was a societal problem—it was time to ask the nation as a whole to take care of those who were suffering. It was grossly unfair to ask the insurance industry—meaning stockholders and insurance policy holders—to shoulder a large proportion of the financial burden imposed by the epidemic. Many stockholders, after all, were just ordinary citizens who had invested in the company in good faith and were entitled to a return that protected their assets. Indeed since insurance companies are widely viewed as relatively nonspeculative investments, much of their stock is held by small investors and in modest trusts and estates.

JOHN RAY'S BILL

Councilman Ray was not persuaded by these arguments. He believed that use of sound methods of risk assessment by insurers—even if they seemed to affect certain groups of people harshly—was fair business practice. But he also believed that use of unsound assessment methods constituted discrimination. As far as he was concerned, use of the ELISA-Western blot protocol as a basis either to deny a person insurance or to charge him or her increased premiums was unsound.

First, Ray argued, FDA-approval of the ELISA specifically stated that the test was inappropriate for any use other than blood bank screening or research. Second, he believed that the test's false positive rate was unacceptable. Third, there had been no time for the development of reliable actuarial studies: the disease, which was believed to have a latency period of perhaps seven years or more, had first been identified only five years before, and the antibody tests had been in use for less than a year. There were no solid numbers upon which to base morbidity and mortality predictions, a point he presumed the insurance industry conceded, as they hadn't yet produced any actuarial studies.

Ray drafted a bill that he thought would complement existing regulations by ending discrimination against those testing HIV-positive and taking into account the insurance industry's need to assess risk. If enacted, the bill would make it illegal for health, life, and disability insurers to request or require anyone to take any kind of AIDS screening test. If the insurer somehow discovered that an applicant had received a positive test result in the past, it would be illegal either to deny coverage or to charge higher premiums on the basis of that knowledge. Issuing policies having exclusions or reductions of benefits for the treatment of AIDS or any disorders associated with HIV infection (unless the exclusions or reductions applied to other illnesses generally) would be illegal. Redlining of people thought to belong to groups at high risk for HIV infection would also be illegal. But insurers would be allowed to deny coverage to those people already diagnosed as suffering from AIDS, and could order tests for applicants who had other symptoms of AIDS present to the extent that only a test result was needed to complete an AIDS diagnosis consistent with the Centers for Disease Control definition.

Five years after the bill's enactment as law, these restrictions would essentially drop away. At that point, insurers wishing to use any AIDS screening test could apply to the district superintendent of insurance for permission to charge those applicants testing positive increased premiums. If the district commissioner of public health found that the test was "reliable and accurate," and the superintendent of insurance determined that the premium increase was "fair, reasonable, nondiscriminatory, and related to actual experience or based on sound actuarial principles applied to analysis of a substantial amount of scientific data collected over a period of years," permission would be granted and insurers would be free to require the test.

Ray cited several precedents for his bill. During 1985, California, Florida, and Wisconsin had enacted insurance testing bans. (California's law prohibited use of the ELISA but allowed use of another, more general immune response test; Florida's law was ambiguous and the subject of much debate in that state; Wisconsin's law prohibited use of the ELISA until the state medical examiner declared it a worthy test.) At least eight other states prohibited insurance discrimination on the basis of exposure to diethylstilbestrol (DES), which had been linked to vaginal and cervical cancers, or on the basis of genetic traits such as sickle cell anemia (primarily affecting blacks) or Tay-Sachs disease (primarily affecting Jews).

The Bill Gets a Hearing

At hearings held by the Committee on Consumer and Regulatory Affairs, January 28, 1986, representatives of the DC Committee on AIDS Issues testified that they had evidence of redlining by insurers and knew of cases in which people had been denied coverage on the basis of positive antibody tests. If this practice continued, they argued, those who did develop AIDS would have to rely on publicly financed health care.

Insurance Superintendent Marguerite C. Stokes testified that it was impossible for insurers to carry out usual risk assessment procedures on those testing positive because there was no known actuarial data on their life experiences. However, she also testified that, as usual, insurers should be allowed to discover pre-existing conditions. But this discovery process should be limited to the questions, "Do you have AIDS?" or "Have you ever been medically diagnosed as having AIDS?"

Two representatives from the district health care community also spoke in favor of Ray's bill. The District of Columbia Hospital Association (whose members stood to gain revenue if more patients were covered) supported the bill. Senior Vice President Calbrieth L. Simpson put it this way:

> To allow insurance companies to discriminate against a particular category of patient simply because it requires intensive medical treatment would run counter to the whole purpose of insurance and would establish a terrible precedent of subjecting any group of patients, regardless of disease, to be denied coverage because of a determination that their disease was too costly or socially unacceptable.

The DC General Hospital Ad Hoc Committee on AIDS chairman also spoke in support of the bill, citing principles of equal access to health care and the cost of AIDS treatment already absorbed by the hospital.

Only one insurer testified in favor of Ray's bill—Blue Cross and Blue Shield for the National Capital Area. BC/BS's representatives testified that neither in the district nor anywhere else in the nation did BC/BS demand physical examinations, blood tests, or answers to questions concerning health or "lifestyle" from applicants for group coverage or, during thirty-day annual open enrollment periods, from applicants for non-group coverage. During the rest of the year, applicants for non-group coverage were asked broad health questions, but none of the questions concerned AIDS or lifestyle.

Two large insurance trade associations sent representatives to speak against Ray's bill. Karen Clifford, counsel for the Health Insurance Association of America, explained the insurers' need to use screening tests when facing the fact that the AIDS epidemic was still spreading. Without use of the tests, she testified, insurers were confronted with the possibility of financial catastrophe. According to Clifford, the bill

> ignored the most basic and traditional principles of insurance and accords both AIDS victims and those at risk for developing AIDS a position not granted to individuals afflicted with or at risk of developing cancer, heart disease, or any other illness.

Presenting life insurers' arguments to the committee were the legislative director of the American Council of Life Insurance (which represented the 629 companies writing 95 percent of the country's life insurance), Kemper Life Insurance Companies' vice president and medical director, Dr. Gary Graham, and Northwestern Mutual Life Insurance Company's associate medical director, Dr. Robert Gleeson. Gleeson echoed Clifford's position that the bill discriminated against other insurance applicants:

> If an insurance company is permitted to obtain information about an applicant suffering from any one of dozens of diseases—heart attacks or anemia, to name just two—why should the carrier of the AIDS virus be given special treatment and a total exemption from relevant tests?

Graham reported that Kemper had been using the antibody tests in all states except California and Wisconsin since October 1985. Use of the test was not discriminatory, he said:

> By requiring these tests on all blood samples, we affirm our underwriting practice of not discriminating on the basis of sexual preference. By requiring the test nationwide, we have not redlined any city or locality where there is a known incidence of AIDS.

If Kemper were denied the ability to use the test, he continued, premiums for individual policies would become unreasonable. He predicted that Kemper would pull out of the district if Ray's bill were passed.

Ray asked Clifford, Graham, and Gleeson why the insurers hadn't pulled out of California or Wisconsin, and why the insurers' predictions of large premium surcharges and loss of coverage hadn't come true there. Clifford responded that it was still too early to assess the impact of the testing bans in those two states, so that premium increases might yet occur. Ray surmised that there had been little impact on the health insurance market for two reasons. First, he said that the per-patient AIDS-care cost estimates of $150,000 publicly quoted by the insurance industry were inflated. He told Clifford that he had obtained minutes from an August 14, 1985, ACLI and HIAA joint meeting citing an HIAA report that estimated per-patient costs of $35,000. Clifford replied that the $35,000 estimate was preliminary and was expected to be increased. Ray secondly predicted that the costs arising from those testing positive who did eventually develop AIDS would have a minuscule effect on premiums because the cost would be spread across a huge pool of people.

Ray also expressed continuing reservations about the adequacy of the tests. He brandished a memo attached to the HIAA report that he had obtained, written by the chairman of a drafting group on legislation and supporting documents for the industry position on testing. The memo stated that:

> Most aspects of antibody testing are very confused and unsettled at the present time.... A person may test positive with Abbott's [one manufacturer's] ELISA and negative with Electro-Nucleonics' [another manufacturer's]....Commercial manufacturers are scrambling for market share by making improvements of one kind or another. Products that we see today will probably not exist tomorrow. Perhaps some persons testing positive today may test negative tomorrow (and vice versa) by virtue of modified or replaced tests.

In all of this, the insurance companies could not argue on free-market principles that they should be left alone. Insurers were exempt from federal anti-trust laws, but subject to a number of regulations, varying from state to state, designed primarily to guarantee that insurers could fulfill their contractual obligations. To conduct business in the district, life and health insurers had to submit records to the superintendent proving that they had sufficient reserves to cover policies and were otherwise financially viable. The superintendent also looked over their actuarial tables and loss experiences each year to ascertain that their premium rates were "fair and reasonable." Furthermore, the district had outlawed premium and benefit differences based on race, and had mandated that treatment for alcohol and drug abuse and mental illness be included in regular health coverage.

John Ray is one of four members of the council elected at-large. Eight others are elected by wards. He is a black with a citywide base in a predominantly black city. He chairs the Consumer and Regulatory Affairs Committee considering the AIDS/Insurance issue and has a professional background, as an attorney, dealing with insurance firms. In past elections, he has had support from Washington's substantial gay community, though he has not been unusual in attracting such support. His appeal, however, has been broad. There is speculation that he might be a future mayoral candidate. Ray knows that, because of its high incidence among intravenous drug users as well as gays, AIDS is an increasingly prominent issue in the black community. At least one black minister has taken the view that testing should be permitted.

As Ray considers both the policy and the politics, how determined should he be to see that the ban on HIV testing become a part of District of Columbia statutes?

Comment

Did the Arizona legislature make a moral mistake in defunding most organ transplants? To answer this question, we need to consider the practical alternatives open to the legislature: no funding of transplants at all, partial funding (of all transplants), full funding (of some or all transplants), or funding of a more comprehensive health insurance program. Distinguish between the choices available to individual representatives and those available to the legislature as a whole. How should an individual legislator view the alternative suggested by Representative Resnick—extend the funding of AHCCCS with greater "notch group coverage," but postpone the decision to fund organ transplants until the legislature can consider a catastrophic health care policy? How should one assess, from the perspective of the legislature as a whole, Dr. Schaller's worry that a decision to fund transplants might convert AHCCCS from a program for poor people into a catastrophic health program for the general public?

Try to identify the moral principles that underlie the arguments made by various physicians and legislators, and then consider objections to them. What principle, for example, supports Dr. Kirschner's *"Titanic"* concept of medicine, which favors broad-based health care for the poor over organ transplant coverage? Assess the conception of the public good in Kirschner's argument that it is "unacceptable [for government] to use. . . limited resources in a way that really doesn't further the public good." Can a vote against funding heart transplants be morally defended on grounds that funding will encourage too many heart patients to move to Arizona? Can a vote in favor of funding be defended partly on the grounds that funding will benefit a state medical school that excels in heart transplantation?

Schaller and the AHCCCS team claim that a decision to fund kidney, cornea, and bone transplants, but not heart, liver, and bone marrow transplants, is "easily defensible" because of the medical and economic differences between the two sets of services. What (if any) is the moral relevance of these differences?

Part of the controversy focused on whether the legislature was deliberately trading-off transplant funding for notch group expansion (as the press suggested) or whether they simply did not want to appropriate the funds necessary to fund both (as Dr. Icenogle claimed). How would you decide whether a legislature is "trading off" one health need for another or declining to spend more on total health care? What is the moral difference between these approaches? How should a legislator decide how much money the government should spend on health care? Representative English suggests that the criterion is what the public is willing to pay for health care. Is this a sufficient standard? A necessary one? For what reasons is health care properly considered a more important good than some other goods funded by government? Which others? How much access to health care is enough?

Assess Representative Wilcox's claim that the refusal to fund Dianna Brown's transplant was "grossly discriminating." Is the differential treatment people receive by virtue of their state residence equally troubling, as Senator Stephens suggests? Or are differences in treatment acceptable as long as they "benefit the most residents of the state of Arizona," as Senator Todd argues? Explain how we should (and should not) distinguish between those health care services that must be funded and those that need not be funded, to satisfy the principle of distributive justice. Compare and contrast the justice of the following: (1) funding treatment for different diseases on the basis of total cost; (2) funding treatment for different diseases on the basis of cost-effectiveness; (3) funding treatment for people suffering from the same disease on the basis of survival rates; (4) funding treatment for people suffering from the same disease on the basis of future productivity; (5) funding basic health care for poor citizens; (6) funding basic health care for all citizens; (7) funding basic and catastrophic health care for all citizens. Before you conclude that only the last avoids injustice, you need to answer the argument that it too is likely to be discriminatory by reducing funds available for other basic human services, such as welfare, education, and police protection.

Should the Arizona legislature be faulted for the process by which it made the decision to defund organ transplants? What might have been gained and what lost had the legislative debate (or the committee deliberations) been more extensive and more public?

The AIDS-testing case complicates the distinction between the health services that government should fund and those that people should be free to buy on the market. The issue before the District of Columbia Council concerned the right of the government to regulate the private market in health insurance. When is preventing discrimination a sufficient reason for regulating the private market? What does nondiscrimination require in this case?

Assess the moral force of each of the following arguments for placing a ban on AIDS-testing by insurance companies: (1) the test does not conform to standard insurance underwriting practices; (2) the test's accuracy and predictive value have not as yet been adequately established; (3) the test has an unacceptably high rate of false positives and could therefore make healthy people uninsurable; (4) insurance companies do not yet have reliable actuarial studies on which to base their rates; (5) the test would make an entire group of people uninsurable; (6) the test would shift the costs of treating AIDS patients substantially to the District government; (6) there is precedent for bans on testing and antidiscrimination statutes in other states (though no precedent specifically for a ban on AIDS-testing).

Which (if any) of these arguments are essential to the case against AIDS-testing? Which are consistent with the policy favored by Council member Ray, who wanted to prohibit AIDS-testing but to permit insurers to deny coverage to people already diagnosed as suffering from AIDS? (He would also permit insurers to order tests for applicants who had other symptoms of AIDS.)

Consider the following arguments in defense of the insurance industry's use of AIDS-testing: (1) AIDS-testing would eliminate even the temptation to "redline"; (2) the government rather than private insurance companies should bear the cost of treating AIDS patients; (3) other consumers of health insurance should not be asked to subsidize AIDS patients; (4) a ban on AIDS-testing discriminates against people suffering from other diseases (such as cancer and diabetes) that disqualify them from regular coverage; (5) a ban on AIDS-testing will eventually destroy the market in health and life insurance; (6) insurance companies avoid discrimination on the basis of sexual preference by requiring nationwide AIDS-testing on all blood samples.

Try to formulate the criteria by which to judge when (if ever) it is nondiscriminatory to charge an applicant higher than average rates for insurance. What legislation on this issue should Council member Ray and the District Council support, and why?

Recommended Reading

The most consistent statement of libertarian theory is Robert Nozick's *Anarchy, State and Utopia* (New York: Basic Books, 1974), especially pp. 149–231. For the libertarian case against government subsidies for medical care, see Loren E. Lomasky, "Medical Progress and National Health Care," in Marshall Cohen et al. (eds.), *Medicine and Moral Philosophy* (Princeton, N.J.: Princeton University Press, 1981), pp. 115–38; and Robert Sade, "Medical Care as a Right: A Refutation," *New England Journal of Medicine,* 285 (1971), pp. 1288–92. See also "Letters to the Editor in Response to Sade," *New England Journal of Medicine,* 286 (1972), pp. 488–93.

John Rawls' *A Theory of Justice* (Cambridge, Mass.: Harvard University Press, 1971) is the most systematic statement of egalitarianism. See especially pp. 90–108 and 221–34. For a Rawls-influenced defense of distributing health care based on need, see Norman Daniels, "Health-Care Needs and Distributive Justice," in *Medicine and Moral Philosophy,* pp. 81–114, and his fuller statement in *Just Health Care* (Cambridge, England: Cambridge University Press, 1985). For an assessment of the egalitarian case, see Amy Gutmann, "For and Against Equal Access to Health Care," in Ronald Bayer et al. (eds.), *In Search of Equity: Health Care Need and the Health Care System* (New York: Plenum Press, 1983), pp. 43–68. Peter Singer provides a sophisticated utilitarian case for a national health service in "Freedoms and Utilities in the Distribution of Health Care," in G. Dworkin et al. (eds.), *Markets and Morals* (Washington, D.C.: Hemisphere Pub., 1977), pp. 149–73.

On AIDS, see Ronald Bayer, *Private Acts and Social Consequences: AIDS and the Politics of Public Health* (New York: Free Press, 1989), and Christine Pierce and Donald Van De Veer (eds.), *AIDS: Ethics and Public Policy* (Belmont, Calif.: Wadsworth, 1988).

7 Equal Opportunity

Introduction

> Imagine a hundred yard dash in which one of the two runners has his legs shackled together. He has progressed 10 yards, while the unshackled runner has gone 50 yards. How do they rectify the situation? Do they merely remove the shackles and allow the race to proceed? They could say that "equal opportunity" now prevailed. But one of the runners would still be 40 yards ahead of the other. Would it not be the better part of justice to allow the previously shackled runner to make up the 40-yard gap; or to start the race all over again?—Lyndon B. Johnson

Deciding what is the better part of justice in a footrace is easy. The social problem that President Johnson intended his analogy to address is difficult: What employment policies does justice require in a society with a history of discrimination? The problem is hard in part because the stakes are so high. Jobs are a means to income, power, prestige, and self-respect. Yet the race for employment cannot be started over again, and employers may not be obliged to help those who have been shackled by discrimination make up the distance in the ongoing race.

The most widely accepted principle governing the allocation of jobs in our society is nondiscrimination. The nondiscrimination principle has two parts. The first stipulates that the qualifications for a job be relevant to its social function. The second specifies that all qualified candidates be given equal consideration for the job.

This simple statement of the principle masks the complexity of its application in particular cases. What qualifications are relevant, for example, to the job of teaching mathematics in a public high school? Knowledge of mathematics clearly is relevant, but the job should not necessarily go to the candidate who knows the most mathematics. Just as relevant to the job but much harder to measure is teaching ability. Certain personality traits—ability to get along with other teachers or to win the respect of students—also predict success on the job. But it would be unfair to refuse to hire blacks or women because other teachers cannot get along with them or because some students have less respect for them.

We must therefore add a proviso to the principle of relevance: candidates should not be disqualified on grounds of prejudice.

Equal consideration certainly prohibits employers from refusing to look at a candidate just because the person is a woman or black. But it may also require employers to actively seek applications from women and blacks if they are not applying for jobs because of past discrimination. Equal consideration therefore may require different treatment for different categories of people: more active recruitment for blacks and women than for white males and more active recruitment for blacks than for women.

Proponents of preferential hiring—the selection of basically qualified persons of a disadvantaged group over more qualified persons of an advantaged group—reject the nondiscrimination standard. They correctly point out that the standard does not permit employers to choose less qualified candidates for a job because they are underrepresented in the workforce or have been discriminated against in the past. Although they concede that nondiscrimination would be the right procedure in a just society, they argue that only preferential treatment can satisfy the principle of fair equality of opportunity in a society burdened by a history of injustice.

There are two distinct interpretations of how preferential hiring remedies past discrimination. The first is that preferential hiring makes up the distance that women and minorities have lost in the race for employment by giving them the jobs they would have had if they had not been discriminated against. Critics argue that preferential hiring is at best an imperfect means of achieving this goal because the most qualified women and minorities often have suffered the least past discrimination. On the second interpretation, preferential hiring provides compensation or restitution for past injuries. Critics of this view question whether jobs are the most effective or fairest means of compensation. They suggest that the costs of preferential hiring are inequitably distributed and the benefits are rarely directed toward those who have suffered the most.

The cases in this section illustrate two types of policies intended to promote justice of hiring—policies designed to remedy a private company's particular history of discrimination, and policies designed to remedy more broadly based discrimination by providing proportionate representation in the public sector. In judging the AT&T settlement, which affected the jobs of thousands of people, we must rely partly upon statistical summaries and generalizations concerning the past employment practices and future goals of the employer. In judging the proposal before the Pasadena city council, which affects far fewer people, we must rely almost entirely on statistics showing underrepresentation in the workforce and generalizations about past discrimination not only (or even primarily) by the city government but also by society at large. In both cases, even when we are concerned with justice to individuals, we must attend to the general categories in which policy speaks.

Affirmative Action at AT&T

Robert K. Fullinwider

I. Introduction

On January 18, 1973, American Telephone and Telegraph Company (AT&T) entered into an agreement with several agencies of the federal government to implement what was called by the judge who approved it the "largest and most impressive civil rights settlement in the history of this nation."[1] Over a six-year period AT&T spent millions of dollars and undertook extensive overhaul of its personnel policies to carry out the terms of the agreement.

Several pieces of litigation flowed directly from the agreement itself. Moreover, the government used its "victory" over AT&T as the springboard for further successes, gaining affirmative action agreements with Delta Airlines later in 1973 and with the Bank of America and several trucking companies in 1974. Also in the same year it won an agreement with nine steel companies, representing 73 percent of the steel industry, which resulted in a backpay settlement of $31,000,000 and extensive changes in the employment practices of the companies.[2]

The case began in late 1970 when AT&T applied to the Federal Communications Commission (FCC) for an increase in long distance rates. In December of 1970, the Equal Employment Opportunity Commission (EEOC) asked to intervene in the proceedings. The EEOC had been created by Title VII of the Civil Rights Act of 1964 to enforce the Title's prohibition of employment discrimination. At the time EEOC sought to intervene in the FCC hearings it had received more than 2,000 individual charges of illegal discrimination against AT&T.[3] Because the FCC's own rules prohibited discrimination in the industries it regulated, the EEOC decided to take advantage of the pending rate hearing to press a case against AT&T on many grounds, accusing it of violating equal pay and anti-discrimination legislation as well as FCC rules.

In January 1971, the FCC decided to establish a separate set of hearings on the employment practices of AT&T and to allow the intervention of EEOC. The hearings were to determine if AT&T's practices violated equal employment opportunity policies and to "determine. . .what order, or requirements, if any, should be adopted by the Commission."[4] During sixty days of hearings, involving 150 witnesses and hundreds of exhibits, a voluminous record of AT&T employment practices was created.[5]

EEOC charged that AT&T engaged in widespread sex segregation of jobs. Males were consistently channeled away from "female" jobs and females away from "male" jobs; transfers and promotion policies maintained the segregation; most of the lowest paying jobs were "female" jobs; and women were paid less than men when they did comparable work.

Of AT&T's 800,000 employees in 1970 (encompassing those employed by AT&T and its Bell System companies but excluding Western Electric and Bell Labs), more than half were women. Yet women comprised only 1 percent of career management personnel. Those women who held career management positions were generally limited to staff positions, without supervisory functions. Upper management personnel were drawn from two sources. On one hand, they were recruited into management training courses from colleges and universities. Company policy limited or excluded women from these courses. Secondly, management personnel were also recruited from within the Bell companies, primarily from craft positions. These were "male" occupations.[6]

At the nonmanagement level, operator, clerical, and inside sales jobs were considered "female" jobs; craft and outside sales jobs were considered "male." Men and women applicants were given different tests and channeled into different divisions.

> Since women were not allowed to take the tests, they could not qualify for craft jobs in the Plant Department. When openings arose in the Plant Department, women employees with seniority were not permitted to bid on them.[7]

Of the more than 400,000 women employed by AT&T in 1971, 80 percent of them were in three job categories: operator, clerical, and administrative (secretarial). Each of these were overwhelmingly "female" jobs. Sex-segregation of jobs was in fact more extensive within the Bell Companies than within the nation as a whole.[8]

The jobs that women worked in were lower paying than the jobs men worked in even when they did the same work. The inside craft job of "frameman" was a male job in all companies except Michigan Bell, where it was called "switchroom helper" and was a female job. When it finally concluded its affirmative action agreement with the government, AT&T had to give $500,000 in pay raises to the switchroom helpers at Michigan Bell to bring their wages to the level they would have been paid had they been male framemen.[9]

The EEOC also accused AT&T of discriminating against blacks and other minorities. Of the 72,000 blacks employed in 1970, 80 percent were female. Black males were few and held the lowest-paying "male" nonmanagement jobs. There were extremely few blacks in management positions. Hispanics were likewise poorly represented in the workforces of those Bell companies located in areas of the country with high Hispanic populations.[10]

In 1971, as the EEOC and the company prepared for the hearings, they also began informal negotiations, encouraged by the administrative law judge, to find a basis for settling the case without formal proceedings. The negotiations continued on an intermittent basis throughout 1971 and 1972 as the hearings were conducted. During this period the Department of Labor issued Revised Order #4. This was a set of rules to implement Executive Order 11246, issued by President Johnson in 1965. It required all federal contractors as a condition for retaining or acquiring federal contracts to take "affirmative action" to assure nondiscrimination in employment practices. The Executive Order assigned to the Secretary of Labor the responsibility of designing and enforcing rules to implement the Order. Revised Order #4 contained rules which required contractors to create affirmative action plans containing goals and timetables for the hiring and upgrading of "under-utilized" groups—minorities and women. The Department of Labor assigned to Government Services Administration (GSA) the authority to administer Revised Order #4 in the telephone industry.

In the winter of 1972, AT&T submitted an affirmative action plan to GSA. Six months later, without consulting EEOC, GSA approved the plan. EEOC protested to the Solicitor of the Department of Labor, who set aside the GSA approval and joined EEOC in its negotiations with AT&T.[11]

EEOC had by this time filed charges against AT&T in three different federal courts. The hearings before the FCC still held open the possibility it would take regulatory action against AT&T. Moreover, the new participation of the Labor Department meant that AT&T's status as a federal contractor could be jeopardized unless it produced a satisfactory affirmative action plan. Faced with dim prospects of resisting successfully on three fronts, AT&T

agreed to a consent decree in January, 1973, which was approved by the federal District Court in Philadelphia, one of the jurisdictions in which EEOC had filed charges. Without formally admitting any wrongdoing, AT&T agreed to undertake to increase the representation of women and minorities in job categories in which they were underrepresented and to compensate through back-pay and wage increases those who were putatively victims of its past discriminatory practices. In return, the government agreed to suspend its legal and administrative actions.

II. The Consent Decree

There were two elements to the agreement embodied in the January, 1973, consent decree. AT&T would first pay $15,000,000 in back-pay to 13,000 women and 2,000 minority men, and would make additional wage adjustments for 36,000 women and minorities.[12] As it worked out, the wage adjustments amounted to $30,000,000 the first year, for a total outlay of $45,000,000. (On March 30, 1974, AT&T and the government signed a second consent decree, which covered management personnel, calling for an additional $30,000,000 in backpay and wage adjustments for 25,000 persons.)

Second, the company formulated a Model Affirmative Action Plan which altered its recruiting, transfer, and promotion policies, and which set hiring and promotion "targets" or "goals" for fifteen job classifications. The ultimate minority goals for each Bell company were set in accordance with the minority ratio in the local labor force. The ultimate female goals were set at 38 percent for most job classifications in which they were underrepresented.[13] Accomplishment of these ultimate goals would result in proportional representation of minorities and women in all the job classifications in which they were underrepresented—that is, would result in minorities and women being employed in the same proportions to their numbers in the relevant labor force. The objective was "statistical parity."

To move toward the ultimate goals, yearly intermediate "targets" were formulated for each Bell company and each job classification by means of an elaborate formula. Based on estimations of yearly hiring and promotion opportunities in a classification, the current percentage of minorities or women in that classification, and the ultimate goal for that classification, yearly goals could be formulated.[14]

For example, suppose in job X at Central Bell 10 percent of the workers were female. Since the ultimate goal for females in X is approximately 40 percent (this is the level of female participation in the nation's workforce), the company was only at 25 percent of "full utilization" (proportional representation). By a special formula, this percentage was to be multiplied by a factor of 2 and the resulting percentage be the goal for female new hires for the year. If, for example, there were ten openings anticipated for the coming year in X, five of those hired would have to be women.

The hiring and promotion goals, consequently, required hiring and promotions at rates proportionately greater than the availability of women and minorities in the relevant labor pools or promotion pools. This was clearly expressed in the Model Affirmative Action Plan:

> The Equal Employment objective for the Bell System is to achieve, within a reasonable period of time, an employee profile, with respect to race and sex in each major job classification, which is an approximate reflection of proper utilization....
>
> This objective calls for achieving full utilization of minorities and women at all levels of management and nonmanagement and by job classification *at a pace beyond that which would occur normally....*[15]

An important feature of the Model Plan, which facilitated this accelerated hiring and upgrading, was provision for an "affirmative action override." In accord with its union contract, the company's promotion criteria called for "selection of the best qualified employee and for consideration of net credited service...."[16]

Where employees were equally qualified, length of service was supposed to be decisive. The "affirmative action override" permitted (and required) both criteria—"best qualifications" and "longest service"—to be defeated whenever adhering to them did not allow the company to meet its goals (targets). In a supplemental order signed in 1976, the obligation of AT&T in regard to its affirmative action goals was expressed thus:

> ...to the extent any Bell System operating company is unable to meet its intermediate targets in [non-management] job classification 5-15 using these criteria [i.e., best qualified, most senior], the Decree requires that...selections be made from any at least basically qualified candidates for promotion and hiring of the group or groups for which the target is not being met....[17]

Thus, the consent decree and the Model Plan quite clearly envisaged the use of racial and sexual preferences. The intermediate targets or goals of the operating companies in the Bell System were mandatory; and the companies could and must hire or promote less qualified and less senior persons over more qualified and more senior persons if this was what it took to achieve the intermediate targets.

Since the consent decree applied to 800,000 employees for six years, it is not hard to imagine that there were numerous instances in which employees or applicants were preferred over others because of their race or sex. It is difficult to establish exactly how frequently AT&T resorted to racial or sexual preferences. The company changed the way it defined "affirmative action overrides" during the duration of the decree, it avoided careful counting, and it never classified as overrides any preferences given in management jobs (classifications 1-4).[18]

Two observers report 28,850 overrides in 1973–74, although they differ on how many there were in 1975–76. The first claims there were about 12,000, the second that there were approximately 6,600.[19] A third observer reports 70,000 overrides during the four-year period.[20] It would probably be a reasonably conservative conjecture that over the full 1973–79 life of the consent decree, and counting both non-management and management jobs, at least 50,000 times AT&T gave a racial or sexual preference in hiring or promoting someone. AT&T achieved 90 percent of its intermediate goals in 1974, 97 percent in 1975, and 99 percent thereafter.[21]

In January, 1979, the consent decree expired. AT&T retained most features of its program, aiming in the future to continue efforts toward the long-range goal of approximate proportional representation. It did, however, drop the affirmative action override from its repertoire of affirmative action tools.

III. RESULTS

As a consequence of the implementation of the Model Plan, considerable progress was made in increasing the representation of women and minorities in jobs from which they had been largely excluded in the past. For example, between 1973 and 1979 there was a 38 percent increase in the number of women employed in the top three job classifications (officials and managers), while there was only a 5.3 percent increase in the number of men. Women made significant strides in sales positions, increasing in numbers by 53 percent (a growth rate seven times faster than that of white males), and in inside crafts, increasing by 68 percent (white males were decreasing by 10 percent).[22] In the outside crafts, the number of women grew by 5,300 while the number of men declined by 6,700. Only in clerical positions did the number of women grow at a lesser rate than men.[23]

Black and Hispanic males also made gains in management and sales positions and inside crafts. In each case their growth rate exceeded the rate of total growth in these jobs.

Although women made important strides in status and mobility at AT&T, the total number of women employed actually declined between 1973 and 1979. At the end of 1972, AT&T employed 415,725 women (52.4 percent of all employees); at the beginning of 1979, it employed 408,671 women (50.8 percent of all employees). This overall decline was not inconsistent with the consent decree. The decree had two aims in regard to women. One was to move women in significant numbers into previously "male" jobs. The other was related: to break down the stereotype of "male" and "female" jobs at AT&T. Both aims were promoted by acting to increase the number of men in the administrative (i.e., secretarial), clerical, and operator jobs. This both worked against the stereotyping and allowed the company to significantly increase the share of women in other job categories without at the same time raising even higher their share of the total workforce.[24]

Two examples illustrate the steps AT&T took to break down the sex-segregation of earlier years. For one thing, the company made clerical positions entry level jobs for men. In 1973, 17 percent of men hired in the Bell companies entered through clerical positions, while 83 percent entered through craft positions. In 1979, 43.7 percent of men hired entered through clerical positions, while only 56.3 percent entered through crafts. Overall, the percentage of men in clerical roles grew from 5.9 percent to 11.1 percent.[25]

Secondly, the company made valiant efforts to increase the number of women in outside crafts. As a result of its efforts, by 1979 4.7 percent of outside craft workers were women, a 550 percent increase from 1973. This achievement was not without its difficulties or costs. The company inaugurated new pole-climbing courses, instituted new safety procedures, modified equipment for use by women, and recruited aggressively. Even so, the company was never faced with a superfluity of female applicants for outside jobs. There were high rates of female failure in the pole-climbing course, and high rates of attrition among those females who worked in the outside jobs. Accident rates for women were two to three times those of men.[26] In its new affirmative action program after the consent decree expired in 1979, AT&T decided to slow its integration of women into outside crafts.

IV. Costs and Benefits

The affirmative action program with its override provision generated unhappiness and lowered morale among white male employees, who viewed themselves as victims of "reverse discrimination and blocked opportunity." One survey indicated most white male employees were antagonistic toward the program.[27] It is easy enough to understand how perceptions of "reverse discrimination" could occur. In 1976, for example, fully two-thirds of all promotions went to women.[28] Instances in which the override resulted in very qualified and senior men being passed over in favor of inexperienced women doubtlessly occurred often enough to provide ample gripe material on the male grapevine. Thousands of grievances were filed within the company and there were two dozen reverse discrimination law suits.[29]

The most important law suits were by the major Bell union, the Communications Workers of America (CWA), which attempted without success to overthrow the affirmative action override.[30] In an unusual case, one AT&T worker, Daniel McAleer, did manage to win $7,500 in damages from the company as a result of his being passed over for promotion in favor of a woman. The court, which upheld his claim of reverse discrimination, explained:

> This is a sex discrimination case. Plaintiff...was denied promotion by American Telephone & Telegraph Co. (AT&T). He was entitled to promotion under the provisions of a collective bargaining agreement but the job was given to a less qualified, less senior female solely because of her sex.[31]

The disgruntlement of male employees was not the only negative effect of the affirmative action program. One observer reported in *Fortune* that "two different telephone consultants...believe the consent decree had done some damage to AT&T's efficiency."[32] The decree resulted in some promotions of inexperienced and inadequately trained persons. There was some lowering of quality standards and the development of "double standards of discipline and performance." Minorities and women were able to air grievances outside of regular channels, and supervisors were more reluctant to discipline or complain about women and minority workers. The supervisors' authority and power were eroded in other ways too, especially by the centralization of personnel decisions in the personnel offices. Previously, supervisors had considerable say about who got promoted.

The policy of forcing men to enter through clerical positions resulted in increased turnover, as did the efforts to increase the number of women in the outside crafts. There, the high attrition and accident rate of women probably resulted in some general decline in performance. However, overall turnover for all employees at AT&T appeared to have actually declined between 1973–1979.[34]

The affirmative action override, requiring the use of racial and sexual preferences, certainly contained the potential of pitting white against black, male against female. Racial and sexual hostility could have been inflamed. However, despite the widespread disgruntlement of white males with the affirmative action program, there appears to have been little adverse impact on employee relations.[35]

On the other hand, AT&T has reaped benefits from the consent decree. A company that employs 800,000 people has a voracious need for labor; and by virtually doubling its pool from which to fill its crafts, sales, and management jobs, the company has a richer source of talent to draw upon than before. Large numbers of qualified and ambitious minorities and women are now able to compete with white males for jobs, with a resulting increase often in the quality of those who win the competition.

Personnel departments, as a result of the need to monitor and manage the achievement of the affirmative action goals, have taken over much of the role in promoting and upgrading workers. Although a negative effect of this is erosion of the authority of supervisors, a positive effect is the greater objectivity and rationality that has been brought to the promotion process. The affirmative action plan and its goals have forced AT&T to be very much clearer about qualification and training standards for career advancement, and this has benefitted both company and workers.[36]

V. THE ISSUE POSED

That white male employees suffered lowered morale under the AT&T affirmative action program is not by itself morally significant. People can be disgruntled by changes which are perfectly legitimate or even morally mandatory. Whites, for example, might resist being supervised by blacks out of prejudice and hatred; or males might resent being bossed by perfectly qualified females. The disgruntlement of employees is more than just a management problem if it is based on *legitimate* grievances. In the case of the AT&T affirmative action program, there is no question that direct and explicit sexual and racial preferences were given in order to fill hiring and promotion goals. The representational aims of the affirmative action program could not otherwise have been accomplished. As a result, the expectations of achievement and advancement were frustrated for many persons because they turned out to be the wrong color or sex.

Is it reasonable or permissible to advance such representational aims by policies which select by race or sex? Aren't such policies unfair to some individuals? In an attitudinal survey taken in 1978, one AT&T worker offered this lament:

> One thing that really bothers me is moving up in the company. I am white, male, twenty-five. I am not a brain, but average. I have a lot of drive and want to get ahead. I have just been notified there is some kind of freeze which will last 3 or 4 months.
>
> [Note: frequently, when a goal couldn't be met, all promotions would be frozen until a person of the right sex or race could be found for the next slot.] In that time, if I am passed over, the company will go to the street. *This is not fair. I work for the company but my chances are less than someone on the street.*"[37]

One irony of the AT&T program was that this "unfairness" was not always confined to white males. As we have noted, a central feature of the consent decree was the aim that male participation in "female" jobs would increase just as female participation in "male" jobs increased. Thus, the Model Plan called for male hiring quotas in clerical jobs, with the ultimate goal of having 25 percent males in this category of jobs. (An informal goal called for 10 percent male operators.)[38] Affirmative action override thus was not applied only against white males; it was actually on occasion applied against women as well.

One AT&T employee, Bertha Biel, went to court when she was passed over for advancement so that a man could be selected. The court record tells the story:

> The employee, a female records clerk, on March 29, 1973 applied for a promotion to the position of operations clerk, a higher-paid job, when it became available. In January of 1973, however, the Company had conducted a work force analysis, required by the terms of the Title VII decree, and determined that males were underutilized in clerical positions. Under the decree the position of operations clerk falls into job class 11, a clerical job title which had traditionally been filled by females. The decree required the establishment of male hiring goals for this job class. In October 1973 the Company had one job class 11 opening to be filled for the remainder of the year. It had not met its intermediate goals for that year since no males had sought the opening. Accordingly, it filled its last opening for the year by hiring a male not previously employed by the Company.[39]

The court held against Bertha Biel and for the company. Thus, Bertha Biel could join the 25-year-old male worker's lament: "This is not fair. I work for the company but my chances are less than someone on the street."

On one level, it may seem a legal puzzle that a program like AT&T's which used sexual preferences against both men and women, as the occasion dictated, could be held by courts to be an appropriate expression of a law which says that it is an unlawful practice for an employer "to discriminate against any individual with respect to his compensation, term, conditions, or privileges of employment, because of such individual's race, color, sex, or national origin. . . " (Title VII, Civil Rights Act of 1964, 42 U.S.C. 20002[2]). On another level, we are confronted with the question whether—judicial approval aside—the AT&T program was morally acceptable and an expression of a just social policy. Questions of fairness and justice were central to many of the complaints by AT&T workers and to the litigation by the unions. Likewise, decisions about the moral rightness (or at least moral tolerability) of the affirmative action program were made by management, judges, and government officials involved in its implementation. Moreover, the AT&T consent decree occurred in the midst of an ongoing public debate about the morality of "reverse discrimination."

NOTES

1. *EEOC* v. *AT&T*, 365 F. Supp. 1105 (1973), at 1108.

2. See *United States* v. *Allegheny-Ludlum Industries*, 11 FEP Cases 167 (1975); Phyllis A. Wallace, "What Did We Learn?" in Phyllis A. Wallace, ed., *Equal Employment Opportunity and the AT&T Case* (Cambridge, Mass.: MIT Press, 1976), p. 278.

3. Phyllis A. Wallace and Jack E. Nelson, "Legal Processes and Strategies of Intervention," in Wallace, ed., *Equal Employment Opportunity*, p. 243.

4. Ibid., p. 246.

5. 365 F. Supp. at 1109.

6. Wallace, *Equal Employment Opportunity*, p. 4; Judith Long Laws, "The Bell Telephone System: A Case Study," in Wallace, ed., *Equal Employment Opportunity*, pp. 160–61.

7. Laws, "Bell System," p. 154.

8. Ibid., p. 157.

9. Wallace and Nelson, "Legal Processes," p. 252; and Wallace, "The Consent Decree," in Wallace, ed., *Equal Employment Opportunity*, pp. 273–74.

10. Wallace, "Equal Employment Opportunity," in Wallace, ed., *Equal Employment Opportunity*, p. 258; Herbert R. Northrup and John A. Larson, *The Impact of the AT&T-EEO Consent Decree* (Philadelphia: The Wharton School, University of Pennsylvania, 1979), pp. 6–7 and tables pp. 41–65.

11. Wallace and Nelson, "Legal Processes," pp. 243–51.

12. Wallace, "Consent Decree," p. 272. The text of the decree is given on pp. 283–96.

13. Carol Loomis, "AT&T in the Throes of 'Equal Employment,'" *Fortune* 99 (Jan. 15, 1979), p. 47. The ultimate female goal for the outside crafts was set at 19 percent.

14. For details, see Northrup and Larson, "Impact," pp. 19–22.

15. FEP 431: 82. Emphasis added.

16. *EEOC* v. *AT&T*, 13 FEP Cases 392 (1976), at 402.

17. 13 FEP Cases at 402.

18. Loomis, "AT&T," p. 54. "All personnel executives interviewed testified that it [giving preference] has been both regular and often has been the only way the targets could be met." Northrup and Larson, "Impact," p. 57.

19. Loomis, "AT&T," p. 54; Northrup and Larson, "Impact," p. 14.

20. Jerry Flint, "In Bell System's Minority Plan, Women Get Better Jobs, But Total Number of Female Workers Drops," *New York Times*, July 5, 1977, C13.

21. Loomis, "AT&T," p. 50; Northrup and Larson, "Impact," p. 12.

22. Northrup and Larson, "Impact," pp. 25, 53, 55, 65.

23. Ibid., pp. 59, 61.

24. Since women compose about 40 percent of the U.S. labor force, they were already overrepresented—in gross numbers—at AT&T. The problem was not the lack of women employees, but the segregating of them.

25. Northrup and Larson, "Impact," pp. 59, 64.

26. Ibid., pp. 60–62; Loomis, "AT&T," p. 50.

27. Northrup and Larson, "Impact," p. 78.

28. Ibid., p. 80; Loomis, "AT&T," p. 54; Flint, "Bell System's Plan," p. C13.

29. 13 FEP Cases at 418; Loomis, "AT&T," p. 54.

30. See *EEOC* v. *AT&T*, 365 F. Supp. 1105 (1973); *EEOC* v. *AT&T* 506 F. 2d 735 (1974); *EEOC* v. *AT&T*, 13 FEP Cases 392 (1976).

31. *McAleer* v. *AT&T*, 416 F. Supp. 435 (1976), at 436.

32. Loomis, "AT&T," p. 57.

33. Northrup and Larson, "Impact," p. 76.

34. Loomis, "AT&T," p. 57; Northrup and Larson, "Impact," p. 68.

35. Northrup and Larson, "Impact," p. 79.

36. Ibid., pp. 68, 232; Loomis, "AT&T," p. 57.

37. Northrup and Larson, "Impact," p. 78. Emphasis added.

38. Loomis, "AT&T," p. 47; Northrup and Larson, "Impact," p. 58.

39. *Telephone Workers Union* v. *N.J. Bell Tel.*, 584 F. 2d 31 (1978), at 32.

Comment

Consider the evidence in 1971 for past discrimination by AT&T. The statistics on the numbers of women and blacks in various job categories are an important part of the evidence, but they prove nothing by themselves. What additional information makes, or would make, the charge of discrimination against AT&T morally compelling?

Consider separately the justifications for the two elements of the consent decree of January 1973: (1) back-pay and wage adjustments and (2) the Model Affirmative Action Plan. Was the government right to require both elements, or would only one have been preferable?

An advocate of nondiscrimination might criticize the consent decree for requiring AT&T to institute preferential hiring rather than to pursue a policy of nondiscrimination in the future. What would a policy of nondiscrimination require of AT&T? Try to specify in as much detail as possible nondiscriminatory qualifications for the various job categories. Consider, for example, whether length of service with the company is a discriminatory standard. Also, try to specify what a nondiscriminatory policy of recruitment would be.

What are the best reasons for rejecting a policy of nondiscrimination? Would the fact that such a policy takes a long time to break sexual and racial stereotypes and to achieve a balanced workforce be a good reason? How do we decide how long is too long?

Next consider what is morally questionable about the affirmative action override instituted by AT&T. Which, if any, of the following effects of the override can you justify:

(1) bypassing more qualified men from outside the company;
(2) bypassing more qualified men for promotion from the inside;
(3) discriminating against women for clerical jobs;
(4) decreasing efficiency of service and increasing prices to consumers?

Some critics of preferential hiring argue that it is just to use affirmative action goals (employment targets based on predictions of how many women and minorities will be hired if practices are nondiscriminatory) but unjust to use quotas (places reserved for women and minorities regardless of their relative qualifications). Is the distinction between goals and quotas clear in the AT&T plan? Is the use of either, or both, morally justifiable?

Affirmative Action in Pasadena

Pamela Varley

Early in 1985, the Pasadena city council (formally called the Board of Directors) was asked to extend the city's affirmative action protections to Armenian-Americans. At the time, the Southern California city of 130,000 had an Armenian population of 13,000—the most rapidly growing community of Armenians anywhere in the country. If they approved the proposal, the councillors would be setting a national precedent. No other city had ever before named Armenians a "protected class" under affirmative action law. In the past, Pasadena's Affirmative Action Office had designated women, blacks, Hispanics, Asians, native Americans, Pacific Islanders, and the handicapped as the classes to be protected — the same groups covered by federal law.

The city council sent the proposal to its Human Relations Committee for review in January. In early March, the committee returned the question to the council with a recommendation. The matter was scheduled for a vote on March 19.

THE ORDINANCE

Pasadena's affirmative action ordinance, enacted in 1980, required city administrators to take positive action "the goal of which is to see that protected classes are represented in the work force to the same extent that they are represented in the relevant labor market." (The "relevant labor market" means those able and willing to perform the duties of any given job.) The Affirmative Action Office was to work actively with city administrators to establish hiring goals and timetables, to arrange for training and upgrading of protected class members, and to monitor and report on the city's progress. (See Exhibit 1.) When contracting for supplies or services, city administrators were to recruit bids from minority- and women-owned firms and to require that any city contractor be an equal opportunity or affirmative action employer. (See Exhibit 2.) There was some talk of strengthening this part of the law by giving minority- and women-owned businesses a percentage differential in bidding competitions. Local businesses were already given such a differential. Thus, if enacted, all minority- and women-owned businesses would receive some advantage, and local minority- and women-owned firms would enjoy an even greater advantage.

PROFILE OF PASADENA

In spring of 1985, about 25 percent of Pasadena's population was black, 22 percent was Hispanic (and that number was growing), 10 percent was Armenian, 6 percent was Asian, and 37 percent was white (and neither Hispanic nor Armenian). (Throughout this case, we use "white" to mean "white and not belonging to a designated ethnic minority.") The white population was mostly middle class to wealthy and wielded disproportionate control over city affairs. Of the seven members of the city council, for instance, six were white — five men and one woman. The other councillor was a black woman. In addition, top management positions in the city were held predominantly by white men, although a few inroads had been made; the Police Chief was a black man; the Deputy City Manager, an Armenian man; and both the Finance Director and Assistant City Manager were white women.

On the whole, black and Hispanic residents were the city's most economically disadvantaged population groups. The Asian population was economically mixed. (Newly arrived Southeast Asian refugees were in the worst straits, although their economic status tended to improve quickly.)

The Armenian community, too, was mixed — culturally and politically as well as economically. About half the Armenians in Pasadena were immigrants or descendants of immigrants who arrived in the United States between 1895 and 1925. On the whole, they had assimilated, were economically well off, and tended to be moderate to conservative politically. The others had immigrated within the last five to ten years from Beirut and other Middle Eastern cities, and were struggling economically, some living in low income enclaves. Many had held professional jobs in the Middle East, but encountered difficulty finding similar work in Pasadena due in part to language and cultural barriers.

Fighting to retain their identity as Armenians, these newcomers had not assimilated and in fact, felt ambivalent or negative about assimilation. In addition, they were polarized on the question of their lost Armenian homeland. One Armenian city administrator estimated that about 10 percent felt allegiance to Soviet Armenia despite its domination by the U.S.S.R. Another 50 percent strongly supported an independent Armenia and were allied with the Pasadena chapter of the Armenian National Committee (ANC). And roughly 40 percent were neutral or quiet on the question.

Proponents of the Proposal

The idea of extending affirmative action protection to Armenians grew out of several incidents in which Armenians had either applied for city jobs or contracts and been turned down, or had been fired from city jobs. Some Armenian candidates for city positions claimed that they had been weeded out of the complex multi-interview process for city jobs because they "talked with an accent."

The case that received the most attention was a competition among tow companies for the right to remove illegally parked cars from city streets. This contract was quite lucrative: when a vehicle owner could not pay off his/her tickets or towing charge, the tow company could take possession of the car. According to one city councillor, the city's Police Department had never gone through a formal competitive bidding process to award the contract in the past, instead granting it as a matter of tradition to a company called S.M. Ward & Son, owned by a prominent, well-connected white businessman. Under pressure from the city council, the Police Department put the service out to bid in 1985. The criteria for judging the competitors were the amount of the tow charge, the ability to provide prompt, round-the-clock service, and the capacity to store impounded cars. Two Armenian firms competed with Ward's for the contract. The largest of the two, Johnnie's Tow Service, had already won towing contracts with the local sheriff and highway patrol, and offered to charge less than Ward's for its tow jobs. The Police Department, however, awarded its towing contract to Ward's, reasoning that there was no compelling reason to make a change and that Johnnie's already had its hands full with its other towing obligations.

This incident spurred two local activists to action: Bill Paparian, an Armenian-American lawyer and member of the city council's Human Relations Committee, and Rick Cole, a white progressive city councillor. Although his family had lived in the United States for several generations, Paparian had formed an alliance with Armenian newcomers in the ANC and frequently represented them as an attorney. Thus the ANC, with Paparian as its spokesperson, began pushing for "protected" status for Armenians under the city's affirmative action ordinance. Paparian noted that Armenians made up 10 percent of the city population, yet less than one percent of the city work force: only three of the city's 1470 employees were Armenian. Other minority or protected groups tended to be underrepresented as well—particularly at top management levels—but not as underrepresented as the Armenians: 25 percent of the city work force was black, 16 percent was Hispanic, 5 percent was Asian, and 31 percent was female. (See Exhibit 3.)

Paparian's proposal was actively supported by Cole, who was working to break up what he saw as a well-entrenched "old boy network" in Pasadena. By extending affirmative action to Armenians, Cole believed that—in addition to opening job opportunities to a broader group—the council would increase the base of support for affirmative action, draw the Armenian newcomers into progressive politics, and ultimately strengthen the city's progressive coalition of young liberals and minority groups.

THE QUIET OPPOSITION

There was little public opposition to Paparian's proposal, but behind the scenes, a number of people were upset about it—among them, established Armenian-Americans who were embarrassed at the suggestion that Armenians required preferential treatment under law. Many of them had fought long and hard to convince their neighbors that they were not inferior or "different," and they worried that being designated a "minority group" would set them back. In addition, the defenders of Soviet Armenia—while they did not play a major role in the debate—opposed the proposal sponsored by their ANC rival.

Some black and feminist activists also opposed the move, fearing that—by increasing the pool of individuals protected by affirmative action—the city would dilute the impact of the program. Already, roughly 75 percent of the city's population was officially covered by affirmative action. The affirmative action law had only been in effect for five years, and blacks in particular felt they were just beginning to win some hard-fought battles in the city. According to John Kennedy, president of the Pasadena chapter of the NAACP (National Association for the Advancement of Colored People), only in the early 1980s were blacks finally able to secure jobs in the Police and Fire Departments. At about the same time, the city narrowly voted to change election laws to allow for greater minority representation on the city council, "but the City of Pasadena has not given up anything without a fight," Kennedy added.

In addition, Kennedy and other activists felt that affirmative action was intended to redress longstanding, deep-rooted discrimination in the United States. "Never was affirmative action intended to right the wrongs of atrocities that occurred in Turkey," he argued, referring to the Turkish government's bloody 1915 genocide of 1.5 million Armenians. By casting too wide a net, the activists feared, the city council would "trivialize" its affirmative action policy. Already the idea of treating Armenians as a protected class had generated some snickering about town. After all, people wondered, why should Armenians be singled out for protection when a number of Armenians in Pasadena were well off if not affluent?

THE RECOMMENDATION OF THE HUMAN RELATIONS COMMITTEE

When the Human Relations Committee considered Paparian's proposal in early March, Paparian—a member of the committee—gave a strong pitch for it. In the end, the committee members concluded that in fact, recent Armenian immigrants were encountering discrimination within the city. In addition, they argued, most recent immigrants confronted prejudice and employment problems. Thus, on March 4, the committee recommended that the city council extend affirmative action protection not only to Armenians, but to any immigrant who had been living in the United States fewer than fifteen years. Two weeks later, with this recommendation in hand, the city council was scheduled to make its decision.

EPILOGUE

On March 19, 1985, the Pasadena city council voted 6 to 0 with one abstention to extend affirmative action protection to Armenian-Americans. (The councillors did not seriously consider the recommendation of the Human Relations Committee to extend affirmative action protection to any recent immigrant.) If anything, however, the question became more controversial during the intervening two years, particularly in the area of city service contracts. A Pasadena citizens' task force on affirmative action began to consider a proposal to give women- and minority-owned firms a 3 to 5 percent differential in bidding for city contracts, but some minority activists did not believe the differential should be given to Armenian-owned firms. Thus, even two years later, the matter was still not fully resolved.

Meanwhile, however, in the next round of contract awards, the Police Department split the city's towing contract between Ward's and Johnnie's. And in May 1987, attorney Bill Paparian made a successful run for a city council seat in a district with a high concentration of Armenian residents, unseating a three-term incumbent.

EXHIBIT 1. PASADENA'S AFFIRMATIVE ACTION ORDINANCE:
AFFIRMATIVE ACTION IN CITY EMPLOYMENT, CHAPTER 2.39

AFFIRMATIVE ACTION
IN CITY EMPLOYMENT

2.39.010 Short title.

This chapter shall be known as the "affirmative action in city employment ordinance." (Ord. 5483 § 1 (part), 1980)

2.39.020 Scope.

The principles of equal opportunity in employment are applicable to all city employment, through Section 802 of the city Charter. In addition, the following equal opportunity employment laws apply, by their terms, from time to time, to city employment:

A. California Fair Employment Practices Act, as amended, Labor Code Section 1410 et seq.;

B. Title VII, Equal Employment Opportunity, of the Civil Rights Act of 1964, as amended, 42 U.S.C. Section 2000e et seq.;

C. Age discrimination in Employment Act of 1967, as amended, 29 U.S.C. Section 621 et seq.;

D. Section 504 of the Vocational Rehabilitation Act of 1973, as amended, 29 U.S.C. Section 701 et seq.

This chapter sets forth specific procedures for all city employment and employees. In addition, this chapter provides a specific mandate for the development of affirmative action plans to cover all city employment. (Ord. 5483 § 1(part), 1980)

2.39.030 Policy statement of city.

This chapter together with the rules and regulations promulgated thereunder and the affirmative action plans generated pursuant to the provisions of this chapter and the rules and regulations promulgated thereunder is a restatement of and supersedes the Affirmative Action Program of the city, dated May 1973, and adopted by Resolution No. 1812 on June 19, 1973, and reaffirmed by the board by oral motion on October 10, 1978.

The policy of the city shall be to provide equal opportunity employment to all persons and not to discriminate against any applicant or employee because of race, religious creed, color, national origin, ancestry, handicap, sex, or age. In the awareness that the intent of this policy is not necessarily fulfilled with the mere prohibition of discriminatory practices, the city will continue to take affirmative action to review all of its employment practices to assure the fulfillment of its stated commitment. (Ord. 5483 § 1 (part), 1980)

2.39.040 Definitions.

Whenever used in this chapter the following words shall have the meanings indicated:

A. "Affirmative action" means the taking of a positive action by an employer, the goal of which is to see that protected classes are represented in its work force to the same extent that they are represented in the relevant labor market. It is an extension of the concept of equal opportunity employment.

B. "Affirmative action employer" means an employer that practices affirmative action.

C. "Affirmative action officer" means a person designated by the city manager to administer, monitor and enforce the provisions of this chapter and to oversee the city's affirmative action activities.

D. "Affirmative action plan" means a written plan documenting an employer's affirmative action program.

E. "Affirmative action program" means the aggregate of the actions taken by an employer to achieve affirmative action.

F. "Age" means over the age of forty.

G. "Discrimination" means disparate treatment, policies or practices which perpetuate in the present the effects of past discrimination, policies or practices having disparate impact not justified by business necessity or bona fide occupational qualifications, and failure to make reasonable accommodation to an applicant's or employee's religious observances or practices.

H. "Employer" means the city.

I. "Employment practices" means any solicitation of, or advertisement for employees or employment; any action resulting in changes in grade or work assignment in the place or location of work; any determinations affecting the layoff, suspension or termination of employees, the rate of pay or other form of compensation including vacation, sick leave and compensatory time; any decisions affecting the selection for training including apprenticeship programs, the grant of employee benefits and participatory activities and promotions; any actions taken to discipline employees for infractions of work rules or employer requirements; functional reorganization; and any other actions which affect the terms and conditions of employment. The term "functional reorganization" includes the employment decisions with respect to increases or decreases in staff brought about by changes in management organization but shall not include the actions or consideration giving rise to such changes or the alteration or modification of the duties, responsibilities, or authority of existing staff.

J. "Equal Opportunity Employer" means an employer who practices equal opportunity employment.

K. "Equal Opportunity Employment" means the utilization of employment practices by an employer that do not discriminate against any protected class.

L. "Goals" means numerical objectives established by an employer with respect to the employer's hiring and promotion goals, the purpose of which is to correct any statistically significant underutilization of a protected class as identified by the employer's utilization analyses.

M. "Handicapped individual" means a person who (1) has a physical or mental impairment which substantially limits one or more of such person's major life activities, (2) has a record of such impairment or (3) is regarded as having such an impairment.

N. "Medical condition" means any health impairment for which a person has been rehabilitated or cured, based on competent medical evidence.

O. "Protected class" means a group of persons which is identified with respect to the race, religious creed, color, national origin, ancestry, handicap, medical condition, sex or age of its members.

P. "Relevant labor market" means that pool of workers, for each position that an employer maintains, that is ready, willing, and possesses the requisite skills to perform the tasks, functions, and duties of the position. The relevant labor market varies as a function of the skills required for the positions and the salary and benefits associated with the position.

Q. "Timetables" means the scheduled times for implementing goals. (Ord. 5483 § 1 (part), 1980)

2.39.045 Exemption.

The transition of employees of the Pasadena community development commission into city employment shall be exempt from the provisions of this chapter if the director of employee and community services agency finds and documents that the city position to be filled:

A. Was caused by the transfer of a redevelopment function from the Pasadena community development commission to the city and the duties of the position will remain essentially the same as the prior Pasadena community development commission position:

B. Is identical to the current Pasadena community development commission position; i.e., the job description is the same and the compensation is the same or shall be made so within a one-year period. (Ord. 5523 § 1, 1981)

2.39.050 Affirmative action plans.

A. The affirmative action officer, in conjunction with all department and agency heads, shall develop an affirmative action plan covering all city employment in accordance with the provisions of this chapter and the rules and regulations promulgated thereunder.

B. The ability and success of management personnel in meeting their affirmative action and equal employment commitments shall be an important factor in determining the amount of their management merit benefit which is provided for in the salary resolution. For department and agency heads, the affirmative action and equal employment commitments include the goals and timetables established under Section 2.39.090 for that portion of the city's work force under their control. The city manager may provide for further sanctions under the personnel rules and regulations the city manager establishes under Section 2.39.050. Failure to achieve the goals and timetables shall be determinative unless a good-faith effort to achieve the goals and timetables has been documented. (Ord. 5495 § 1, 1980: Ord. 5483 § 1 (part), 1980)

2.39.060 Elements of the plan.

The affirmative action plans developed pursuant to this chapter shall contain the following elements:

A. Policy statement;

B. Utilization analyses;

C. Goals and timetables;

D. Employment practices;

E. Internal and external dissemination and reporting;

F. Internal auditing and monitoring. (Ord. 5483 § 1 (part), 1980)

2.39.070 Policy statement.

The policy statement shall be the second paragraph of Section 2.39.030. (Ord. 5483 § 1 (part), 1980)

2.39.080 Utilization analyses.

Utilization analyses of the work force of the city shall be conducted annually by the affirmative action officer in accordance with rules and regulations promulgated by the affirmative action officer but shall, in general, include the following for each analysis:

A. An analysis of the work force in question by job classification groupings using the EEO-4 or similar categories, to determine the extent to which those protected classes identified by race, color, national origin, or sex are represented therein.

B. A comparison of the work force statistics developed in subsection A of this section with the equivalent statistics for the relevant labor market for the same job classification groupings to determine any statistically significant under-utilization. (Ord. 5483 § 1 (part), 1980)

2.39.090 Goals and timetables.

A. Goals and timetables for the work force of the city shall be established annually by thc affirmative action officer, in conjunction with each department or agency head with respect to that portion of the city's work force under their control, to correct any statistically significant under-utilizations identified by the utilization analysis described in Section 2.39.080.

B. Goals and timetables shall be established in accordance with rules and regulations promulgated by the affirmative action officer and shall be based on projected turnover rate, evidence of which is historical turnover rate. (Ord. 5483 § 1 (part), 1980)

2.39.100 Employment practices.

A. The director of personnel and employee relations, in conjunction with each department and agency head with respect to that portion of the city's work force under their control, shall continually review the city's employment practices to assure the practices do not discriminate against any protected class.

B. The director of personnel and employee relations shall take positive action to assure that vacant positions which will be opened to the public are advertised in media directed towards protected classes. Affirmative action principles, upward mobility, career service concepts, and morale of current city employees shall be considered when deciding whether to open a position to the public.

C. The director of personnel and employee relations, in conjunction with each department and agency head with respect to that portion of the city's work force under their control, shall take positive action to assure that the selection process for filling vacant positions does not have an adverse impact on a protected class, except to the extent that the limiting criteria are job-related. Oral examination boards should include persons who are members of protected classes.

D. The director of personnel and employee relations, in conjunction with each department and agency head with respect to that portion of the city's work force under their control, shall take positive action to assure discipline is uniformly applied to employees without respect to the employee's membership in a protected class. The affirmative action officer or the officer's designee shall participate in the disciplinary process, except for advisory arbitration to the city manager, of any employee who requests such participation and who alleges by way of defense that the disciplinary action proposed is a result of or is excessive because of the employee's membership in a protected class; the management person imposing discipline shall, in such cases, confer with the affirmative action officer or the officer's designee prior to making a final decision.

E. The director of personnel and employee relations and the affirmative action officcr, in conjunction with each department and agency head with respect to that portion of the city's work force under their control, shall, to the extent that funds have been budgeted therefor, provide such training for city employees as is necessary to upgrade the employees' potential for promotion. Such training should emphasize the needs of the various protected classes. (Ord. 5483 § 1 (part), 1980)

2.39.110 Internal and external dissemination and reporting.

A. The affirmative action officer and the director of personnel and employee relations, in conjunction with each department and agency head with respect to that portion of the city's work force under their control, shall take positive action to assure that applicants to and employees of the city are fully informed on the city's commitment to affirmative action and equal opportunity employment and the city's affirmative action plan.

B. All management personnel shall be instructed in the principles and practices of affirmative action and equal opportunity employment and their responsibilities thereunder.

C. All solicitations or advertisements for applicants for employment placed by or on behalf of the city shall include the following statement:

Equal Opportunity – Affirmative Action Employer

D. The affirmative action officer shall prepare an annual report on the progress achieved under the city's affirmative action plan which shall be presented to the board of directors at one of its regular meetings; the presentation shall include a provision for public comment. Such report shall include the utilization analyses, the goals and timetables, the progress made in achieving the goals and timetables, and suggested corrective actions, if any. (Ord. 5483 § 1 (part), 1980)

2.39.120 Internal auditing and monitoring.

The affirmative action officer shall establish internal auditing and monitoring mechanisms to assure that the city's affirmative action plan meets the requirements of this chapter and the rules and regulations promulgated thereunder and to assure that the commitments set forth in the plan are met. (Ord. 5483 § 1 (part), 1980)

2.39.130 Enforcement.

This chapter creates no private cause of action within the public and may only be enforced by the city. (Ord. 5483 § 1 (part), 1980)

2.39.140 Rules and regulations.

The affirmative action officer shall promulgate rules and regulations to carry out the provisions of this chapter and shall generate or collect statistics on the representation of those protected classes identified by race, color, national origin, or sex within the relevant labor market for various job classification groupings using the EEO-4 or similar categories. Such rules and regulations shall be reviewed by the director of personnel and employee relations, the city attorney and the city manager, prior to submission to the board of directors, to assure that they are compatible with the city's personnel practices, the rules and regulations established by the city manager pursuant to Section 2.26.050, and applicable local, state and federal law. Such rules and regulations shall be submitted to the board of directors, within ninety days after the adoption of the ordinance codified in this chapter, and shall not become effective until approved and ordered filed by the board. (Ord. 5483 § 1 (part), 1980)

EXHIBIT 2. PASADENA'S AFFIRMATIVE ACTION ORDINANCE: AFFIRMATIVE ACTION IN CONTRACTING, CHAPTER 4.09

AFFIRMATIVE ACTION IN CONTRACTING

4.09.100 Rules and regulations.

4.09.010 Short title.

This chapter shall be known as the "affirmative action in contracting ordinance." (Ord. 5482 § 1 (part), 1980)

4.09.020 Policy

The policy of the city is to promote the principles of equal opportunity employment and affirmative action in its contracting and to recruit vigorously and encourage persons, and businesses owned by persons, who are members of a protected class to make proposals and bids for its contracts. In addition, the following equal opportunity employment laws apply, by their terms, from time to time, to city contracting:

A. California Fair Employment Practices Act, as amended, Labor Code Section 1410 et seq.;

B. Title VII, Equal Employment Opportunity, of the Civil Rights Act of 1964, as amended, 42 U.S.C. Section 2000e et seq.;

C. Age Discrimination in Employment Act of 1967, as amended, 29 U.S.C. Section 61 et seq.;

D. Section 503 of the Vocational Rehabilitation Act of 1973, as amended, 29 U.S.C. Section 701 et seq.;

E. Executive Order 11246, issued September 24, 1965, Equal Employment Opportunity;

F. Executive Order 11375, issued October 17, 1967. Amended Executive Order 11246 to cover sex discrimination. (Ord. 5482 § 1 (part), 1980)

4.09.030 Definitions.

Whenever used in this chapter the words "affirmative action," "affirmative action employer," "affirmative action officer," "affirmative action plan," "affirmative action program," "age," "discrimination," "employment practices," "equal opportunity employment," "equal opportunity employer," "goals," "handicapped individual," "medical condition," "protected class," "relevant labor market," and "time tables" shall have the meanings indicated in Chapter 2.39.

In addition to the definitions incorporated from Chapter 2.39, the following words, when used in this chapter, shall have the meanings indicated:

A. "Awarding authority" means the board of directors or any city employee who is authorized to award a contract on behalf of the city.

B. "Contract" means any contract for labor, material, supplies, or services entered into by the city.

C. "Contractor" means any person who submits a bid or proposal to the city or who has entered into a contract with the city.

D. "Employer" means a contractor or subcontractor, as the context requires.

E. "Nondiscrimination requirements" means those contract requirements set forth in Sections 4.09.060, 4.09.070, and 4.09.080.

F. "Subcontract" means a written subcontract on a contract with the city, regardless of tier.

G. "Subcontractor" means a person who enters into a subcontract. (Ord. 5482 § 1 (part), 1980)

4.09.040 Exemptions.

A. The following contracts are exempt from the provisions of this chapter:

1. Contracts for labor or services rendered by any city officer or employee;

2. Contracts for labor, material, supplies or services furnished by one city department to another city department;

3. Contracts with other governmental entities for labor, material, supplies, or services.

B. The following contracts may be exempted, in whole or in part, from the provisions of this chapter by the awarding authority:

1. Contracts for material and supplies available from one person.

2. Contracts for labor, material, or supplies for actual emergency work;

3. Contracts relating to the acquisition, disposal, or lease of real property;

C. Contracts or subcontracts for which the city's interests are best served by exemption may be exempted in whole or in part. Such determination may be made as follows:

1. By the affirmative action officer for contracts or subcontracts up to $2,500;

2. By the affirmative action officer, with the approval of the city manager for contracts or subcontracts up to $10,000;

3. By the board of directors for any contract or subcontract or class of contracts or subcontracts.

Any determination which results in a total exemption must be made prior to the release of the request for proposals or invitation for bids and the exemption shall be noted therein.

This "best interests" exemption process shall only be used to exempt contracts or subcontracts for which the affirmative action and equal opportunity employment results attainable are substantially outweighed by the cost of achieving compliance or to exempt contracts or subcontracts where the policy to further affirmative action and equal opportunity employment is substantially outweighed by another city policy which benefits city residents.

D. Whenever a contract or subcontract is exempted, in whole or in part, from the provisions of this chapter by subsections B or C of this section, the highest authority approving such exemption shall document the basis for the exemption and that the exemption is bona fide in view of the city's policy set forth in Section 4.09.020. (Ord. 5482 § 1 (part), 1980)

4.09.050 Nondiscrimination certificate.

A. Every contractor submitting a bid or proposal to the city, which, if accepted, would result in a contract subject to competitive bidding, shall submit a nondiscrimination certification with its bid or proposal unless it has an approved nondiscrimination certification on file with the city. Failure to do so will cause the bid or proposal to be deemed nonresponsive. This requirement shall not be waived by the city.

B. No contract shall be awarded until the contractor has submitted to the city or has on file with the city a nondiscrimination certification acceptable to the city.

C. All nondiscrimination certifications shall be subject to the approval of the affirmative action officer or the officer's designee. Such approval shall be effective for one year from the date of approval provided the contractor or subcontractor does not breach its stated nondiscrimination commitment.

D. Nondiscrimination certifications shall be submitted for all subcontractors prior to the award of the subcontract. (Ord. 5546 § 1, 1981: Ord. 5482 § 1, 1980)

4.09.060 Nondiscrimination clause.

A. Every contract, regardless of the amount of consideration, shall contain a nondiscrimination clause whereby the contractor agrees that it shall not discriminate against protected classes in its employment practices during the term of the contract.

B. Every contract, regardless of the amount of consideration shall require the contractor to include such a nondiscrimination clause in each of its subcontracts.

C. The preferred wording of the nondiscrimination clauses is set forth in subsection A of Section 4.09.070. (Ord. 5482 § 1 (part), 1980)

4.09.070 Requirements for contracts or subcontracts in excess of $1,000.

Every contract and subcontract for which the consideration is in excess of $1,000 shall contain the following provisions, which shall be designated as the "Equal Opportunity Employment Practices Provisions" of such contracts and subcontracts.

A. Contractor certifies and represents that, during the performance of this contract, the contractor and each subcontractor will adhere to equal opportunity employment practices to assure that applicants and employees are treated equally and are not discriminated against because of their race, religious creed, color, national origin, ancestry, handicap, sex, or age.

B. Contractor agrees that it will, in all solicitations or advertisements for applicants for employment placed by or on behalf of the contractor, state that it is an "Equal Opportunity—Affirmative Action Employer" or that all qualified applicants will receive consideration for employment without regard to their race, religious creed, color, national origin, ancestry, handicap, sex or age.

C. Contractor agrees that it will, if requested to do so by the city, certify that it has not, in the performance of this contract, discriminated against applicants or employees because of their membership in a protected class.

D. Contractor agrees to provide the city with access to and, if requested to do so by the city, through its awarding authority or affirmative action officer, provide copies of all of its records pertaining or relating to its employment practices, to the extent such records are not confidential or privileged under state or federal law.

E. Contractor agrees to recruit vigorously and encourage businesses owned by persons who are members of a protected class to bid on its subcontracts.

F. Nothing contained in this contract shall be construed in any manner so as to require or permit any act which is prohibited by law.

No contract or subcontract shall be divided into parts for the purpose of avoiding the requirements of this section. (Ord. 5482 § 1 (part), 1980)

4.09.080 Requirements for contracts or subcontracts in excess of $10,000.

In addition to the requirements of Section 4.09.050:

A. No contract or subcontract, in excess of $10,000, whose performance requires labor and services shall be awarded until the contractor or subcontractor has submitted an affirmative action plan acceptable to the city. The affirmative action officer or the officer's designee shall be responsible for the approval of affirmative action plans submitted pursuant to this section. Such approval shall be effective for one year from the date of approval provided the contractor does not breach its stated affirmative action commitment. This section shall not apply to contracts or subcontracts which will be accomplished by 3 persons or less.

B. The required affirmative action plan shall, as a minimum, contain the following:

1. A utilization analysis which shall include the following:

a. An analysis of the contractor's or subcontractor's work force, by job classification groupings using the EEO-1 or similar categories, to determine the extent to which those protected classes identified by race, color, national origin, or sex are represented therein.

b. A comparison of the work force statistics developed in paragraph a of this subdivision with the equivalent statistics for the relevant labor market for the same job classification groupings to determine any statistically significant underutilizations. This requirement shall not apply to affirmative action plans for contracts or subcontracts performed outside the Los Angeles-Long Beach Standard Metropolitan Statistical Area.

2. Goals and timetables to correct any underutilizations shown by the analysis. This requirement shall not apply to affirmative action plans for contracts or subcontracts performed outside the Los Angeles-Long Beach Standard Metropolitan Statistical Area.

3. The methods by which the contractor or subcontractor will disseminate the affirmative action plan within its company and to its employment applicants, its subcontractors, and the public.

4. The methods the contractor or subcontractor will use to assure that protected classes are represented in its applicant flow to the same extent that they are represented in the relevant labor market.

5. The methods the contractor or subcontractor will use to assure that its hiring, promotion, training, discipline and other employment practices do not discriminate against protected classes.

6. A statement by the contractor's or subcontractor's highest management person that it will adhere to the letter and spirit of all federal, state and local equal employment laws.

C. Every contractor submitting a bid or proposal to the city, which if accepted would result in a contract with the city subject to this section, shall submit its affirmative action plan with its bid or proposal unless it has an approved affirmative action plan on file with the city. Failure to do so will cause the bid or proposal to be deemed nonresponsive. This requirement will not be waived by the city in awarding any contract.

D. Contractors may, with the prior approval of the affirmative action officer or the officer's designee, submit a copy of its affirmative action plan as prepared for another governmental entity in lieu of the plan required by this section.

E. Contractor agrees to recruit Pasadena residents initially and to give them preference, if all other factors are equal, for any new positions which result from the performance of this contract and which are performed within the city. (Ord. 5546 § 1, 1981: Ord. 5482 § 1 (part), 1980)

4.09.090 Penalties for noncompliance with the nondiscrimination requirements of a contract.

A. The failure of any contractor to comply with the nondiscrimination requirements of its contract shall be a breach of its contract and shall be deemed to be a material breach. Such failure shall only be established upon a finding to that effect by the awarding authority, on the basis of its own investigation or that of the affirmative action officer or the officer's designee. No such finding shall be made except after notice of the alleged violation and an opportunity to be heard has been given to the contractor. The contractor may be given an opportunity to cure such breach.

B. A contractor aggrieved by the finding of the awarding authority may appeal such finding to binding arbitration in accordance with rules and regulations promulgated by the affirmative action officer. No penalties shall be imposed pending deposition of such appeal.

C. Upon a finding duly made that the contractor has failed to comply with the nondiscrimination requirements of its contract, its contract may be cancelled, terminated or suspended, in whole or in part, by the awarding authority, and all moneys due or to become due under the contract may be retained by the city. Further, the city may sue to recover any moneys paid to a noncomplying contractor by the city and shall be entitled to court costs and attorneys' fees if it is the prevailing party.

In addition thereto, such breach may be the basis for a determination by the awarding authority that the contractor is an irresponsible bidder. In the event of such determination, such contractor shall be disqualified from being awarded a contract with the city for a period of two years, or until it shall establish that it is ready, willing, and able to comply with the provisions of this chapter.

D. This chapter creates no private cause of action within the public and may only be enforced by the city. (Ord. 5482 § 1 (part), 1980)

4.09.100 Rules and regulations.

The affirmative action officer shall promulgate rules and regulations to carry out the provisions of this chapter and shall generate or collect statistics on the representation of those protected classes identified by race, color, national origin, or sex within the relevant labor market for various job classification groupings using the EEO-1 or similar categories. Such rules and regulations shall, so far as practicable, be similar to those adopted in applicable federal executive orders. Such rules and regulations shall be reviewed and approved by the city attorney and city manager, prior to submission to the board of directors, to assure that they are compatible with the city's contracting practices and local, state and federal law. Such rules and regulations shall be submitted to the board of directors within 90 days after the adopting of the ordinance codified in this chapter and shall not become operative or effective until approved and ordered filed by the board. (Ord. 5482 § 1 (part), 1980)

EXHIBIT 3. ETHNIC COMPOSITION OF THE PASADENA CITY WORK FORCE IN 1980 & 1985*

1980 Work Force

	Number	*Percent*
White male	644	41%
White female	272	17%
Black male	259	17%
Black female	126	8%
Hispanic male	131	8%
Hispanic female	64	4%
Asian male	37	2%
Asian female	17	1%
Other	5	–
Total	1555	100%

1985 Work Force

	Number	*Percent*
White male	546	37%
White female	243	17%
Black male	245	17%
Black female	116	8%
Hispanic male	160	11%
Hispanic female	80	5%
Asian male	51	3%
Asian female	20	1%
Indian male	5	–
Indian female	1	–
Other	3	–
Total	1470	100%

*Full-time employees only.

Comment

The immediate issue before the Pasadena city council was whether to extend affirmative action protection to Armenian-Americans. But the case also invites an assessment of the city's general policy of offering affirmative action protection to specific groups.

Begin by assuming that the city council will not consider changing its general policy of affirmative action for "protected" groups of city residents. What is the strongest argument for extending "protected" status to Armenian-Americans? Assess the relevance of the following considerations offered by proponents of the extension: (1) Armenians make up 10 percent of the city population but less than 1 percent of the city work force; (2) Armenians are more underrepresented than any other minority or protected group; (3) Johnnie's Tow Service offered to charge less for its tow jobs but was not awarded the Police Department's contract; (4) Extending protection to Armenian-Americans would increase support for affirmative action and strengthen the city's progressive coalition of young liberals and minority groups.

John Kennedy resisted the extension, arguing that affirmative action was originally intended to redress deep-rooted discrimination in the United States. Is there a principled reason for an affirmative action policy to redress the effects of past discrimination suffered in the United States but to ignore discrimination suffered elsewhere? Or is the most defensible purpose of Pasadena's affirmative action policy something other than redressing past discrimination?

To answer these questions, we have to examine Pasadena's general policy of affirmative action. The explicit rationale for the policy is "to provide equal opportunity employment to all persons and not to discriminate against any applicant or employee because of race, religious creed, color, national origin, ancestry, handicap, sex, or age." The ordinance also affirms an "awareness that the intent of this policy is not necessarily fulfilled with the mere prohibition of discriminatory practices." Why does equal opportunity employment demand more from the government than mere prohibition of discriminatory practices? How much more? To justify the city's policy of equal opportunity employment, must one show that the city itself engaged in or encouraged discrimination in the past? That businesses in the city did so? The rules governing contracts and subcontracts in excess of $1,000 (4.09.070) and those in excess of $10,000 (4.09.080) both do more than merely prohibit discriminatory practices, and yet they impose different requirements. Can the differences be justified?

Can the percentage differential that the city offers in bidding competitions to local businesses be justified on grounds of equal employment opportunity? On any other moral grounds? Consider how the percentage differential in favor of minority- and women-owned firms might best be defended. Formulate and then assess the strongest critique of this part of Pasadena's affirmative action policy.

Should the city councilors have seriously considered the recommendation to extend affirmative action protection to any recent immigrant? To any poor resident of Pasadena? What policy would you have recommended to the city council had you been on the Human Relations Committee?

Recommended Reading

Michael Walzer's *Spheres of Justice* (New York: Basic Books, 1983), pp. 129–64, is one of the few theoretical works that includes a specific discussion of principles governing the distribution of jobs in a just society. Also, see Ronald Dworkin, *A Matter of Principle* (Cambridge, Mass.: Harvard University Press, 1985), Part 5, "Reverse Discrimination."

Judith Jarvis Thomson defends preferential hiring when candidates are equally qualified in "Preferential Hiring," in Marshall Cohen et al. (eds.), *Equality and Preferential Treatment* (Princeton, N.J.: Princeton University Press, 1977), pp. 19–39. Robert Simon criticizes Thomson's limited defense in "Preferential Hiring: A Reply to Judith Jarvis Thomson," in *Equality and Preferential Treatment*, pp. 40–48. George Sher considers whether preference may be given to a candidate who is less than the best qualified person for a job in "Justifying Reverse Discrimination in Employment," in *Equality and Preferential Treatment*, pp. 49–60. See also Alan Goldman, "Affirmative Action," in *Equality and Preferential Treatment*, pp. 192–209; and Robert Amdur, "Compensatory Justice: The Question of Costs," *Political Theory*, 7 (May 1979), pp. 229–44. Robert Fullinwider provides a clear summary of the principal arguments on both sides of the controversy in *The Reverse Discrimination Controversy* (Totowa, N.J.: Rowman and Littlefield, 1980). Also, see Robert K. Fullinwider and Claudia Mills (eds.), *The Moral Foundations of Civil Rights* (Totowa, N.J.: Rowman and Littlefield, 1986).

8 Liberty and Paternalism

Introduction

Paternalism is interference with a person's liberty with the aim of promoting his or her own good. John Stuart Mill rejected paternalism absolutely: "because it will be better for him to do so" or "because it will make him happier" never justifies restricting the liberty of a sane adult. Yet most people value other goods, such as health and happiness, along with liberty. And sometimes they can secure these goods, or their future liberty, only if society restricts their present freedom of choice. When Mill considers specific examples where important interests other than liberty are at stake, he abandons his absolutist prohibition against paternalism. He defends preventing someone from crossing an unsafe bridge and approves outlawing slavery based on voluntary contract.

Recognizing that some people always and all people sometimes are incapable of exercising liberty, many contemporary political theorists accept an even broader range of paternalistic restrictions on adult behavior than Mill did. They would favor, for example, banning the use of harmful drugs and requiring the use of seat belts and motorcycle helmets. Others, condemning the rapidly growing intrusion of government into the lives of citizens, defend Mill's explicit absolutism. The controversy in political theory parallels the challenge of paternalism in contemporary politics: can government protect the welfare of its citizens without denying their claims to freedom?

We might begin to meet this challenge by justifying paternalistic intervention only if it satisfies these criteria: (1) the decisions it restricts are already unfree; (2) the intervention is minimally restrictive in time and effect; and (3) the person whose freedom is restricted could accept the goal of the intervention were his or her decisions unimpaired. But to state these criteria is not to solve the problem of paternalism, especially as it arises in public policies that affect many people and have uncertain consequences. When are the decisions of a group of people unfree? How limited must an intervention be (and how limited can it be while still being effective)? In what sense must the affected individuals accept its purposes? Must they all accept it or only a majority?

"Legalizing Laetrile" illustrates each of these problems in deciding whether a paternalistic policy is justifiable. New Jersey legislators and public health officials disagreed about whether cancer patients exercise free choice in deciding to use Laetrile. They differed over what is the least restrictive yet effective means of protecting patients against medical fraud. And they offered competing accounts of what people who use Laetrile really want: an effective cure for cancer, psychic comfort, or both. Many of the same issues posed by Laetrile continue to arise in more recent controversies over the regulation of other new and potentially dangerous drugs that offer hope for victims of diseases such as AIDS.

The debate over the "Do-It-Yourself Kit for AIDS Testing" centers neither on what potential consumers of the kit really want (an accurate and private test for the AIDS virus) nor on whether their decisions (in choosing between professional and do-it-yourself testing) would be unfree. In contrast to the consent-based criteria for justifying paternalism that we suggested earlier, the FDA's rationale for proposing a ban on the kits is welfare-based: people should be protected from an unnecessary risk of false testing and from the psychic trauma of the truth. The question of whether to permit AIDS-testing kits, which the FDA had not finally decided by the spring of 1989, invites an evaluation of two contrasting approaches to justifying paternalism.

Paternalism in public policy raises not only the problem of a hard choice among competing goods, but also a dilemma of process: who has the authority to make paternalistic decisions and by what procedures should they make them? We may agree that the policy is correct, but criticize the way it was made. In the Laetrile case, our answer to the question of whether citizens should be free to use Laetrile still leaves open a series of questions concerning the process by which the decisions about Laetrile were made. Did the legislators who voted for legalization in the hope and expectation that the Department of Health would delay effective passage of the bill act ethically? Once the Laetrile law was passed, did Department of Health officials act correctly in interpreting the law as they did and in enforcing the guidelines for testing and manufacturing the drug as strictly as the law permitted? In the case of the AIDS-testing kit, is the FDA right to hold public meetings before rendering its final decision? What should be discussed at the meetings? To what extent (if at all) should the FDA's final decision depend on the opinions expressed in those meetings?

To answer these questions, we must consider the moral duties of legislators and bureaucrats in a democracy. In one theory of democracy, attributed to Joseph Schumpeter, the only moral duty of politicians is to preserve the institutional arrangements that make possible the ongoing competitive struggle for the people's vote. A second democratic theory, associated with Mill, offers a more demanding ideal of representation, which would hold legislators and bureaucrats who have broad discretion accountable for particular policies. Because legislators and high-level bureaucrats wield so much power over so many people, we can insist that they give citizens sufficient information to assess their decisions, especially on salient and controversial issues such as legalizing Laetrile and marketing a test kit for AIDS.

Legalizing Laetrile

Marion Smiley

Laetrile (also known as vitamin B-17, or Amygdalin) is a derivative of the apricot pit and has been promoted during the last twenty-five years as a cure, treatment, or prophylaxis for cancer. It has also been promoted as a treatment for red blood cell deficiencies, for sickle-cell anemia, for various parasitic diseases, and for arthritis. In 1963 the FDA banned the use of Laetrile on the grounds that Laetrile is not *effective* in the treatment of either cancer or other health problems. Despite the ban, public support for Laetrile grew. In 1977 the FDA conducted further tests on Laetrile and reaffirmed its ban. Although the Supreme Court in 1979 sanctioned in certain respects the FDA's authority to ban Laetrile, the controversy has not been finally resolved. Moreover, the issues raised in the controversy go beyond the matter of Laetrile and are likely to arise in other instances of government regulation in the future. This case study describes the history of the FDA's involvement in the regulation of Laetrile; summarizes the scientific and ethical arguments that have been offered by the proponents and opponents of the drug; and provides an account of the controversy as it evolved in the state of New Jersey.

Laetrile and the FDA

Dr. Ernest Krebs, Sr., who discovered Laetrile in 1920, at first considered it to be too toxic for use in the treatment of cancer. In 1937, Dr. Krebs' son, Ernest Krebs, Jr., "purified" the drug to meet his father's standards of toxic safety, and shortly thereafter, father and son went into the Laetrile business together.

According to Krebs, Jr., cancer cells contain a large amount of an enzyme that releases cyanide from Laetrile. Once released, this cyanide supposedly kills the cancer cells. Laetrile would not kill the normal cells as well, Krebs claimed, because normal cells do not contain nearly so much of the cyanide-releasing enzyme as do cancer cells.

Although the FDA never shared Krebs' view of apricot pits, the agency took no legal measure against the proponents of Laetrile until 1962. The FDA in that year charged Krebs, Jr., with violating the new drug provisions of the Federal Food, Drug and Cosmetic Act; the law provided for the first time that all drugs approved by the FDA must be effective, as well as safe. After many unsuccessful attempts to obtain FDA approval of Laetrile as a drug, Mr. Krebs, Jr., claimed that Laetrile was not really a *drug* but instead was a vitamin. He argued that Laetrile was vitamin B-17, the very vitamin needed to prevent and treat cancer (cancer itself now being conceived of as a disease of vitamin deficiency). The advantage of promoting Laetrile as a vitamin was that in this form it would be exempt from the FDA's drug laws.

In early 1974, the FDA took legal action against two vitamin B-17 products, Aprikern and Bee-Seventeen; the FDA maintained that even if Laetrile were a vitamin, it would also still be a drug and therefore susceptible to FDA drug regulation. In 1975 a federal court judge in California held that vitamin B-17 was not even a vitamin, and he placed the manufacturers of Aprikern and Bee-Seventeen under permanent injunction. In 1976 a federal court judge in New Jersey went a step further and concluded that the promotion of vitamin B-17 products constituted a "fraud on the public" and was therefore to be prohibited.

In response to these legal actions, the proponents of Laetrile changed their account of the nature of Laetrile, or vitamin B-17. Proponents of Laetrile for the most part no longer advertise vitamin B-17 as an independent cure for cancer. Instead, they offer vitamin B-17 as part of a more general regimen that often includes large doses of vitamin C, enzymes of various sorts, and sometimes even transcendental meditation. Furthermore, the proponents of Laetrile do not currently claim that it can cure cancer. Instead, they argue that it can prevent cancer or control it.

On April 8, 1977, Laetrile proponents were successful in a case involving *Mr. Glen L. Rutherford et al.* v. *The United States of America et al.* in the U.S. District Court for Western Oklahoma. Judge Luther Bohanon ruled that any cancer patient certified by affidavit to be terminally ill should be allowed to use Laetrile. On May 10, 1977, Judge Bohanon issued a subsequent order specifying both the format of the affidavit to be used and the amount of Laetrile that each patient may import.

In opposition to Judge Bohanon's orders, the FDA on August 5, 1977, ruled once again against the use of Laetrile. Donald Kennedy, Commissioner of the FDA, based his decision to keep Laetrile off the market on both scientific and ethical arguments. First, he argued, qualified experts still do not recognize Laetrile as a safe and effective drug. He further argued that doctors who deal with cancer patients find that the patients turn to legitimate therapy too late, having delayed while trying Laetrile. Furthermore, he observed, another substantial group of cancer victims avoids effective treatment altogether and uses Laetrile instead.

Addressing himself to the "freedom of choice" issue, the Commissioner argued that "the very act of forming a government necessarily involves the yielding of some freedoms in order to obtain others." Applying this principle to the Laetrile issue, he wrote:

> . . . in passing the 1962 amendments to the Food and Drug Act—the amendments that require a drug be proved effective before it may be marketed—Congress indicated its conclusions that the absolute freedom to choose an effective drug was properly surrendered in exchange for the freedom from danger to each person's health and well-being from the sale and use of worthless drugs.[1]

In response to the FDA ruling, Judge Bohanon in December of 1977 permanently enjoined the FDA from interfering with the use of Laetrile. The FDA appealed to the Supreme Court and, on June 18, 1979, the Supreme Court overturned Judge Bohanon's decision. The Court argued that Congress had included the safety and effectiveness clauses in the federal Food, Drug, and Cosmetic Act in order to protect all citizens—including the terminally ill. The concept of safety, it maintained, is not without meaning for terminal patients: "a drug is unsafe for the terminally ill, as for anyone else, if its potential for inflicting death or physical injury is not offset by the possibility of therapeutic benefit." Furthermore, "the effectiveness of a drug does not necessarily denote capacity to cure; in the treatment of any illness, terminal or otherwise, a drug is effective if it fulfills, by objective indices, its sponsors' claim of prolonged life, improved physical condition or reduced pain."[2]

Laetrile and the Scientific Arguments

Several major studies have tested Laetrile's effectiveness, and virtually all of them have concluded that Laetrile is useless in the treatment of cancer. In 1953, the Cancer Commission of the California Medical Association found Laetrile to be completely ineffective as a cancer cure. Ten years later, when the California Department of Health reported to the public that Laetrile was ineffective in the treatment of cancer, California banned the drug. That same year, the *Canadian Medical Association Journal* reported that two formulations of Laetrile—one an American product, the other produced in Canada—were completely ineffective in the cure of cancer. The Canadian study itself inspired further testing of Laetrile. Between 1957 and 1975, the National Cancer Institute tested Laetrile on five different occasions and concluded on each occasion that Laetrile was useless in the treatment of cancer. Likewise, between 1972 and 1976, the Sloan-Kettering Institute in New York City reached similar conclusions in thirty-seven separate tests of Laetrile.

Whereas these earlier studies generally showed only that Laetrile is ineffective, more recent work has suggested that the drug may be unsafe as well. Recent animal experiments have shown Laetrile to be potentially toxic because of its cyanide content. Furthermore, at least thirty-seven cases of poisoning and seventeen deaths have resulted from the use of Laetrile by humans. Dr. Joseph F. Ross, Professor of Medicine at the UCLA School of Medicine, testified at the July 12, 1977, Senate Hearing on Laetrile that when released in the gastrointestinal tract, the cyanide content of Laetrile interferes with the body's ability to use oxygen, and hence can produce cyanosis, dizziness, stupor, coma, nausea, vomiting, shock, or death. Dr. Robert C. Eyerly, Chairman of the Committee on Unproven Methods of Cancer Management, maintains that the presence of Laetrile in American society poses a danger for children. According to Dr. Eyerly, the ingestion of five capsules of Aprikern or two packets of Bee-Seventeen can be fatal to a child.

Scientific evidence in *support* of Laetrile's safety and effectiveness has been rare. Two scientific papers are sometimes cited in support of the drug. The first paper, however, has been criticized by a committee of university biochemists, who found in the paper twenty-five statements based on erroneous facts or false assumptions. The second paper has had a better reception in scientific circles. But its author, Dr. Harold Manner of Chicago's Loyola University, cautioned the Senate Committee against accepting his conclusions until the results upon which he based those conclusions could be replicated.

Laetrile and the Argument from Free Choice

Many proponents of the drug in recent years have chosen to defend the use of Laetrile on ethical or political grounds. They argue that to restrict the use of Laetrile is to violate the individual's right to free choice in medical treatment. The group that has become the most powerful supporter of this position is itself called the Committee for Freedom of Choice in Cancer Therapy. In 1978, it claimed to have 450 chapters and 23,000 members. Other groups which have come to the support of Laetrile include the International Association of Cancer Victims and Friends, the Cancer Control Society, and the National Health Federation—all alleged to be right-wing organizations, some with the backing of the John Birch Society.

While the position of these groups is essentially that individuals should have the right to choose their own medical treatment, the groups differ on how extensive such a right to choose should be. Some believe that individuals should be able to obtain any drug that they themselves wish to use—regardless of whether that drug may have been deemed unsafe or ineffective. Other more moderate proponents of Laetrile agree that the safety clause should be retained in its present form, but argue that instead of banning drugs found to be ineffective, the FDA should require manufacturers to print a "statement of ineffectiveness" on the label of, say, every bottle of Laetrile tablets sold over the counter or by prescription. Still other Laetrile supporters think that the drug should be dispensed by prescription only. Finally, some supporters maintain merely that Laetrile should be prescribed only to patients who have been certified "terminally ill."

The supporters of the legalization of Laetrile do not all favor the use of Laetrile itself. Many believe that Laetrile is a fraud but that it should still be legalized. Laetrile should be legalized, they argue, because its prohibition constitutes a violation of individuals' right to free choice. Representative Steven Symms, Republican from Idaho, expresses some of the antipaternalist perspective that underlies this view:

> Freedom is the issue. The American people should be allowed to make their own decisions. They shouldn't have the bureaucrats in Washington, D.C. trying to decide for them about what is good and what is bad, as long as it is safe....
>
> The FDA is typical of what you get in regulatory agencies—a very protective mentality by bureaucrats who want to protect their own jobs and their own positions. It's easier for them to say "No" to a product—Laetrile or anything else—than it is to say "Yes." The FDA is simply not faced with the urgencies of patient care....
>
> Stringent drug regulation for society as a whole limits therapeutic choice by the individual physician, who is better able to judge risks and benefits for the individual patient.[3]

Similarly, Robert Bradford, president of the Committee for Freedom of Choice in Cancer Therapy, testified:

> The FDA must get off the backs of physicians, cancer patients, and ourselves. What, in the name of humanity, is the agency doing? Whom does it represent? Surely, not the people....
>
> Rest assured, gentlemen, that the people demand Laetrile, and they are going to have it, whether Big Brother likes it or not.[4]

What do "the people" think about drug regulation and Laetrile? Cambridge Reports, Inc., surveyed consumer attitudes concerning drug regulation. One of the questions asked was:

> Some people say companies should tell us in plain English what the possible dangers are in a product, as they do on cigarette packages, and then leave it to us, as individual consumers, to decide whether or not we want to use the product. Would you agree or disagree?

Eighty-two percent of the respondents agreed, 9 percent answered that they were unsure, and 9 percent disagreed. In a study more directly related to Laetrile, a Harris Poll indicated that Americans oppose the ban on Laetrile by a 53 to 23 percent margin.[6]

The proponents of Laetrile repeatedly invoke the individual's right to free choice in medical treatment, including the right to choose foolishly. As one individual in favor of legalizing Laetrile wrote:

> If the people want to use unapproved or home remedies it is their right to do so. If they want to delay conventional and possibly life-saving treatment then it is their right to do so, foolish and tragic as it might be.[7]

The FDA and most of the medical profession disagree with this position. They argue that the legalization of Laetrile will actually *decrease* the opportunities for free choice. In the first place, they maintain that the choice of a product (medical or otherwise) is not a *free* choice if the product in question is a fraud. In the words of one high-ranking FDA official:

> Laetrile is the most unattractive kind of fraud. It is making some people very rich on the basis of promises that, according to all available evidence, are false, and are known by many of the proponents of Laetrile to be false. The major promoter has a very seamy record and there are hints of ties to right-wing paramilitary groups in the case of the Wisconsin operation.[8]

In the second place, they argue that choices made under extreme emotional stress are not really free. Cancer patients and their families are often forced to make choices when they are under such emotional stress, and these choices, therefore, cannot be considered wholly free. Moreover, they argue that choices made under emotional stress—if unwise—can in effect decrease the possibilities for free choice in the future.

The opponents of Laetrile further insist that, whether toxic or not, Laetrile is unsafe simply because it is ineffective. As Dr. Daniel S. Martin, research associate of the Institute of Cancer Research of Columbia University, has stated:

> [N]o worthless drug is without harm; a patient's choice of Laetrile, to the extent that such a choice delays or interferes with swift diagnosis and prompt effective treatment, is potentially fatal.[9]

Dr. Martin cites a number of cases (documented by the American Cancer Society) in which patients with treatable cancer abandoned conventional therapy for Laetrile. By the time these patients realized that Laetrile was not working, their chances for recovery were either poor or nil. Summarizing and broadening the position of the opponents of the legalization of Laetrile, Arthur A. Checchi writes:

> It is in the public interest for legislators to leave basic decisions concerning the safety and efficacy of specific procedures to experts who are qualified to make such judgments rather than to laymen who are not....
>
> In debating special legislation for products such as Laetrile, we must consider who are the likely purchasers and users of the questionable products: it is the desperate with serious diseases not entirely treatable by recognized procedures; and unfortunately, there is a growing group of people in our society which distrusts the government, big industry and our scientific institutions....
>
> There can be Freedom of Informed Choice only where the persons making the judgment have the basic training and understanding of the issues to make that choice. That person must be qualified. Unfortunately, the average person is not....
>
> The gullible, like children, should be protected from those who exploit them![10]

Laetrile in New Jersey

While the interstate manufacture of drugs comes under the jurisdiction of the FDA, the control of the intrastate manufacture of drugs falls to the regulatory agencies of each state. Hence, when a New Jersey company announced its plans to manufacture Laetrile in the state of New Jersey, the New Jersey Commissioner of Health became responsible for deciding whether these plans could be carried out. The responsibility was an unusual one for the Commissioner since drugs are rarely manufactured on an intrastate basis. Furthermore, since the New Jersey State Department of Health never had to review new drugs before, the state never bothered to revise the New Jersey drug law in accordance with the changes the federal drug law made in 1962. Unlike its federal counterpart, the New Jersey drug law requires that a new drug be examined only for its safety, not for its efficacy.

The situation posed a dilemma for the Commissioner, Dr. Joan E. Finley. On the one hand, she strongly believed that Laetrile should not be allowed on the market (agreeing with the FDA that if a drug were to be allowed to be sold, it should first be proved effective as well as safe). On the other hand, she was forced by New Jersey law to examine Laetrile only for its safety.

Without waiting for the Commissioner's decision on Laetrile, three New Jersey State Assemblymen on May 2, 1977, introduced a bill to legalize Laetrile. The bill, A-3295, introduced by Assemblymen Gregario, Deverin, and Karcher, read:

> 1. No duly licensed physician shall be subject to any penalty or disciplinary action by any state agency or private professional

> organization solely for prescribing, administering or dispensing amygdalin, also known as Laetrile or Vitamin B-17, to a patient who has made a written request for such substance.... [The form on which the request is made must include the statement] "Amygdalin has not been approved as a treatment or cure of cancer by the United States Food and Drug Administration.... Neither the American Cancer Society, the American Medical Association, nor the Medical Society of New Jersey recommends use of Amygdalin (Laetrile) in the treatment of any malignancy, disease, illness or physical condition.... There are alternative recognized treatments for the malignancy, disease, illness or physical condition from which I suffer which he [my doctor] has offered to provide...."
>
> 2. No duly recognized pharmacist shall be subject to any penalty or disciplinary action ...for dispensing amygdalin...labelled with the following statement: "Amygdalin has not been approved as a treatment or cure of any malignancy, disease, illness or physical condition by the United States Food and Drug Administration."
>
> 3. No health care facility or employee thereof may restrict or forbid the use of, refuse to administer, or dispense amygdalin, when prescribed by a physician....
>
> 4. No person shall be held liable to any civil or criminal penalty solely for the manufacture...in this state of amygdalin....
>
> 5. The State Department of Health shall maintain records concerning the use of the substance amygdalin...and shall make periodic studies concerning the efficacy of such substances in the treatment of cancer.[11]

Debate on the bill lasted only two days. Arguing against the bill, the Commissioner insisted that the New Jersey drug law is "archaic" and that it should be changed to include some requirement for effectiveness; this change would prohibit drugs such as Laetrile from making their way onto the market.[12] Also testifying against Laetrile were representatives of the FDA and the Public Health Council of the State of New Jersey.

Most of those testifying, however, supported the legalization of Laetrile. One group testified on behalf of friends and relatives who had cancer and who had allegedly been helped by Laetrile or who now sought the "right to hope" that it supposedly provides. Assemblyman Gregario himself fell into this category; he described at length his father's bout with cancer and his own decision to take Laetrile as a preventative treatment for cancer. Then there were representatives from the Committee for Freedom of Choice and Options, Inc. Both of these representatives stressed the individual's right to freedom of choice in medical treatment and the ever-increasing intrusion of government into the lives of citizens.[13]

Outside the hearing room, several members of the federal and state health agencies argued that only they were capable of deciding whether individuals should be allowed to use Laetrile. Many state legislators and assemblymen maintained, on the contrary, that only individuals by themselves or through their legislators were competent to make such decisions.

Donald Foley, Deputy Commissioner of Health for the State of New Jersey and the department official chiefly responsible for drug regulation in the state, argued that his department should have the authority for decisions concerning the legalization of Laetrile. First of all, he argued, "drugs differ from mere commodities; they are life-saving and life-endangering; and therefore decisions concerning them should be made by those who can best judge them." Second, "the public isn't as informed as they think they are. They're not dumb, but when they read the label they don't understand what they read. They don't know chemistry." Third, individuals with cancer are under emotional stress and therefore cannot always act in a rational manner when choosing their medical treatment. According to Foley, "some of them are in such an emotional state that if you told them that they would be cured if they jumped off the Brooklyn Bridge, they would jump. This is what we want to stop."[14]

Many of the scientists and pharmacists in the Health Department favored giving individuals more free choice than Foley's position permitted. But even they agreed with Foley that the department itself should regulate the use of Laetrile.[15] Thomas Culkin, a department pharmacist concerned with the Laetrile issue, articulated a typical middle position between free choice and government regulation. While he agreed that "individuals must be allowed free choice if they are to be considered adults," he argued that "to talk about freedom without also talking about the regulation of those who might take advantage of that freedom is foolish.... This is one reason why the safety clause of our regulations is so important." He continued, "If Laetrile is proven safe, individuals should be able to use it if they want to." In this instance, the "state's job should be one of educator and not father."[16]

Many state legislators went further than Culkin in their commitment to free choice: "only the individual can know what is good for himself" and "while the Health Department is certainly necessary up to a point [to ensure safety], beyond that point it starts to get in the way of the individual's ability to function."[17] Legislators also warned of the general tendency of bureaucracies to stifle medical innovation. As one assemblyman commented on the FDA, "It is not their fault, they just have so much to deal with that it takes them twenty years to get to a drug which could have saved thousands of lives by then.... If the drug is safe, why not let people use it and then we'll find out whether it's effective or not."[18]

On January 10, 1978, the bill to legalize Laetrile passed by a wide margin in both houses. Governor Byrne signed the bill one day later, stating that

> I recognize that the drug Laetrile is not a proven cure for cancer. Clearly, it is no more than a source of psychic comfort to cancer patients.... Yet I do not believe that people should be deprived of its use; and I have faith in the medical profession that it will not be abused and that cancer patients will be advised of proven and recognized cancer treatment methods.[19]

Asked why the Laetrile bill passed so easily, health officials and legislators cited in addition to the ideological and emotional factors discussed above, several more purely political factors. First, the bill came up for a vote at the very end of the legislative session, when almost everyone was fatigued and eager to go home. Second, political bargaining had taken place; some legislators voted for the Laetrile bill only to ensure support for their own bills that would be voted on later.

A third reason for the bill's relatively easy passage, also revealed by interviews, is that several legislators knew all along that, regardless of whether or not the bill were enacted, Laetrile almost certainly could not be manufactured in New Jersey for at least seven or eight years. The legislators knew that the New Jersey Department of Health had the intention and the authority to prolong the procedure for testing the safety of Laetrile. For at least a few legislators, the prospect of an eight-year period during which Laetrile would not be allowed on the market was sufficient to overcome any qualms they had about voting for the Laetrile bill.

Laetrile in New Jersey, according to Deputy Commissioner Foley, is "on hold, and will be for at least seven or eight more years to come...until we can prove it is safe enough for the people of New Jersey." Some people contend that the Department of Health is merely stalling. Foley disagrees, but adds that "although we are not stalling (it's simply that testing takes a long time and we have a backload), I think that the seven or eight years it will take to complete the Laetrile tests may be enough time for people to come to their senses.... Hopefully by then they will have taken it upon themselves to vote down Laetrile."[20]

IMPLEMENTING THE LAETRILE LAW

The state Health Department delegated to its Bureau of Drugs the responsibility for implementing and enforcing the Laetrile Act.

The state official who is the Director of the Bureau of Drugs is a nationally recognized scientist and administrator. He has published many professional articles concerning drugs, and has recently been elected president of a multistate health association. Because of his professional stature, any Laetrile actions he takes may be followed by other officials in states that have Laetrile laws.

The Director, on the basis of the available scientific evidence, emphatically believes that "Laetrile is not only worthless in the treatment of cancer, but that it is a health fraud; and worse still, citizens in the state are foregoing conventional cancer treatment in favor of Laetrile with fatal results."

The Laetrile Act did not change any existing drug laws in the state. The old state drug law does have a safety requirement for intrastate "new drugs." However, this part of the law has not been enforced in over twenty years because the FDA safety regulations were applied in the state. These regulations require an extensive animal work-up on the toxicity and toxicology of all new drugs prior to distribution in interstate commerce. The extent of *just* intrastate use of a drug is illustrated by the Director's comment that "he can only remember during the past twenty years, only two requests for state approval of a new drug...and in both cases he convinced the applicant not to apply."

However, two applications have recently been received by the Division of Drugs for approval to manufacture Laetrile in the state. One application is from a chemical company which has found a method to synthesize Laetrile. The other application is from a company in Mexico which is currently manufacturing the drug and wishes to set up a subsidiary plant in the state. Both companies have followed up their initial requests with phone calls and letters.

Prior to any definitive response to the two manufacturers, the state Director of the Bureau of Drugs has, with the *concurrence* of the Health Commissioner, promulgated, *without public hearings,* regulations under the existing "old" state drug laws pertaining to the safety of intrastate new drugs. In essence, the state has adopted by reference the FDA regulations pertaining to safety requirements of new drugs.

In order to satisfy the very strict "safety tests" regulations, a sponsor would have to initiate a complete animal study which could take several years and cost several hundred thousand dollars. "In effect," the Director said, "even if a company were to do this, the approval and legal use of Laetrile in the state could be delayed from three to eleven years. The FDA experience is that it takes an average of seven to eight years for a 'new drug' to be approved."*

The Director, under the quality control authority of the Laetrile Act, has also, with the concurrence of the Health Commission and without public hearings, adopted by reference the Good Manufacturing Practices (GMPs) regulations of the FDA.

These regulations require that Laetrile manufacturers have *adequately* equipped facilities, *adequately* trained technical and professional personnel, the *necessary* analytical controls and *adequate* record keeping methods. Laetrile not manufactured under conforming methods or in conforming facilities is considered adulterated and will be seized and destroyed by the state.

*This time frame also includes satisfying the efficacy requirements for new drugs which may require two to three years of testing.

These GMP regulations rigidly interpreted could also further delay the distribution of Laetrile in the state.

The Director has said that the Health Department interprets the legislative intent as requiring safety testing. He commented, "The legislature is aware of both of these new regulations but, as of yet, is not cognizant of the FDA experience in terms of granting 'new drug' approval (the average of seven to eight years it takes) or the state intention 'literally' to enforce GMPs on Laetrile manufacturers if and whenever necessary."

The Department's actions, the Director has stated, have been taken in effect "so that the state will have time to realize that Laetrile is a most dangerous hoax and health fraud and will repeal the law." In the meantime, he believes that "lives will be saved by conventional cancer treatments rather than lost because of Laetrile."[21]

Notes

1. HEW Release, Aug. 4, 1977.
2. *U.S.* v. *Rutherford*, 61LEd 2d 68, 99 S Ct (1979).
3. Representative Steven Symms, quoted in *U.S. News and World Report*, June 13, 1977, p. 51.
4. Arthur A. Checchi, "The Return of the Medicine Man: The Laetrile Story and the Dilemma for State Legislators," *Association of Food and Drug Officials Quarterly Bulletin*, April 1978, p. 94.
5. Cambridge Reports, Inc., 1978.
6. Lewis Harris, *The Harris Survey* (New York: Chicago Tribune-New York News Syndicate, 1977).
7. Editorial, *Buffalo Courier Express*, June 15, 1977.
8. Interview with anonymous official.
9. Dr. Daniel S. Martin, *Philadelphia Inquirer*, Feb. 12, 1978.
10. Checchi, "Medicine Man."
11. Assembly Bill No. 3295 introduced May 2, 1977, with Senate Committee amendments adopted on Jan. 10, 1978.
12. New Jersey State Assembly Hearing on A3295, New Jersey State Document 974.90 N222, 1977, p. 3.
13. Ibid., pp. 6–40.
14. Interviews with Donald Foley, Dec. 7, 1978, and Jan. 11, 1979.
15. Interviews with New Jersey Department of Health administrators, scientists, and pharmacists, Jan. 8 through Jan. 16, 1979.
16. Interview with Thomas Culkin, Jan. 10, 1979.
17. Interviews with New Jersey state legislators, Jan. 8 through Jan. 16, 1979.
18. Ibid.
19. Governor Brendan Byrne, quoted in the *Trenton Times*, Jan. 11, 1977, p. 2.
20. Interview with Donald Foley, Jan. 11, 1979.
21. The preparation of this case benefited greatly from the work of Robert Rich.

AIDS Testing at Home

Ted Aaberg

During 1986 and 1987, more than a dozen individuals or companies expressed their intention to market a do-it-yourself kit for testing for the HIV virus associated with AIDS. For less than $40, anyone would be able to purchase the kit by mail order or at a drug store without prescription, and use it in the privacy of his or her own home. The typical kit would consist of a lancet to prick a finger, a vial to contain the blood sample, and a pre-addressed package in which to send the sample to an authorized laboratory, which would report the results by return mail or by phone. This procedure, its promoters say, offers a significantly less expensive and much more convenient method than the usual alternatives—a trip to the doctor's office or a visit to the hospital. It also would be more likely to preserve confidentiality.

In March 1988, the Food and Drug Administration announced that it was "limiting the marketing of blood collection kits [known as "AIDS home test kits"] at this time to those intended for professional use only."[1] Under the agency's policy, kits would be approved only if they meet these criteria:

> 1. Kits are labeled and marketed for professional use only within a health care environment (e.g., hospitals, medical clinics, doctor's offices, sexually transmitted disease clinics, HIV-1 counseling and testing centers, and mental health clinics;
> 2. Kits provide for the collection of a venipuncture or other appropriately validated sample by one who is recognized by a State or local authority to perform such procedures;
> 3. The testing sequence for all samples collected with the kits includes use of a licensed screening test for HIV-1 antibody and, for those samples testing positive by the screening test, the use of an additional more specific test (i.e., Western blot or comparable test). It is recommended that a licensed test which is more specific for HIV-1 antibody be utilized. However, the agency may accept a properly validated unlicensed test until licensed tests are more widely available;
> 4. The instructions for sample collection, storage, shipping, and testing conform with, or are validated as the equivalent to the package insert instructions for the specific licensed HIV-1 antibody test kit used to test samples; and
> 5. All results of testing are reported directly to a professional health care provider for reporting and interpretation of the result to the person requesting the test, as well as for counseling of the individual.[2]

Although many press accounts interpreted the FDA's action as effectively banning the kits,[3] FDA officials insist that the decision is not a ban but concerns only "what type of kit we will consider for approval."[4] Furthermore, the criteria are intended to be only temporary until public hearings can be held.

One of the FDA's major objections to the kits appears to be that they do not ensure that individuals who test "positive" will receive the personal counseling that they need to cope with the extreme psychological stress such results usually cause. The FDA also believes that the risk of incorrect diagnoses is too great if trained technicians do not take the blood samples.

The FDA is not alone in its opposition to the kits. Officials at the Centers for Disease Control also emphasize the potential harm to the individual taking the test. Dr. Richard George, responsible for part of the CDC's AIDS program, argues that counseling is necessary to explain the meaning of a positive test result. The result should not be interpreted as necessarily implying that one is "ill" or that "death is around the corner." He also questions the accuracy of a home test, not only because the test taker may "botch the test," but also because the laboratory will not usually have the individual's medical history that should be part of any adequate diagnosis.[5] Another CDC official, Dr. Peter Drotman, doubts that the kits are necessary: hundreds of free public health clinics across the country are now providing high quality testing, along with professional counseling. The clinics, furthermore, have had long experience with sexually transmitted diseases, and can point to an excellent record of maintaining confidentiality.[6]

The CDC also believes that counseling can help prevent the spread of the disease:

> Counseling and treating persons who are infected or at risk for acquiring HIV infection is an important component of prevention strategy. Most of the estimated 1 to 1.5 million infected persons in the United States are unaware that they are infected with HIV. The primary public health purposes of counseling and treating are to help uninfected individuals initiate and sustain behavioral changes that reduce their risk of becoming infected and to assist infected individuals in avoiding infecting others.[7]

Outside the government, opinion is divided. The American Medical Association in 1985 praised "home-use in vitro devices" as having "great potential for broadening the base of knowledge and understanding of the American people about their own health."[8] But the AMA also expresses concern about such tests, stating that they should be carefully scrutinized before being permitted on the market. They should be subjected to strict criteria based on this premise: ". . .as the potential harm both to the individual and to society would increase upon occurrence of inaccurate test results, misinterpretation of test results or failure to follow up properly and in a timely fashion on such results, the requirements for demonstration of safety and efficacy should increase commensurately."[9]

The FDA's position has been criticized for undermining the Public Health Service's goal of encouraging more extensive testing throughout the population. One of the manufacturers who wishes to market the kit comments: "We don't understand the FDA's position at all. We were under the impression that the federal government was *for* mass, anonymous testing."[10] Other critics see the FDA's decision as part of a government "plan to remain in complete control of testing and of knowledge of the results."[11]

Critics of the FDA decision also argue that banning the kits would take away the individuals' right to have confidential knowledge about their own health. The kits virtually guarantee privacy, while the current health system cannot, as even FDA officials admit.[12] The CDC notes that "disclosures of HIV-testing information [can be] deliberate, inadvertent or simply unavoidable" in the current system. Confidentiality may be breached because of the wide scope of "need-to-know situations, because of the possibility of inappropriate disclosures, and because of established authorization procedures for releasing records. . . ."[13]

The most general objections to the FDA policy invoke the specter of an authoritarian bureaucracy forcing citizens to conform to its view of what is good for them. "In essence, the Federal Government is enunciating the right to ban for general use a simple medical test because the public cannot be trusted with the results. . .the agency had never before used a potential psychic trauma as a justification for restricting sales of a medical product."[14]

In response to these and other public criticisms of its policy, the FDA announced that it would hold a public meeting in the spring of 1989 to "provide an opportunity for all interested persons to make their views known to the FDA and to allow thorough discussion of the issues." The views expressed at the meeting will be considered "in the development of final policy and regulatory decisions" concerning the kits.[15] The meeting was to cover these topics:

A. Topic 1: Blood Collection Kits

1. *Collection and shipping of blood samples by laypersons.* Improper sample collection, preparation, and shipment could adversely affect the accuracy of HIV-1 antibody test results. In addition, it is possible, although most unlikely, that improper sample collection and transport might result in transmission of infection or injury. Therefore, comments are solicited on the ability of laypersons to safely and adequately collect and package these samples for shipment.

2. *Return of test results directly to the person from whom the sample was collected.* Some manufacturers have proposed systems in which the HIV-1 antibody test results would be returned directly to the person from whom the sample was collected. The results of in vitro diagnostic tests often require interpretation (e.g., under what circumstances false-negative or false-positive results might occur) and must be integrated into an overall assessment of a person's medical status. Before returning the results of testing for evidence of infection with HIV-1 to any person other than a health professional, adequate instructions for interpretation of the test results would have to be developed. Comments are solicited on

whether such information could be adequately provided.

3. *Counseling outside of a medical health care environment.* This topic is related to the issue of proper interpretation of and followup on test results. There is agreement among medical experts that adequate counseling regarding the test results should be part of HIV-1 testing. Comments are solicited regarding the ability to provide effective pre- and post-test counseling in a setting outside the health care environment.

4. *Availability of blood collection systems.* The availability of blood collection systems as over-the-counter (OTC) devices could increase the number of samples tested by making systems more readily available. Comments are solicited on whether blood collection systems should be available as OTC devices.

B. Topic 2: Kits for Collection and Home Testing of Blood for Evidence of HIV-1 Infection

Some have discussed the possibility of developing test kits with which laypersons could not only obtain their own specimen at home, but also perform testing for evidence of HIV-1 infection. FDA invites comments on issues related to these types of kits. Such issues would include whether the kits should be made available OTC, whether laypersons can reliably and safely perform the test, whether laypersons can adequately interpret the test results, and whether that interpretation in the absence of a medical professional is appropriate.[16]

NOTES

1. "Blood Collection Kits Labeled for Human Immunodeficiency Virus Type 1 (HIV-1) Antibody Testing; Home Test Kits Designed to Detect HIV-1 Antibody; Open Meeting," [Docket No. 88N-0319] *Federal Register* Feb. 17, 1980, p. 7280.

2. Ibid.

3. "Banned at Home: An FDA Ruling on AIDS Tests," *Time* (April 18, 1988), p. 26, and "Home Kits for AIDS Virus Testing Virtually Ruled Out by the F.D.A.," *New York Times* (April 8, 1988), p. A15.

4. Telephone interview with Debra Henderson, special assistant to the director of the Center for Biologics, Research and Evaluation, FDA, Feb. 1, 1989.

5. Telephone interview with Richard George, chief of Developmental Technology Section, AIDS Program, CDC, Feb. 17, 1989.

6. Telephone interview with Peter Drotman, assistant to the director of AIDS Program, CDC, Feb. 17, 1989.

7. Centers for Disease Control, U.S. Department of Health and Human Services/Public Health Service, "Public Health Service Guidelines for Counseling and Antibody Testing to Prevent HIV Infection and AIDS," *Morbidity and Mortality Weekly Report* (Boston, Mass.: Massachusetts Medical Society) Aug. 14, 1987, p. 509.

8. Letter from James H. Sammons, Executive Vice President, American Medical Association, to Jerome A. Donlon, FDA, Oct. 14, 1985.

9. Ibid.

10. "AIDS Tests for Home Use Prohibited: Accuracy, Trauma Worry Officials," *Washington Post* (April 8, 1988), p. A1.

11. Ibid.

12. Telephone interview with Debra Henderson, Jan. 4, 1989.

13. Centers for Disease Control, p. 514.

14. "Banned at Home," p. 26.

15. "Blood Collection Kits," *Federal Register,* pp. 7280–81.

16. Ibid.

Comment

The Laetrile case is best analyzed, first, by deciding whether the legislators voted for the best policy and, second, by judging the process by which they and Department of Health officials legalized Laetrile but delayed its approval.

The first step in judging the content of the decision to legalize Laetrile is to decide whether the legislature's explicit policy was paternalistic. Avoid the common tendency to describe all cases of justified paternalism as nonpaternalistic. Mill, for example, denies that intervention in the case of the person crossing the unsafe bridge is paternalistic "for liberty consists in doing what one desires, and he does not desire to fall into the river." But if the person wants to cross the bridge and if we thwart his desire in order to save his life, then our intervention is paternalistic. Determining whether a restriction on freedom is paternalistic therefore must be separated from the question of whether the restriction is justified.

Also, be careful not to conflate the problems of paternalism and democracy by labeling any democratic decision paternalistic simply because its effect is to limit the freedom and protect the interests of a minority. A law whose purpose is to satisfy the preferences of a democratic majority may not be paternalistic if, for example, its purpose is to restrict the majority's freedom. Was the ban on Laetrile such an instance?

Was the decision to make Laetrile available only by prescription the best one? Consider the major alternatives available to the legislature: permitting the sale of Laetrile over the counter, with or without mandatory labeling; and banning its production and sale, with or without exceptions for the terminally ill.

What policy should someone support who, like Representative Symms, believes that "freedom is the only issue"? What restrictions on the availability of Laetrile are necessary and sufficient to create free choice?

If you have doubts about the absolute value of freedom, even of informed choice, you will consider paternalistic alternatives to the free market. The policy explicitly endorsed by the legislature does not leave the choice up to the market: doctors stand between buyers and sellers. May we assume, as Symms seems to, that by permitting doctors to prescribe Laetrile, patients are free to choose among therapies by choosing among doctors?

Are claims that cancer patients cannot understand the choice among the therapies and suffer from severe emotional stress sufficient to justify a complete ban on Laetrile? Is it plausible to maintain that those whose freedom is restricted by a ban nevertheless accept the goal of governmental intervention or would accept it if their decision-making faculties were not impaired?

In judging the process by which the Laetrile policy was enacted and implemented, keep in mind the distinction between content (was the right policy adopted?) and method (was it adopted rightly?). The legislators had democratic authority to determine the policy on Laetrile. Are there any grounds for criticizing how they made their decision? Consider whether citizens who supported (or opposed) the legalization of Laetrile had sufficient means for holding their representatives accountable.

Suppose a legislator reasoned as follows: "I will vote for legalizing Laetrile because I am reasonably sure that even if the law is passed, Laetrile will not be marketed for at least seven years. If I vote against legalization, I will probably lose the next election to Joe Smith whom I know to be incompetent and corrupt. Therefore, it is in the public interest, as well as my own, to concede to my opponents on this issue, despite the fact that I firmly believe that their position is wrong." The legislator votes for legalization and it passes by one vote. Evaluate his action.

Bureaucratic discretion in the Laetrile case, as in the AIDS-testing case and many others, is great. In the Laetrile case, it gave officials of the Department of Health and the Bureau of Drugs scope to act on their own moral judgments about the value of Laetrile. If the Bureau of Drugs could have tested Laetrile for safety in less than seven or eight years, should it have acted as quickly as possible, or should it have drawn the testing period out as long as was legally possible in deference to the intent of those legislators with whom the director morally agreed? To what extent should Foley have looked at his duties from the perspective of a legislator when he was making (rather than merely implementing) policy? If Foley had a duty of accountability like that of a legislator, what did that duty require of him in this case?

In the AIDS-testing case, the nonelected officials at the FDA recognized that they were making policy and had assumed some of the duties of legislators. They decided, for example, to consult broadly and hold public meetings before they rendered a final decision. What other duties, if any, does this kind of policy-making role require of FDA officials? Should the FDA be making policy at all? Assess the alternatives.

The rationale behind the FDA's proposed policy to ban the marketing of AIDS-testing kits is clearly paternalistic. Is the paternalism justified? To answer this question, we should attend to the two different welfare-based arguments offered by FDA officials: (1) people should be protected from an unnecessarily high risk of false testing; and (2) people should be protected from the trauma of learning a dreadful truth without the aid of psychological counselling. Is there a morally significant difference between protecting people from paying for tests that are excessively unreliable and protecting them from the psychic trauma accompanying accurate (as well as inaccurate) information? Should FDA officials consider whether the people who are likely to seek AIDS tests would consent to both kinds of protection? If actual or hypothetical consent should be a factor, how should the FDA go about determining whether people consent? If consent is inappropriate, according to what criteria should the FDA draw the line between justified and unjustified paternalism? Develop a set of criteria based on individual welfare that could guide a paternalistic policy; then evaluate the relative merits of welfare-based and consent-based criteria for justifying paternalism.

Use your evaluation to assess the strongest arguments for and against the FDA's decision to ban the do-it-yourself kits. Then assess the alternatives to the blanket approval of the do-it-yourself kits defended by the commercial laboratories and the absolute ban proposed by the FDA.

If you were testifying at the public meeting set by the FDA, what would you say on each of the topics on the agenda? On other topics not on the agenda? If you were an FDA official, what would you expect to learn from such a meeting?

Recommended Reading

The classic source on paternalism is Mill's *On Liberty,* Introductory, chapters 4 and 5. For modern discussions, see Gerald Dworkin, "Paternalism," *Monist* 56 (1972), pp. 64–84, reprinted in R. Wasserstrom (ed.), *Morality and the Law* (Belmont, Calif.: Wadsworth, 1971); Joel Feinberg, *The Moral Limits of the Criminal Law,* vol. 3, *Harm to Self* (New York: Oxford University Press, 1986); John Kleinig, *Paternalism* (Totowa, N.J.: Littlefield and Adams, 1984); Dennis F. Thompson, "Paternalistic Power," in *Political Ethics and Public Office* (Cambridge, Mass.: Harvard University Press, 1987), ch. 6; and Donald VanDeVeer, *Paternalistic Intervention: The Moral Bounds of Benevolence* (Princeton, N.J.: Princeton University Press, 1986). More generally, see Gerald Dworkin, *The Theory and Practice of Autonomy* (New York: Cambridge University Press, 1988).

On the ethics of democratic representation, Mill is, once again, a good place to start. See his *Considerations on Representative Government* (Indianapolis: Bobbs-Merrill, 1958), chapters 5–8, 12, and 15. Compare Joseph Schumpeter, *Capitalism, Socialism and Democracy* (New York: Harper and Row, 1975), pp. 240–83. A useful commentary is Hanna Fenichel Pitkin, *The Concept of Representation* (Berkeley: University of California Press, 1972), chapters 7–10.

On AIDS, see the Recommended Reading in Chapter 6.

9 Liberty and Life

Introduction

The idea that all persons have a right to life commands widespread support in this country. But what beings possess this right is one of the most divisive questions of our recent political history. The "pro-life" movement defends the fetus's right to life while "pro-choice" groups defend a woman's right to abortion. They disagree on questions of both personal morality (whether having an abortion is moral) and political morality (whether abortion should be legal).

The structure of the pro-life argument is:

The fetus is a person.
It is wrong to kill a person (except in self-defense).
Abortion is therefore wrong (unless a mother's life is at stake).
It should therefore be illegal.

The typical pro-choice argument has a parallel logic supporting the opposite conclusion:

The fetus is not a person, but is part of a woman's body and significantly affects her life.
A woman has a right to control her own body and life.
Abortion therefore is a woman's right.
It should therefore be legal.

The two sides are divided by fundamentally different perceptions of what a fetus is, perceptions that seem impervious to change by rational argument. Each views the perception of the other as "not simply false, but wildly, madly false—nonsense, totally unintelligible and literally unbelievable" (Roger Wertheimer). While philosophers may not even in principle succeed in resolving this controversy, they can hope to make a more modest contribution. They may be able to show that the premises of each side support less extreme conclusions on the level of both personal and political morality.

Some philosophers have argued that even if the fetus is a person, its death may be justifiable. Self-defense is not the only justification for letting an innocent person die. One is not obligated to save an innocent person at great personal sacrifice if one is not otherwise responsible for the person's situation. On this view, the basic premise of the pro-life position leads to a less absolutist stance against abortion: abortion is permissible in cases of rape and incest. Other writers have suggested that even if abortion is wrong at the level of personal morality, it may still be right for a liberal state to legalize it when the public is so divided over its morality.

Philosophers also have criticized the internal logic of the extreme pro-choice position. They have argued that the right of a woman to control her body is not absolute: it does not include the right to destroy for trivial reasons what is admittedly a potential life. And the pro-choice position is not, as its proponents often argue, neutral as a political morality. Giving all women a choice between having and not having an abortion is still, for those who believe that the fetus is a person, giving women the right to kill innocent people. To the pro-life advocates this choice is immoral, just as for those who do not believe that the fetus is a person, outlawing abortion is immoral because it restricts a woman's right to control her own body and her freedom more generally.

The political morality of abortion is complex because no policy can be morally neutral, and neither side can rationally convince the other of the moral superiority of its position. Political philosophers have suggested several ways of dealing with situations of this kind. One is to consider a compromise that is fair to both sides, though not fully satisfying the moral claims of either. Another is to find a method of decision-making that is procedurally fair, even if its results favor one side of the moral controversy. Despite the vast literature on abortion, neither of these alternatives has been examined with sufficient care.

The cases on abortion in this chapter add moral complications to an already difficult political issue. Given that abortion is now legal in this country under most circumstances, should the government subsidize abortions for poor women? Most people who believe that abortion is a woman's right also argue that the government should subsidize it for poor women. But critics point out that having a right to free speech, for example, does not obligate the state to provide anyone with a subvention for publication. Most pro-life advocates argue that, even if the law permits some women to obtain abortions, there is no reason for the government to subsidize the taking of innocent lives. Yet some who believe that abortion is morally wrong dissent from this view on grounds that the exercise of legal rights should not be effectively withheld from the poor. In the congressional debate over funding, these and other moral positions are passionately represented. Califano's account of his position while he was secretary of the Department of Health, Education and Welfare raises yet another issue in political ethics: what should a public official do when the policy he may be instructed to enforce violates his own moral principles?

The conflict between life and liberty has taken on unforeseen dimensions in the newly expanding commercial practice of surrogate parenting, leaving state governments without standards for resolving the conflict in one of its poignant forms—the dispute over who are the rightful parents of a newly born child. Any legislation that settles this conflict will also have a profound effect on the more fundamental issue of whether government should sanction the commercial (or noncommercial) practice of surrogate parenting in the first place. The first proposal for legislative reform reprinted here recommends legalizing and enforcing contracts for surrogate parenting. Prepared by the staff of the New York State Senate Judiciary Committee, the recommendation is based on the view that enforcement

of suitably designed surrogate contracts will both secure the welfare of children born under such contracts and satisfy standards of informed consent required for valid private contracts. The second proposal, presented by the New York State Task Force on Life and the Law, rejects this view. The Task Force concludes that the commercialization of human reproduction is against the best interests of children, degrades women, and (more generally) conflicts with the public good. The Task Force therefore recommends that the legislature declare surrogate contracts void and unenforceable. Anyone who wishes to understand the conflict between the value of life and liberty presented by the practice of commercial surrogacy must come to terms with the differing moral perspectives represented by these two proposals.

Administering Abortion Policy

Joseph A. Califano, Jr.

The abortion issue marked my initiation by public controversy as Secretary of Health, Education, and Welfare.

It was certainly not the issue I would have chosen to confront first. The abortion dispute was sure to make enemies at the beginning of my tenure when I particularly needed friends; guaranteed to divide supporters of social programs when it was especially important to unite them; and likely to spark latent and perhaps lasting suspicions about my ability to separate my private beliefs as a Roman Catholic from my public duties as the nation's chief health, education, and social service official.

The issue whether Medicaid should fund abortions for poor women was more searing than many I faced, but it was quintessentially characteristic of the problems confronting HEW. The abortion dispute summoned taproot convictions and religious beliefs, sincerely held and strenuously put forth by each side, about the rights of poor people, the use of tax dollars, the role of government in the most intimate personal decisions. The pro- and anti-abortion forces each claimed that the Constitution and the American people were on its side, and each truly believed that it was protecting human life. Wherever those forces struggled to prevail—in the courts, the Congress, the executive regulatory process, the state legislatures, and city councils—there were HEW and its Medicaid program. And there was no neutral ground on which HEW or its Secretary could comfortably stand, for any decision—to fund all, or none, or some abortions—would disappoint and enrage millions of Americans who were convinced that theirs was the only humane position.

The controversy exposed me to the world of difference between being a White House staffer—however powerful—and being a Cabinet officer, out front, responsible not only to the President as an advisor but also to the Congress and the American people. It was one thing to be Lyndon Johnson's top domestic policy advisor crafting Great Society programs, but not accountable to the Congress and not ultimately responsible. It was quite another to be the public point man on an issue as controversial as federal financing of abortions for poor people.

Lyndon Johnson had held his White House staff on a particularly short leash. We spoke only in his name—explaining what he thought, how he felt, what his hopes and objectives for America were. "The only reason Hugh Sidey [of *Time*] talks to you is to find out about me, what I think, what I want. He doesn't give a damn about you," Johnson so often told us, "so make sure you know what I think before you tell him what you think I think." Indeed, during my lengthy press briefings on new legislative programs, as Johnson read early pages of the instantly typed transcript in his office, he sometimes sent messages to me to correct statements or misimpressions before the briefing ended.

Cabinet officers, of necessity, function with less detailed and immediate presidential guidance. It goes with the territory for a Cabinet officer to put a little distance between himself and the President, particularly on such controversial issues as abortion. Presidents expect, as they should, that their Cabinet officers will shield them from as much controversy as possible so that precious presidential capital can be spent only for overriding national objectives the President selects.

Jimmy Carter first talked to me about abortion when we lunched alone in Manchester, New Hampshire, in early August 1976. He expressed his unyielding opposition to abortion and his determination to stop federal funding of abortions. He asked me to work with Fritz Mondale to make his views known to the Catholic hierarchy and influential lay Catholics. Mondale was using his Minnesota friend Bishop James Rausch, who was then the general secretary of the National Conference of Catholic Bishops, to get Carter's view across, and Charlie Kirbo would be quietly communicating with Terence Cardinal Cooke in New York, but Carter said he wanted a "good Catholic" to spread the word of his strong opposition to abortion. I was impressed by the sincerity and depth of Carter's views on abortion and I found his determination to get credit for those views politically prudent in view of the inevitable opposition his position would incite. It later struck me that Carter never asked my views on the subject, and I never expressed them. Our conversation simply assumed complete agreement.

The assumption was well grounded. I consider abortion morally wrong unless the life of the mother would be at stake if the fetus were carried to term. Under such tragic and wrenching circumstances, no human being could be faulted for making either choice, between the life of the mother and the life of the unborn child. Those are the only circumstances under which I considered federal financing of abortion appropriate.

During the 1976 presidential campaign, I never had to reconcile my beliefs as a Catholic about abortion with any potential duty to obey and execute the law as a public servant. In promulgating Carter's view, like any proponent of a presidential candidate, I took as a given his ability to translate that view into law or public policy. Since my conversations were with those who opposed abortion, no one asked me what Carter would do if the Congress enacted a different position into law.

In talks with Monsignors George Higgins and Francis Lally, and others at the Catholic Conference, I sought to convince them that Carter shared their view. Higgins was an old friend from the Johnson years and he helped get Carter's position better known in the Catholic community. But Higgins confided that nothing short of a firm commitment to a constitutional amendment outlawing abortion would satisfy the conservative elements of the Catholic hierarchy. When I reported this to Mondale, he expressed doubt that

Carter would—or should—go that far, particularly since in January 1976 he had said he did "not favor a constitutional amendment abolishing abortion." I agreed.

Eventually, in response to the numerous questions on abortion during the campaign and after a meeting with Catholic bishops in Washington on August 31, 1976, Carter said that he had not yet seen any constitutional amendment he would support, but he "would never try to block. . .an amendment" prohibiting abortions. He added pointedly that any citizen had the right to seek an amendment to overturn the Supreme Court's 1973 *Roe* v. *Wade* decision, which established a woman's constitutional right to have an abortion, at least in the first trimester of pregnancy.

In November 1976, after the election, as Mondale, Tip O'Neill, and other friends reported conversations in which Carter or his close advisors such as Jordan and Kirbo were checking on my qualifications, it became clear that I was a leading candidate for the HEW post. Then, for the first time, I had to focus on the depth of my personal religious belief about abortion: As Secretary of Health, Education, and Welfare, would I be able, in good conscience, to carry out the law of the land, even if that law provided for federal funding of all abortions? I asked myself that question many times before others began asking it of me.

Both my parents are devoutly religious Catholics. Their influence and my education at St. Gregory's elementary school in Brooklyn, at the Jesuit high school Brooklyn Prep, and at the College of the Holy Cross had provided me not only with some intellectual sextants but with a moral compass as well. Like many Catholic students and young lawyers in the 1950s, I had read the works of John Courtney Murray, a leading Jesuit scholar and philosopher. His writings on the rights and duties of American Catholics in a pluralistic society and the need to accommodate private belief and public policy were guides for liberal Catholics of my generation. But even with this background, it was an exacting task in modern America to get clarity and peace in my private conscience while satisfying the legitimate demands of public service and leadership.

The abortion issue never came up in the Johnson administration. But family planning, even the aggressive promotion of the use of contraceptives to prevent pregnancy as a government policy, was an issue I had confronted in those years. President Johnson was an ardent proponent of birth control at home and abroad. He repeatedly rejected the unanimous pleas of his advisors from Secretary of State Dean Rusk to National Security Advisor Walt Rostow to ship wheat to the starving Indians during their 1966 famine. He demanded that the Indian government first agree to mount a massive birth control program. The Indians finally moved and Johnson released the wheat over a sufficiently extended period to make certain the birth control program was off the ground.

Johnson spoke so often and forcefully about birth control that the Catholic bishops denounced him publicly. He sent me to try to cool them off. Working discreetly with Monsignor Frank Hurley, then the chief lobbyist for the Catholic Conference in Washington, we reached an uneasy off-the-record truce: If LBJ would stop using the term "birth control" and refer instead to the "population problem," which allowed increased food production as a possible solution, the bishops would refrain from public attacks on him. Johnson agreed, and spoke thereafter of "the population problem"—but with equal if not greater vigor.

During my years with Lyndon Johnson, and the legislative fights to fund family planning services through the Public Health Service and the War on Poverty, I had to relate my private conscience to public policy on family planning. The alternatives of teenage pregnancy, abortion, mental retardation, poverty, and the like were far worse than providing access to contraceptives; to expect all citizens to practice premarital celibacy or all married couples to use the rhythm method was unrealistic in America's increasingly sexually permissive society. I was able to reconcile my private conscience with public policy. I concluded that it made sense for government to fund family planning programs that offered and even encouraged artificial birth control. I had no moral qualms about such a policy in a pluralistic society so long as it respected individual dignity and religious belief. The Catholic bishops disagreed with Johnson. But among theologians there was a great diversity of opinion about the moral propriety of birth control in various personal situations; I inclined to the more liberal position.

Abortion was a far more difficult issue. Here I faced my own conviction that abortion was morally wrong except to save the life of the mother, that medically unnecessary abortions offended fundamental standards of respect for human life. It is one thing temporarily to prevent the creation of a human life; quite another level of moral values is involved in discarding a human life once created. With abortion, I had to face direct conflict between personal religious conviction and public responsibility.

I was to learn how difficult it would be to preserve the precious distinction between public duty and private belief. Setting forth my own and the President's view of appropriate public policy on federal funding of abortion, putting the issue in perspective, relating it to considerations of fairness, and striving to separate my own personal views from my responsibilities as a public official once the Congress decisively acted on the legislation were to be matters of enormous complexity and lonely personal strain. Whatever inner strength I mustered from my own religious faith, the public anguish would not be eased by the fact that I was the only Catholic in the Carter Cabinet.

The anti-abortion, right to life groups and the pro-abortion, freedom of choice organizations had turned the annual HEW appropriations bill into the national battleground over abortion. The issue was whether, and under what circumstances, HEW's Medicaid program to finance health care for poor people should pay for abortions. It would be debated and resolved in the language of the HEW appropriations law, and the regulations implementing the law. This made the Secretary of HEW an especially imposing and exposed figure on the abortion battlefield.

With the Supreme Court's *Roe* v. *Wade* decision in 1973, HEW's Medicaid program promptly began funding abortions for poor women as routinely as any other medical procedure. By 1976, estimates of the number of HEW-funded abortions ranged as high as 300,000 per year. The furies that the *Roe* decision and its impact on HEW's Medicaid program set loose turned abortion into a legal and political controversy that the courts and the Congress would toss at each other for years. The federal financing of an estimated 300,000 abortions set off an emotional stampede in the House of Representatives in 1976, led by Republican Representative Henry Hyde of Illinois, and reluctantly followed by the Senate, to attach a restriction to the 1977 HEW appropriations bill prohibiting the use of HEW funds "to perform abortions except where the life of the mother would be endangered if the fetus were carried to term."

Before the restriction took effect, pro-abortion groups obtained an injunction from Federal District Judge John F. Dooling in Brooklyn, blocking its enforcement until he could decide whether the Supreme Court decision in *Roe* v. *Wade* established an obligation of the federal government to fund abortions, as a corollary to the right to have them performed.

Whatever the courts ultimately ruled, the abortion issue would continue to be a volatile inhabitant of the political arena. Sincerely held as I believe it was, Carter's stand was also a critical part of his election victory. Betty Ford's strong pro-abortion views and Gerald Ford's ambivalence were thought by Carter to have hurt the Republican candidate.

But Carter's appointment of pro-abortionist Midge Costanza as a senior White House aide and his strong support of the Equal Rights Amendment and other feminist causes gave women's groups some hope that his position would be softened. The pro-lifers were suspicious because Carter's colors blurred on the litmus test of supporting a constitutional amendment outlawing abortion. With pro- and anti-abortion advocates poised to battle for the mind of the administration, I prepared for my confirmation hearings on January 13, 1977.

From my religious and moral convictions, I knew my conscience. From my training at Harvard Law School and my life as a lawyer and public servant, I knew my obligation to enforce the law. But on the eve of becoming a public spokesman for myself and the administration, I sought the reassurance of double-checking my moral and intellectual foundation. I consulted an extraordinary Jesuit priest, James English, my pastor at Holy Trinity Church in Georgetown. He came by my law office on the Saturday morning before the confirmation hearing. He sat on the couch against the wall; I sat across the coffee table from him. I told him I wanted to make one final assessment of my ability to deal with the abortion issue before going forward with the nomination. If I could not enforce whatever law the Congress passes, then I should not become Secretary of Health, Education, and Welfare.

Father English spoke softly about the pluralistic society and the democratic system, in which each of us has an opportunity to express his views. Most statutory law codifies morality, he noted, whether prohibiting stealing or assault, or promoting equal rights, and the arguments of citizens over what the law should be are founded in individual moral values. He said that my obligation to my personal conscience was satisfied if I expressed those views forcefully.

I postulated a law that any abortion could be funded by the federal government, simply upon the request of the woman. He said that so long as I tried to pursue the public policy I believed correct, then I was free—indeed, obliged if I stayed in the job—to enforce that permissive law. I was relieved, comforted by his quiet assurance. As I thanked him for coming by, he mentioned an expert in this field, Father Richard McCormick, a Jesuit at the Kennedy Institute of Bioethics at Georgetown, whose advice I might find helpful.

On the following Monday evening, January 10, representatives of the National Women's Political Caucus sat on the same red couch Father English had occupied. It was the most intense of a series of meetings with various special interest groups.

As the women filed through the door to my office, I shook hands with each one. Their eyes seemed cold and skeptical, and reflected deep concern, even when they smiled. The warm welcome with which I greeted them masked my own foreboding about the imminence of the clash on abortion.

The discussion began on common ground: the failure of the Nixon and Ford administrations to enforce laws prohibiting sex discrimination. One after another, the representatives of each group in the women's political caucus attacked the enemy: discrimination in the Social Security system (in terms far more forceful than Jimmy Carter's quaint accusation that the benefit structure encouraged senior citizens to "live in sin"), in the federal income tax system, and on the nation's campuses. Most mentioned female appointments at HEW, but since they knew I was searching for qualified women, they did not linger on the personnel issue. Margot Polivy, a tough and talented attorney litigating to eliminate discrimination in women's athletics, pressed her case for HEW enforcement of Title IX, the law prohibiting sex discrimination at educational institutions that receive federal funds.

I shared most of the views the women expressed on these subjects and they knew it. When are they going to stop circling their prey, I thought, and ask about abortion?

Dorothy Ross, a committed feminist who had been helping me recruit for HEW jobs, was seated at my left. She had told me abortion would be the key topic and I wanted to get it over with. Then one of the women put the question: "What's your view on abortion?"

I had decided to make my view unmistakably clear. It was important to state my position on abortion before the Senate confirmation hearings. No senator should be able to claim that his vote was cast for my confirmation without knowing my view on this subject. But in the tension of the moment, it was not easy or pleasant to get the words out.

"I believe abortion is morally wrong," I said softly and firmly. "That is my personal belief."

There was a brief moment of breathtaking at the depth of conviction in my voice. Then the women responded.

"Would you deny federal funds for abortion?" one woman angrily asked.

"I oppose federal funding for abortion." The circling was over. The questions were accusations called out like counts in an indictment.

"The Supreme Court gives a woman a right to an abortion. You would deny that right to poor women?"

"You'd deny a woman her constitutional right?"

"How can you be a liberal and hold such a view?"

"Suppose the woman's life is at stake?"

"What about rape or incest?"

"Suppose the child would be retarded, a vegetable?"

"Are you going to impose your religious views on HEW?"

The questions came with such furious vehemence that I had to interrupt to respond.

"Look," I said, "I have no intention of imposing my personal view on anybody. I am prepared to enforce the law, whatever it is."

"But how could you possibly," one of the women asked, "when you have such strong personal views, such religious commitment?"

"There's nothing wrong with religious commitment," I fired back, "and nothing about it prevents me from enforcing the law."

The women made no attempt to disguise their anger or their suspicion. I wanted to end the meeting before it further deteriorated. The subject was even more volatile than I had anticipated. I was shaken by the obvious depth and genuineness of their emotional and intellectual conviction, and the difficulty of some of the questions they had raised. But there was nothing to be gained by heated exchanges. If there were no other matters on their minds, I suggested we conclude the meeting. They were just as anxious as I to cut off discussion: they, out of a desire to report to their colleagues and plan strategy; I, out of relief.

The parting was superficially amicable, but the battle lines had been drawn. Washington's feminist network buzzed with reports of the meeting throughout that evening and the next day. Late that Tuesday afternoon I was told that the women's groups would attack my nomination on the basis of my stand on abortion.

By Wednesday, the day before my confirmation hearing, the National Abortion Rights Action League had asked to appear, on behalf of fourteen groups which supported federal funds for abortion, before both Senate committees scheduled to hear me testify on my nomination.

As I drove to my office early on Thursday morning, the radio news broadcasts were announcing that Senator Robert Packwood of Oregon, a staunch proponent of Medicaid-funded abortions and member of the Finance Committee which had jurisdiction over my nomination, would question me closely on abortion and might well oppose my nomination unless I changed my reported views.

I needed a much more sophisticated grasp of the political code words on abortion. I knew my own position, but the Senate hearing rooms of Washington were paneled and carpeted with good intentions and clear views ineptly expressed by well-meaning witnesses. I wanted to be sure I could maneuver through the verbal and emotional minefield of pro- and anti-abortionists. It was imperative for those in the abortion controversy, from Cardinal Cooke to National Abortion Rights Action League Executive Director Karen Mulhauser, to understand the words I spoke as I meant them, and I wanted to be confident that I knew what they would hear when I spoke. Far more careers have been shattered in Washington because of what people say than because of what they do—and far more often through words spoken by inadvertence or ignorance than by design.

As I parked my car, I recalled Father English's recommendation of Father Richard McCormick as an ethicist well versed in the abortion controversy. I called him as soon as I got to the office. I told him I had only a few minutes before leaving for the Senate hearing. I quickly reviewed the old ground with him, the obligation to enforce a law contrary to my personal view. Then I moved to some of the harder questions, about pursuing a public policy for our pluralistic country that differed from my personal beliefs.

"What about rape and incest? In terms of public policy, it seems to me that when a woman has been the victim of rape or incest, a case can be made to permit an immediate abortion."

"First of all," McCormick responded, "the woman may be able to solve the problem if she acts fast enough without even getting to an abortion. Even after fertilization but before implantation in the uterus, there are things like twinning and possible recombination of fertilized eggs. These things create doubt about how we ought to evaluate life at this stage. It may take as long as fourteen days for the implantation process to end."

"Do you mean that from an ethical point of view, you don't see any abortion problem for up to two weeks?" I asked.

"I mean there are sufficient doubts at this stage to lead me to believe it may not be wrong to do a dilation and curettage after rape. It's very doubtful that we ought to call this interruption an abortion. Absolutist right to life groups will still complain. But serious studies support this. The pro-abortionists feel very strongly about rape and incest."

"Suppose the doctor says the child will be retarded, or severely handicapped physically?"

"That is a much more difficult question. The Church would not permit an abortion, and the right to life and pro-abortion groups feel deeply here," McCormick replied.

"And what about some severe or permanent damage to the mother's health short of death?"

"That's another tough question in public policy terms. The Church would oppose abortion."

"Well, it's going to be an interesting morning," I mused aloud.

McCormick summed up rapidly. "You should always keep in mind three levels of distinction here. First, there is the personal conscience and belief thing. Second, there is what the appropriate public policy should be in a pluralistic democracy, which could be more liberal on funding abortions than one would personally approve as a matter of conscience or religious conviction. Actual abortion for rape and incest victims might be an example here. And third, there is the obligation of the public official to carry out the law the nation enacts."

"So I could pursue a policy for the country that funded abortion for rape and incest victims even though the Church—and I as a matter of personal and religious conviction—opposed abortion under those circumstances."

"Yes, you could."

I thanked him and rushed out of the office to my confirmation hearing.

I had to walk past a long line of people waiting to get into the standing-room-only Senate Finance Committee room in the Dirksen Building. Inside the door I had to weave through spectators and climb over legs to get to the witness table. The lights of all three networks were on me, sporadically augmented by clicking cameras and flashing bulbs from photographers sitting and kneeling on the floor in front of me. Seated behind their elevated and curved paneled rostrum, the committee members and staff looked down at me.

The hearing began promptly at 10:00 A.M. After fifteen minutes in which I made a brief opening statement and received some generous praise from Chairman Russell Long, Senator Packwood began:

"Mr. Califano, you know I have some strong feelings about abortion.... What is your personal view on abortion?"

The cameras turned on me.

I began by expressing my recognition of the difficulty of the abortion issue and the sincerity and depth of feeling on all sides. I noted that Carter and I shared identical views on the subject, although we came from quite different religious, cultural, and social backgrounds. I then set forth my views:

"First, I personally believe that abortion is wrong.

"Second, I believe that federal funds should not be used for the purpose of providing abortions.

"Third, I believe that it is imperative that the alternatives to abortion be made available as widely as possible. Those alternatives include everything from foster care to day care, family planning programs to sex education, and especially measures to reduce teen-age pregnancies.

"Finally, we live in a democratic society where every citizen is free to make his views known, to the Congress or to the courts. If the courts decide that there is a constitutional right in this country to have an abortion with federal funds, I will enforce that court order. If the Congress changes its mind and amends the statute which it has passed, or passes other laws which direct that funds be provided for abortion, I will enforce those laws. I will enforce those laws as vigorously as I intend to enforce the other laws that I am charged with enforcing if I am confirmed, including laws against discrimination against women on the basis of sex in Title IX, the Title VI laws."

Packwood pressed: "You are opposed and would be opposed to federal funds for abortions under any circumstances...if the life of the woman is jeopardized, if the fetus is carrying a genetic disease?" I testified I did not oppose federal funding of abortion where carrying the fetus to term endangered the life of the mother. That was not as far as Packwood wanted me to go.

Packwood continued: "What I am really interested in, Mr. Califano, what I would hope is that your feelings as a person would not interfere with the law, the enforcement of the laws." I assured him that my personal views would not interfere with my enforcement of the law.

Packwood asked what my recommendation would be for legislation in the future. The same as Carter's, I responded. "We would recommend that federal funds not be used to provide abortions" in Medicaid or any other program.

Packwood's first-round time was up. The tension in the room eased a little as other senators asked questions on Social Security, balancing the budget, eliminating paperwork, busing, race discrimination, a separate department of education, Medicare and Medicaid management, handicapped rehabilitation programs, fraud and abuse in the welfare program, older Americans, alcoholism, and other matters prompted by special interest constituencies and the concerns of Americans that HEW intruded too deeply in their lives. The ever-present staffers whispered in senators' ears and passed their slips of paper from which senators read questions.

Texas Senator Lloyd Bentsen tried to lighten the atmosphere as he began: "Mr. Chairman, I am very pleased to see Mr. Califano here. I have known him for many years and have a great respect for his ability, intelligence, integrity, and judgment—until he took this job." The room burst into laughter.

At about noon, it was Packwood's turn again. When our eyes engaged, it was a signal for all the buzzing and rustling in the room to stop. As I expected, he went right to abortion, asking how I would change the law if I had the power to do so. I told him that President Carter and I would support the ban on the use of federal funds for abortions except where the mother's life was at stake. "That is the position. . .of the Carter administration," I concluded, quoting from one of the President-elect's campaign statements.

Packwood felt so strongly about the issue his face went florid with anger.

I thought for an instant about raising the issue of rape and incest, but immediately decided against it. This abortion controversy would be with me and the President for a long time and I didn't want to go any further than absolutely necessary without careful thought.

With his blue eyes blinking in disbelief, Packwood's voice rose: "If you had a choice. . .your recommendation would be that no federal funds will be used for those two hundred and fifty or three hundred thousand poor women, medically indigent, mostly minorities, who could not otherwise afford abortions?"

I reiterated: that would be my recommendation and the position of the administration. When I expressed the need to provide alternatives to abortion, Packwood interrupted: "How do you deal with teen-age pregnancies once the teen-ager is pregnant?" I said we needed more sensitive, decent human alternatives, treating the pregnant teen-ager as a person, letting her remain in school or continue her education in a home. I also recognized the need for better sex education and more effective family planning programs.

Packwood expressed support for all such programs. Then, his voice again rising, he said, "What we are saying, as far as the Carter program goes, with all the planned parenthood facilities, all the homes for unwed mothers, all the decent facilities to take care of them, if that woman wants to have an abortion and is poor and cannot afford it, tough luck." The last two words came out in angry disgust.

I could hear the whir of the television cameras.

"Senator, what I am saying is that we should reduce these cases to the greatest extent possible."

Packwood repeated for the television evening news: "Still, tough luck, as far as federal help is concerned."

I noted that "the federal government is not the only source of all funds," and private organizations were free to finance abortions. I then reminded Packwood that the administration position "is what the Congress has said in the Hyde amendment. The Senate and the House. . .voted for that amendment last year."

He asked whether the administration would oppose funding abortions in a national health insurance program. I said it would.

Packwood shook his head in apparent despair. We come to this issue from such different premises, I thought. To him, it is unfair for the government not to fund abortions for poor women when the Supreme Court has established a constitutional right to an abortion in the first trimester. To me, there is no question of equity. I thought abortion was wrong for women who could afford it unless the life of the mother was at stake, so I had no misgivings on grounds of equity in opposing the use of public funds to pay for abortions for poor women, as a matter of statutory law. Where the life of the mother was endangered, I favored public funding of abortions for the poor. The constitutional right to an abortion in the first trimester did not, in my mind, carry with it the right to public funding. The Constitution guarantees many precious rights—to speak and publish, to travel, to worship—but it does not require that the exercise of those rights be publicly funded.

Packwood cited Carter's hedging during the campaign and asked about a constitutional amendment to reverse the Supreme Court decision striking down state abortion laws. I responded that I opposed any constitutional amendment on abortion. "We run to the Constitution to stop busing, we run there on prayers in schools. We have to stop running to the Constitution to solve all of our problems." Packwood, still unsatisfied, had no further questions.

As the television crews disassembled their cameras, Senator Harry Byrd launched an attack on HEW's interference in local schools with excessively detailed civil rights questionnaires, and asked me about my support for voluntary charitable organizations.

The hearing before the Senate Finance Committee lasted so long that I had less than an hour before the Senate Committee on Labor and Public Welfare session began early in the same afternoon. Within fifteen minutes of its start, Senator Jacob Javits of New York asked about my ability to carry out the law, in view of my personal beliefs. I told Javits I had no qualms of conscience about my ability to enforce the law, "whatever the law is."

After a two-and-one-half-hour interlude of questions on civil rights enforcement, the isolation of HEW from the rest of the nation, welfare reform, busing, museums, education funding, biomedical research, national health insurance, conflicts of interest, animal testing of drugs, lack of coordination among Cabinet departments, and HEW's unresponsiveness to state and local government, Maine Democratic Senator William Hathaway returned to abortion. He characterized my position as being "morally and unalterably opposed to abortion," and then asked: "Does this mean that your convictions are so strong that if Congress should enact a law, whether it is national health insurance or whatever, that did provide federal funds for abortion, that you would recommend to President Carter that he veto such legislation?"

I hedged to get time to answer this unexpected question. I had never discussed this situation with Carter and I did not want to box the President in by simply saying I would or would not recommend a veto. "I do not think President Carter, in terms of his own views, needs my advice on whether to veto that legislation."

As Hathaway pressed, asking what I would recommend if Carter sought my advice and how active a role I would take, I decided to finesse the question. "I cannot answer that question. Laws come over with lots. . .of provisions in them, and whether one provision is of such overriding importance in terms of the national administration's policy that the bill ought to be vetoed. . .is something very difficult to judge in the abstract." There was no way I would judge this issue now.

Hathaway sensed what I was thinking and helped out by noting the difference between a national health insurance program that the administration wanted with abortion funding being the only unwelcome provision and a bill that simply provided federal funds for abortion.

He then asked whether I would lobby the Congress against legislation which permitted federal funds to be spent for abortion. I told him that the administration would lobby against such legislation.

Hathaway expressed concern about anyone forcing his religious or other beliefs on the public, citing as examples a Christian Scientist HEW Secretary who did not believe in modern medicine, or a vegetarian Secretary of Agriculture who did not believe food stamps should be spent for meat. I responded firmly that if I had the slightest hesitation about enforcing whatever law the Congress passed, I would not be sitting in front of him.

Hathaway didn't question that. His concern was that no individual "should enforce his particular religious or moral beliefs into the policy-making area." I responded that "the Congress had made a judgment last year that restricting federal funds for abortions was a matter appropriate for legislation." As to my personal views, I was expressing them so every senator who had to vote on my confirmation would know them.

Unlike the exchange with Packwood, the exchange with Hathaway ended on a conciliatory note. He appreciated my candor and hoped that I would maintain an open mind during the course of the debate on abortion.

But neither the press nor the American public was prepared for any conciliation on this issue. Before I had departed the hearing room the first of some 6,473 letters and telegrams and hundreds of phone calls, unyielding on one side or the other, began arriving at my office. That evening, the *Washington Star*'s front page headlined: ANGRY SENATOR BLASTS CALIFANO ON ABORTION. The story featured Packwood's questioning and his "tough luck" comment. It did report my commitment to enforce the law vigorously, and it questioned an assumption that Packwood and Hathaway had made—that the woman's right to an abortion established in *Roe* v. *Wade* implied a right to federal funds to pay for the procedure. Earlier in the week, during oral arguments before the Supreme Court on pending abortion cases, several Justices had questioned any such right to funds. There were indications that the Court would throw the scalding issue back into the legislative-executive political process. That possibility only enhanced the significance of my views—and President Carter's.

That evening Carter telephoned me: "How did the testimony go today?"

"All right, I think, Mr. President," I responded hesitantly. "I hope I didn't create any problems for you."

"What did they ask you about?"

"Most of the questions were on your campaign promises, like welfare reform and national health insurance, and then typical special interest questions about HEW's constituencies and busing. I testified for seven hours. But the fireworks came in the thirty minutes of questioning about abortion."

"I saw what you said in the paper and on television. You hang tough. You're saying the right things."

"Thank you, Mr. President."

In public comments outside the hearing, Packwood expressed deep concern and anger. Javits predicted a long and contentious struggle over the issue. And Karen Mulhauser of the National Abortion Rights Action League said it was "unthinkable" that a leading civil rights attorney "would openly discriminate" against indigent women. "We really didn't know until this week how extreme Califano's views were," she added. The lead editorial in the *Washington Post,* my former law client, was headed "Mr. Califano on Abortion," and took after me and my new boss: "The fact that each man reached this conclusion as a matter of personal conviction makes the conclusion itself no less troubling. For, personal or not, the effect of their common position would be to deny the poor what is available to the rich and not-so-rich. To argue as they do, that the emphasis should be on other medical services and/or pregnancy services does not address this inequity."

On Inauguration Day, January 20, 1977, the new President sent the nominations of the nine Cabinet members-designate whose hearings were completed to the Senate for confirmation. Eight were swiftly confirmed. Senator Packwood denied the Senate the necessary unanimous consent to consider my nomination that day.

Majority Leader Bob Byrd called my nomination to the Senate floor on January 24. Packwood was vehement. He said I held my views so passionately, so vigorously, that "I think it is impossible that Mr. Califano will be able to fairly administer the laws involving abortion, assuming that the Supreme Court says women. . .continue to have a right to an abortion, and that they continue to have a right to federal funds to help them."

Javits shared Packwood's view favoring federal funds for abortion, but he felt my qualifications in other areas merited my being confirmed. Other Republicans, from Senate Minority Leader Howard Baker to arch-conservative Carl Curtis, the ranking minority member of the Finance Committee, supported the nomination. The debate was brief, the vote 95 to Packwood's 1. Strom Thurmond was the first to phone to tell me of the Senate confirmation and congratulate me.

I called to thank each senator who had spoken on my behalf. Then I thought about Packwood. I felt that he had been petty in holding my nomination up four days, and that there had been an element of grandstanding in it. However, I had to accept the fact that his beliefs on abortion were as sincerely held as mine. From his point of view, putting that extra spotlight on me may have provided a little insurance that I would be careful to enforce a law that funded abortions more widely than I considered appropriate. I had been confirmed overwhelmingly, and I had to deal with him as a member of the Senate Finance Committee that had jurisdiction over such key HEW programs as Social Security, Medicare, Medicaid, and welfare. I swallowed a little hard and called him: "Bob, I understand your view on abortion. But I'm now Secretary and you and I agree on virtually every other social issue. I hope our differences on abortion won't prevent us from working together." Packwood, clearly surprised, thanked me for the call.

In a *New York Times* editorial on January 31 condemning my position on abortion, one element struck me as amusing: "Mr. Califano's statement in one sense represents his personal opposition to abortion. In another sense, it is a free political ride, earning credit for the administration from abortion foes without his having any real decision to make. It was Congress, though sharply split, which last fall decreed the ban on Medicaid funds for abortions. It is the courts, now scrutinizing that ban, which will decide. And Mr. Califano has pledged, as he must, to carry out the orders of the courts." I could understand the point of the editorial, but I hardly considered my experience before the Senate committees a free ride.

The abortion issue would track me for most of my term as HEW Secretary. I shortly discovered that, like Champion and Shanahan, few, if any, of my colleagues at HEW shared my view or the President's on abortion. Everyone in the top HEW management who expressed his opinion disagreed with mine. Only at the Christmas open house, when they streamed through my office to shake hands and have a picture taken, would HEW employees—mostly the blacks or Catholics—whisper, "Don't let them kill those black babies," or "God bless you for your stand against abortion."

The same was true at the White House. A few staff members, such as Midge Costanza, were publicly outspoken in favor of federal funding for abortion. Shanahan called me on July 15, 1977, and said she was going to a meeting at the White House, set up by Midge Costanza to organize the women in the administration to urge Carter to change his position on abortion. Shanahan said they might draft a petition asking to see Carter and setting forth their views. I was incredulous that a White House staffer would organize such a meeting. I had no question about Shanahan's loyalty, but was appalled at Costanza's judgment and seriously questioned her loyalty to Carter. Two of the other top appointees at HEW, Assistant Secretary for Human Development Services Arabella Martinez and Assistant Secretary for Education Mary Berry, also went to the meeting.

A story was in the *Washington Post* on the morning following the Friday afternoon meeting. Jody Powell called Shanahan at about 11:00 A.M. "I just wanted to find out what right you all think you had to have a meeting like that in the White House?" Before Shanahan could respond, he answered, "No right, none at all."

"We have a right to express our views," Shanahan began.

Powell snapped, "At least General Singlaub [who disagreed with the President's policy in Korea] resigned. I can respect him."

"I did not give up my First Amendment rights when I joined the administration," Shanahan shot back.

Powell was incensed. "Most of these turkeys wouldn't have a job if it weren't for the President."

Shanahan spoke firmly, in the tense, modulated tone her voice often assumed when all her energy was devoted to maintaining her composure: "These women left damn good jobs to join the administration. Most are better qualified than men who got jobs of the same rank."

"Not you, Eileen, I don't include you," Powell responded defensively to the former economic correspondent for the *New York Times*, "but these turkeys would not have jobs if the President hadn't given them one."

When Shanahan told me about this conversation later that afternoon, she was still trembling with indignation and rage. Fortunately, she found great satisfaction in her work and she and I had developed a relationship of sufficient respect that she decided not to resign.

I assumed Carter would be enraged when he heard about the women's meeting—and he was, privately, and at the Cabinet meeting on Monday, July 18: "I don't mind vigorous debate in the administration. As a matter of fact, I welcome it," Carter said, "but I do not want leaks to the press or attacks on positions we've already established. If the forty women had listened to my campaign statements, they should know my position." Carter then contrasted Commerce Secretary Juanita Kreps and HUD Secretary Pat Harris with the group of women who met with Midge Costanza. Kreps raised her hand to speak. The President recognized her. In her soft-spoken, polite, and respectful manner, she said: "Mr. President, I appreciate the intent of your comment about me and I, of course, am loyal to you as we all are."

What well-chosen words, I thought. "But"—Kreps paused to make certain we were all appropriately postured on the edge of our Cabinet chairs—"you should not take my absence from the meeting of the women as an indication of support for the administration's position on abortion."

Carter seemed somewhat surprised, not at Kreps's position, but at the quiet firmness with which she expressed her view in front of the Cabinet and the "barber shop" patrons (as I sometimes thought of the crew of aides and note-takers that sat against the wall in the Cabinet Room). From across the Cabinet table, Pat Harris promptly agreed with Kreps, but promised to keep her views within the official family. The President, so uncomfortable that he almost sounded defensive, indicated he was of course not talking about "Juanita and Pat," and reiterated his desire for "full debate," but he insisted on "complete loyalty" once an administration decision was made.

When the President walked in to begin the Cabinet meeting two weeks later, on August 1, the first Costanza had attended after her women's meeting, he put his arm around her, kissed her, and said, "Nice to see ya, darlin."

Whatever distance the President wanted from me on other policies, like school integration, the anti-smoking campaign, or Social Security cuts, he held me at his side whenever he spoke of abortion: during a March 1977 Clinton, Massachusetts, town meeting and on a Los Angeles television show in May 1977 ("Joe Califano, who is Secretary of HEW, feels the same way I do against abortions"); in Yazoo City, Mississippi, in July 1977 ("...the Secretary of HEW agrees with me completely on this issue..."); at a Bangor, Maine, town meeting in February 1978 ("Joe Califano, who is head of HEW, is a very devout Catholic.... I happen to be a Baptist, and his views on abortion are the same as mine"); with college and regional editors and at general press conferences.

There were demonstrations, first in front of the building where my law office was located, then at the corner of Independence Avenue and Third Street, S.W., where the HEW headquarters and my offices were. The demonstrations, always peaceful but with increasingly sensational placards during 1977, were, as I looked out my window, a constant reminder of the potential of this issue to consume my energies to the detriment of other programs. A week after my confirmation, on January 31, 1977, Karen Mulhauser led a contingent of marchers from the National Abortion Rights Action League, carrying signs ("Califano Will Enslave Poor Women") that, however overdrawn they seemed to me, conveyed how many Americans felt. Coupled with the personal turmoil the issue stirred in several key managers I had recruited, both men and women, I decided it was imperative to set an overall tone and strategy from the beginning.

I was a bureaucratic child of the 1960s, acutely sensitive to the potential of an issue that touches on human life to kindle a consuming movement—as the military draft fueled the anti-Vietnam War movement. On abortion, the issue was life itself: If we all believed that life began at the same time, there would be no debate on abortion. If all citizens believed life begins at the moment of conception, then they would consider it intolerable for their national government to permit, much less fund, abortion because it involves the elimination of life. If, however, the body politic unanimously believed that life does not begin until the second or third trimester, or that there is no life until the fetus can be viable separate from the mother's body, then it would offend social justice for the government of such a single-minded people not to fund abortions for the poor when rich and middle-class women could easily obtain them to avoid serious illness or the later creation of retarded or physically handicapped life. However, the American people are far from unanimous in their view of when life begins; indeed, disagreement on that issue has been so strong it spawned as bitter a social and political dispute as the 1970s produced.

I concluded that it was not sufficient simply to express my view clearly and consistently, but that it was also essential to communicate the certainty with which I held it. Any hedging would only encourage those who disagreed to hope for a change that would not be forthcoming, and those who agreed to take steps to stiffen my resolve. By repeatedly and clearly setting forth my position, I could perhaps deflect the resources of some of the pro- and anti-abortion partisans to other targets they felt they had the opportunity to influence or the need to bolster.

My second conclusion was that I must do all I could to avoid unnecessary provocation. My obligation was to keep some measure of political decorum in this emotional debate. I did not have the luxury of an outside antagonist to be flip or hyperbolic. I refused to see or speak before pro-life groups who wanted to give me awards or roses, and I tried (not always with success) to avoid crossing picket lines or confronting demonstrators directly. In 1977, this involved going to a lot of places through the back door.

I had to display a calm and reasoned approach because of my obligation to enforce whatever law the Congress ultimately passed or the courts eventually declared constitutional. On this issue, above all, it was not enough for me to be fair; it was critical for the interested people to perceive they were being fairly treated.

Maintaining a sense of integrity was important not only to the public, but to the professionals in the department. HEW's Center for Disease Control was charged with the surveillance of communicable diseases. Most commonly identified with monitoring and reporting on influenza or other communicable diseases, the center was also responsible for surveillance of abortions and abortion-related deaths in the United States. In October 1977, at the peak of the legislative debate over Medicaid funding for abortion, there were reports that an Hispanic-American woman had checked into a McAllen, Texas, hospital with complications from an abortion improperly performed in Mexico. There were allegations that the woman was covered by Medicaid and had been told by a Texas doctor that if she had only come a few weeks earlier, she would have been eligible for Medicaid funding for an abortion, but now the law prohibited it. The woman died within a few days of being admitted to the hospital.

I called Bill Foege, whom I had recently appointed director of the center, and asked him to check out the reports. He came to Washington and nervously told me that while it was difficult to establish the facts because the woman might have gone to Mexico to keep the abortion secret, she had received two Medicaid-funded abortions before the Hyde amendment took effect. "So we may have a confirmed death from an abortion improperly performed on an otherwise Medicaid-eligible woman," Foege said, resting his paper on his lap as though trying to produce relief from a tension that still persisted.

I studied him silently for a moment and then realized that he was concerned about my view of the center's role in keeping abortion statistics.

"Look," I said, "you must understand this: I want you to keep statistics as accurately as you can, to investigate as meticulously as you can. Our obligation—whatever my views—is to set the facts before the Congress and the people. Particularly on an issue like this, we must maintain the integrity of HEW's data. The only way to deal with an issue this hot is to be accurate."

His face brightened in relief. "That's just the way I feel," he said.

While I could not predict the route or timetable, I sensed that the abortion issue was inexorably headed for my desk. On June 20, 1977, the Supreme Court decided in *Beal* v. *Doe* and *Maher* v. *Roe* that the federal government had no constitutional obligation to fund discretionary abortions that were not medically necessary. Like so many ardently awaited Supreme Court decisions, this one created as much controversy as it resolved. The Court had cleared the way to having the Hyde amendment go into effect, thus restricting Medicaid funding to abortions where the life of the mother would be endangered if the fetus were carried to term. The Court had also moved the debate back into the political arena, to the floors of the House and Senate and the HEW regulatory process.

I asked my staff to prepare a guideline to implement the Hyde amendment. Judge Dooling in Brooklyn would now have to withdraw his order blocking enforcement of that amendment and I wanted to be ready to issue the necessary instructions the same day the judge acted. Any delay would only give the pro- and anti-abortionists more time to demonstrate. If I could act immediately, there would be only one day of newspaper and television coverage.

As we planned to move as quickly and quietly as possible, the President was hit with a question about the Supreme Court decision at his July 12 press conference. I was signing routine mail, casually watching the televised conference, when Judy Woodruff of NBC News caught my attention with a question asking how "comfortable" the President was with the recent Supreme Court decision "which said the federal government was not obligated to provide money for abortions for women who cannot afford to pay for them." The President reiterated his view that "I would like to prevent the federal government financing abortion."

Woodruff followed up: "Mr. President, how fair do you believe it is then that women who can afford to get an abortion can go ahead and have one and women who cannot afford to are precluded?"

In an echo of a statement by John Kennedy, the President answered, "Well, as you know, there are many things in life that are not fair, that wealthy people can afford and poor people can't. But I don't believe that the federal government should act to try to make these opportunities exactly equal, particularly when there is a moral factor involved."

I had been leaning back in my chair and almost went over backward. I was stunned at the President's response. It was clear to me that he had no idea of the bitter reaction his comment would incite. It couldn't have been deliberate. At worst, it was an on-the-spot, clumsy attempt to appeal to fiscal conservatives and right-to-lifers; at best it was an inept, off-the-top-of-his-head answer to a question for which he was not prepared. Within an hour Eileen Shanahan was in my office, tears of anger welling in her eyes, to tell me that the press wanted my comment on the President's "life is unfair" remark. "None, none, none," I said.

The only person who told me she agreed with the comment of the President was Eunice Kennedy Shriver, who wrote me on July 15: "In terms of the equity argument, I think the President's answer is satisfactory." It was one of the few times I can recall disagreeing with the political judgment of this extraordinary woman. She had become and remained a dedicated and politically persistent participant in the abortion controversy, an energetic opponent of federal funding.

In July, unknown to the public, to most of the antagonists prowling the halls of Congress with roses and hangers and, indeed, to most congressmen and senators, a secret compromise remarkably close to the agreement the House and Senate would reach in December was beginning to take shape in the mind of Eunice Kennedy Shriver. She called me, as she was undoubtedly calling others, in the middle of the month, three weeks after the Supreme Court tossed the issue back to the Congress. She had "some language that might be acceptable to both the House and Senate" and end the widespread access to abortion. "We've got to face the rape and incest argument, don't you think?" And, spraying words in her staccato Massachusetts accent, she added: "We also have to deal with serious damage to the mother—physical damage, not this fuzzy psychological stuff."

Eunice read me some language and concluded, "I'm sending this over to you, personally and confidentially, and you can use it as your own."

Just as I was about to hang up, she added, "And Joseph, when we get over this, we need a teen-age pregnancy bill. I'm getting Teddy to introduce it and I want the two of you to work together on it." Eunice was working on a bill to fund centers to help teen-agers who were pregnant (she was so well connected within HEW that I got her revision of my draft testimony in support of the bill before I even received the draft from the departmental staff). Impressed by a Johns Hopkins program that helped teen-agers deal with their babies and avoid having more, she wanted to duplicate it around the nation. But even there she stood firmly on abortion. When the teen-age pregnancy bill was being considered in 1978 and HEW Deputy Assistant Secretary Peter Schuck was quoted as saying states might give funds to clinics providing abortions if they were providing services to pregnant teenagers, Eunice sent me a strong letter: "I certainly have not worked on this bill for three years under the assumption that abortion services would be provided under the bill. . . . I will not continue, quite frankly, if abortion services are permitted under this legislation." Due in large measure to her lobbying on the Hill, when the bill was eventually enacted, no abortion services were funded under it.

The confidential proposal Eunice Shriver sent me suggested modifying the Hyde amendment to prohibit the use of funds to perform an abortion, except in cases of rape and incest, where necessary to save the life of the mother, or where the mother has an organic disease that would cause grave damage to her body if the pregnancy were continued to term. Under her proposal, she estimated that only a thousand to fifteen hundred abortions per year would be performed under Medicaid, mainly involving mothers with severe heart or kidney disease or severe diabetic conditions. "I am told," her letter concluded, "that 80 percent of the abortions performed under Medicaid would be eliminated by this language."

There were few takers for the Shriver compromise in July, but before the abortion legislation saga ended in December 1977, the House and Senate would agree on language reflecting her influence and access to key members.

On August 4, 1977, Judge Dooling reluctantly lifted his injunction against enforcing the Hyde amendment. Within hours, I announced that HEW would no longer fund abortions as a matter of course, but would provide funds "only where the attending physician, on the basis of his or her professional judgment, had certified that the abortion was necessary because the life of the mother would be endangered if the fetus were carried to term."

The House and Senate Conferees' report on the Hyde amendment approved funding for termination of an ectopic (fallopian tube) pregnancy, for drugs or devices to prevent implantation of the fertilized ovum on the uterus wall, and for "medical procedures for the treatment of rape or incest victims." I had asked Attorney General Griffin Bell to interpret that language. His opinion concluded that the Hyde amendment and the quoted language prohibited funding abortion for rape or incest (unless the life of the mother was threatened), but permitted funding for prompt treatment before the fact of pregnancy was established.

On the same day Judge Dooling lifted his injunction and I issued my guidelines under the Hyde amendment to the 1977 HEW Appropriations Act, the Senate voted by a lopsided 60 to 33 to permit payment for abortions under a broad "medically necessary" standard in 1978. Earlier that week the House had voted 238 to 182 to retain the strict Hyde amendment language.

And on the same August 4th day, the Defense Department revealed that it had funded 12,687 abortions at military hospitals between September 1, 1975, and August 31, 1976. The Pentagon policy was to fund abortions for members and dependents for reasons of physical and mental health. The *Washington Post* story reporting military abortion statistics also noted that federal employees were entitled to abortions under the general health plans, but no records were kept of the number of abortions performed for them and their dependents.

In this state of chaos and division, the House and Senate left Washington for their August recess. When the Congress reconvened in September, high on its agenda was the House and Senate Conference on the Labor-HEW appropriations bill.

There are two ways to block federal funding of a particular activity otherwise authorized. One is to pass a statute that prohibits the federal government from acting. Such legislation must be referred to the authorizing committees of the Senate and the House; normally those committees would be required to hold hearings and report the legislation before it was eligible for consideration on the floor. That can be a long and tedious process—with no certainty that the legislation will ever get to the floor of both Houses for a vote. The authorizing committee can block consideration by simply holding the bill.

The other way to block federal funding for a specific purpose is through the appropriations process, either by not providing funds, or by attaching a rider to an appropriations bill, stating that none of the appropriated funds can be spent for the proscribed activity. The appropriations rider has the same practical force as authorizing legislation, and it offers a significant advantage to legislators: Each year the appropriations bills for the executive departments must be reported by the appropriations committees and acted on by the Congress if government is to continue functioning. The disadvantage is that, unlike substantive, authorizing legislation, the appropriations rider comes up for review each year.

Until the mid-1960s, there were few such riders. By and large, House and Senate parliamentarians ruled them out of order because "substantive legislation" was not permitted on appropriations bills. But as the government funded more activities, the lines between substantive legislation and limits on the uses of federal funds became increasingly hard to draw. The more controversial the activities funded by the appropriations bill, the more frequent the attempt to restrict spending by riders.

No bill attracted more politically aggressive, true-believing interest groups than the annual HEW appropriations bill. It had become honey for a host of political bees: riders prohibiting loans or grants to students who crossed state lines to incite to riot (a hangover from the Vietnam War), forbidding the use of funds for busing, limiting the use of funds to obtain civil rights enforcement information from schools. Senator Warren Magnuson, Chairman of the Senate Appropriations Committee, told me during my first month in office, "Joe, you won't recognize the appropriations hearing for HEW. It has attracted the Goddamnedest collection of kooks you ever saw. We've got to stop all these riders. Make them go to the authorizing committees." But Magnuson's outburst was to prove nothing more than exasperated hope. For during the fall of 1977, he would be involved in the bare-knuckled, prolonged fight over the abortion rider on the HEW appropriations bill.

Some facts about abortions also helped inflame the issue. In 1975, the nation's capital had become the first city in America where abortions outnumbered births. As the congressional recess ended in September 1977, the District of Columbia government revealed that in 1976, legal abortions obtained by District residents totaled 12,945—an unprecedented one-third more than the city's 9,635 births. And 57 percent of the abortions—7,400—were paid for by the Medicaid program before the Hyde amendment went into effect on August 4. The high abortion rate in Washington, D.C., reflected the nationwide abortion rate among blacks, which was double that among whites.

With the Congress returning to Washington, the pro-abortionists moved to counter the right to life roses. On September 7, pro-abortion leader Karen Mulhauser announced a campaign to mail coat hangers to Representative Daniel Flood, the Pennsylvania Democrat who chaired the HEW appropriations subcommittee, and other anti-abortion members.

The first meeting of the House and Senate all-male cast of conferees on September 12 broke up almost as soon as it started. Magnuson and Massachusetts Republican Senator Edward Brooke (who, like Packwood, strenuously fought to fund abortions under Medicaid) vowed that they would not return to the conference table until the House voted on the Senate version of the abortion rider. House Committee Chairman Flood initially refused. But, under pressure from his colleagues who feared that funds for important HEW programs and paychecks for federal employees would be interrupted if no appropriations agreement were reached, Flood took the Senate proposal to fund abortions where "medically necessary," to the House floor. On September 27, the House overwhelmingly rejected the Senate language, 252 to 164.

Then Flood took Magnuson up on his earlier commitment to compromise if the House would first vote on the Senate language. But Magnuson was not prepared to give much and House conferees ridiculed his attempt to cover genetic disease, with statements that his suggestion would permit abortions where the child had a blue and brown eye. At one point Magnuson proposed limiting funding to situations where the life of the mother was at stake, cases of rape or incest, and situations involving "serious permanent health damage." When I heard about his proposal, I suspected the fine hand of Eunice Shriver. But Flood's initial reaction was scathing. "You could get an abortion with an ingrown toenail with that Senate language," and it went nowhere.

After House Speaker Tip O'Neill complained that only pro-abortionist Magnuson and Brooke attended the conference for the Senate, thus making compromise near-impossible with the dozen House members usually present, more Senate conferees went to the meetings. The conversation became more civil, but the conferees were no closer to agreement as September 30, the end of the fiscal year and the end of HEW's authority to spend money, arrived.

Up to that point I had decided to stay out of the congressional fight over abortion. The administration view was well known. The President did not want to be part of any compromise that was more permissive than his anti-abortion campaign statements. It was one thing to carry out whatever law the Congress passed, quite another to take an active role in easing the restriction. Carter was committed to the former; he wanted no part of the latter.

Popular sentiment, reflected in the polls, was with the strict House view, and many pro-abortionists realized that. On October 6, for example, Normal Dorsen, head of the American Civil Liberties Union, in opposing a constitutional convention, cited his concern that a nationwide convention might be used to outlaw abortion completely. With that kind of popular support, the House was likely to hold to the strict limits on federal funding for abortions that Carter favored.

Moreover, my conversations with members of Congress had led me to the conclusion that I could be of little, if any, help in drafting the substance of an eventual compromise. Abortion was such a profoundly personal issue that neither I nor a President who, during his first nine months of office, had already lost a good deal of respect on the Hill, would have much influence with individual members.

Only once had I come close publicly to entering the debate during this time. I understood the depth of conviction and humane values that motivated most abortion advocates, but I was deeply offended by the cost-control, money-saving argument pushed by the staunchly pro-abortion Alan Guttmacher Institute, the research arm of the Planned Parenthood Federation of America. In late September, the Institute published a report claiming that the Hyde amendment would cost the public at least $200 million, for the first year of their life, to take care of children who could have been aborted under Medicaid. I wanted to denounce this kind of argument in severe terms: it was appallingly materialistic and represented a selfish failure to confront moral issues as such. But in the interests of being firm yet not provocative, I waited until I was asked about it at a press conference to express my views, and then did so in muted tones.

Now, however, I had to get into the congressional fight. On October 1, I was compelled to eliminate all hiring and overtime and virtually all out-of-town travel by HEW's 150,000 employees. I also warned that they might receive only half their pay in mid-October unless the House and Seante resolved the appropriations fight over abortion. It was, so far as we could tell, unprecedented at the time for a department to have no authority to operate or spend money after the first of the new fiscal year.

Despite the situation, the conferees again failed to reach agreement on October 3, and postponed any further action until October 12, after the Columbus Day recess. That postponement jeopardized beneficiaries of HEW programs and the pay of Department employees. Across the nation, state rehabilitation agencies for the handicapped were running out of money to process claims for Social Security disability benefits; New York State would be unable to meet its payroll for employees to process disability determinations; Texas intended to furlough 612 employees on October 12; Idaho would have no money for its nutrition and community services program for the aged.

I called Tip O'Neill and Bob Byrd on October 10th, and asked them to try to break the abortion deadlock in order to avoid severe human suffering. The next day I sent them a letter and made it public. It was, the letter charged, "grossly unfair to hold the vulnerable people of our nation and thousands of federal and state employees hostage" in the congressional dispute over the use of federal funds for abortions. If the Congress could not agree on abortion language, I urged them to pass a Continuing Resolution to give me authority to spend in early 1978 at the end-of-1977 level in order to continue HEW programs that people depend on each day. The Senate opposed a Continuing Resolution because it would also keep the Hyde amendment in effect.

I sent telegrams to the state governors alerting them to imminent funding terminations so they would press their congressmen and senators to act. I asked Labor Secretary Ray Marshall to tell the Congress and the public of the dangers of continuing to hold up 1978 funding, since his department's appropriations were tied to the HEW bill. Marshall announced that further delay could force many states to stop processing unemployment insurance claims and halt federally funded job and health safety programs. At my suggestion, President Carter told the congressional leadership on the morning of October 12 that, while we all recognized what an emotional issue abortion was, the paychecks of federal employees should not be held up while Congress tried to resolve it. House Appropriations Committee Chairman George Mahon warned of "chaos in some parts of our government." By October 13, after wrangling with each other and some spirited debate on the House floor, both legislative bodies passed a Continuing Resolution to provide funds for fifteen days until the end of the month.

On Sunday, October 16, I was scheduled to appear on the ABC-TV program *Issues and Answers*. On the Saturday morning preceding the program, I called the President to review the administration's position on abortion. The President said that his position had not changed since the campaign.

"One issue in sharp dispute is how to handle victims of rape or incest," I said, asking whether he objected to funding abortions for rape or incest victims and referring to his July 12, 1977, press conference. There Carter had said that the federal government "should not finance abortions except when the woman's life is threatened or when the pregnancy was the result of rape or incest. I think it ought to be interpreted very strictly."

I asked the President whether his "very strictly" interpretation was related to the dispute between House and Senate conferees over medical procedures short of abortion for rape or incest performed shortly after the act, as distinguished from outright abortion. Carter said he was unaware of the dispute, but wanted to stay out of it. I said that it might not be possible for me to do that. Then leave the administration position ambiguous on this issue, he suggested. "Above all I want people to understand I oppose federal funding for abortion in keeping with my campaign promise."

The words had the texture of the three dimensions that came into play when Carter discussed abortion with me: his deep personal belief, his sense (particularly in the first year) that he would violate some sacred trust if he did not adhere to his campaign statements, and his insistence on getting the political plusses out of issues that had such significant political minuses as well.

ABC White House correspondent Sam Donaldson asked the first question on the program the next day: What was the administration's position on abortion? I recited the administration position opposing federal funds for abortions "except where the life of the mother is endangered if the fetus were carried to term, or for treatment as a result of rape or incest."

After Bettina Gregory asked about teenage pregnancy, Donaldson pressed for precision on the issue of rape or incest. "The House position. . .would not even allow abortions to be financed in the case of rape or incest, unless someone comes forward and it can be established that there is not yet a pregnancy that has been medically found. Is that reasonable?"

Trying to satisfy the President's desires, I responded: "In the case of rape or incest, you would assume that the individual would come promptly for treatment and that is a matter of several days. Doctors and experts disagree on it. It can be days or a couple of weeks."

Donaldson noted that the House would allow a dilation and curettage only where an abortion was not involved, and asked if I agreed. I hesitated, then in pursuit of the President's overriding objective to be anti-abortion, responded: "Yes, that is the way I feel; that is the way the President feels. He made that clear during the campaign repeatedly, as you are well aware, covering him during the campaign."

I then recalled my own desire to cool the debate, and added: "This is a very difficult issue; it is a very complex issue; it is a very emotional issue. There are strong feelings on all sides. I think in terms of the nation as a whole what is important is that this issue is being debated in every state in the union. . . in city after city. The way to reach a consensus in a democracy is to have people talk about it, where they live; and that is happening now in this country. . .the issue should be debated in more places than in the House and Senate."

When the Continuing Resolution ran out on October 31, House and Senate conferees agreed to language which would permit federal funding for abortion in cases of rape, including statutory rape of minors, or incest, where a prompt report was made to appropriate authorities. They were still split over Senate language which would permit abortions "where grave physical health damage to the mother would result if the pregnancy were carried to term." By the next day, however, the House conferees wanted only forced rape covered. The Senate conferees were furious, and the conference broke up in acrid charges of bad faith. This skirmish marked the first time the House conferees had agreed on abortion, as distinguished from treatment before the fact of pregnancy was established, in any rape situation. Nevertheless, with their conferees unable to agree, the House and Senate voted another Continuing Resolution, giving members a three-week respite from the issue until December 1.

But there was no respite from the demonstrations. Without fail, during the week pickets marched outside HEW. The signs got more vivid; the crude printing crueler. There were the color pictures from *Life* magazine and the roses and hangers, which had become calling cards for the protagonists. The rhetoric was increasingly sprinkled with harsh accusations of "murder" by each side—of killing unborn children by Medicaid abortion, or poor mothers by back-alley abortion. Some placards accused me of being a "murderer of poor women."

Wherever I went, pickets greeted me. When I spoke in Oregon at a Democratic political fundraiser, several hundred demonstrators from both sides paraded outside the Hilton Hotel. The Oregon Legislative Emergency Board was scheduled to decide in ten days whether to replace lost federal abortion funds with state money. The pro-abortionists angrily accused me of trying to inject my own views into the Oregon fight, which I had not heard of until arriving in Portland.

The sincerity of the Oregon demonstrators and others like them took its toll on me: earnest pleas of both sides were moving. None of the lighthearted sidebars that accompanied most demonstrations—even some during the Vietnam War—were present during pro- and anti-abortion rallies. When I avoided demonstrators by going out a side entrance, as I did that evening in Oregon, I felt like a thief in the night, denying these committed marchers even the chance to know they had been at least heard, if not heeded.

The most vehement demonstration took place in New York City's Greenwich Village on Saturday afternoon, November 12. It was my most draining emotional experience over the abortion issue.

New York University President John Sawhill invited me to receive NYU's University Medal. The award ceremony was to consist of a brief talk and an extended question and answer period. As the day approached I was told that pro-abortionists planned a major demonstration. When I arrived at the NYU Law School in Washington Square, there were several thousand demonstrators. They were overwhelmingly pro-abortion; the handful of right-to-lifers there said they had heard of the demonstration only the evening before and had no chance to mobilize their supporters. Bella Abzug reviled the "white-male dominated White House." Speaker after speaker attacked me for "imposing my Roman Catholic beliefs on poor women." "Our bodies, ourselves" protesters chanted to the beat of a big drum. "Not Califano's."

The crowd was so large and noisy, I could hear it clearly when I entered the law school around the block from the demonstrators. As I reached the back entrance, ACLU Chairman Norman Dorsen, a friend of twenty-five years, greeted me with a broad smile on his face. "It took Califano to bring the sixties back to NYU," he cracked. We all chuckled at that welcome, which broke the tension for the next few minutes.

When Dorsen, who was to moderate the question and answer period, Sawhill, and I entered the auditorium, my right arm and hand were in a cast, held by a sling, due to an operation on my thumb the week before. The auditorium was crushingly overcrowded. Every seat was taken; every inch of wall space lined with standees. The antagonism of the audience was so penetrating I could physically feel it as I sat on the elevated stage. Even the cast on my arm will evoke no sympathy here, I thought.

Sawhill spoke first about me. He then turned to give me the medal. As I rose to receive it, the last row of the audience unfurled a huge pro-abortion banner across the back of the auditorium. Fully half the audience stood and held up hangers, many with ends that had been dipped in red nail polish. When the medal was presented, at least a hundred people in the audience turned their backs to me. Many of them remained in that position throughout the entire ninety minutes of my speech and the question and answer session that followed.

The question period was largely devoted to abortion, with many emotional statements and speeches. None, however, struck me more forcefully than that of an intense woman who picked up on a comment I had made earlier that year. On the Sunday, March 20, NBC program *Meet the Press,* Carol Simpson had queried me at length on abortion and the adequacy of the administration program for alternatives to abortion. In the course of one extended response, I observed: "I have never known a woman who wanted an abortion or who was happy about having an abortion. I think it is our role to provide for those women the best we can in terms of family planning services, of day care centers for their children, of health, and prenatal services to make sure children are born healthy, and all the decent things in life that every child in this country deserves, whether it is health care or a clean home or a decent schooling, and we will do our best to do that."

To my left, about halfway down the aisle in the NYU auditorium, a woman rose to the microphone. Her head was tilted sideways, her eyes spilled over with anger, even hatred. "Look at me, Mr. Califano," she shouted with defiant emotion. "I want you to see a woman who wanted an abortion. I want you to see a woman who was happy at having an abortion. I want you to see a woman who had an abortion two weeks ago and who intends to have another abortion."

The room fell into total silence as the tone of her voice became that kind of gripping whisper everyone can hear even when they don't want to: "I want you to go back to Washington knowing that there are women who are happy to have had abortions, knowing that there are women who want abortions. I don't ever want you to make a statement like the one you made saying that you have never known a woman that wanted to have an abortion or never known a woman who was happy about having an abortion. You have now met one."

So draining was the emotional experience at NYU, that afterward, when I got into the car to Kennedy Airport to depart for England, Germany, and Italy to look at national health programs—my first trip abroad as Secretary of HEW—I instantly fell asleep and did not wake up until the driver shook me to say we had arrived at Kennedy.

The abortion issue followed me to Europe. There were questions in England and the Italians were in the midst of their own volatile parliamentary debate on the issue. The latent suspicion of my Catholicism again surfaced in Rome. Immediately after my audience with Pope Paul VI, several reporters called at the Hassler Hotel to see if the Pope talked to me about abortion. He had not mentioned the issue. His focus was on the failure of the food-rich nations such as the United States to feed the world.

I returned to Washington on Thanksgiving eve. I knew the abortion issue would erupt again when the latest Continuing Resolution expired. But I was not prepared for the news the *Washington Post* brought me on the Sunday after Thanksgiving. Connie Downey, chairperson of an HEW group on alternatives to abortion, had written a memo expressing her views to her boss, Assistant Secretary of Planning and Evaluation Henry Aaron. The *Post* headlined the most sensational portion of an otherwise typical HEW memo: TASK FORCE HEAD LISTS SUICIDE, MOTHERHOOD, AND MADNESS: ABORTION ALTERNATIVES CITED IN HEW MEMO.

The memo, written more than four months earlier on July 18, contained this paragraph: "Abortion is but one alternative solution to many of the problems . . . which may make a pregnancy unwise or unwanted. . . . It is an option, uniquely, which is exercised between conception and live birth. As such, the literal alternatives to it are suicide, motherhood, and, some would add, madness. . . ."

The memo had never reached me, but its leak provided a dramatic reminder of the potential for turmoil within HEW and raised the curtain on the final act between the House and the Senate on the fiscal 1978 HEW appropriations bill.

Returning from Thanksgiving recess, the House leadership was determined to press for a compromise. They did not want the Christmas checks of federal employees to be short. Appropriations Committee Chairman Mahon called me on November 29 to say he had decided to take the leadership completely away from Flood, who ardently opposed federal funds for abortion. "He's just implacable on the subject," Mahon said, distraught. "I'm retiring, but this kind of conduct is a disgrace to the House. We all look asinine."

In secret negotiations with Senator Brooke, Mahon eventually produced the compromise on December 7. The House voted twice within less than four hours. The first time members rejected a Mahon proposal and voted 178 to 171 to stand by their strict position against all funding for abortions except those needed to save the mother's life. Minutes later Mahon, dejected but determined, won speedy approval of new language from the Rules Committee and rushed back to the House floor. The House reversed direction and adopted the new and relaxed standard, 181 to 167. Within two hours, with only three of its hundred members on the floor, the Senate acceded to the House language and sent the measure to President Carter for his signature.

Under the measure, no HEW funds could be used to perform abortions, "except when the life of the mother would be endangered if the fetus were carried to term, or except for such medical procedures necessary for the victims of rape or incest, when such rape or incest has been reported promptly to a law enforcement agency or public health service; or except in those instances where severe and long-lasting physical health damage to the mother would result if the pregnancy were carried to term when so determined by two physicians."

Senator Brooke described the outcome as "not really acceptable to either side, but it makes some progress." Representative Hyde said that the measure "provides for the extermination of thousands of unborn lives." Senator Javits called the action "a major victory for women's rights." ACLU Chairman Dorsen characterized it as "a brutal treatment of women with medical needs for abortion." Any relief I felt at seeing at least some resolution was lost in the knowledge that the protagonists would rearm to battle over the regulations I had to issue.

As soon as President Carter signed the $60 billion appropriations bill on December 9, it landed on my desk, for the final provision of the compromise language stated: "The Secretary shall promptly issue regulations and establish procedures to ensure that the provisions of this section are rigorously enforced."

The antagonists turned their attention to me. Magnuson and Brooke wrote and called with their permissive interpretation. Robert Michel, ranking Republican on the Appropriations Committee, wrote with his strict view. Dan Flood called and other members—and their even more aggressive staffs—pressed for their interpretation of words such as "medical procedures," "promptly reported," "severe and long-lasting physical health damage," and "two physicians."

There was no way in which I could avoid becoming intimately involved in making key decisions on the regulations. I decided personally to read the entire 237 pages of self-serving and often confused congressional debate and to study the ten different versions of this legislation that were passed by either the House or the Senate.

To assure objectivity, to balance any unconscious bias I might harbor, and to reduce my vulnerability to charges of personal prejudice, I assigned the actual regulation writing to individuals who did not share my strong views about abortion and, more importantly, who stood up for their own views and did not hesitate to tell me when they thought I was wrong. The bulk of the work was done by Richard Beattie, the Deputy General Counsel of HEW, and HEW attorneys June Zeitlin and David Becker, all of whom opposed any restrictions on federal funding of abortions. I also asked the Attorney General to review independently the regulations we drafted at HEW. Once they were in effect, I would establish a detailed auditing system to assure compliance and fulfill the congressional mandate "to ensure that the provisions of this section are rigorously enforced."

Finally, I decided not to consult the President about the regulations. Carter had enough controversial problems on his desk without adding this one. My responsibility under the Constitution and under our system of government was to reflect accurately the law passed by the Congress. Neither Carter's personal views nor mine were of any relevance to my legal duty to ascertain what Congress intended and write regulations that embodied that intent.

In pursuit of my overall goal of cooling the temperature of the debate, I wanted to issue the regulations more "promptly" than anyone might expect. Not relying solely on my own reading of the congressional debates, I asked the lawyers for a thorough analysis of the legislative history. We then spent hours discussing and debating what the Congress intended on several issues, frustrated by the conflicting statements in the congressional record. We determined that for rape and incest victims, the term "medical procedures" as used in this new law now clearly included abortions; that a "public health service" had to be a governmental, politically accountable institution; that short of fraud we should accept physicians' judgments as to what constituted "severe and long-lasting physical health damage"; that the two physicians whose certification was required must be financially independent of each other; and that the rape or incest victim need not personally make the required report to public authorities. We resolved a host of other issues as best we could against the backdrop of the heated and confusing congressional debate. They were wearing days, because I felt the law was too permissive, and its provisions were in conflict with my own position. I revisited many decisions several times, concerned, on overnight reflection, that I had bent too far to compensate for my personal views and approved inappropriately loose regulations, or that I was letting my personal views override congressional intent.

By far my most controversial determination was to define "reported promptly" in the context of rape and incest to cover a sixty-day period from the date of the incident. Even though the Attorney General found the judgment "within the permissible meaning of the words within the Secretary's discretion," there was a storm of controversy over this decision.

There were widely varying interpretations on the floor of the House and the Senate. Most of the legislative history on the Senate floor was made by pro-abortion Senators Magnuson and Brooke. They spoke of "months" and "ninety days" to make the period as long as possible. On the House side, Mahon and other proponents of the compromise spoke of "weeks" and "thirty days" as they cautiously maneuvered this difficult piece of legislation to passage. On the floor of Congress, pro- and anti-abortionists could express their views and protect their constituencies. But I had to select a number of days and be as certain as possible that it would stick.

After extensive internal discussion and spirited argument within the department, I concluded that a sixty-day reporting period was within the middle range of the various time limits mentioned in the debates. The dominant issues during debate were access to abortions and prevention of fraud. The sixty-day period was long enough for a frightened young girl or an embarrassed woman who might not want to report a rape or incest, or one in shock who psychologically could not, to learn whether she might be pregnant and to make the report to public authorities. Sixty days was also prompt enough to permit effective enforcement of the law.

I was ready to issue the regulations during the third week of January 1978. On Monday, January 23, the annual March for Life to protest the 1973 Supreme Court abortion decision was scheduled to file past HEW en route from the White House to the Capitol. I decided to delay issuing the regulations until later in the week. The participants were outraged at the House-Senate compromise. As march leader Nellie Gray saw it, "The life issue is not one for compromise and negotiation. Either you're for killing babies or you're against killing babies."

I issued the regulations on January 26. Attorney General Bell concluded that they were "reasonable and consistent with the language and intent of the law." The *New York Times* editorialized that I had "done [my] duty. . . . He has interpreted the nation's unfair abortion law fairly. . . . On several controversial issues Mr. Califano and his lawyers have performed admirably, hacking their way through a thicket of ambiguities in the law that passed a bitter and divided Congress in December after months of heated debate."

The right to life lobby disagreed. Thea Rossi Barron, legislative counsel for the National Right to Life Committee, called the regulations an example of "a rather blatant carrying out of a loophole to allow abortion on demand." The pro-life groups were particularly disturbed about the sixty-day reporting period for victims of rape or incest. But the most severe critic of that provision was Jimmy Carter.

In testifying before the House Appropriations Committee on the morning of February 21, 1978, less than a month after issuing the regulations, Chairman Flood and Republican Robert Michel pressed me to provide an administration position on tightening the restrictions on abortion.

I called the President during the luncheon break. The President wanted the reporting period for rape or incest shortened. He was "not happy" with the sixty-day time period in the regulations. "I believe such instances are reported promptly," he said coolly.

I told him that the sixty-day period was my best judgment of what Congress intended in the law. Carter "personally" believed sixty days permitted "too much opportunity for fraud and would encourage women to lie."

"But what counts is what the congressional intent is," I argued.

The President then said he thought the regulations did not require enough information. He particularly wanted the doctor to report to Medicaid the names and addresses of rape and incest victims. The President was also inclined to require reporting of any available information on the identity of the individual who committed the rape or incest. Carter said, "Maybe some women wake up in the morning and find their maidenhead lost, but they are damn few. That actually happened in the Bible, you know."

"Perhaps we can tighten the reporting requirements," I responded, somewhat surprised at his Biblical reference. "Do you have any strong feelings on the legislation itself?"

Carter expressed some strong feelings: "I am against permitting abortions where long-lasting and severe physical health damage might result. I think that might permit too much of a chance for abuse and fraud. I want to end the Medicaid mills and stop these doctors who do nothing but perform abortions on demand all day."

When I testified that afternoon, I gave the House Appropriations Subcommittee some indication of the administration's views and agreed to submit a letter with the administration's position the next day.

After preparing a draft, I called the President and reviewed my proposed letter for the committee word by word. The letter set the administration position as stricter than the December compromise of the Congress. The administration opposed funding abortions in situations involving "severe and long-lasting physical health damage to the mother." The President and I compromised on the rape and incest paragraph: "In the case of rape or incest, we believe that present law requires the sixty days specified in the regulation as the period Congress intended for prompt reporting. In order to reduce the potential for fraud and abuse, it may be advisable to reduce that period to a shorter period of time."

Just as he was hanging up the phone, Carter again directed me to tighten the reporting provisions on rape and incest. "I want rules that will prevent abortion mills from simply filling out forms and encouraging women to lie."

I changed the regulations to require that the names and addresses of both the victim and the person reporting the rape or incest, and the dates of both the report and the incident, be included in the documentation for Medicaid funding. This change drew immediate fire from the National Organization for Women's National Rape Task Force, but it was well within my discretion under the law and consistent with the congressional intent.

Yet the President was still not satisfied. He wanted the sixty-day reporting period shortened, regardless of congressional intent. He raised the issue again two months later at the Camp David Cabinet summit of April 17, 1978, sharply criticizing "the regulations HEW issued on abortion" among a series of actions by Cabinet officers with which he disagreed.

The concern of the President and others that the regulations were too loosely drawn in the rape and incest area has not turned out to be justified. During the first sixteen months under the law and regulations, until shortly before I left HEW, only 92 Medicaid abortions were funded for victims of rape or incest. The overwhelming majority of Medicaid-funded abortions—84 percent of 3,158 performed—were to save the life of the mother; 522 were to avoid severe and long-lasting health damage to the mother. Eunice Shriver's estimate of 1,000 to 1,500 Medicaid-funded abortions each year was not too far off, particularly when compared with the 250,000 to 300,000 abortions estimated to have been performed annually under Medicaid in the absence of any funding restrictions.

I came away from the abortion controversy with profound concern about the capacity of national government, in the first instance, to resolve issues so personal and so laced with individual, moral, and ethical values. The most secure way to develop a consensus in our federal system is from the bottom up. But once the Supreme Court established a woman's constitutional right to an abortion against the backdrop of federally funded health care programs, the issue was instantly nationalized. As each branch acted—the Congress with the Hyde amendment, the executive with its regulations, and the Supreme Court in its opinions—the mandates from the top down generated as much resentment as agreement. This is true even though, by 1978, many states had more restrictive provisions on abortion funding than the national government.

In 1978, the Congress extended abortion funding restrictions to the Defense Department budget. In 1979, it applied an even stricter standard to both HEW and Defense appropriations, by eliminating funding in cases of long-lasting physical health damage to the mother, thus funding abortions only when the life of the mother is at stake or in cases of rape or incest, as Carter and I proposed for HEW in February 1978. The Supreme Court in the *McRae* case upheld the constitutionality of the Hyde amendment in June of 1980, concluding that the right to an abortion did not require the government to provide the resources to exercise it and that the Congress could restrict the circumstances under which it would pay for abortions. Months later, the Senate and House agreed to place tighter restrictions on Medicaid funding of abortions. Under the 1981 appropriations legislation, such funding is permitted only where the mother's life is at stake, in cases of rape reported within 72 hours and in cases of incest. That legislation permits the states to be even more restrictive; they are "free not to fund abortions to the extent that they in their sole discretion deem appropriate." Similar language was attached to the Defense appropriations bill.

Conforming the Defense and HEW appropriations bills provides the same standards for most of the federal funding arena. So long as the Congress acts through the appropriations for each department, however, rather than by way of across-the-board authorizing legislation, there will be inconsistencies. Even within HEW, the abortion funding policy has been a quilted one. The restrictions do not apply to disabled citizens whose health bills are paid by Medicare, because that program is financed out of

Social Security trust funds, not through the HEW appropriations bill. Nor do the funding limits apply to the Indian Health Service; though administered by HEW, funds for the Indian Health Service are provided in the Interior Department appropriations bill. The Congress has begun to move to prohibit the use of federal funds to pay for abortion through federal employee health insurance. The inevitable challenges in court to new restrictions and the recurrent debate in the Congress assure continuing turmoil and controversy over the abortion issue.

In personal terms, I was struck by how infinitely more complex it was to confront the abortion issue in the broader sphere of politics and public policy in our pluralistic society than it had been to face it only as a matter of private conscience. I found no automatic answers in Christian theology and the teachings of my church to the vexing questions of public policy it raised, even though I felt secure in my personal philosophical grounding.

I was offended by the constant references to me as "Secretary Califano, a Roman Catholic" in the secular press when it wrote about the abortion issue. No such reference appeared next to my name in the stories reporting my opposition to tuition tax credits favored by the Catholic Church or my disputes with the Catholic hierarchy on that issue.

I was dismayed by the number of Catholics and diocesan papers that attacked me for the regulations I issued on abortion. Their attack so concerned Notre Dame president, Father Theodore Hesburgh, that he urged me to speak about the conscience and duty of a Catholic as a public offical at the commencement in South Bend in 1979. The assumption of many bishops that I could impose my views on the law passed by the Congress reflected a misunderstanding of my constitutional role at that stage of the democratic process. As it turned out, like the President's, their assumption that the sixty-day reporting period for rape or incest constituted a legal loophole was as ill-founded in fact as it was in law.

Throughout the abortion debate, I did—as I believe I should have—espouse a position I deeply held. I tried to recognize that to have and be guided by convictions of conscience is not a license to impose them indiscriminately on others by one-dimensionally translating them into public policy. Public policy, if it is to serve the common good of a fundamentally just and free pluralistic society, must balance competing values, such as freedom, order, equity, and justice. If I failed to weigh those competing values—or to fulfill my public obligations to be firm without being provocative, or to recognize my public duty once the Congress acted—I would have served neither my private conscience nor the public morality. I tried to do credit to both. Whether I succeeded is a judgment others must make.

Funding Abortion

U.S. House of Representatives

[The debate excerpted here took place on the floor of the House of Representatives on September 9, 1988, on a motion to reject a Senate amendment (proposed by Senator J. James Exon, Democrat, Nebraska) that permitted the use of federal funds in state-run Medicaid programs for abortions in cases of rape or incest. The relevant part of the Senate amendment specified that funding would be

Reprinted from *Congressional Record,* Sept. 9, 1988, pp. H 7350–H 7359.

permitted "for such medical procedures necessary for the victims of rape or incest, when such rape or incest has been reported promptly to a law enforcement agency or public health service." It also stated: "nor are payments prohibited for drugs to prevent implantation of the fertilized ovum, or for medical procedures necessary for the termination of ectopic pregnancy; provided, however, that the several states are and shall remain free not to fund abortions to the extent that they in their sole discretion deem appropriate, except where the life of the mother would be endangered if the fetus were carried to term."]

Mr. OBERSTAR [Democrat, Minnesota]. Mr. Speaker, a few weeks ago while driving along I saw a bumper sticker on a car that said, "A fetus is a little human." I think that goes to the essence of this debate. Mr. Speaker, what we are talking about is a human being.

America has come to be known as the disposable society, but that should not include people, the elderly in their sunset years; it should not include the retarded, nor the handicapped, and we certainly should not discard children before they are born.

Dr. Bernard Nathanson, a New York obstetrician-gynecologist, was a founder of the National Abortion Rights League. He was a militant abortion rights supporter before the U.S. Supreme Court decision. Nathanson founded and served as director of the first and largest abortion clinic in the United States. A year and a half and 60,000 abortions later, he resigned as head of that clinic. He wrote:

> I am deeply troubled by my own increasing certainty that I have in fact presided over 60,000 deaths. There is no longer serious doubt in my mind that human life exists within the womb from the very onset of pregnancy.
>
> The infinitely agonizing truth is that in an abortion we are taking life.

Mr. Speaker, a few years ago I conducted a hearing in which a doctor recounted the story of a patient who in his words was poor, raped, black, pregnant, and teenaged.

"As I talked with her," he said, "she made it very clear that abortion was not ever a consideration."

She said, "I couldn't do that to something that is half of me."

What public policy question could be more vital to the well-being of society than whether a fetus is human. It is an established biological fact that the existence of a human being begins at conception and that the individual so created remains a human being throughout every stage of biological development thereafter.

But there are some forms of life that people are concerned about enough to protect, to change the law so that vulnerable life can be protected. In Arizona a person can be fined $300 for destroying a Gila monster egg. In that same State, there is no fine for destroying a 28-week-old unborn human being.

The focus of this debate, however, is language to provide for Federal funding of abortion in cases of rape or incest. This issue must be addressed with dignity, with sensitivity and respect for the victims, both mother and potentially unborn child.

Rape is a violent crime against a woman, an innocent victim, a defenseless woman. Abortion is also a violent destruction of equally innocent human life, the unborn, including the unborn resulting from rape, but it is also a fact that prompt medical treatment following rape prevents pregnancy. In correspondence with the former chairman of the subcommittee on then HEW, Mr. Flood, a physician wrote: "As an emergency room physician, I would like to share with you my knowledge about treatment of rape and incest victims, rape treated in the emergency room of hospitals. No competent doctor would expose a woman to the hazards of an abortion when a simple medical curettage is available to prevent pregnancy in rape. The patient is given estrogen for 5 days, which makes it impossible for the woman to conceive."

Life must not become a privilege reserved for the strong and denied to the old, to the retarded, to the handicapped or to the voiceless and the voteless among us, the unborn.

In this throwaway society of ours, what we ought to throw away is the junk ethic that dismisses the unborn simply as a mass of cells, simply a collection of tissue that can be discarded without remorse, as a hindrance or as a nuisance. That ethic and the legal framework provided by the Supreme Court decision in Roe versus Wade does more than destroy unborn human life. It literally has a corrosive effect upon the very fabric of society and demoralizes society itself.

We should resolve to show a strength of principle that will restore meaning to life, the right to life of the unborn, including those who may be the progeny of a pregnancy that results tragically from rape or incest.

Taking innocent unborn life will not ease the abuse of rape, ease the abuse created when an innocent female victim is brutalized. It will not apprehend the rapist. It will not heal the emotional scars of that violent crime.

Mr. Speaker, we should stay with the House position and reject the position of the other body.

Mr. GREEN [Republican, New York]. . . .

Let me at the outset say that I understand the depth of feeling of those who support the motion and who feel that abortion should be permitted only when the life of the mother is in danger. I understand the sincerity with which those who advocate that position come to the floor.

I wish they would understand that there are some of us who feel with equal fervor that to force a woman who has been raped to carry to term the fetus that is the product of that rape is an act of horrible cruelty second only to the rape itself.

Now, I know that obviously that position is one that morally is inconsistent with the position of those who are supporting the motion, but I suggest to you it is certainly an understandable, defensible position, and one which I would hope those who do not like abortion would nonetheless understand.

So recognizing the terrible dilemma that we face when a woman is raped and a pregnancy results from that, I would hope that they would at least acknowledge that there is enough moral controversy, that that is a decision as to what should happen to the product of that rape that is best left to the woman's own conscience, the woman's own relationship to God. If you believe that, as I do, I would only hope that you would vote no, so that we can sustain the Senate position.

Mr. HOYER [Democrat, Maryland]. . . .

Mr. Speaker, this is an issue on which the opinions of Members are deeply held and on which the consequences to individuals are very substantial. Those on both sides of this issue will talk about the consequences to other human beings.

First of all, let me take a brief time to explain what this is. The other body added an amendment overwhelmingly to their bill which said in the instances—the sole instances—where a pregnancy results as the result of the rape of a woman, or where a pregnancy results from an incestuous attack, in that instance and in the other instances which are presently in the law where the life of the mother is in the balance, in those instances alone, poor women will, like other women who do not need public assistance, [be] allowed to use public funds for abortion services.

There was an additional provision in that bill, interestingly, and language that we have adopted some four times between 1980 and 1982, which says that a State will have the option still to opt out to say no not even in these instances of vicious sexual attack will we exempt a woman from carrying the child of her attacker however psychologically damaging that may be, however permanently damaging that may be.

This amendment simply makes those sole exceptions, and no broader.

I think, Mr. Speaker, this is the appropriate and sensitive and humane step for us to take. We disagree, we understand. I would ask, therefore, that the motion be defeated.

Mr. SMITH [Republican, New Jersey]. . . . Mr. Speaker, clearly rape and incest are unconscionable assaults on women and children. While abortion likewise is a violent assault on an innocent unborn child, I believe that the Federal Government should not be paying for any person to be assaulted, whether he or she is born or unborn.

Mr. Speaker, as I have listened to this debate, and especially as it has proceeded over the years on rape and incest, I am always struck by how the abortion proponents have attempted to frame the debate. We have, of course, in America, abortion on demand, a million and a half children killed each and every year, a staggering and overwhelming number.

It is deeply regrettable that not one of these little persons are to the abortion proponents worth legally protecting. Clearly, this position of supporting abortion on demand from fertilization throughout the total 9 months of pregnancy has scant support in our Nation. So the abortion proponents are not focusing on their extreme position of destroying unborn children for any reason any time prior to birth. No, they are focusing on advocating abortion where pregnancy results from rape or incest. They focus on a situation which rarely occurs, but which is so emotionally laden that they appear to have a reasonable position, while their opponents are painted as being unreasonable.

The fact of the matter is, Mr. Speaker, the proabortion position, notwithstanding its surface appeal, is the unreasonable position and is also the unjust position.

Since 1973, those who promote the violence of abortion have had their season of child deaths, a staggering 22 million have perished. I believe this is a national scandal.

Mr. Speaker, I am encouraged that in the last few years and months that the truth seems to be penetrating society. There seems to be a growing recognition of what abortion is and what it does to the woman, as well as what it does to the baby.

Mr. Speaker, those of us who support life care and we care deeply for both the women and their children. We care, regardless of the circumstances of a person's beginning or his race or creed or whether or not that child is handicapped or suffers some other anomaly, because all human life is so precious.

Mr. Speaker, is it not odd that when we talk about human rights so often in this Chamber that the most basic and most fundamental of all human rights, the right to life, is the one that this country does not respect?

Mr. Speaker, to be sure, we care, those of us in the prolife movement, and we are absolutely repelled by the fact that each day in America some 4,000 unborn children are killed. They are torn apart. They are cut apart. They are poisoned and they are asphyxiated by abortion procedures. This is indeed a national scandal.

We care, Mr. Speaker, and publicly stand for the unborn child, not only when it is convenient to do so, like when the child is wanted or when the child is planned or when the child is perfect, but we also stand for the child when it is most difficult to do so. Clearly, a child is a child and his or her worth is not diminished one iota by the circumstances of that beginning. That again is the truest definition of human rights.

Mr. Speaker, finally, if Members vote to reverse the current Hyde language, children will surely die. I urge a "yes" vote, sustain the House position, sustain the Hyde amendment.

Mr. MOLLOHAN [Democrat, West Virginia]. . . .

Mr. Speaker, one of the frustrations of debating the larger issue of abortion is that the two opposing sides are not usually divided over questions of logic. After many years of debate over the general issue of abortion, only a few still question the existence of life before birth. Life begins at conception.

The opposing sides reach their respective positions on abortion based on what value they place on human life at any particular stage of development. Debate over this fundamental question can be difficult, because we do not always agree on the logical framework we should use to answer the question.

The more narrow question before us today, however, is different; whether to allow Medicaid funding of abortion in cases of rape and incest can, regardless of one's view on abortion, be logically answered in only one way, in the negative. It is not a difficult analysis.

Mr. Speaker, those of us who vote on the prolife side have determined that life is worth protecting at every stage of development. Abortion is wrong. It is the taking of human life, life that the sovereign, the Government, has an interest in protecting. The majority of Members of both Houses share this view, as evidenced by repeated adoption of the Hyde amendment. We believe abortion is wrong, and consequently we believe that Federal money should not be used to support it. If you adopt our premise that unborn life is valuable, and therefore abortion is fundamentally wrong, there is no logical reason for allowing exceptions in cases of rape and incest.

Regardless of the tragic circumstances of conception, exceptions in cases of rape and incest.

Regardless of the tragic circumstances of conception, abortion remains the taking of human life. Concede us that point and you must reject an effort to carve out a rape and incest exception.

As an individual Member you may disagree with our premise, but Congress as a whole by adopting the Hyde amendment adopts our premise as its starting point. A prolife Member and a Member who supports abortion should agree logically on this point. There is no basis for compromising the integrity of the Hyde amendment. You either vote for the Hyde amendment or you vote against it. You do not, however, search for some middle ground that logically cannot exist, and you do not vote for the Exon amendment.

Mrs. BOXER [Democrat, California]. Mr. Speaker, will the gentleman yield?

Mr. MOLLOHAN. I yield to the gentlewoman from California.

Mrs. BOXER. Mr. Speaker, I thank the gentleman for yielding to me.

Does the gentleman feel there ought to be an exception for life of the mother if the life of the mother is endangered, then it is permissible to grant an abortion to the woman?

Mr. MOLLOHAN. Indeed, and that is implicit—explicit in the Hyde amendment, because, if the gentlewoman will allow me to finish my answer, when we have two competing lives in being, it is logical to opt for the mature life in being.

Mrs. BOXER. There are two competing lives, and the gentleman comes down on the side of the life of the mother rather than the life of the fetus?

Mr. MOLLOHAN. Indeed, as the Hyde amendment does, and the Congress has affirmed numerous times.

Mrs. BOXER. Let me ask my friend this question. Let us take a situation where a husband and a wife are in the privacy of their own home. An intruder comes in, a rapist, rapes the woman, almost kills her, murders the husband. The woman survived is pregnant, and this gentleman is saying that that woman should be forced to have that child of the murderer; is that correct?

Mr. MOLLOHAN. We have equally tragic situations that the gentlewoman is describing presenting extremely tough choices, the tragic situation of destroying by dismembering the unborn life and shattering the life of the mother who has been raped by that person. What I am simply saying is that I am answering the question and that is the proposition that the gentlewoman is proposing creates these tremendously difficult choices. Just to make one point which can be answered based upon what premise the gentlewoman starts with, and that is if we have a life and how much value we place on that life.

Mrs. BOXER. Mr. Speaker, I respect the gentleman, and I respect his opinion, I honestly do.

Mr. MOLLOHAN. We express our opinions on this very difficult issue.

Mrs. BOXER. But I just want to make the point so that there is no misunderstanding that a woman who is raped by the murderer of her husband will be forced to have that child, and I just want to make that the point for the record. . . .

Mr. OBEY [Democrat, Wisconsin]. Mr. Speaker, I have voted on this issue about 60 times, and I have to say that I have come to accept and agree with the legitimacy of the argument that in almost all circumstances Federal dollars should not be used to finance abortions.

The question is what happens to a woman who is raped or who is the victim of incest. This amendment deals only with the question of rape or incest. It does not endorse or recommend in any way abortions in those circumstances. If it did, I could not personally support it.

My wife and I lost two babies, and I do not believe that abortion in the case of rape or incest is the answer. But as a man that is easy for me to say.

All this amendment says is that when a woman is raped or is the victim of incest, she, not I or you, should be able to make the choice in accordance with her own conscience without regard to whether she is rich or poor, if the State in which she resides allows the choice. That is all this amendment does, and reasonable people ought to be able to agree on that.

Mr. WEBER [Republican, Minnesota]. . . . Mr. Speaker, the National Right to Life Committee has called this vote the most important prolife vote of the 100th Congress. We should ask ourselves why that is, because we have cast other votes on this important and emotional issue. I suggest there are a few reasons why this vote, of all of those votes that we have cast in this Congress, is considered the most important prolife vote.

First of all, because it would make a shift in a longstanding existing policy. Particularly Members who have not had to vote on this in the past, and there are many, should understand that fact. The Hyde amendment has been the law of the land since it was passed in 1977. We have not had to vote on it in about 5 years.

We are talking about upsetting a long, well-established, and, in my judgment, proven policy.

The second reason why it is the most important prolife vote of this Congress is because the Hyde amendment is, indeed, working as planned. We used to pay, in this country, for over 300,000 abortions per year. Taxpayers, many of whom were deeply opposed to abortion for moral reasons, were forced to use their taxpayer dollars to pay for abortions. That is not happening anymore.

Furthermore, the terrible effects that were predicted by many on the initial passage of the Hyde amendment have not come to pass. Large numbers of women have not been forced to seek back-alley abortions or lose their lives because of the passage of the Hyde amendment as was predicted on its initial passage in 1977. Those problems simply did not arise.

Third, the same problems that were foreseen by many at the attempt to pass the exceptions for rape and incest back in 1977 would arise if those exceptions were written into law today.

Law enforcement officials from many parts of the country opposed the insertion of a rape-and-incest exception in 1977, and since then, because they believe it would cause large numbers of people to report false rapes, false cases of incest, in order to have the Government pay for their abortions. Even Gloria Steinem on the other side of the issue obviously said that a rape-and-incest exception alone would make many women liars. We do not want to complicate that situation, as the Congress wisely decided not to complicate it back in 1977.

Finally, this is the most important prolife vote of the year because the issue is not really rape and incest, and the issue is not really even tax dollars. The issue is life itself. After all, we do not really expect to see a large number of cases paid for under this particular provision that are genuinely the result of rape and incest.

Medical procedures are available, legal in every State, to prevent the woman recently raped or the victim of incest from conceiving a child. That is the answer to the question of the gentlewoman from California who was just involved in the debate.

All in all, it is expected that perhaps the number of abortions resulting from rape and incest may well be in the hundreds, not even in the thousands every year, and certainly not all of those wish to abort. We are talking about a very small number of cases.

The larger issue, here again, is simply the issue of life, the issue of availability of abortion, and the issue of forcing taxpayers to pay for abortions. It is against the standard of taking of a human life that all other actions, even actions as horrible as cases of rape and incest, must be judged, so we urge support for the chairman's position. We urge maintaining a standard that has been established in this country for over 10 years that says that the taxpayers are not going to be forced to pay for abortions against their will. . . .

Mr. VOLKMER [Democrat, Missouri]. Mr. Speaker, I wish to commend the gentleman for his remarks, especially in regard to the question on law enforcement.

What we have here is a potential of making law enforcement look at people, ladies, when they come in, and/or girls when they come in and complain of a rape, the question of whether there actually was rape, whether they should go out and investigate, or is this just for the purposes of getting an abortion funded, that has been something that law enforcement has been very concerned about, and I think everyone should be concerned about, because I think rape is one of the most heinous crimes there is. Yet to then turn around and say that we should relegate that to the fact that is a way to get an abortion because that is what is going to happen, as the gentleman said, even Gloria Steinem has commented what we are trying to do basically with the opposition is to make liars out of women so that they can get an abortion funded by the Government.

I commend the gentleman, and I, too, urge the Members of the House to vote "aye" on the motion of the gentleman from Kentucky. . . .

Mrs. MORELLA [Republican, Maryland]. Mr. Speaker, I rise in support of the Exon amendment, to allow Medicaid funding for abortion services in cases of rape and incest. This amendment would allow Federal funding of abortions only in *promptly reported* cases of rape and incest and contains a State's rights provision to allow each State to determine whether it will fund abortions in cases of sexual assault.

The justice campaign, a national campaign to secure public funding for abortion for the victims of rape and incest, is made up of representatives of a number of religions, including Hebrew, Episcopal, Baptist, Methodist, Unitarian, and Presbyterian congregations. The vast majority of the American public supports this coverage—even many who support the Roe versus Wade decision. Polls taken over the last 15 years indicate that 8 in 10 Americans believe abortion should be an available option for women who have been the victims of sexual assault.

Poor women who are pregnant as a result of rape or incest—victims of brutal acts—should have access to the same health care options as more affluent women. I urge my colleagues to join the justice campaign to preserve the Senate language in supporting the Exon amendment to H.R. 4783. . . .

Mr. EDWARDS [Democrat, California]. . . . Mr. Speaker, I rise in support of the Senate's position.

Mr. Speaker, earlier this summer, our colleagues in the other body did a courageous thing.

By voting to provide Federal funding for abortions in promptly reported cases of rape and incest, the other body was only trying to put into law the views of the vast majority of Americans. The time has come for the House of Representatives to do the same thing.

Recent surveys show that 81 percent of Americans believe abortion services should be available to women who become pregnant as a result of sexual assault. . . .

Mr. Speaker, for the first time since 1979, we have the opportunity to do the decent and humane thing.

I urge a "no" vote. . . .

Mr. DORNAN [Republican, California]. Mr. Speaker, I want to congratulate all of my colleagues for the high tone of this debate. We do not seem to be talking past one another any longer on this issue. We seem to be reaching out to understand one another's position.

One of the most incredible acts of political courage I have ever seen was on America's most-watched television show "60 Minutes." Our current President, Ronald Reagan, was pressed forcefully but politely by one of the star interviewers of our era, Mike Wallace, on this issue of rape/incest and abortion. It was not a direct question. Mike Wallace simply was probing for one of those confessions from a politician. He said: "Mr. President, what is the biggest mistake you have ever made in political life?" I immediately, as a politician, like a baseball player will anticipate a move, I answered in my mind: "Oh, that is for my opponents to tell you, I would rather talk about some of the good things I have done." The President did not say that. He said, and this is almost verbatim: "Mike, that is easy. The biggest mistake I ever made was my first year as Governor of California when I did not really understand in depth the issue of abortion." President Reagan was referring to a bill that bore the name of one of our distinguished colleagues here, Mr. Beilenson, a good friend of mine who is on the opposite side of the issue. Mr. Beilenson was in the State senate in California at that time. President Reagan went on and said: "The Beilenson bill came up in California. I signed it to allow abortion for rape and incest.

"And I didn't realize what I was doing. I opened a Pandora's box." And he said: "And what's happened ever since has been a national scandal." He said it was used as an excuse for unlimited abortion on demand for every cause, and that is the problem that faces this House today.

The rape problem is as tough as we can get on this issue. I happen to have a personal friend whose daughter was raped at noon on a college campus. I believe it was at the instigation of one of America's slimiest pornographers, who offered $400 the night before the rape to anybody who could get a story on my friend's daughter. She was pulled off of the parking lot and into the bushes, and she was raped by three or four students, she cannot remember exactly. The next night her father, who is a nationally known official, held a press conference and said that we have done everything that we can to avoid this pregnancy that our church will allow. He said that: "If my daughter ends up pregnant, she told me from the hospital that she wants to have the baby. She will not commit an act of violence when there is no capital punishment for the men who raped her in an act of violence."

I applaud the cause of Joan Andrews, who I think is a martyr. She is taking her legal punishment for unplugging one of these suction pieces of equipment in modern American life that tears a living child from its mother's womb, and spins the aborted baby into a gel in one of these whirling, razor blade machines. . . .

Ms. SNOWE [Republican, Maine]. . . . Mr. Speaker, I rise in opposition to the motion to insist on the House position.

And I do so, Mr. Speaker, as a Member who has opposed Federal funding of abortion on demand. I subscribed to the notion that the Federal Government should not bear the responsibility to fund abortions for women who choose—who chose—not to take proper precautions.

Rather, it is a question of a woman taking responsibility for her own actions, no matter what income level.

But instances occur, tragic instances, when the choice is taken out of the woman's hands—more accurately, when it is violently and brutally taken from her. A woman who has been raped, or who is the victim of incest, faces enormous physical and emotional consequences. And these are consequences that simply are not of her own making.

Yet women of economic means who have thus suffered have options which we currently deny to low-income women. They have choices in this hideous circumstance that are now withheld. We have made income and economic status the basis by which women contend with the aftermath of rape or incest—as if falling victim to those crimes were not degrading enough.

In this debate, Mr. Speaker, we have spoken in the dispassionate terminology of legislatures as to what lower-income women are being forced to do and contend with. Yet the cruel and agonizing reality of their fate is far removed from such debate.

Further, there is a great deal of talk about "rights," about who has what kind and what take precedence. I would suggest, rather, that we should speak not of rights but of obligations. And there is an obligation in our society toward a rape victim, toward the victim of incest, to provide the basic array of choices in these horrifying circumstances regardless of income.

To preclude women, in the wake of the crudest and most degrading of crimes, from recovering from those crimes simply on the basis of economics goes from the realm of unfairness toward base cruelty.

I urge my colleagues to defeat the motion to insist on the House position. . . .

Mr. FAZIO [Democrat, California]. Mr. Speaker, I rise in strong support of the centrist Senate compromise on this matter, and it is important for Members to realize that the 19 opponents in the Senate were made up of Members on both sides of this issue who could not compromise.

This is really an opportunity to add a small element of compassion to the Hyde amendment, and I mean a small one. Statistics show us that in 1986, 90,000 cases of rape occurred in the United States, and over 100,000 cases of child abuse, some of which were incest. Yet in 1979, the last year in which we were able to gather data on this prior to the enactment of the Hyde amendment, only 72 people qualified for this form of Federal assistance. So we are not talking about an awful lot of people.

But we are talking about a very important principle, and that is why I think the demeanor of this debate is so important.

As the gentlewoman from Maryland [Mrs. MORELLA] said, we are requiring prompt reporting of the crime. This is not a new loophole that people will be able to use to violate the broader Hyde amendment. We are giving the States local control to make decisions about whether they wish to use their State Medicaid funds for this purpose.

But I think we have overlooked one fundamental issue, and that is the question of economic justice. We all know that under the law currently in this country women who wish to have an abortion can have one. I do not think very many of us who are in the affluent element of our society realize what a burden this can be to poor people. An abortion today could cost half the family's monthly income for people who qualify for AFDC, the people we are talking about here today, that 20 percent of our society or less who will fall into the lower-income bracket.

We are talking about economic justice. If the Constitution says that is one of our purposes of being here, if we have said in adherence to the Supreme Court rulings like Roe versus Wade that this abortion concept can exist in our society, we cannot allow this disparity to continue. I ask my colleagues to support the Senate compromise. . . .

Mr. FRENZEL [Republican, Minnesota]. Mr. Speaker, it has been mentioned a number of times on the floor that this is a very narrow kind of compromise. It applies in a very limited number of cases, only on two occasions, after reporting, and the States can undo everything that we might do here today.

I would like to suggest that this is not abortion on demand. It has nothing to do with abortion rights. That matter is determined elsewhere. What we are talking about is whether a poor woman has the same opportunity in the United States as a rich woman. All we are talking about is whether there is an opportunity for the poor to be treated the same way as the rich.

It seems to me that if we have any dedication to equality in this House that we have no other course than to support the Senate amendment. . . .

Ms. PELOSI [Democrat, California]. . . . I rise today in support of Senate language providing Medicaid funded abortions for women whose pregnancy results from rape or incest.

It is ironic and tragic that Medicaid, the very program which was created to provide necessary medical care to poor women, has been transformed into a program that denies poor women who are pregnant access to all available medical options. Poor women who are victims of the brutal crimes of rape or incest should have access to the same legal rights to abortion as other women in our society. Denying them access to these services is nothing but a policy of discrimination against the poor.

In 36 States in this country, no public funds are available to help women whose pregnancies are the result of violence and assault. In an ideal world, abortions would not be necessary. Unfortunately, in the real world, the brutal realities of crimes of aggression such as rape and incest occur with alarming frequency. We have the opportunity today to assist some women on the long road to regaining control of their lives. It is unfair, unreasonable and inhumane to deny them this assistance. I urge my colleagues to oppose any measures to weaken the Senate language restoring Medicaid funding for abortions for women victimized by rape and incest.

Mr. Speaker, I come from a culture as an Italian American, Roman Catholic mother of 5 children of my own who worships children. This has nothing to do, as the gentleman from Minnesota [Mr. FRENZEL] said, with the question of abortion, but it is a question of fairness, and a question of not denying people their rights.

I ask every Member of this body to examine his or her conscience and say if any one of our children or spouses of male Members were confronted with this circumstance of rape or incest, would they deny that member of their family the opportunity to every medical option. I do not think the time is now for hypocrisy, but it is a time to really face the reality and truth of the situation, and not deny to women, just because they lack the financial resources, the same medical options we reserve for our own families and our own spouses. . . .

Mrs. JOHNSON [Republican, Connecticut]. Mr. Speaker, I thank my colleagues from both sides of the aisle for this opportunity to speak on what I consider to be a very, very important matter. Preceding speakers have spoken eloquently to the fact that this is not abortion on demand that we are talking about. This is rather an issue of equity and a deeply human right, which at times life demands that we be allowed to exercise from the deepest reservoirs of our own individual being.

This amendment does not offer abortion on demand. It talks only about incest and rape. It is narrowly drawn. It is thoughtfully drawn with the States rights provisions and the other sections that have been mentioned today.

But what it talks about is not narrow. Rape is not a narrow experience.

Rape is being in fear for your life. Rape is being violently subdued.

Picture your daughter, picture your own wife, picture the terror, picture the pain. I ask Members to take unto yourselves the full responsibility for this vote. I ask Members to know that with a knife at your throat, with fear in your heart, maybe an hour, maybe over an hour, an experience of such extraordinary brutality, and under those circumstances to be penetrated. Yes, we are not talking about assault and battery. Rape is not assault and battery. It is penetration.

Men and women experience this situation very differently. Penetration is different than penetrating.

And that is part of what this is all about. I will tell you that if your 13-year-old daughter—I have three daughters—but picture your sobbing 13-year-old daughter in your arms convulsed in terror and anguish, are you going to ask her day after day to relive that experience? Are you going to make that decision for her? Can every man in the House of Representatives take upon themselves at this moment the right and responsibility to make this kind of decision for every poor woman and child—yes, child—in America?

This bill is about incest. Now, who commits incest? Who is the victim of incest? Female children.

I appreciate the time allotted to me, because I do think this is no ordinary matter. I think—I hope that I have made that plain. We are only asking that under extraordinary, brutal, deeply human situations that that woman, that child, be allowed the same choice as your wife, or your child, because you can pay for it, and because you have the power to choose.

Believe me, rape is not something that is over when it is finished. It is not done when it is done. It is with you the rest of your life. These choices are not choices that can be taken on in the well of the House. . . .

Mr. SCHEUER [Democrat, New York]. Mr. Speaker, the last 4 minutes during which we heard the statement of the lady from Connecticut [Mrs. JOHNSON] constitutes the 4 most deeply moving minutes that I have spent in this Congress in the last 20 years. I must say that all of the debate from both sides of this issue has been thoughtful, has been deeply felt and has dignified this Congress.

Mr. Speaker, I only have a minute. We have heard that abortion is an assault on an innocent unborn life, we have heard that abortion is the taking of a human life, that the issue of life itself is what we are talking about, and that the fetus is a human being.

We have heard that abortion has a corrosive effect on the fabric of society, it takes an innocent life.

However, there is another view to consider. There is the view that I adhere to, the view that abortion is not the taking of human life but a sublime humanitarian act that, in this case, will ease the suffering of human beings.

This does not mean that I am anti-life. I and my colleagues who support a woman's right to choose also support life-sustaining legislation. My colleagues, when you are asked if you are prolife, give them the record of life-sustaining legislation you have supported this year.

Tell them what you are doing to lower the abysmally high infant mortality rate in this country. Point to the health care programs you have supported to curb fatal diseases among the Nation's 37 million citizens without basic health services.

The Children's Defense Fund cited 10 House votes this year as being critical to the physical, mental, and spiritual health of the Nation's children. The bills provided for food, clothing, shelter, education, and health care for children. These are true life-sustaining bills.

Many religious organizations, including the U.S. Presbyterian Church, the Union of American Hebrew Congregations, and the United Church of Christ, support the Exon amendment. Seventy percent of Americans in a Lou Harris poll, commissioned by Planned Parenthood, believe that abortion in this circumstance is acceptable. Our colleagues in the Senate passed the amendment by an overwhelming vote of 73 to 19.

Furthermore, in every single developed nation in the world, with the exception of Ireland, abortion for rape and incest victims is legal. This includes Spain, Italy, and France, three of the most Catholic countries in the world. Not only is abortion legal in this instance, but it has been since the early 1930's.

If a victim of sexual assault wants to terminate her pregnancy she should have that right—regardless of her financial circumstances. Congress should not stand between a woman and her body, especially in cases of rape and incest. . . .

Mr. AuCOIN [Democrat, Oregon]. Mr. Speaker, for the last 15 years in virtually every public opinion poll in this country, the overwhelming majority of Americans have supported the right of rape and incest victims to choose to end the pregnancy that results from that rape or that incest. That is what the polls say.

But today the law of the land is not in step with nor does it represent the mainstream thinking of the American public. The law that this Congress has mistakenly created says that a victim of criminal rape must bear the rapist's child. I think, Mr. Speaker, that not only a majority of Americans, but a majority of the Members of this House honestly, in the bottom of their hearts, believe that is a gross denial of justice.

Rape and incest cases are increasing across this country. Many of those victims of violent sexual assault are young women who are poor and who depend on the Federal Government for their well-being and their health care.

Now some of my colleagues have said that a woman who has been victimized once by conceiving against her will should be also victimized again by her own government and be forced to deliver against her will. Mr. Speaker, I ask, and my colleagues on our side ask for simple compassion. Surely Members of this body think that women are more than incubators for rapists and criminals and perpetrators of incest. If you do believe as we do, you will accept the Senate revision. It exempts rape and incest victims and it requires cases of rape and incest to be promptly reported and that states agree to accept the funds.

These provisions assure that claims of rape and incest are legitimate and that the opportunity for fraud is minimized. These provisions give State governments the option to participate in the policy decisions. And most importantly, it leaves to a violently impregnated woman the moral right to choose for herself whether or not she will deliver the criminal rapist's child.

In the name of compassion, in the name of justice for women who have suffered enough, I urge my colleagues to vote "no" on the motion and to accept the Senate provision. . . .

Mr. HYDE [Republican, Illinois]. Mr. Speaker, I just want to say parenthetically something that the last speaker said about bearing the child of a criminal rapist, that strikes me as the Scarlet Letter, as though the innocent child, the second victim of the rape, somehow must bear the stigma of the criminal act of the father. I have difficulty following the logic of that.

Now we have heard in some painful detail the emotional trauma of what a rape can mean. Let me also say that incest is a form of rape, only it is within the family. Let me say also abortion does not cure that family's situation. Something more has to be done to get the poor victim of the incest away from the perpetrator of the incest and abortion does not go to that at all.

But I think to understand fully this soul-wrenching issue, let us focus for a moment away from the woman, just for a moment, and look at the other victim, the unborn child, and let us try to figure out what an abortion does to that child.

Now it is not a tonsillectomy, it is not an appendectomy; by definition, by intention it is the killing, the killing of an innocent, an innocent human life.

Thomas More when he was beheaded by Henry VIII is noted for a famous line. He said to the axman, "Be careful of my beard, it hath committed no treason." So as his head was cut off, he wanted his beard to maintain its dignity; "it hath committed no treason."

The little baby has not committed a crime, a rape, the little baby is an innocently inconvenient victim along with the victimized woman.

The law protected the rapist. The Supreme Court has said, "You may not impose capital punishment on a rapist." This is cruel and unusual punishment. But you are saying to exterminate, not terminate, a pregnancy—every pregnancy terminates at the end of nine months—exterminate this innocently inconvenient residual of the rape, the product of the rape, the consequence of the rape. Visit on that innocent child the penalty the law will not visit on the rapist. This is really, really what you are saying.

Now let us stipulate on compassion. Let us stipulate—I will, I stipulate that Mr. HOYER, NANCY JOHNSON, VIC FAZIO, everybody has an abundance of compassion. How can you not? We are talking about one of the most traumatic situations in literature, in life. But stipulate, please, that we have compassion too. We have what we like to think is more than a one-dimensional compassion, a compassion that extends beyond sympathy and bleeding for and with and weeping with the victim of the rape, but extends to the innocently inconvenient consequence of that rape.

We want to enlarge the circle of persons for whom society will be responsible, to include within that circle of protection the little stranger, the little intruder who through no fault of his or her own has been made a party to this terribly criminal act. Rape is not over when it is finished, that is right, oh, that is right. But neither is abortion.

Abortion is terminal, abortion is killing.

Now no one, not even a woman who has been raped, God bless her and help her, and we help her and bless her, but nobody has the right to kill another innocent life, nobody. And no circumstances give that God-like power to anybody.

I have heard "picture your own wife or daughter." OK, fair enough. Now I am going to give you a picture, a little newborn baby that you are holding in your arms, think of that when you vote on this issue and ask yourself if you can be an accessory to exterminating that little child because his father committed a crime.

That is as real a picture for you to form in your mind as anything else. It is a matter of focus, of emphasis.

I ask you to extend your compassion to that abstraction that you cannot see, you cannot touch it because it is in the mother's womb, that tiny child of transcendent human value surrounded by a woman who has been victimized but who indeed is a mother.

In the fullest sense of the term, this is a human rights issue and you have in all of these situations conflicting rights, conflicting rights. You have the right of the first victim to have her body free from the consequences of a criminal act of rape. That is over here.

And over here you have the very right to life, itself, the right to live of the second victim, the unborn.

Now when rape and incest occur, a great injustice occurs, an enormous, monstrous, inhumane, humiliating, brutal injustice occurs. In all honesty I cannot say other than that forcing a woman to carry to term the child of the rapist is anything but a terrible injustice.

But that having been said, must we visit another injustice on top of that? Must we superimpose that on this crime of rape by destroying in the womb an innocent preborn child? It is not a tumor, it is not a bad tooth or swollen tonsils. That little microscopic entity is a tiny member of the human family that has committed no treason, has committed no crime, and we must perform an act of virtue, some act of will to transfer due process and the equal protection of the law to the second victim, because that is the second victim. But it is a far greater injustice to kill the child, superimposing that injustice on the injustice of the rape.

We cannot avoid injustice in a rape situation. We cannot avoid injustice in an incest situation. We can ameliorate, we can mitigate, we can help, we can nurture, we can alleviate, but we cannot escape injustice. But why must we compound the injustice by adding to it the extermination of an innocent human life, one that cannot rise up on the street, cannot speak out, cannot defend himself or herself, and cannot escape?

The injustice of rape lasts at least nine months. It is a terrible injustice, but it can be helped psychologically, financially, and spiritually. But abortion is the second injustice. There is the taking of a life, and there is no help for that. There is no remedy for that.

Interestingly enough, we have heard very few statistics on this. We have heard some from the gentleman from Oregon, ambiguous, I must say, and the reason is that there are not any. It is very hard to find out from anybody how many pregnancies result from rape and incest. The answer is that there are very, very few.

Now, on the economic argument that a poor woman should have the advantages of a rich woman, may I suggest that Planned Parenthood gets millions of taxpayer dollars from this Government. Let them pick up the cost for the very few who insist on exterminating their young. They should not make us accessories. They should not make us a part of that double tragedy of rape and exterminating an unborn child.

There are very, very few such pregnancies in this country. We cannot get the statistics. There are studies I can quote for the Members that say it almost never happens. But I must suggest to Members that we should let Planned Parenthood pay for those who insist on punishing the child for the crime of the father. Why must the Federal Government supply the only answer and be an accessory in the extermination of an innocent life?

These are poor women, yes. But there are poor babies. They are defenseless, defenseless babies.

Ethel Waters was a great black actress who passed away a few years ago. She played a famous role in "Cabin in the Sky." I do not know whether many remember it; perhaps only I do, but perhaps some who are a little older will remember it also. She was a great lady, a great person, and she wrote a book about her life that she called "His Eye is on the Sparrow." She said, "My father raped my mother when she was 12, and now they are dedicating a park to me in Chester, Pennsylvania."

Out of great, great tragedy some good can come.

Let me just leave the Members with something that was said by Sam Levinson, the comedian, some years ago. Levinson said, "I believe that each newborn child arrives on Earth with a message to deliver to mankind. Clenched in his little fist is some particle of yet unrevealed truth, some missing clue which may solve the enigma of man's destiny." He has a limited amount of time to fulfill his mission, and he will never get a second chance. Nor will we. He may be our last hope. He must be treated as top sacred.

So as the Members vote on this—and it is not easy—let us not accuse anybody of lacking compassion. Let us consider focusing our compassion beyond what we see and touch and hear and take into consideration the abstract, this little atom of humanity, defenseless and innocent, and let us know that while rape is a terrible thing, an abortion is worse, because rape, with all of its horror, is not killing. Where there is life surely there is hope. But abortion terminates a life, and one of those little lives might have found the secret to cancer, to multiple sclerosis, to world peace; one of those little lives that is now thrown out like a crushed empty beer can.

Mr. Speaker, it is a tough vote. But I plead with the Members to support the gentleman from Kentucky [Mr. NATCHER] and support the gentleman from Massachusetts [Mr. CONTE], who have been like Gibraltars on this issue for years. They are responsible for saving many babies. Yes, the unborn of the rich are at risk. We cannot save them if their mother's want an abortion, because they can go out and buy one. But if we can save the unborn of the poor, occasionally, that is no small achievement.

Mr. DEFAZIO [Democrat, Oregon]. Mr. Speaker, I want to commend the Senate for adopting the Exon amendment which allows Medicaid funding to terminate a pregnancy that is the result of rape or incest in cases that are promptly reported to a law enforcement agency or public health service.

It is an outrage that the victims of brutal physical and mental assault have to carry an unwanted pregnancy to term because they are dependent upon the Federal Government for their health care. For most economically disadvantaged women health care options and choices about abortion are available only if they are financed through programs such as Medicaid.

While the Exon amendment would be a step forward in what has been a backward approach to this issue, the "promptly" reported language in the amendment is a disservice to a majority of women it's supposed to benefit. We are just beginning to realize the alarmingly high incidence of incest. These cases are rarely "promptly" reported. The young victims live in a daily environment of fear, confusion, anger and helplessness. They are unable to defend themselves from the perpetrator and are often led to believe that the situation is their fault. We cannot expect these young women to come forward seeking assistance when we send a message, "don't come knocking on the door of the Federal Government for help if you're poor."

The overwhelming majority of public opinion polls over the past 15 years have found that eight in 10 Americans support availability of abortions for sexually assaulted women. In 1978, my home state of Oregon was the first State to vote on a ballot initiative that would have prohibited the use of public funds for abortions. That measure was defeated. In 1986, the question again appeared on the ballot and the voters again opposed it. Clearly, restricting the availability of abortions for these victims is not the policy that most Americans want.

Mr. Speaker, I urge my colleagues to reconsider this discriminatory policy and, at the very least, allow the use of Federal funds to provide abortion services to poor women who are the victims of sexual assault. I urge my colleagues to vote no on the House language.

Mr. WEISS [Democrat, New York]. Mr. Speaker, I want to express my strong support of the motion to agree to the Senate provision on abortion funding to the Labor, Health and Human Services, Education appropriations conference report for fiscal year 1989. By restoring Federal funding to abortion in the cases of rape and incest, this provision would begin to redress the gross injustices of our current abortion laws.

In 1973, the Supreme Court affirmed that it is a woman's constitutional right to end a pregnancy in its early stages. Yet over the 15 years since then, the Congress has enacted a series of measures that have denied poor women this constitutional right. We cannot continue a policy that condemns women to the trauma of bringing an unwanted child into the world, or to a back alley abortionist, simply because she does not have enough money for a safe abortion.

Mr. Speaker, a woman should have the freedom to make her own decision about a pregnancy that is the result of violence and assault. The highest court in our land has affirmed that right. But the issue before us today is a question of resources and rights. Our Government is straddled with an abortion policy that discriminates against the poor, and we are now presented with the opportunity to remedy this travesty.

Congress has an obligation to assure equality of health care to all our citizens, and I urge my colleagues to join in supporting the motion to restore Federal funding for abortion in the case of rape and incest.

[The House voted 216 to 166 in favor of the motion, thus rejecting the Senate amendment to permit exceptions for rape and incest. The deadlock between the two bodies was overcome when the Senate four days later reversed itself and accepted the House position. The Senate amendment had been attached to a major spending bill for health, education, and labor programs, and many Senators who switched their vote said they wished to insure that federal spending for the programs in the bill, including research for AIDS and other diseases, could begin when the fiscal year starts on October 1. The federal abortion law remained as it had been since 1981, allowing Medicaid financing of abortions only to save the life of the woman.]

Comment

In the Califano case, Father McCormick helpfully identifies three levels of moral questions about abortion: (1) the personal morality of having an abortion; (2) the political morality of legalizing and funding abortion; and (3) the obligations of public officials in carrying out the law. We cannot ignore the first level of personal morality in considering our positions on public policy and the obligations of public officials, but both cases focus on the second and third levels.

Begin with the issue of public policy—whether the government should fund abortions for poor women. Note Califano's responses to a representative from the National Women's Political Caucus: "I believe abortion is morally wrong," and "I oppose federal funding for abortion." Must the second position necessarily follow from the first? Senator Packwood, Judy Woodruff, Congressman Fazio, and Congresswomen Pelosi and Morella all suggest that it would be unfair for the government not to fund abortions for the poor as long as they are legal. They thereby attempt to separate the question of whether abortion should be legal from the question of whether the government should subsidize abortion for poor women once it is legal. Assess the responses of Califano, Carter, and Congressman Hyde to the defense of federal funding on grounds of fairness. Is there any principle other than fairness that would favor funding?

On what moral grounds (if any) can one distinguish between the funding of all legal abortions for poor pregnant women and the funding of only those abortions that terminate pregnancies resulting from rape and incest? Congresswoman Morella argues that "poor women who are pregnant as a result of rape or incest—victims of brutal acts—should have access to the same health care options as more affluent women." Congressman Mollohan argues against the moral relevance of any such distinction: "If you adopt our premise that unborn life is valuable, and therefore abortion is fundamentally wrong, there is no logical reason for allowing exceptions in cases of rape and incest." Are members of Congress who share Mollohan's premise logically bound to accept his conclusion? Assess Congresswoman Pelosi's defense of funding abortions in cases of rape and incest. Must members of Congress who approve of legalized abortion also approve of funding all legal abortions under Medicaid, not just those that result from incest and rape?

One philosopher has suggested that legalizing abortion but not subsidizing it is a fair compromise between the pro-life and pro-choice positions, although it completely satisfies the moral claims of neither. If a compromise is the best solution to the public policy question, are these the right terms? Should the terms of a fair compromise be more or less generous to poor women?

Consider the question of whether Califano was correct in thinking that he could act responsibly in public office while personally opposing abortion. Did he use the correct standard—willingness to enforce whatever law Congress passes—in deciding to accept the position? Having accepted the position, did

Califano act properly in office? Consider the ways in which his opposition to abortion might have affected his conduct in office, including his public statements. Was he justified in interpreting the intent of Congress as he did in writing HEW regulations on funding abortion? Should he have compromised with the President on the paragraph concerning rape and incest?

The moral conflicts Califano faced might have been even more difficult had Congress instructed HEW to fund abortions through Medicaid. Would Califano then have been justified in doing anything to oppose such a policy? Had Califano been committed to the position that poor women have a right to subsidized abortion, what should have been done in the face of congressional action to the contrary? If both the president and Congress are determined to preserve the Hyde Amendment unrevised, are there any circumstances under which someone committed to subsidizing abortions for poor women should accept the office of secretary of Health and Human Services?

Surrogate Parenting in New York—I

New York State Senate Judiciary Committee

[The report excerpted below supported legislation introduced February 3, 1987, by John R. Dunne, deputy majority leader of the New York Senate, and Mary B. Goodhue, chairman of the Senate Child Care Committee. The legislation would have recognized surrogate motherhood contracts as legal and irrevocable in New York. Although initially there was support for the proposal, the sponsors withdrew it later in the session as opposition grew. The legislature then suspended all hearings on the question of surrogacy until the governor's task force could issue its report (see "Surrogacy in New York—II").]

EXECUTIVE SUMMARY

Many American couples, experiencing the problem of infertility, are turning to surrogate parenting to help them create families. It is estimated that over five hundred surrogate births have occurred in the United States, most of them in the last few years. The purpose of this report is to examine the questions presented by surrogate parenting and to determine the appropriate public policy response.

Generally, surrogate parenting involves an agreement between a married couple who cannot have a child and a fertile woman who agrees to be artificially inseminated with the sperm of the husband of the couple, to carry the child to term, and then to surrender all parental rights. The biological father establishes paternity, and his infertile wife legally adopts the child. A fee, as well as all necessarily incurred costs, is paid to the surrogate, and often a fee is paid to an infertility center or other third-party intermediary for making the arrangements.

This process, by itself, involves little or no state involvement. However, the development of surrogate parenting has outpaced the development of law. Conse-

---

From *Surrogate Parenting in New York: A Proposal for Legislative Reform*, prepared by the staff of the New York State Senate Judiciary Committee, John R. Dunne (chairman), and Roberta Glaros (project director), Dec. 1986.

quently, when the courts are called upon to interpret and enforce these agreements, they must decide issues, such as the status of the child, without the guidance of statutes or caselaw.

National attention has focused on cases involving breaches of surrogate parenting agreements. In 1983, a child conceived as the result of a surrogate parenting agreement was born defective, and neither party wanted to accept parental responsibility. More recently, the case of "Baby M," now pending in the New Jersey superior court, involves a surrogate mother's refusal to relinquish parental rights to the child.

In July 1986, Nassau County Surrogate Court Judge C. Raymond Radigan, in the course of an adoption proceeding, ruled on the legality of a surrogate parenting agreement. The major issue was whether the agreement violated state law which prohibits payment of compensation other than medical expenses in adoptions. Judge Radigan concluded that New York State's current laws are ambiguous and provide little guidance to the courts in deciding cases involving surrogate parenting arrangements. In a letter to the chairmen of the judiciary committees of both the Senate and the Assembly, he urged that the legislature examine this issue.

In response to Judge Radigan's request, the Senate and Assembly judiciary committees held a joint hearing in October 1986 to determine what action, if any, the legislature should take in regard to the practice of surrogate parenting. Nineteen witnesses, including legal experts, ethicists, and representatives of religious and feminist groups, provided extremely valuable testimony on the moral, ethical, and legal implications of surrogate parenting. In addition, several witnesses recounted their personal experiences with the practice.

Following the hearing, the Senate Judiciary Committee chairman instructed the committee staff to review hearing testimony, to conduct further research on the subject and to make recommendations regarding legislation to carry out the appropriate public policy. This report outlines the findings of the committee staff and makes recommendations to the legislature with regard to determining a public policy response to the practice of surrogate parenting in New York State.

FINDINGS AND RECOMMENDATIONS

After a careful analysis of the testimony presented to the committee at its hearing and after a careful review of the literature and research into the practice of surrogate parenting, the committee staff recommends that the state recognize surrogate parenting contracts as legal and enforceable. The first and foremost concern of the legislature must be to ensure that the child, born in fulfillment of a surrogate parenting agreement, has a secure and permanent home and settled rights of inheritance. The prospects for achieving this goal will be enhanced if there is informed consent on the part of all parties to the agreement. In addition, legislation should be designed to prevent exploitation of the parties and excessive commercialization of the practice.

The foregoing recommendations are based on the following findings:

1. Surrogate parenting is perceived as a viable solution to the increasingly common problem of female infertility. Thus, the practice is likely to continue in the foreseeable future.

2. In fashioning a response, the legislature must consider the implications of the practice for the parties and for society as a whole. Specifically, the challenge to accepted societal values, the possible physical and psychological harm to participants, and the potential for fraud, manipulation, and coercion of the parties by entrepreneurs must be examined.

3. Clearly, surrogate parenting presents the legislature with the problem of adapting the law to social and technological change. Contract law, adoption law, and

constitutional law obliquely touch upon the subject and provide some basis for legal analysis, but no existing body of law fully or adequately addresses the legal issues raised by the practice of surrogate parenting. The gaps and deficiencies of the law result in the uncertain status of the child born of a surrogate parenting arrangement.

4. In light of the state's interest in ensuring the status of children born under surrogate parenting arrangements, recognition and regulation of the practice is the most appropriate legislative response.

LEGISLATIVE ACTION

The following recommendations are submitted as a framework for correcting the imbalance between the current state of the law and the developing practice of surrogate parenting.

The role of the courts

The keystone to any legislation relating to surrogate parenting must be judicial approval of the surrogate parenting contract prior to insemination of the surrogate mother. The purpose of the court proceeding should be to ensure that the parties are fully aware of their rights and obligations under the agreement. In order to achieve informed consent, the legislation should require that the parties have the benefit of independent legal representation and the availability of counseling by a licensed mental health professional.

Legislation regulating surrogate parenting should also provide for judicial approval of the fees paid to the surrogate mother, attorneys, and the infertility center. In reviewing surrogate parenting contracts, the court should apply a standard of "just and reasonable compensation" to determine that all fees and compensation are equitable, appropriate to the services rendered, and without coercive effect.

Provisional approval

The health and safety of the child and of the surrogate mother require that insemination be performed by a physician licensed by the state and that tests for sexually transmitted diseases be completed before each insemination. For this reason, the court's approval of the contract should be provisional until it receives notice from a licensed physician that he or she has tested the natural father and the surrogate mother for sexually transmitted diseases, that the surrogate has been inseminated with the semen of the intended father, and that conception has occurred. The court's approval of the contract should then become final.

Effect of court approval

Any proposed legislation should make explicitly clear that a child born to a surrogate mother, in fulfillment of a contract approved by the court prior to insemination, shall be deemed the legitimate, natural child of the biological father and his wife. This would supplant any requirement that the wife of the biological father adopt the child. The statutory determination of parenthood may be rebutted by the intended father if paternity tests show conclusively that he is not biologically related to the child.

Remedies for breach

The surrogate mother's agreement to waive parental rights should be irrevocable and enforced at the birth of the child. Prior to delivery, the surrogate mother should be deemed to have full control of the decisions relating to her pregnancy. Surrender of the child should be enforceable through the remedy of specific performance.

Parental obligations, such as support, should be enforceable against the intended parents from the time of conception. Breach of contract, e.g., refusal to accept parental responsibilities, should result in a judgment of support against the intended parents, since they, by operation of the statute, will be the legal parents of the child.

Eligibility

Given the scarcity of empirical evidence about how the surrogacy process affects those involved, it is recommended that the courts recognize as enforceable only those contracts concluded between a surrogate mother and a couple, the female of whom is medically certified as infertile. Legislation should provide for a measure of proof by which medical necessity can be demonstrated to the court. The petition for court review of the contract should be accompanied by the written statement of a licensed physician that the intended mother has a condition which makes conception or birth of a child unlikely or which creates a likelihood that a child of the intended mother will have a mental or physical impairment or disability.

CONCLUSION

These recommendations provide a framework for an effective legislative response to the legal void surrounding the practice of surrogate parenting. Enforcement of the surrogate contract by the state will secure the welfare of children born under surrogate parenting arrangements. Regulation, based on the principle of informed consent, will address the risks associated with the practice. Judicial review and approval of the surrogate parenting contract prior to insemination is crucial to enforcement, regulation, and informed consent and should be considered the keystone of any proposed legislation. . . .

The Development of Surrogate Parenting

Surrogate parenting developed as a response to the desire of infertile couples to have a child with a genetic link to one parent. Its growing popularity is due to recent increases in the incidence of female infertility and to the development of infertility centers which facilitate the process. An examination of the phenomenon of increasing infertility supports the conclusion that, because surrogate parenting meets a perceived need, it will continue to gain in popularity in the foreseeable future.

INFERTILITY AND ITS CAUSES

According to recent studies, infertility is currently on the rise. A 1976 study found that "one in ten couples failed to conceive after at least one year of marriage during which no contraceptives were used."[1] By 1983, however, "one in eight American married couples failed to conceive after one year of trying."[2] Statistical studies generally set the infertility rate at from 12 to 15 percent of the couples wishing to conceive. These figures may be conservative since they generally include only those couples who seek clinical assistance for infertility. They do not include cases in which the couple chooses not to conceive for genetic reasons, the female can conceive but habitually miscarries, the female has had an early hysterectomy, or the female can conceive but would experience a high risk pregnancy.[3]

Medical experts attribute the rising rate of female infertility to a combination of factors. Changing work roles and the availability of contraception have led many women to postpone childbearing. Delaying childbearing allows age-related biological factors to increase the rate of infertility. In addition, the widespread use of intrauterine devices for the purposes of birth control and changing sexual practices have increased the incidence of pelvic inflammatory disease, a leading cause of female infertility.[4]

Increases in infertility in the United States have occurred at a time of moral emphasis on the family. There is some indication that the values of the pro-family movement have "reinforced the social image of infertility as a major health problem."[5] Mental health experts agree that the inability to beget, bear, and raise children has grave psychological and emotional implications for many infertile men and women.[6] As one scholar put it, "infertility often implicates the most fundamental feelings about one's self and one's relationship to the familial unit, and may leave persons feeling handicapped or defective in an area that is central to personal identity and fulfillment."[7] Infertile couples often experience isolation, guilt, marital strife, and a loss of confidence and self-worth.

THE OPTIONS OF THE INFERTILE COUPLE

Infertile couples wishing to create families are faced with a limited number of choices. Conventional medical treatments, including hormonal drug therapies and surgical procedures, cure a certain percentage of infertility. Yet, in 1983, it was estimated that some 500,000 American women had either an absence or blockage of the fallopian tubes or oviducts.[8] Surgical procedures to correct this condition are sometimes recommended, but in a significant number of cases, surgery is unsuccessful.[9]

When conventional medical treatment fails, the infertile couple is faced with two options: adoption or the less conventional medical treatments of artificial conception. Traditionally, adoption has been the primary means of relieving childlessness. For many couples, however, adoption is no longer a satisfactory alternative. Professionals involved in child welfare and adoption attribute this to a decreasing supply of healthy infants available for adoption. According to the National Committee for Adoption,[10] several factors may have contributed to the decrease: (1) the accessibility of birth control, (2) the legalization of abortion, (3) the closure of many comprehensive maternity homes, and (4) greater social acceptance of single mothers and greater willingness of single mothers to rear their own children. Due largely to social acceptance of single mothers, the number of adoptions decreased by 32.4 percent between 1972 and 1982, despite a 13 percent increase in the number of live births and a 77.4 percent increase in out-of-wedlock births.[11]

Reduced availability has resulted in longer waiting periods and more stringent applicant requirements. According to Nassau County Surrogate Judge C. Raymond Radigan, waiting periods in New York State can be as long as seven years.[12] Such waits are typical nationwide.[13]

The combined factors of increasing infertility and decreasing availability of healthy infants for adoption are causing more and more couples to seek nonconventional medical treatment of infertility. Nonconventional or alternative reproductive technologies offer the infertile couple the hope of having a child with a genetic link to one or both partners. The two most common techniques, artificial insemination and *in vitro* fertilization, involve the transfer of the sperm or egg out of the body which produced it to another body or medium in order to facilitate fertilization.

Artificial insemination is the introduction of sperm into an ovulating woman for the purposes of fertilization. The technology is simple; it requires only the mechanical introduction of the sperm into the uterus. For this reason, artificial insemination has a relatively high rate of success and has been common practice for several decades.

In vitro fertilization involves the capture of a mature egg before ovulation and the transfer of that egg to an external medium, such as a petri dish or test tube, where it can be exposed to sperm. If fertilization occurs, the fertilized egg is placed in an incubator until it is developed enough to be implanted in the mother. *In vitro* fertilization is the indicated treatment in cases where scarring of the fallopian tubes prevents natural conception. It has severe disadvantages, however. The overall success rate is about 10 percent, a relatively low figure when compared to artificial insemination. In addition, the procedure can be physically and emotionally stressful for the infertile woman. Cost estimates range from $38,000 to $50,000.[14]

SURROGATE MOTHERHOOD—A VIABLE ALTERNATIVE

Surrogate parenting is not a distinct type of artificial conception technology. Rather, it involves a different application of artificial insemination in order to produce a child when the female of the couple is infertile. The distinguishing feature of surrogate parenting is the involvement of the surrogate mother as the third person.[15]

The use of a surrogate mother is indicated when the wife has a condition which makes the conception or birth of a child unlikely or which creates a likelihood that the child will have a serious mental or physical impairment. In most cases, infertile couples resort to the use of a surrogate only after they have exhausted all other medical options and have been discouraged from adopting by long waiting periods and increasingly stringent requirements.

For some couples, a surrogate mother provides the only means to have a child genetically related to one of them. The waiting period is much shorter than in traditional adoptions, and the infertile wife can participate with her husband in choosing a surrogate agreeable to both. The child born of a surrogate arrangement is reared by a couple who so wanted him that they were willing to participate in a novel process with potential legal and other risks.[16]

The process offers potential benefits for the surrogates as well. A recent study[17] found that the motivations of women applying to become surrogate mothers are complex. Approximately 85 percent indicated that they would not participate without compensation but that money was not their sole motivation. Other factors influencing their decisions included the enjoyment of being pregnant, the desire to give the gift of a baby to an infertile couple, and an emotional need to work through the previous loss of a child by abortion or adoption. A significant number of those studied were sympathetic to the problems of infertility, and some had, themselves, been adopted as children by infertile couples. For many, surrogacy represents an alternative income option. For example, some divorced women with young children have chosen to be surrogates in order to support their children and to remain at home to care for them.[18]

THE ROLE OF THE ENTREPRENEUR

For the couple wishing to create a family through surrogate parenting, the most difficult and important step is finding a suitable surrogate mother. In some cases, the surrogate is a close friend or relative of the couple, and the agreement is private and informal. In other cases, the couple advertises for a surrogate, usually in suburban and university campus newspapers. But, increasingly, childless couples are turning to infertility centers to help them make their surrogate parenting arrangements.

The first infertility center was opened in the 1970s in Los Angeles by an obstetrician, two lawyers, and a psychologist. Over the past ten years, entrepreneurs have responded rapidly to the market opportunity presented by increased infertility. Major centers have opened in Detroit, Philadelphia, Louisville, Columbus, Topeka, and suburban Washington, D.C. Two infertility centers are currently operating in New York City, and one recently opened in Buffalo. A Long Island center, opened in 1983 and managed by a photographer, is apparently no longer in business.[19] Since the practice is not recognized or regulated by any state, there is no reliable information on the number of centers in existence at any one time, the qualifications of the entrepreneurs, or the number of surrogate births arranged by each center.

The couple's first contact with a center is likely to involve a preliminary interview, during which they may discuss their particular problem and receive information and counseling regarding infertility. If they decide to proceed with surrogate parenting, they sign a contract with the center and gain access to its files on available surrogate mothers. When the couple becomes interested in an individual surrogate, the center coordinates an interview, arranges for medical and psychiatric evaluation of the surrogate, and provides legal representation for the couple in contract negotiations. When a contract is concluded, the center arranges a schedule for the insemination of the surrogate. If conception occurs, the center coordinates the legal steps necessary to establish the natural father's paternity and to finalize adoption of the child by the infertile wife.

The most important service provided by the center is recruitment of potential surrogate mothers. Selection and screening practices vary widely from center to center. Some centers carefully interview applicants and require a waiting period of several months between the time the surrogate is interviewed and the signing of a contract with an infertile couple. Other centers keep files on prospective surrogates but regard them as independent agents. In these cases, medical and psychological testing are included as part of the surrogate parenting agreement and are paid for by the infertile couple.

A surrogate parenting contract generally contains three major provisions: (1) the surrogate agrees to bear the child and surrender parental rights at birth; (2) the natural father agrees to accept responsibility for the child; and (3) the natural father agrees to pay all medical expenses incurred and the fees of both the surrogate and the infertility center.[20] Secondary provisions may include agreements regarding counseling; medical, psychiatric and genetic screening; amniocentesis or other tests to detect genetic defects in the fetus; restrictions on such behavior as smoking, drinking, or drug use by the surrogate; and provision for changes in the fee structure in the event of miscarriage or stillbirth. Despite the fact that the contracts may not be enforceable, they make provision for legal remedies in case of breach.[21]

After the surrogate gives birth, the wife of the natural father adopts the child, often travelling to a jurisdiction which has an accommodating step-parent adoption statute. For example, the Florida Step-Parent Adoption Act[22] does not include a residency requirement or a requirement for disclosure of any fee or expense involved in the adoption. Taking the baby out of state for adoption is often viewed as necessary because twenty-four states prohibit the payment of any consideration other than medical expenses in adoptions.[23] Recently, however, contracts developed by infertility centers are signed only by the natural father, the surrogate mother, and her husband, if any. One center operator argues that under this arrangement, the wife of the natural father is not responsible for any of the payments made to the surrogate. Therefore, she can petition to adopt in the state of her residence regardless of any prohibition against compensation in adoptions.[24]...

OPTIONS FOR GOVERNMENTAL RESPONSE

There are three possible legislative responses to the practice of surrogate parenting: inaction, prohibition, and regulation. This section will examine the public policy and constitutional aspects of each option.

LAISSEZ FAIRE: "LET WELL ENOUGH ALONE"

As discussed in the previous section, New York law does not address the issues raised by surrogate parenting. Although certain aspects of existing law may apply to such arrangements and, to some extent, may serve to resolve the question of the status of the child and to define the rights and duties of the parties, there is no certainty.

Some argue that an absence of settled law regarding surrogate parenting does not require immediate remedial action. They argue that in issues where there are deep-seated controversies or unknown factors, it is best to allow the law to develop without legislative intrusion.[56]

The *laissez faire* approach ignores the fact that without legislative action, the rights of the child, including the right to a permanent and stable home environment, are at risk. Breaches of an agreement may result in familial upheaval and protracted custody battles. Therefore, the question of contract enforceability should not be left to the "uncertainties of evolutionary legal development."[57]

Hearing testimony and published articles make it clear that legal experts, ethicists, and mental health professionals, whether they oppose or support surrogate parenting, agree that the legislature should fill the legal void that surrounds the practice.

PROHIBITION

In deciding whether the practice of surrogate parenting should be prohibited, the state must first determine whether such a prohibition would deny a fundamental constitutional right. If a fundamental right is involved, any attempt to impair this right will likely be struck down as unconstitutional, absent any compelling state interests.

Neither the United States nor the New York constitution contains language explicitly stating that a person has a right to have a child. Decisions relating to procreation and self autonomy, however, have been discussed within the context of the "right to privacy,"[58] which has been defined as containing ". . . only personal rights that can be deemed 'fundamental' or 'implicit in the concept of ordered liberty.' "[59]

It is arguable that the desire to have a child falls within this concept of "ordered liberty." The Supreme Court, *in dicta,* has repeatedly discussed the right of procreation in the same context as marriage and marital intimacy.[60] In *Skinner v. Oklahoma,*[61] the Supreme Court struck down Oklahoma's Habitual Criminal Sterilization Act, which provided for the sterilization of criminals convicted of two or more crimes involving moral turpitude. The Court ruled that the statute denied equal protection in that the phrase, "crimes of moral turpitude," was too vague. In its decision, the Court stated that, "[t]his case touches a sensitive and important area of human rights. Oklahoma deprives certain individuals of a right which is basic to the perpetuation of a race—the right to have offspring."[62] Furthermore, "[t]he right of procreation without state interference has long been recognized as 'one of the basic civil rights of man . . . fundamental to the very existence and survival of the race.' "[63] In a later case, *Eisenstadt v. Baird,*[64] the Court stated: "[i]f the right of privacy means anything, it is the right of the individual, married or single, to be free from unwarranted governmental intrusion into matters so fundamentally affecting a person as the decision whether to bear or beget a child."[65] In 1977, the Supreme Court in *Carey v. Population Services, Inc.,*[66] found unconstitutional a statute which prohibited the sale or advertising of contraception because, "[t]he decision whether or not to bear or beget a child is at the very heart of this cluster of constitutionally protected choices. That decision holds a particularly important place in the history of the right of privacy. . . .[67] Most recently, the Court has even hinted that the promotion of child birth, rather than abortion may, in fact, be a legitimate state interest.[68]

From the foregoing, there appears to be ample precedent that the right to have a child is a fundamental right protected by the constitutional right of privacy and that attempts to outlaw surrogate parenting would be construed as unconstitutional interference with that right. The question still remains, however, whether this right of privacy extends to the use of surrogate parenting as a means of procreation. The right of privacy has not yet been interpreted to include a third party,[69] but to prohibit an infertile couple from using a viable alternative such as surrogate parenting may, in fact, preclude those persons from the only reproductive mechanism possible, and, thereby, indirectly deny those persons the right to have a child.

While it is not suggested that the state should encourage the practice of surrogate parenting, it should not prohibit the practice *in toto*, since such a prohibition would perpetuate the legal vacuum which now exists to the detriment of children born of these arrangements.

REGULATION

If it is accepted that the use of surrogate parenting falls within the protections of the right of privacy, then surrogate parenting may only be restricted or denied if there exists a compelling state interest which necessitates such a restriction or denial. "Compelling is, of course, the key word; where a decision as fundamental as . . . whether to bear or beget a child is involved, regulations imposing a burden on it must be narrowly drawn to express only those interests."[70]

The Supreme Court has noted, however, that the right of privacy "is not absolute, and certain state interests may, at some point, become sufficiently compelling to sustain regulation of factors that govern the right. . . ."[71] Surrogate parenting, if accepted as a part of the fundamental right of privacy, involves the interests of several different parties, all of whom may present the state with compelling interests to protect.

Identifying the Interests

The state's principal interest, once it decides to allow surrogate parenting, is to ensure the status of the child who is born of the arrangement. The state's interest in protecting the child would be best met if the status and legitimacy of the child were secured upon birth, thus avoiding the possibility of a protracted custody battle.

Aside from the infertile couple's decision whether to have a child, the surrogate mother's benefits and potential risks should also be assessed. Under the *Roe v. Wade* analysis, the surrogate mother has the right to decide whether or not she will give birth to a child. Under current law, the state does not limit her decision concerning who should inseminate her, nor does it prevent her from giving the child up for adoption. The state has traditionally refrained from interfering with these personal decisions.

The state does, however, have an interest in the health, safety, and welfare of the mother because of a mortality rate involved with bearing a child, a risk of transmission of disease, and the psychological and emotional ramifications of giving up a child.

Finally, the state has an interest in preventing the potential abuses which may accompany the commercialization of childbearing. The abuses of this technique would most likely be associated with the use of surrogate parenting by couples who are biologically capable of producing their own offspring but wish their children to have superior genetic traits or wish to avoid the inconvenience of pregnancy and childbirth.

The state may, in addition to other regulations, justifiably limit the use of surrogacy to couples where the female is infertile. A "medically necessary" standard has been employed before and has constitutional precedence. In the case of *Maher v. Roe*,[72] the Court upheld a Connecticut statute which limited Medicaid reimbursement for abortions to those which were "medically necessary." The Court considered whether the medically necessary distinction resulted in a denial of equal protection under the constitution, in that indigent women who wanted to have a medically unnecessary abortion might be precluded from doing so. The Court upheld the Connecticut regulation because it "placed no obstacles—absolute or otherwise—in the pregnant woman's path to an abortion. An indigent woman who desires an abortion suffers no disadvantage as a consequence of Connecticut's decision to fund childbirth; she continues as before to be dependent on private services she desired."[73]

Similarly, a requirement that the couples using surrogate parenting demonstrate medical necessity does not infringe upon the right of fertile couples to have children, since they may do so naturally. Additionally, couples who wish to use surrogate parenting outside of the recommended statutory framework will not have the benefit of court enforcement of their contracts.

In summary, it is the committee staff's decided conclusion that surrogate parenting is a logical extension of the right to procreate, and accordingly, a part of the constitutional right of privacy. There are state interests and parties to be protected within the surrogate parenting arrangement, which necessitates state regulation of the surrogate parenting process. These restrictions, however, must be narrowly drawn to address the specific concerns of the state.

Recommendations

The fundamental issue considered in this report is whether the state should recognize the surrogate parenting contract as legal and enforceable and, thereby, ensure the legal status of the child. Based on the foregoing findings and analysis, the committee staff recommends that the legislature grant enforceability to surrogate parenting contracts and regulate the practice as set forth below.

THE ROLE OF THE COURTS

Judicial approval of the surrogate parenting agreement prior to insemination of the surrogate mother is the keystone of any legislation relating to the practice of surrogate parenting. For a contract to be enforceable, the parties should be required to apply to the Surrogate or Family Court, prior to insemination, to have the terms of the agreement reviewed and approved by the court.

Promoting the interests of the child

Recognition of the contract as legal and enforceable will ensure the legal status of the child born of a surrogate parenting arrangement for the purposes of determining parental responsibilities and rights of inheritance. If the state grants enforceability to the contract, it has an interest in determining before the agreement is concluded that the child will have a stable and suitable home. For this reason, legislation should authorize the court, at its discretion, to order an independent investigation prior to approval of the agreement. This investigation may include the following information:

(a) the marital and family status, as well as the history, of the intended parents;

(b) the physical and mental health of the intended parents;

(c) the property owned by and the income of the intended parents;

(d) whether either parent has ever been respondent in any proceedings concerning allegedly neglected, abandoned or delinquent children; and

(e) any other facts relating to the familial, social, emotional and financial circumstances of the intended parents which may be relevant to the judge's decision.

Ensuring informed consent

Parties to a surrogate parenting contract agree to acts that have irrevocable consequences and involve physical and psychological risks. Accordingly, the state has an interest in ensuring that the parties are fully aware of their rights and responsibilities under the agreement and have sufficient information to intelligently weigh the risks against the benefits. Informed consent will help to assure that the transfer of parental rights at birth does not produce disruptions in the home environment of the child.

Before approving the surrogate parenting contract, the court should determine the following:

(1) that a physician licensed by the state has examined the surrogate mother and advised her of the physical risks she may assume in the course of insemination, pregnancy, and delivery;

(2) that a licensed mental health professional[74] has determined that the surrogate and her husband, if any, are capable of consenting to the termination of their parental rights and have been counseled about the potential psychological consequences of their consent;

(3) that the surrogate's husband consents to the artificial insemination of the surrogate;

(4) that the surrogate mother and her husband agree to assume parental rights if it is later determined, on the basis of paternity tests, that the intended father named in the agreement is not the true biological father of the child;

(5) that a licensed mental health professional has counseled the intended parents and determined that they fully understand the consequences and responsibilities of surrogate parenting and are prepared to assume parental responsibilities for the child born to the surrogate, regardless of the condition of that child;

(6) that each of the parties has had the advice of independent legal counsel in negotiating the terms of the agreement.

Preventing exploitation

Legislation should allow payment of a reasonable fee to the surrogate mother. A prohibition of compensation would, as a practical matter, be a *de facto* prohibition of the practice itself. According to both hearing testimony and recent studies, most surrogate mothers would not participate in the arrangement without compensation.[75]

Payment of a fee to the surrogate mother does not fall within the scope of Section 374 of the Social Services Law. The prohibition is intended to prevent the coercion of women who are already pregnant or who have already given birth to the child. The surrogate mother arrangement is distinguishable, since the surrogate mother's agreement to relinquish her parental rights occurs prior to conception. In addition, payment is made, not by some third party, but by the biological father who then gains custody of the child. Since the surrogate parenting contract is an agreement between the natural parents of a child, it should be exempted from statutory prohibitions against payment of compensation in adoptions.

Fees paid to the surrogate mother, attorneys, and infertility centers should be subject to judicial approval. In reviewing surrogate parenting contracts, the court should apply a standard of "just and reasonable compensation" to determine that all fees and compensation are equitable, appropriate to the services rendered, and without coercive effect.

Provisional approval

The health and safety of both the child and the surrogate mother require that insemination be performed by a licensed physician and that tests for sexually transmitted diseases be completed before each insemination. For this reason, the court's approval of the contract should be provisional until the court receives a physician's certification that the natural father and the surrogate mother have been tested for sexually transmitted diseases, that the surrogate has been inseminated with the semen of the intended father, and that conception has occurred. The court's approval of the contract would then become final.

EFFECT OF COURT APPROVAL

The legislation should provide that any child born to a surrogate mother, in fulfillment of a contract approved by the court prior to insemination, shall be deemed the legitimate, natural child of the biological father and his wife. This statutory determination of parenthood would supplant any requirement that the wife of the natural father adopt the child. The intended father, named in the agreement, may rebut the statutory determination if paternity tests show conclusively that he is not biologically related to the child.

If either the natural father or his wife dies before the birth of the child, the terms of the contract should not be altered and the statutory determination of legal parenthood should remain in effect as to the survivor. If both intended parents die, the surrogate's consent to relinquish parental rights should be voidable at her option. If she elects to claim parental rights, the child would have inheritance rights from the natural father, but not from his wife. The intended parents should be encouraged to nominate a guardian for the child in the event they both die and the surrogate chooses not to claim parental rights.

CONTRACT ENFORCEMENT AND REMEDIES FOR BREACH

The surrogate mother's agreement to waive parental rights must be irrevocable and enforced at the birth of the child. Prior to delivery, the surrogate mother is deemed to have full control of the decisions relating to her pregnancy. Surrender of the child should be enforceable through the remedy of specific performance.

Parental obligations, such as support, should be enforceable against the intended parents from the time of conception. Breach of contract, e.g., refusal to accept parental responsibilities, should result in a judgment of support against the intended parents, since they will be the legal parents of the child by operation of the statute.

Breach of other provisions of the contract may be handled as the parties see fit in the terms of the contract. It is very important, however, that the monetary damages for breach of these provisions be limited to the amounts contained in the contract. No cause of action should be created for emotional distress or mental anguish due to the conduct of the parties during the contract period.

ELIGIBILITY

Surrogate parenting is the only solution to infertility for a couple when the woman cannot conceive or carry a child to term or would pass on a genetic defect. The same cannot be said for the use of a surrogate mother when the female of the couple is fertile. Although there are no documented cases of surrogacy for nonmedical reasons, the possibility exists that a couple may choose to employ a surrogate as a matter of convenience.

Given the scarcity of empirical evidence about how the surrogacy process affects those involved, it is recommended that the courts recognize only those contracts concluded between a surrogate mother and a couple, the female of whom is medically certified as infertile. Legislation should provide for a measure of proof by which medical necessity can be demonstrated to the court. The petition for court review of the contract should be accompanied by a statement signed by a licensed physician that the intended mother has a condition which makes conception or birth of a child unlikely or which creates a likelihood that a child of the intended mother will have a mental or physical impairment or disability.

CONCLUSION

Any surrogate parenting law must recognize the benefits the practice provides for infertile couples and resolve the present uncertainties regarding the legal status of the child. In order to ensure the smooth and peaceful transition of parental rights at birth, the law must ensure that all parties know, in advance, their rights and obligations under the agreement so that they may give informed consent to its provisions. In addition, the law must attempt to limit the possible abuses of the practice while preserving, to the greatest extent possible, the right of privacy in reproductive matters. It is submitted that the foregoing statutory recommendations meet these requirements.

NOTES

1. Aral and Cates, *The Increasing Concern with Infertility,* 250 J.A.M.A. 2327, 2327 (1986).

2. Center for Disease Control, *Infertility, United States, 1983,* 34 *Morbidity and Mortality Weekly Report* 197 (1985).

3. Ontario Law Reform Commission, *Report on Human Artificial Reproduction and Related Matters* 10-11 (1985).

4. Aral, *supra* note 1, at 2329.

5. *Id.* at 2330.

6. Menning, *The Emotional Needs of Infertile Couples,* 34 Fertility and Sterility 313, 314–315 (1980).

7. Robertson, *Embryos, Families and Procreative Liberty: The Legal Structure of the New Reproduction,* 59 S. Cal. L. Rev. 939, 945 (1986).

8. Grobstein, Flower, Mendeloff, *External Human Fertilization: An Evaluation of Policy,* 222 Sci. 127, 127 (1983).

9. *Id.*

10. National Committee for Adoption, *Adoption Factbook: United States Data, Issues, Regulations and Resources* 18–19 (1985).

11. *Id.* at 18.

12. *In Re Baby Girl L.J.* 123 Misc. 2d 972 (1986).

13. There is some indication that such long waiting periods can be shortened to as little as three to nine months when the adoption is arranged individually rather than through a public or private agency. According to the National Committee for Adoption, individually arranged adoptions are more likely now than they have been in the past fifteen to twenty years. Groups, such as the National Committee for Adoption, are concerned that quicker placements may be achieved by eliminating the safeguard procedures used by public and private agencies.

14. Grobstein, *supra* note 8, at 130.

15. Another form of surrogacy involves the surrogate gestational mother, who provides the gestational, but not the genetic, component of reproduction. The wife's egg is fertilized with her husband's sperm through *in vitro* fertilization, and the resulting pre-embryo is transferred to another woman who gestates and gives birth to the infant for the infertile couple. In these cases, the child is biologically related to both the husband and the wife, but not to the surrogate. This application of technology is indicated in cases where the wife has certain uterine problems, implantation difficulties, chronic miscarriage, or health problems that would make pregnancy harmful or lethal.

16. American Fertility Society, Ethics Committee, *Ethical Considerations of the New Reproductive Technologies,* 46 Fertility and Sterility, Supplement 1, 1s, 64s (1986).

17. Parker, *Motivation of Surrogate Mothers: Initial Findings,* 140 Am. J. Psychiatry 117, 118 (1983).

18. American Fertility Society, *supra* note 16, at 64s.

19. *New York Times,* Nov. 20, 1983, at 18.

20. The following fee structure is common: $6,500 to $10,000 for the infertility center, $10,000 for the surrogate mother, all medical expenses not covered by a surrogate's health insurance, $300 for psychiatric evaluation of the surrogate, travel expenses for the surrogate, term life insurance for the surrogate, $400 for an attorney for the surrogate, $400 for maternity clothes, $500 for paternity tests, and $500 in attorney's fees for the adoption.

21. Brophy, *A Surrogate Mother Contracts to Bear a Child,* 20 J. Fam. L. 263, 264 (1981-82).

22. Florida Step-Parent Adoption Act, F.S. Sec. 63.04 (2) (d).

23. Katz, *Surrogate Motherhood and the Baby-Selling Laws,* 20 Colum. J. L. & Soc. Prob. 1, 8 (1986).

24. Brophy, *supra* note 21, at 264.

...

56. Graham, *Surrogate Gestation and the Protection of Choice,* 22 Santa Clara L. Rev. 291, 318 (1982).

57. Ontario Law Reform Commission, *supra* note 3 at 103.

58. *Griswold v. Connecticut,* 381 U.S. 479 (1965), in which the court struck down a statute making it a crime for a married couple to use contraceptives.

59. *Roe v. Wade,* 410 U.S. 113, 152 (1973). (A Texas statute which outlawed abortions was found unconstitutional as it related to abortions performed throughout the entire term of pregnancy.)

60. *Ibid.,* at 159.

61. 316 U.S. 535 (1942).
62. *Ibid.*, 536.
63. *Maher v. Roe*, 432 U.S. 464, 472 (1977), citing *Skinner v. Oklahoma*, at 541.
64. 405 U.S. 438 (1972).
65. *Ibid.*, at 453.
66. 431 U.S. 678 (1977).
67. *Ibid.*, at 678.
68. *Harris v. McRae*, 448 U.S. 297, 325 (1980).
69. *Griswold v. Connecticut, Roe v. Wade, supra.*
70. *Carey v. Population Services, Inc., Id.* at 683.
71. *Carey, Id.* at 683.
72. *Supra* 432 U.S. 464.
73. *Ibid.*, at 474.
74. A mental health professional may be a psychiatrist, psychologist, clinical social worker, or a marriage, family, and child counselor.
75. Parker, *supra* note 17, at 118.

Surrogate Parenting in New York—II

New York State Task Force on Life and the Law

[The report excerpted below was released on May 28, 1988 by a twenty-nine-member task force appointed by Governor Mario M. Cuomo. During the same week, Assemblywoman Helene Weinstein introduced legislation to enact most of the task force's recommendations. The recommendations were still under consideration in the legislature in the spring of 1989.]

Executive Summary

PART I: THE MEDICAL, LEGAL AND SOCIAL CONTEXT

Surrogate parenting is not a technology, but a social arrangement that uses reproductive technology (usually artificial insemination) to enable one woman to produce a child for a man and, if he is married, for his wife. Surrogate parenting is characterized by the intention to separate the genetic and/or gestational aspects of child bearing from parental rights and responsibilities through an agreement to transfer the infant and all maternal rights at birth.

The well-publicized Baby M case has given surrogate parenting a prominent place on the public agenda. Nonetheless, the reproductive technologies used in the arrangements—artificial insemination and, increasingly, in vitro fertilization—also pose profound questions about the ethical, social and biological bases of parenthood. In addition, the procedures to screen donors raise important public health concerns. The Task Force will address these issues in its ongoing deliberations and recognizes that they form part of the context within which surrogate parenting must be considered.

Legal questions about surrogate parenting, although novel in many respects, arise within the framework of a well-developed body of New York family law. In particular, policies about surrogate parenting will necessarily focus upon two basic concerns in all matters involving the care and custody of children—the protection of the fundamental right of a parent to rear his or her child and the promotion of the child's best interests.

The Supreme Court of New Jersey has ruled that paying a surrogate violates state laws against baby selling. Surrogacy agreements may also be found invalid because they conflict with comprehensive statutory schemes that govern private adoption and the termination of parental rights.

In New York, it is uncertain whether surrogate parenting contracts are barred by the statute that prohibits payments for adoption. If not, it is probable that the

From *Surrogate Parenting: Analysis and Recommendations for Public Policy*, by the New York State Task Force on Life and the Law, May 1988.

surrogate could transfer the child to the intended parents by following private adoption procedures. If a dispute about parental rights arises before the surrogate consents to the child's adoption, custody would probably be determined based on the child's best interests. Regardless of the outcome, the court ordinarily will have no basis for terminating the parental status of either the surrogate or the intended father.

The right to enter into and enforce surrogate parenting arrangements is not protected as part of the constitutional right to privacy. Surrogate parenting involves social and contractual—rather than individual—decisions and arrangements that may place the rights and interests of several individuals in direct conflict. The commercial aspects of surrogate parenting also distinguish the practice from other constitutionally protected private acts. Constitutional protection for the right to privacy is diminished when the conduct involved assumes a commercial character.

The social and moral issues posed by surrogate parenting touch upon five central concerns: (i) individual access and social responsibility in the face of new reproductive possibilities; (ii) the interests of children; (iii) the impact of the practice on family life and relationships; (iv) attitudes about reproduction and women; and (v) application of the informed consent doctrine.

Surrogate parenting has been the subject of extensive scrutiny by public and private groups, including governmental bodies in the United States and abroad, religious communities, professional organizations, women's rights organizations and groups that advocate on behalf of children and infertile couples. Of the governmental commissions that have studied the issue, many concluded that surrogate parenting is unacceptable. In this country, six states have enacted laws on surrogate parenting, four of which declare surrogate contracts void and unenforceable as against public policy.

PART II: DELIBERATIONS AND RECOMMENDATIONS OF THE TASK FORCE

As evidenced by the large body of statutory law on custody and adoption, society has a basic interest in protecting the best interests of children and in shielding gestation and reproduction from the flow of commerce.

When surrogate parenting involves the payment of fees and a contractual obligation to relinquish the child at birth, it places children at risk and is not in their best interests. The practice also has the potential to undermine the dignity of women, children and human reproduction.

Surrogate parenting alters deep-rooted social and moral assumptions about the relationship between parents and their children. The practice involves unprecedented rules and standards for terminating parental obligations and rights, including the right to a relationship with one's own child. The assumption that "a deal is a deal," relied upon to justify this drastic change in public policy, fails to respect the significance of the relationships and rights at stake.

Advances in genetic engineering and the cloning and freezing of gametes may soon offer an array of new social options and potential commercial opportunities. An arrangement that transforms human reproductive capacity into a commodity is therefore especially problematic at the present time.

Public policy should discourage surrogate parenting. This goal should be achieved through legislation that declares the contracts void as against public policy. In addition, legislation should prohibit fees for surrogates and bar surrogate brokers from operating in New York State. These measures are designed to eliminate commercial surrogacy and the growth of a business community or industry devoted to making money from human reproduction and the birth of children.

The legislation proposed by the Task Force would not prohibit surrogate parenting arrangements when they are not commercial and remain undisputed. Existing law permits each stage of the arrangement under these circumstances: a decision by a woman to be artificially inseminated or to have an embryo implanted; her voluntary decision after the child's birth to relinquish the child for adoption; and the child's adoption by the intended parents.

Under existing law on adoption, the intended parents would be permitted to pay reasonable expenses associated with pregnancy and childbirth to a mother who relinquishes her child for adoption. All such expenses must be approved by a court as part of an adoption proceeding.

In custody disputes arising from surrogate parenting arrangements, the birth mother and her husband, if any, should be awarded custody unless the court finds, based on clear and convincing evidence, that the child's best interests would be served by an award of custody to the father and/or genetic mother. The court should award visitation and support obligations as it would under existing law in proceedings on these matters.

To date, few programs have been conducted by the public or the private sector to prevent infertility. Programs to educate the public and health care professionals about the causes of infertility and the measures available for early detection and treatment could spare many couples from facing the problem. Both the government and the medical community should establish educational and other programs to prevent infertility. Resources should also be devoted to research about the causes and nature of infertility. . . .

Devising Public Policy on Surrogate Parenting

THE FRAMEWORK FOR PUBLIC POLICY

Contemporary American society is characterized by its pluralism. That pluralism embraces the rich and varied threads of different religious, moral and ethnic traditions. It requires a continued effort to express one's own world view and to understand those of others.

One hallmark of a pluralistic society is its commitment to individual freedom and to the right of individuals to choose their own path among the many different traditions and values that make up our social fabric. In particular, certain freedoms considered basic to the expression of personal identity and selfhood are accorded special deference. In the framework of our Constitution, this deference is shown by requiring government neutrality or non-interference with rights deemed fundamental, unless government can show a compelling interest.

Our social policies and law, however, reflect more than the celebration of individual liberty. A broad if seldom articulated consensus of shared values shapes and enriches our common experience. We therefore acknowledge society's interest in protecting and promoting those social values and institutions it deems primary to its collective life. The issue of surrogate parenting confronts society with the need to weigh the competing claims of individuals involved in the arrangements and to strike an appropriate balance between the individual's freedom to make reproductive choices and other social and moral values.

Decisions about family life and reproduction are intensely private. The rights of adults to make reproductive choices have therefore been granted special protection and status.

Proponents of surrogate parenting assert that the right to enter into such an arrangement is part of the fundamental right to reproduce. They maintain that there is no conclusive or compelling evidence that surrogacy causes tangible harm to individuals. They argue that, without such evidence, society lacks any legitimate basis for intervention. In assessing what constitutes "tangible" harm, proponents dismiss appeals to shared norms and values as vague or symbolic, and hence inappropriate as the basis for public policy. Finally, proponents suggest that pluralism is best promoted by safeguarding and extending the rights of individuals.

The Task Force does not accept these assumptions as the basis for public policy for surrogate parenting. The surrogate contract is not part of a fundamental right supported on constitutional grounds or defensible as a basic moral entitlement. The claims of surrogates and intended parents to reproductive freedom in the context of surrogate arrangements are attenuated in several ways: by the commercial nature of the arrangements; by the potential conflicts between the rights of parties to the surrogate contract; and by the risks of harm to other individuals.

Many individual rights, like freedom of speech or the right of consenting adults to engage in sexual relations, are constrained when they enter the stream of commerce. They lose their strictly private or privileged stature and the claim they exert on society to non-interference and deference. The same holds true for the decision to conceive and bear a child. Society protects that choice when made privately and without financial incentives. Consistent with that protection, society is free to deny women the opportunity to make money from their gestational capacity and to deny others the right to pay someone else to reproduce.

Unlike privacy protections guaranteed to single individuals, surrogate parenting contracts involve potentially conflicting claims between individuals. These potential conflicts may place the surrogate's right to bodily integrity in conflict with a contractual obligation to submit to invasive medical procedures. Most obviously, the surrogate and the intended parents may have competing and irreconcilable claims to parental status and rights. The Task Force concluded that surrogate parenting arrangements also carry the risk of harm to others. Most serious are the potential risks to the children born from such arrangements. Members of the surrogate's family, including the surrogate's other children, might also be harmed.

Once it is recognized that surrogacy is outside the scope of the basic right to reproduce, the arguments by the proponents of surrogacy lose much of their force. Since the right to enter into a surrogate contract is not a fundamental right, society has no obligation to marshall evidence of tangible harm before devising policy on surrogate parenting arrangements. Proponents of surrogacy correctly point out that the risks to children or to the surrogates are unproven—no empirical data exists to confirm these predictions because the practice is so novel. Nonetheless, society can conclude that the potential or likely risks of a practice outweigh the benefits conferred without awaiting broad-scale social experimentation.

Moreover, surrogate parenting touches upon basic values and relationships in our private and collective lives: the interests of children, the role of the family, attitudes about women, and the potential commercialization of human reproduction. Society need not cast aside widely held norms or values about these issues in formulating public policy on surrogate parenting. As long as fundamental rights are not infringed, society can promote and protect a broadly shared vision of the public good. Indeed, our existing laws relating to such areas as the family, medical treatment and criminal sanctions, embody shared social values. Through these laws, society establishes a widely accepted framework within which individuals pursue a more particularized vision of the goods of life.

When no fundamental right exists, the possibilities for government intervention are broad. However, the possibility of such intervention does not render it desirable. Indeed, some strongly favor governmental neutrality on all issues when harm to individuals cannot be demonstrated. Under liberal political theory, this neutrality is viewed as the best assurance that individuals will be unhindered in pursuing their own moral choices.

Yet, even if society wished to adopt a neutral stance with regard to all social policies, it is clear that "neutral" alternatives for policy on surrogate parenting cannot be fashioned. Legislation that upholds the contracts lends the authority of both the courts and the legislature to enforce the agreements. Alternatively, legislation to void the contracts and withdraw the state's active involvement from the arrangements also cannot be considered neutral. Finally, government inaction, while neutral in theory, is not neutral in practice. When disputes arise, the parties will seek relief from the courts, forcing the articulation of public policy on a case-by-case basis. More significantly, however, the practice will proliferate through the existing commercial channels that have sprung up to promote it. The vacuum left by the absence of publicly articulated goals and values will be filled by the practices and mores of the marketplace. The result will not be neutral in any sense nor will the impact be limited to the commercial sector. Instead, the attitudes and practices that guide our most private relationships will be refashioned by commercial standards.

Society has a basic interest in protecting the best interests of children and in shielding gestation and reproduction from the flow of commerce, as evidenced by the large body of statutory law on custody and adoption. A "neutrality" that would leave such fundamental goods vulnerable to the dictates of the marketplace is contrary to the public interest.

AN ASSESSMENT: THE SOCIAL AND MORAL DIMENSIONS OF SURROGACY

The Task Force deliberated at length about the social, moral and legal issues posed by surrogate parenting. Its members began the deliberations with a wide diversity of opinion.

Ultimately, they reached a unanimous decision that public policy should discourage surrogate parenting. Divergent and sometimes competing visions form the basis for this conclusion. Their judgments are informed by different values, concerns and beliefs. The unanimous support for the conclusion reached is no less remarkable because of the diversity of opinion that underlies it.

The Task Force members share several basic conclusions about surrogate parenting. First, when surrogate parenting involves the payment of fees and a contractual obligation to relinquish the child at birth, it places children at risk and is not in their best interests. Second, the practice has the potential to undermine the dignity of women, children and human reproduction. Many Task Force members also believe that commercial surrogate parenting arrangements will erode the integrity of the family unit and values fundamental to the bond between parents and children.

The Task Force concluded that state enforcement of the contracts and the commercial aspects of surrogate parenting pose the greatest potential for harm to individuals and to social attitudes and practices. The conclusions and concerns expressed below relate primarily to these two aspects of surrogacy.

The Interests of Children

The Sale of Babies. Many Task Force members view surrogate parenting as indistinguishable from the sale of children. They reject the practice as morally and socially unacceptable because it violates the dignity of children and the societal prohibition against the purchase and sale of human beings. That prohibition rests on basic premises about the nature and meaning of being human and the moral dictates of our shared humanity. One such premise is respect for the inherent dignity and equality of all persons. Allowing one person to purchase another contravenes this premise and should be rejected regardless of the intentions or motivations of those involved.

The fact that it is the child's father who purchases the child from the child's mother (or, at the least, purchases her right to have a relationship with her child) does not change the character of the arrangement. Euphemisms like "womb rental" or "the provision of services," developed in part as marketing techniques, disserve the public by seeking to obscure the nature of the transaction. The intended parents do not seek a pregnancy or services as the ultimate object of the arrangement; they seek the product of those "services"—the child.

The surrogacy contracts themselves make this intent unmistakably clear. For example, the contract between Mary Beth Whitehead and the Sterns specified that the Infertility Center would hold $10,000 in escrow for Mary Beth Whitehead. If Mary Beth Whitehead had suffered a miscarriage prior to the fifth month of pregnancy, she would not have received any money under the contract. If she had a miscarriage subsequent to the fourth month of pregnancy or if the child died or was stillborn, her compensation would have been $1,000, an amount completely unrelated to the "services" performed. Likewise, if testing indicated that the fetus had genetic or congenital anomalies and Mary Beth Whitehead had refused to have an abortion and had carried the child to term, she would have received little or no compensation. Finally, all doubt about the nature of the contract is removed by virtue of the fact that Mary Beth Whitehead was not entitled to any compensation for her "services" alone; she was only entitled to compensation if she surrendered the product of those services—the child.

The Risks Posed. The Task Force concluded that surrogate parenting presents unacceptable risks to children. First, the fact that the practice condones the sale of children has severe long-term implications for the way society thinks about and values children. This shift in attitudes will inevitably influence behavior towards children and will create the potential for serious harm.

Surrogacy also poses more immediate risks to children. Under the arrangement, children are born into situations where their genetic, gestational and social relationships to their parents are irrevocably fractured. A child may have as many as five parents, or, frequently, will have at least four—the mother and her husband and the father and his wife. Where the birth mother has no genetic link to the child, the child has two mothers.

In contemporary family life, many children are denied the benefit of an ongoing relationship with both their biological parents. High divorce rates and the growing number of unwed mothers leave many children with a close connection to only one parent. When remarriage occurs, children are raised in a reconstituted family unit that does not share the bonds of genetic relationship. The same has always been true for children relinquished at birth or thereafter and raised by adoptive parents. Although some children thrive in these situations, others face greater risk of emotional harm or loss.

Unlike divorce or adoption, however, surrogate parenting is based on a deliberate decision to fracture the family relationship prior to the child's conception. Once parenthood is fragmented among persons who are strangers to one another, there is no basis to reconstruct the family unit or even to cope with alternative arrangements in the event conflict arises.

A child may be caught in the cross-fire of a fractious and lengthy court battle between his or her parents during the early years of the child's life, when stability and constant nurturing are vital. Alternatively, where the bonds of kinship are attenuated, children who are born with physical or mental anomalies are far more likely to be abandoned by both parents. Potentially, neither parent will have a bond with the child at birth; the mother because she successfully preserved her emotional distance and the father because he has not shared the pregnancy and has no relationship to the child's mother. While legislation or contractual agreements can apportion financial responsibility, they cannot compensate for the high risk of emotional and physical abandonment these children might face. Other potential dangers for children include the harm from knowing their mothers gave them away and the impact on brothers and sisters of seeing a sibling sold or surrendered.

Advocates of surrogate parenting suggest that any risks to children are outweighed by the opportunity for life itself—they point out that the children always benefit since they would not have been born without the practice. But this argument assumes the very factor under deliberation—the child's conception and birth. The assessment for public policy occurs prior to conception when the surrogate arrangements are made. The issue then is not whether a particular child should be denied life, but whether children should be conceived in circumstances that would place them at risk. The notion that children have an interest in being born prior to their conception and birth is not embraced in other public policies and should not be assumed in the debate on surrogate parenting.

The Dignity of Women and Human Reproduction

The gestation of children as a service for others in exchange for a fee is a radical departure from the way in which society understands and values pregnancy. It substitutes commercial values for the web of social, affective and moral meanings associated with human reproduction and gestation. This transformation has profound implications for childbearing, for women, and for the relationship between parents and the children they bring into the world.

The characterization of gestation as a "service" depersonalizes women and their role in human reproduction. It treats women's ability to carry children like any other service in the marketplace—available at a market rate, based on negotiation between the parties about issues such as price, prenatal care, medical testing, the decision to abort and the circumstances of delivery. All those decisions and the right to control them as well as the process of gestation itself are given a price tag—not just for women who serve as surrogates, but for all women.

The Task Force concluded that this assignment of market values should not be celebrated as an exaltation of "rights," but rejected as a derogation of the values and meanings associated with human reproduction. Those meanings are derived from the relationship between the mother and father of a child and the child's creation as an expression of their mutual love. Likewise, the meaning of gestation is inextricably bound up with the love and commitment a woman feels for the child she will bring into the world.

In a surrogate arrangement, the intended parents seek a child as a way to deepen their own relationship and to establish a loving bond with another human being. In the process, however, the birth mother uses the child as a souce of income and, in turn, is used by the intended parents as a vehicle to serve their own ends. They seek the biological components of gestation from her while denying the personal, emotional and psychological dimensions of her experience and self. If she succeeds in denying her emotional responses during this profound experience, she is dehumanized in the process. If she fails, her attachment to the child produces a conflict that cannot be resolved without anguish for all involved.

Proponents of surrogate parenting urge that neither the surrogate nor the intended parents should be denied their right to choose the arrangement as an extension of their claim to reproductive freedom. Yet protection for the right to reproduce has always been grounded in society's notions of bodily integrity and privacy. Those notions are strained beyond credibility when the intimate use of a third person's body in exchange for monetary compensation is involved.

Women who wish to serve as surrogates would not be limited in their private choices to conceive and bear children—they would only be denied the opportunity to make money from their gestational capacity. Some Task Force members believe that this limitation is justified by the possibility of exploitation, especially in relation to poor women inside and outside of this country. They fear the creation of a class of women who will become breeders for those who are wealthier.

Other Task Force members concluded that the risk of exploitation could be minimized, but remained concerned about the potential loss to society. They believe that societal attitudes will shift as gestation joins other services in the commercial sphere; the contribution and role of women in the reproductive process will be devalued. Abstracted from the family relationships, obligations and caring that infuse them with meaning, gestation and human reproduction will be seen as commodities. Advances in genetic engineering and the cloning and freezing of gametes may soon offer an array of new social options and potential commercial opportunities. An arrangement that transforms human reproductive capacity into a commodity is therefore especially problematic at the present time.

The Family

The Family Unit. The family has long been one of the most basic units of our society—a repository of social and moral tradition, identity and personality. It provides the structure and continuity around which many of our most profound and important relationships are established and flourish.

Social and economic forces have challenged the traditional family unit. At the same time, high divorce rates and the incidence of unwed parents have changed the permanence of the family in the lives of many. Yet, these trends do not alter the importance of the family in our personal and communal lives.

Surrogate parenting allows the genetic, gestational and social components of parenthood to be fragmented, creating unprecedented relationships among people bound together by contractual obligation rather than by the bonds of kinship and caring. In this regard, surrogate parenting, like prenuptial agreements, has been viewed as an extension of a more general social movement from status (or kinship) to contract as a basis for ordering family relationships and the reproductive process.

Although some individuals now choose to shape aspects of their personal relationships with the principles and tools of contract law, society should not embrace this trend as a prescriptive standard. It embodies a deeply pessimistic vision of the potential for human relationships and intimacy in contemporary society. It promotes legal obligations as the touchstone for our most private relationships instead of fostering commitments forged by caring and trust. Rather than accept this contractual model as a basis for family life and other close personal relationships, society should discourage the commercialization of our private lives and create the conditions under which the human dimensions of our most intimate relationships can thrive.

The Relationship of Parent and Child. Surrogate parenting alters deep-rooted social and moral assumptions about the relationship between parents and children. Parents have a profound moral obligation to care for their offspring. Our legal and social norms affirm this obligation by requiring parents to care for their children's physical and emotional well-being.

Surrogate parenting is premised on the ability and willingness of women to abrogate this responsibility without moral compunction or regret. It makes the obligations that accompany parenthood alienable and negotiable.

Many of the Task Force members concluded that society should not promote this parental abdication or the ability of some women to overcome the impulse to nurture their children. Some Task Force members reject all third party donation to the reproductive process because it encourages adults to relinquish responsibility for biological offspring. Other Task Force members distinguish surrogacy from gamete donation because of the surrogate's direct and prolonged relationship to the child she bears.

Surrogate parenting also severs the second prong of the legal relationship that binds parents and children—parental rights. In fact, the practice involves unprecedented rules and standards for terminating both parental status and rights, including the right to a relationship with one's own child. Under existing law, parental rights cannot be denied without a showing of parental unfitness. This high standard embodies society's respect for the rights that flow from parenthood and the relationship those rights seek to protect.

Surrogate parenting rejects that standard in favor of a contract model for determining parental rights. Many Task Force members view this shift as morally and socially unacceptable. The assumption that "a deal is a deal," relied upon to justify this drastic change in public policy, fails to recognize and respect the significance of the relationships and rights at stake.

The Relationship Between the Spouses. Some Task Force members reject surrogate parenting and all third party donation to the reproductive process because they violate the unity and exclusivity of the relationship and commitment between the spouses. According to this view, procreation reflects the spiritual and biological union of two people; children born of that union manifest the uniqueness of the marital relationship. The involvement of a third person as surrogate or as gamete donor contravenes the spiritual and human values expressed in marriage and in the procreative process.

Some Task Force members also believe that an imbalance may be created in the marital relationship when only one parent is genetically related to the child. This imbalance may generate tension in the family unit rather than enrich the relationship between the spouses.

The Waiver of Fundamental Rights

Under the laws of New York and other states, parental rights and status cannot be irrevocably waived in advance of the time the rights will be exercised. By placing these rights as well as others beyond the reach of an advance agreement that is legally enforceable, society seeks to preserve those rights and the values they embody.

Many Task Force members believe that parental rights, including the right to a relationship with one's own child, deserve this special status. They do not view this as a limitation of individual freedom, but as a societal judgment about how that freedom is best protected.

The Task Force's proposal is consistent with existing adoption laws, which provide that a woman cannot consent to her child's adoption until after the child is born. Surrogate parenting should not be allowed to dislodge this long-standing public policy.

Informed Consent

Many of the Task Force members support the nonenforceability of surrogate contracts, in part because they believe that it is not possible for women to give informed consent to the surrender of a child prior to the child's conception and birth. Some commentators have argued that this conclusion diminishes women's stature as autonomous adults. The Task Force members reject that assertion.

The debate on surrogate parenting focuses on the ability of women to make informed choices—not because women differ from men in making important life decisions, but because women alone can bear children. The inability to predict and project a response to profound experiences that have not yet unfolded is shared by men and women alike. This inability often stems from the capacity for growth and an openness to experience in our relationships with others. These qualities are a positive and dynamic part of our humanness.

Denying women the opportunity to change their minds does not accord them respect; it limits their options and freedoms. Other avenues exist to inform or influence social attitudes about women. These avenues can be explored without penalizing women by demanding a degree of certainty and irrevocability we do not demand of men or women in making other vital life choices.

Many Task Force members believe that enforced removal of a child from the child's birth mother under a surrogate contract involves severe consequences for the birth mother. Studies have shown that many women who voluntarily relinquish children for adoption face a lingering and deep sense of loss. The harsh consequences of a poorly informed decision to relinquish one's child require a rigorous standard for consent before consent should be considered truly informed. This is why the adoption laws do not permit an expectant mother to surrender her child for adoption and insist that she await the child's birth before making such a decision. While some women have been able to anticipate their response in advance of the child's conception, the long gestational process and the child's birth, others have not. Our policies must recognize that many women may not be able to give informed consent in these circumstances.

RECOMMENDATIONS FOR PUBLIC POLICY

At the outset of its discussion about surrogate parenting, the Task Force recognized that society could choose any one of five broad directions for public policy, subject to constitutional constraints that might apply. Essentially, society could seek to prohibit, discourage, regulate or promote the practice or could take no action.

The Task Force proposes that society should discourage the practice of surrogate parenting. This policy goal should be achieved by legislation that declares the contracts void as against public policy and prohibits the payment of fees to surrogates. Legislation should also bar surrogate brokers from operating in New York State. These measures are designed to eliminate commercial surrogacy and the growth of a business community or industry devoted to making money from human reproduction and the birth of children. They are consistent with existing family law principles on parental rights and reproduction.

The Task Force proposes that surrogate parenting should not be prohibited when the arrangement is not commercial and remains undisputed. The Task Force concluded that society should not interfere with the voluntary, non-coerced choices of adults in these circumstances. Existing law permits each stage of these voluntary arrangements: a decision by a woman to be artificially inseminated or to have an embryo implanted; her decision after the child's birth to relinquish the child for adoption; and the child's adoption by the intended parents. The proposed legislation would also not bar the payment of reasonable medical and other expenses to surrogates, if the payment is made as part of an adoption and is permitted by existing law.

The Task Force evaluated and rejected the option of upholding the contracts under the regulatory models proposed in many states. This regulatory approach squarely places the state's imprimatur on the surrogate arrangement. It employs the authority of both the legislature and the courts to uphold the contracts. Through these two powerful branches of government, society would be enmeshed in a long series of dilemmas and problems posed by the practice.

The regulatory approach has been justified and supported as the only way to protect the children born of surrogate parenting. The practice is seen as a trend that cannot be inhibited given the existence of the underlying technologies and the intense desire of infertile couples to have children, a desire that now fuels a growing black market in the sale of children. According to this view, regulation does not facilitate surrogacy, but merely accepts and guides its inevitable proliferation.

The Task Force found this justification for regulating and upholding the practice unpersuasive. The difficulty of discouraging a practice does not dictate social acceptance and assistance. Society has not legalized the purchase and sale of babies to establish a better marketplace for that activity despite the fact that both the children and intended parents might be better protected. The laws against baby selling embody fundamental societal values and doubtlessly minimize the practice even if they do not eliminate it.

Public policy on surrogate parenting should also reflect basic social and moral values about the interests of children, the role of the family, women and reproduction. A commitment by society to uphold the contracts removes the single greatest barrier to those considering the practice. In contrast, voiding the contracts, banning fees, and prohibiting brokering activity will drastically reduce the number of persons who seek a commercial surrogate arrangement. Given the potential risks to the children born of surrogacy, children are best served by policies designed to discourage the practice.

The Task Force members feel deep sympathy for infertile couples, many of whom experience a profound sense of loss and trauma. Nevertheless, the Task Force concluded that society should not support surrogacy as a solution. The practice will generate other social problems and harm that reach beyond the infertile couples who seek a surrogate arrangement.

While treatment is increasingly sought by and available to infertile couples, few initiatives to prevent infertility have been taken by the public or the private sector. The Task Force recommends that measures should be undertaken to reduce the incidence of infertility through public education and public support for research about its causes. Broader awareness among health care professionals and members of the public about the causes of infertility, especially infertility related to sexually transmitted diseases, could prevent some couples from ever facing the problem. Other couples would benefit from an increased understanding of the causes of infertility and new treatments for it.

Appendix

Proposed Surrogate Parenting Act

1. Definitions

(a) *Birth mother* shall mean a woman who gives birth to a child pursuant to a surrogate parenting contract.

(b) *Genetic father* shall mean a man who, by virtue of his provision of sperm, is the father of a child born pursuant to a surrogate parenting contract.

(c) *Genetic mother* shall mean a woman who, by virtue of her provision of an ovum, is the mother of a child born pursuant to a surrogate parenting contract.

(d) *Surrogate parenting contract* shall mean any agreement, oral or written, whereby a woman agrees either:

> (i) to be inseminated with the sperm of a man who is not her husband; or
>
> (ii) to be impregnated with an embryo that is the product of an ovum fertilized with the sperm of a man who is not her husband,

and to surrender the child.

2. PUBLIC POLICY

Surrogate parenting contracts are hereby declared contrary to the public policy of the State of New York and are void and unenforceable.

3. COMMERCIAL SURROGACY PROHIBITED

(a) No agency, association, corporation, institution, society, organization, or person shall request, accept or receive any compensation or thing of value, directly or indirectly, in connection with any surrogate parenting contract; and no person shall pay or give to any person or to any agency, association, corporation, institution, society or organization any compensation or thing of value in connection with any surrogate parenting contract.

(b) This subdivision shall not be construed to prevent a person or other entity from accepting, receiving, paying or giving money or other consideration

> (i) in connection with the adoption of a child provided such acceptance or payment is also permitted by section 374.6 of the Social Services Law and paid pursuant to section 115.7 of the Domestic Relations Law; or
>
> (ii) to a physician for reasonable medical expenses for artificial insemination or in vitro fertilization.

(c) Any person or entity who or which violates the provisions of this subdivision shall be guilty of a misdemeanor for the first such offense. Any person or entity who or which violates the provisions of this subdivision, after having been once convicted of violating such provisions, shall be guilty of a felony. . . .

Comment

The authors of both proposals agree that governments must not restrict the basic liberties of citizens, but they disagree about whether the capacity to enter into a surrogate parenting contract constitutes a basic liberty. Analyze the grounds on which the Judiciary Committee staff concludes that the use of commercial surrogacy falls within the sphere of basic liberties. The Task Force argues that "the claims of surrogates and intended parents to reproductive freedom . . . are attenuated in several ways: by the commercial nature of the arrangements; by the potential conflicts between the rights of parties to the surrogate contract; and by the risks of harm to other individuals." Each of these considerations should be weighed against the claims of reproductive freedom.

First, consider the argument that the right to reproductive freedom is constrained when reproduction becomes commercialized. Many critics agree with the state senator from Michigan who has called surrogate parenting "baby-selling, pure and simple." Yet some surrogate mothers claim that their reasons for bearing a child are not purely or primarily financial but also benevolent. Why should the fact that a woman is paid to bear a child affect her freedom to enter into a surrogacy arrangement? Is the payment for surrogacy morally different from the payment for legal adoption? Some advocates of surrogacy argue that rather than degrading poor women, surrogacy can make them better off; prohibiting commercial surrogacy denies poor women the opportunity to earn money for an otherwise legal service. Do you agree? Assess the strongest argument against your conclusion.

Second, examine the potential conflicts among the parties to a surrogacy contract. To what extent can the conflicting claims of the surrogate mother and the intended parents be avoided by designing a contract that conforms to the standards of informed consent? The Task Force suggests that due to the very nature of pregnancy and childbirth, women cannot give knowing and informed consent to relinquish a child before birth. Yet the Judiciary Committee staff outlines a series of measures designed to ensure that all parties "are fully aware of their rights and responsibilities under the agreement and have sufficient information to intelligently weigh the risks against the benefits." Are these measures sufficient to ensure informed consent? Necessary? Try to devise other measures that might better satisfy the standard of informed consent. Why is it important that the standard be satisfied before enforcing a contract?

Third, analyze the risks of harm to the individuals affected by surrogacy arrangements. Should a state weigh the risks of harm to the adult parties as heavily as the risks to the children born as a result of surrogacy contracts (and other children affected by such contracts)? In assessing the effects on children, the Judiciary Committee staff emphasizes the value of bringing into the world desperately wanted children who would otherwise not have been conceived. The Task Force focuses on the potential harm caused by the commercialization of child bearing, not only on those children, but also on other children, women, and families. Is there a way of reconciling these perspectives or deciding between them?

Recommended Reading

Most of the philosophical literature on abortion focuses on the personal morality of abortion. A good place to start is a widely discussed article by Judith Jarvis Thomson, "A Defense of Abortion," in Marshall Cohen et al. (eds.), *The Rights and Wrongs of Abortion* (Princeton, N.J.: Princeton University Press, 1974), pp. 3–22. John Finnis, "The Rights and Wrongs of Abortion," in *The Rights and Wrongs of Abortion,* pp. 85–113, takes issue with Thomson's qualified defense of abortion. See also Steven L. Ross, "Abortion and the Death of the Fetus," *Philosophy & Public Affairs,* 11 (Summer 1982), pp. 232–45; and L. W. Sumner, *Abortion and Moral Theory* (Princeton, N.J.: Princeton University Press, 1981).

On the question of what the government's position on abortion should be, see Roger Wertheimer, "Understanding the Abortion Argument," in *The Rights and Wrongs of Abortion,* pp. 23–51; and George Sher, "Subsidized Abortion," *Philosophy & Public Affairs,* 10 (Fall 1981), pp. 361–72. A utilitarian case in favor of legalizing abortion and a critique of other approaches is in Jonathan Glover, *Causing Death and Saving Lives* (New York: Penguin Books, 1977), chapters 4, 9–11. Considerations favoring political compromise are highlighted in Mary Ann Glendon, *Abortion and Divorce in Western Law: American Failures, European Challenges* (Cambridge, Mass.: Harvard University Press, 1987).

Philip Abbott criticizes the way philosophers have treated the abortion issue in "Philosophers and the Abortion Question," *Political Theory,* 6 (Aug. 1978), pp. 313–36. Roger Wertheimer, "Errata: A Reply to Abbott," *Political Theory,* 6 (Aug. 1978), pp. 337–44, responds. In light of this debate, Amy Gutmann examines what moral philosophy can contribute to resolving political problems such as abortion in "Moral Philosophy and Political Problems," *Political Theory,* 10 (Feb. 1982), pp. 33–48.

Most of the literature on surrogacy focuses on the legal issues. For an excellent overview of these questions, see Martha A. Field, *Surrogate Motherhood* (Cambridge, Mass.: Harvard University Press, 1988). For a philosophical argument against commercial surrogacy, see Elizabeth Anderson, "Is Women's Labor a Commodity? The Case Against Surrogate Motherhood," *Philosophy & Public Affairs,* 18 (Fall 1989). Also, see Margaret Jane Radin, "Market Inalienability," *Harvard Law Review,* 100 (June 1987), pp. 1849–1937; and Joan Heifetz Hollinger, "From Coitus to Commerce: Legal and Social Consequences of Noncoital Reproduction," *Journal of Law Reform,* 18 (Summer 1985), pp. 865–932. For a critical examination of competing standards for determining the best interests of children of relevance to commercial surrogacy, see Jon Elster, "Solomonic Judgments: Against the Best Interest of the Child," *The University of Chicago Law Review,* 54 (Winter 1987), pp. 1–45. More generally, see Peter Singer and Deane Wells, *Making Babies: The New Science and Ethics of Conception* (New York: Scribner, 1985).